Articulating Hidden Histories

Articulating Hidden Histories

Exploring the Influence of Eric R. Wolf

EDITED BY

Jane Schneider
Rayna Rapp

UNIVERSITY OF CALIFORNIA PRESS
Berkeley   Los Angeles   London

University of California Press
Berkeley and Los Angeles, California

University of California Press
London, England

Library of Congress Cataloging-in-Publication Data

Articulating hidden histories : exploring the influence of Eric R.
   Wolf / edited by Jane Schneider, Rayna Rapp.
       p.   cm.
   Includes bibliographical references.
   ISBN 0-520-08581-7 (cl.: alk paper).—ISBN 0-520-08582-5 (pbk.:
alk. paper)
   1. Ethnology—Philosophy.   2. Wolf, Eric R., 1923–
3. Political anthropology.   4. Economic anthropology.   5. History,
Modern.   I. Schneider, Jane, 1938–   .   II. Rapp, Rayna.
GN345.A77   1995
306'.01—dc20   94-22055
                                                            CIP

Printed in the United States of America

1   2   3   4   5   6   7   8   9

The paper used in this publication meets the minimum requirements of American
National Standard for Information Sciences—Permanence of Paper for Printed Library
Materials, ANSI Z39.48-1984 ∞

CONTENTS

PART III • IN THE MARKET'S WEB: RISK AND RESPONSE

PART IV • NATIONAL INTEGRATION AND DISINTEGRATION

PART V • POLITICAL ECONOMY AND CULTURAL IDENTITY

ACKNOWLEDGMENTS

This book grows out of a wider project to explore the influence of Eric R. Wolf, whose books, teaching, and critical evaluations have touched several cohorts of scholars. Besides those listed in the present table of contents, participants in the project include several colleagues and friends whom we particularly wish to thank: Elizabeth Brumfiel, Robert Canfield, John Cole, Gwendolyn Hall, Tom Hall, Philip Kohl, Antonio Lauria-Perricelli, Thomas Patterson, Barbara Price, Peter Schneider, Ann Stoler, Carlos Vélez-Ibañez, Soon Young Yoon, and the late Archibald Singham. Each wrote papers or gave advice relevant to the themes herein developed; each also encouraged our effort in a variety of ways. A special debt is owed to Roger McConochie, one of Wolf's students from the "Ann Arbor days," who sparked the organization and timing of the project.

Aleeze Sattar, a graduate student at the New School for Social Research in New York, undertook the responsibility of developing two bibliographies for this volume: a unified bibliography for all of the contributors and a specialized bibliography listing Wolf's publications to 1992. Her keen understanding of the complexities of this task and great good cheer have earned our unending gratitude. At the Graduate School of the City University of New York, Gerald Creed and Pamela Wright provided editorial advice and assistance, and Michael MacDonald constructed, for Wolf, a comprehensive curriculum vita. We sincerely thank them as well.

Our greatest debt is to our teacher and friend of many years, Eric Wolf. A political and moral, as well as intellectual, compass through several troubled decades of the late twentieth century, he has inspired us, and all of the authors herein.

PART ONE

Introduction

ONE

Introduction:
The Analytic Strategies of Eric R. Wolf

Jane Schneider

At the American Anthropological Association Meeting of 1991, three sessions explored the influence of Eric R. Wolf's scholarship on the field of anthropology and related disciplines. Participants included two generations of students trained directly by Wolf, as well as others who, although their ideas matured elsewhere, were beneficiaries of his interest in their projects over many years. Out of the 1991 sessions the title for this book, "Articulating Hidden Histories," evolved. Here, I use these words to frame what I think are the analytic strategies of Eric Wolf, working from back to front.

The first word is "histories." For Wolf, historical processes are preeminently political and economic, reinforced through ideology. Concentrations of political and economic power generate "forces" or "vectors" with enormous potential to disrupt human arrangements over a wide field. These disruptions put people at risk, demand that they cope, and provoke oppositional responses that at times succeed. Yet even the revolutionary overthrow of a particular concentration of power can end up with the "subjugation and transformation" of the social groups in whose name the revolutionaries struggled. This point was made by Wolf in *Peasants* (1966a, 92–93, 109), a book that predated by twenty years the uprisings against revolutionary socialist regimes in Eastern Europe. It was reiterated in his essay "Freedom and Freedoms: Anthropological Perspectives," delivered to the University of Capetown in 1990. There Wolf compares liberal and Jacobin models of freedom. As a radical faction at the time of the French Revolution, the Jacobins conceived of the state "not as a potential threat to liberty, but as the very embodiment of 'the people's will' to freedom." Yet they, and revolutionary parties after them, were unable to install their principles or protect their gains from foreign and domestic enemies without adopting measures "quite contrary to their initial sentiments" (1990a, 9, 11).

Conclusions such as these are not born of cynicism but rather derive from a profound sense that concentrations of power, however they might be achieved, will continue to act disruptively out of their location in a competitive, ever-changing, and unevenly developed "field of forces." At times Wolf has used the terms "structure" or "structural power" to refer to power complexes (e.g., 1990*b*, 586–587). He is, however, self-consciously ambivalent about this architectural metaphor, with its implication of fixity. A bibliographic note in *Europe and the People without History* expresses appreciation of the French structural Marxists for expanding on the mode of production concept, yet regrets their abandonment of the Hegelian language of dialectical contradictions in favor of a teleology of "structural causality" (1982*a*, 401). Consistent with this is Wolf's conscious borrowing of metaphors from physics rather than architecture: vectors, forces, and fields of force are frequently evoked in his writing.

Some anthropologists balk at the concept "forces" for being too abstract, disembodied, and determinative. Yet powerful forces like militarized chiefdoms, merchant and industrial companies, banking houses, and governmental regimes (whether tributary, capitalist, or socialist) are conceptualized by Wolf as human products and repositories of human agency, having developed out of historical processes of political-economic-ideological competition. Their seeming impersonality derives from the open-ended and inherently unstable fields within which they are constrained to operate, for any particular concentration of power provokes others into being, with which it must then contend. Wolf's essay "Cycles of Violence" (1987*a*) strongly suggests that the issue is not one of impersonal determinants so much as it is the unpredictable, ever-changing moves of strategizing and self-justifying powerholders in a "world of multi-tiered conflicts."

This means, of course, that ideational phenomena belong to the world of politics and economics; they are not its product or "superstructure." Put differently, foci of accumulation require ideological definition in their very operation; ideology organizes the material and political practices of those who would deploy power. Nor does a concern with "forces" or "vectors" preclude recognizing religion as a realm of symbolic communication contributing to the realms of politics and economics. Appreciating Mart Bax's concept, "religious regime," Wolf emphasizes that religion also generates vectors, at once economic, political, and sanctifying (see Wolf 1984*a*, 1991*a*). Yet of all the forces or vectors that play, and have played, in the fields of interaction we call history, those associated with mercantilism and capitalism are seen to pose the "greatest single threat" (1990*b*, 587). Under capitalism, the "Cycles of Violence" essay argues,

> arrangements of power and order are predicated not upon stable and enduring foundations, but upon an economic base forever trembling and subject to major quakes. . . . If capitalism has a special relation to the development of political freedom as we know it, it also exercises an extraordinarily destabilizing power in its continuous search for higher profits and sustained capital ac-

cumulation. Capital forever abandons older sectors of the economy and re-
locates in new and more promising industries and areas ... [;] in its continuous and often unpredictable movements, it also continuously shakes up the
foundations of human existence, and as a result also calls into question over
and over again the capacity of power groups to wield power and to maintain
it. (1987a, 147–148)

I belabor Wolf's image of a trembling and quaking field of forces, intrinsic to world history but vastly more disruptive under capitalism, in
order to expand on the word "histories"—in particular the choice of the
plural form—in the title of this book. Much of anthropology asks whether
locally situated, powerless peoples—classical anthropological subjects—can
exercise "agency" in relation to the "structures" that would dominate them.
This is not Wolf's definition of the problem. His starting point is an open-
ended, unpredictable, interaction sphere, whose very fluidity among competing, and often contradictory, forces enlarges the possibilities for empowerment from below. Local and regional histories abound, built up out
of the organizational or tactical power of "operating units" with the help
of leadership and personal persuasion (see Adams 1975; Wolf 1990b, 586).
Moreover, there are circumstances under which such mobilizations can
enter the force-field as significant vectors.

Peasant Wars of the Twentieth Century, published in 1969, exemplifies this
process, its chapters covering the rural groups and wider coalitions that supported revolutions in six countries: Mexico, Russia, China, Algeria, Cuba,
and—of particular concern to Americans of that time—Vietnam. Rather
than present his subjects as romantic champions of social justice, restorers
of a "moral economy," Wolf took pains to locate them in relation to regionally specific histories, each history the source of distinctive social and
cultural forms. David Hunt, in his essay for this volume, poignantly reminds us how the resulting vision of peasant rebels partook at once of
tragedy and hope: "Coming at a moment when many Americans saw the
Vietnamese as scarcely human, this affirmation was an extraordinary act of
political courage and human sympathy.... There was both grandeur and
humility in his demonstration that a new language, a new science, was
needed to understand these rural revolutionaries."

At the time of the Vietnam war, Eric Wolf was among those who illustrated the potentialities of local agency through political activism as well as
scholarly writing. William Gamson, in a retrospective study (1991), describes how Wolf participated in the invention and planning of the first
"teach-in" on the war in Vietnam. During this all-night event, held on the
campus of the University of Michigan, 24 March 1965, Wolf also spoke to
packed audiences about the exigencies of peasant life. "Teaching-in"—
that is, using the "down time" of the university to develop new, critical
ideas and understandings—became a highly effective strategy in the mobilization of American college students against the war. Here too was a local

history that mattered. It was reinforced in 1970–1971 when, as chair of the newly formed Ethics Committee of the American Anthropological Association, Wolf took a strong and controversial position on ethnographic research that abetted or could abet counterinsurgency (see Wakin 1992).

If the theory at hand makes room for even the most singular of local moves, it also anticipates the eclipse or compromise of oppositional social action. Quite apart from overt repression, failures of nerve are likely, as actors panic over the realization that what they do has effects they never intended and cannot control. In both *Peasant Wars* and its predecessor, *Peasants*, Wolf wrote sympathetically about groups whose members could not rebel because, without land and other resources, to do so would have jeopardized their households' survival. A recent essay on ethnicity (Wolf 1992*a*) laments anthropologists' lack of attention to the constraints that emerge as struggling groups, constructing symbolic representations, seek to elicit a deeper commitment. Yet ambivalence and failure are no excuse for ignoring or trivializing the continuous production of alternative ways of being and alternative points of view. On the contrary, because the alternatives that percolate around the edges of every social force demand constant vigilance and energy on the part of those who would suppress them, they deserve our closest attention. The point about them, as histories, is not their insignificance, but the tragedy and alienation that frequently accompany their course. The essay by Ashraf Ghani which follows touches on the sense of tragedy in Wolf's work, relating it to Wolf's personal experiences of Nazi Germany and World War II.

If local histories are significant notwithstanding their frequently alienating and unanticipated outcomes, why have we used the word "hidden" in our title? Here, it is worth specifying the purpose of *Europe and the People without History*, Wolf's most comprehensive book, whose title raises a similar paradox. As Joan Vincent has put it (1990, 402), this substantial volume was written "specifically to expose what historians' and sociologists' accounts of the historical process left out." Toward this end, *Europe* begins by historicizing the concept of the "autonomous, self-regulating and self-justifying society and culture [that] has trapped anthropology inside the bounds of its own definitions" (1982*a*, 18). Self-justifying notions of social order and political process in sociology and political science are similarly revealed to be history-bound and Eurocentric. For all these disciplines, Wolf cites as a formative moment their nineteenth-century "rebellion" against a common parent, political economy. Freed from it, each developed a partial perspective. Yet the revolt was incomplete, for political economy's focus on "production, class, and power" continued as a subterranean agenda—an unproductive, because unacknowledged, dialogue with the ghost of Marx.

Recovering the political economy agenda means, for Wolf, reunifying the social science disciplines. In a 1983 speech about his goals to the University

Faculty Senate of the City University of New York, he concluded that "it is only when we integrate our different kinds of knowledge that the people without history emerge as actors in their own right. When we parcel them out among the several disciplines, we render them invisible—their story, which is also our story, vanishes from sight" (Wolf 1983*f*, 5). Among the disciplines, there would yet be a division of labor in which anthropology would chart the histories of peoples well-studied by ethnographers—the peasants and kin-ordered groups of Latin America, Asia, and Africa; their counterparts in Europe who were transformed by the "political unification and cultural homogenization" of nineteenth-century state making; and globally recruited working classes. Often ignored or caricatured by other scholars and devalued by a wider public, such peoples "are thought by many to have no history" (Wolf 1983*f*, 1).

Clearly, if histories have been "hidden," then the first word of our title, "articulating," refers to their recovery. This means defining written and oral historical "records" as among the sources to be mined by anthropologists. It means systematic use of archaeology, linguistics, ethnographic observation, and interviewing to discern a yet richer past. And it means listening for the histories that others produce for themselves. Because much of the past is unknowable, however, and because both records and memories are partial, Wolf has also sought to model historical interactions. For him, the local social fields that generate "hidden" histories are enmeshed in "webs" or "nets" of relations that connect their actors to a wider context. Revisiting his concept of the "closed corporate peasant community" in 1986, he described himself as striving to comprehend "local and parochial relationships in terms of wider unfolding economic and political processes, while trying simultaneously to grasp how human beings in [these local] communities responded to these processes through culturally informed action and action-involved cultural forms" (1986*b*, 328).

For Wolf, undervalued peoples are not only "among the makers of the modern world, and among its shakers," but knowing their histories is also a way "to recover a significant part of ourselves, so that we may gain more effective knowledge of the world which all of us, with our shared history, inhabit together" (Wolf 1983*f*, 5). This brings us to a second sense of the word "articulating"—the linkages of an increasingly globalized totality. Occasionally, Wolf has been taken as a "world-system" theorist, bent on demonstrating unequal exchanges between "core," "peripheral," and "semiperipheral" regions, differentially capable of producing high-profit goods and services. But, although he is ever aware of unevenness in the world distribution of profit and power, he faults this approach for obliterating the "range and variety" of the micropopulations "habitually investigated by anthropologists" (Wolf 1982*a*, 23).

If anything, the very concept "periphery" reifies difference, as if the ordering of power in the world had a teleology in which Europe, or more precisely, North Atlantic Europe, had been destined to ascend to "core" status and stay there. Such thinking masks the contradictory reality, attended to by Wolf, that Europeans were "peripheral" to more developed power complexes for centuries, whereas of late they have had to take note of new and potent accumulation processes in Asia. Because his analysis begins with an open field of forces, with relational sets and internal contradictions, he is receptive to the possibility that new complexes might well appear, contra any fixed notion of a core-periphery hierarchy. It is this openness that most profoundly marks his dynamic, processual approach to what history is about.

Not only does the use, here, of "articulation" differ from a world-system outlook, it is also at variance with the multiple usages of the French structural Marxists. In the 1970s, philosophers and anthropologists of this school explored new applications of the mode of production concept, delineating several types or modes that had been absent, or underdeveloped, in the writings of Marx and Engels, and exploring the terms of their coexistence with capitalism. In their language, the colonial and imperial projects of Europeans brought the capitalist mode into "articulation" with other modes, variously labeled by such general terms as "Asiatic," "African," "precapitalist," or by more restrictive designations such as "hunting and gathering," "horticulture," "slavery," and so on. William Roseberry, with his usual clarity, reviews the attempt of Pierre-Philippe Rey to map out stages of articulation between capitalist and noncapitalist modes, as well as other applications of this term (1989, 155–175).

In *Europe and the People without History*, Wolf, too, makes use of the mode of production concept, arguing that, because it is a powerful tool for analyzing the differentiation and appropriation of social labor, it usefully guides us to a fuller consideration of relationships of class and power. Yet he eschews the typological fixity and structural determination implied by Rey and others. Their anthropology, he suggests, shows a tendency "to collapse all culture and cultural diversity into the elements of the mode of production. Furthermore, they reify modes of production into timeless essences, which are then allowed to reproduce themselves or conjugate ('articulate') with one another without reference to historical time or circumstance" (1982a, 401). Wolf opts instead for no more than three comprehensive modes, each internally differentiated and capable of much variation. The three—kin-ordered, tributary, and capitalist—are not so much structured entities as heuristic devices for sorting out divergent processes of power and wealth accumulation, these processes in turn fostering divergent patterns of social inequality and ideological justification. Moreover, all three are dynamic. Change, growth, and development emerge from kin-ordered and tributary relations, and from their interactions, as well as from the much touted restlessness of capitalism. To be discovered are the articulations among the foci of accumulation, both within and across the three modes.

Having related the words of the title to Wolf's theoretical orientation, I turn to a note on methods, for the authors included in this volume consider themselves indebted on this level as well. We might begin by noting that the anthropologist working under the influence of Wolf is strongly oriented toward empirical research aimed at revealing a good sociocultural map. To be discovered and described are various social groupings or classes, extant and in formation, their relationships with one another, and the connection of these relationships to the division of social labor. This does not mean seeking out bounded collectivities. The concept "group" for Wolf shades into "alliance" and "coalition"—social forms that permit the simultaneous pursuit of several roles and are "sufficiently loosely structured to exempt the participants [from commitment] in a period of severe trial" (1966a, 80). Nor is people's means to a livelihood the only research question. More often it is cultural phenomena or, in Wolf's words, the "on-going dialectical interpenetration" of social behavior and symbolic form (1986b, 327), which are under investigation. But no issue of this sort can be addressed adequately without considering its reciprocal relation with the ecological, economic, and organizational context.

For many researchers influenced by Wolf, groups and the interactions of groups are best discerned in a local setting—usually a community or region—but these localities are conceptualized in a particular way. Rather than discrete or bounded, such small-scale entities are viewed as affected by, and affecting, wider processes, the historical unfolding of which must also be grasped. Until recently, many social scientists short-circuited this step through the convenient but misleading before-and-after dualism of tradition and modernity, perhaps glossed as precapitalist and capitalist, or precolonial and colonial eras. Today, this dichotomy has given way to another—the modern and postmodern—which similarly collapses the processes of an earlier epoch into a single, seamless trajectory, while raising the possibility of history's equally seamless endgame. Eschewing these shortcuts, Wolf shows us what the anthropologist can learn about particular local histories if those histories are charted in relation to the large-scale transformations of, let us say, the last three hundred years. Researchers in his tradition generally want to know what happened in their research site during times of tributary and mercantile expansion, European or other colonialism and imperialism, political and religious movements for national independence, neocolonial or other development initiatives, and the related processes now unfolding.

Depending on the research problem, the setting might transcend a locality or region. For example, Wolf has always been interested in the political and cultural processes of national and religious integration—processes through which a group or groups promote and maintain their understandings against the assertion of alternatives. Although such processes are central to the writings of Antonio Gramsci, it is interesting to note his minimal use of Gramsci's concept, "hegemony." For Gramsci, as for Wolf, the cultural "work" of hegemony is accomplished by specific social groups—class fractions, organic intellectuals, Catholic priests—but many others who have embraced the term describe hegemonic phenomena in relation to a simplified social landscape, consisting for the most part of dominators and dominated. To Wolf, ever skeptical of dualisms, the word "hegemony" too often glosses over the sociology of cultural construction that needs to be investigated.

Both this sociology and the point about chronological depth are evident in Eric Wolf's most recent explorations into the German catastrophe under National Socialism. Going back to the creation of the Holy Roman Empire, he traces the historical development of a particular rendering of *Gemeinschaft*, characterized by hierarchically ordered estates of noblemen, town-dwellers, and peasants, for whom various rights and obligations were codified in obsessive detail. Although differently manifested from region to region, the codified groups everywhere excluded a large unchartered society "of people in despised occupations or people who lacked local roots ... tanners, shepherds, linenweavers ... and the perennial sojourners in Christendom, the Jews"(1992*b*, 4). Thirty years of religious war and the war-driven efforts of the princes to extract ever-higher taxes, then the headlong rush into capitalism to meet the challenge of the industrializing, colonizing giants of England, France, and the Netherlands, are shown to have reactivated and intensified age-old battles over "honor and belonging," especially as Prussian bureaucrats set about creating the "iron cage" of German unification. Hermann Rebel's essay in this volume is similarly concerned with the long-term salience, in Germany, of symbolically marked and ritually guarded boundaries between successful and dishonorable or polluting social elements.

Wolf's method is not just historical; it is also self-consciously comparative. Once one has examined a problem or process in a particular locale, it is necessary to hold that case against others, mulling over the following questions: How does what is locally observed compare with phenomena in other places where the same or similar forces are present and operating? What about similar places subjected to contrasting forces? Two well-known examples illustrate these alternatives. One is the 1957 article on the "closed corporate peasant community." This classic essay begins by outlining the similar cultural-structural features that characterized communities in central Java and highland Mesoamerica during and after the colonial period, then proceeds to contrast these features with those of communities in China, Uganda, and other regions of Latin America. "These casual contrasts," Wolf wrote, suggest that "the kind of peasant community appears to respond to forces which lie within the larger society to which the community belongs rather than within the boundaries of the community itself" (1957, 236). In the case of Mesoamerica and Java, communities with the specific features of communal land jurisdiction, restrictive membership, and wealth-leveling institutions, had crystallized in response to a particular pattern of conquest emphasizing forced settlement on restricted land and a legal arrangement that treated each locale as a relatively autonomous, tribute- and labor-supplying corporation.

A book with John W. Cole, *The Hidden Frontier* (1974), compares two neighboring villages in the alpine reaches of Northern Italy which "share very similar modes of adaptation to a common mountainous environment," but had interacted dialectically with a contrastive "play of forces" over much of their medieval and modern history (1–3). A central sociocultural difference between them was the assertion by the inhabitants of German-speaking St. Felix of a preference for eldest-son inheritance, as opposed to the Italian-speaking Trettners' preference for partibility. In actuality, inheritance practices converged: the eldest son among St. Felixers was often driven off the land in favor of a younger sibling, whereas Trettners' practice of out-migration for work or education often left only one sibling as de facto heir.

The research problem thus became one of accounting for difference not so much in actual behavior as in the "template of ideas for the ordering of social life" (Wolf and Cole 1974, 19). The authors trace the interactions over several centuries between each village and its wider economic, political, and ideological field. Because, in the one case, relevant forces derived from German-speaking concentrations of power associated with the Austro-Hungarian Empire, whereas in the other they derived from Romance-speaking city-states and the nation-state of Italy, the division was profound, shaping not only the divergent ideologies of inheritance, but a broader contrast in ethnic identity and the ways it would be used. All told, the contrasts are shown to have influenced different responses to the combined agricultural mechanization and expanding urban labor markets that affected both communities in the 1960s.

In pursuing such comparisons, Wolf always expects to be surprised, to stumble on anomalies, to discover instances that do not fit into a pattern. Self-described as one who "loves facts," he appears never to tire of being exposed to yet another set of human arrangements, whether these are unheard of ways of stabilizing power or newly recorded rituals for drinking tea. Possessed of an enormous curiosity, he is a prodigious reader and listener, predisposed to harvest examples from even the most humble sources. One sees the results of this industry in his general essays, such as the 1990 Distinguished Lecture to the American Anthropological Association, which typically spill out a cornucopia of well-selected marvels, provoking wonder at cultural variation. Far from collections of exotica—trophies of the ethnographic enterprise—these arrays help make a case for human possibilities.

Finally, and most important, Wolf guides the researcher to locate anthropological concepts—peasant, society, culture, class, community, kinship, tribe, race, ethnic group, nation-state—in relation to the social milieus out of which they grow and change through time. As Raymond Williams insists at the end of *Marxism and Literature* (1977), words like these are not definitional, but denote ongoing social processes and problems, embedded in history. What concepts can do depends on where they come from and the uses they serve, peasantry being a telling example. It matters whether peasants are apprehended through the lens of a Kroeber-Redfield world, a Chayanov-Narodnik world, or the world that Wolf shared with his mentor Julian Steward and colleague Sidney Mintz. Understanding the difference means learning about these separate worlds—their historically particular academic institutions and the concerns of their wider publics.

Among the concepts to receive Wolf's attention, one stands out, and that is "culture"—the central tool of anthropology. From a 1950 thinkpiece on the nation-state, outlined in the introduction to part 3 of this volume, to the Capetown Freedom lecture and beyond, he has questioned anthropology's romance with this term. Especially familiar, perhaps, is his criticism of Robert Redfield's folk society notion of peasant culture as value-saturated, timeless, and homogeneous (1964, 53–87; see also Silverman 1979; Vincent 1990, 367–375). Diagnostic, too, is Wolf's exploration of the culture concept's intellectual and political history in a small book called *Anthropology* (1964, 16–19). Drawing on the work of Norbert Elias, whom he heard lecture in an internment camp in England (see Ghani, this volume), Wolf there elaborates on the contrast between "culture" and "civilization" in German usage, relating the divergence to that nation's unusually sharp division, when compared with France and England, between bourgeoisie and aristocracy in the seventeenth and eighteenth centuries.

Filtered through the German Enlightenment and later Romantic philosophers—enhanced, especially, by the historicity and intuitive methods of Wilhelm Dilthey—culture as a foil for the French-influenced "march of reason," culture as romantic, "informal and internal" (Wolf 1964, 19), made its way into Boasian anthropology in twentieth-century North America. Wolf's critique of its subsequent development parallels his critique of Redfield: that is, except for Alexander Lesser (who argued for "open fields" of interaction), the Boasians wrongly assumed the existence of internally homogeneous and coherent units, each capable of producing its own worldview, its particular patterning of mind. Epitomized by the "culture and personality" texts of Margaret Mead and Ruth Benedict, and by their forays into "national character" studies, this tendency needed an antidote, which Wolf found in Anthony Wallace's call (1961) to think of culture as the "organization of diversity," rather than as uniform essences, replicated through time. This antidote, and the reasons for it, underlie all the methods outlined above.

This volume gathers together twenty papers. An overarching essay by Ashraf Ghani examines the concept of power in Wolf. There are then four parts, whose respective introductions follow below. These take up four major themes: peasants, responses to risk in contemporary North America, national integration, and relations between political economy and cultural identity. Sharing a sense that history is at once hopeful, tragic, and surprising, the respective essays demonstrate the sweep and continuance, intellectually and politically, of Eric R. Wolf's influence.

PEASANTS: CONCEPTS AND HISTORIES

Nowhere are the possibilities of comparative history more clearly brought out than in Eric Wolf's contributions to peasant studies. I have already made note of two—his analysis of the closed communities of Mesoamerica and Java, and his analysis of the contrasting ethnicities of Alpine Northern Italy—but there are others. In his first book, published in 1959, Wolf undertook to reconstruct several centuries of divergence between Mexico's broadly defined regions of north, center, and south, making note, as well, of local variations within them. A student of Julian Steward and admirer of Karl Wittfogel, he paid close attention to the different environmental potentialities and limitations of these regions; indeed the title, *Sons of the Shaking Earth*, evokes the environmental challenge to human existence of periodic earthquakes. Drawing on archaeological information, however, the book compared not only different ecological "adaptations," but increasingly distinct processes of tributary state formation, the interactions of which affected European colonization and, eventually, the contrasting revolutionary traditions of Emiliano Zapata and Pancho Villa. All told, *Sons of the Shaking Earth* synthesizes not only Mexican history, but the comparative histories of Mexico's divergent regions.

Using a strategy of comparison, *Peasant Wars of the Twentieth Century* arrives at a tentative theory regarding the revolutionary potential of "middle peasants"—a category defined by Lenin and Chayanov as cultivators who have relatively secure access to modest landholdings worked with family labor. Following Hamza Alavi (1965), Wolf found these peasants to possess at least a minimum of the "tactical freedom required to challenge their overlord"— a condition that also pertained for less well-endowed peasants in marginal areas (1969*a*, 291). Paradoxically, middle peasants were also the "main bearers of peasant tradition ... [a] culturally conservative stratum" (292). Wolf resolved the paradox by demonstrating the exceptional vulnerability of precisely these groups to commercial capitalism in each of the cases being compared. Another paradox was left unresolved: that in each example of revolution, middle peasants entered into coalitions and alliances with other groups, especially the intelligentsia, whose goals included the abolition of the old order which they, the middle peasants, were committed to preserve.

In elaborating concepts like "the closed corporate peasant community" and "middle peasants," Wolf consistently warned his readers against reification; his purpose was to illuminate historical processes, not identify fixed categories. The same warning pervades the presentation of peasant possibilities in his 1966 book, *Peasants*. It is worth revisiting chapter 3 of that book for an example of how one can systematize knowledge without entering into a taxonomic exercise that reifies types.

To some extent, chapter 3 characterizes peasants in the way that Marx did when he applied the famous "sack of potatoes" metaphor to the rural population of France. Wolf emphasizes their need to sustain autonomous households, committing both the energy and the emotions of family members to a round of productive and ceremonial activities intended to ensure the reproduction of the immediate family over time. Another publication of the same year (1966*b*), "Kinship, Friendship, and Patron-Client Relations in Complex Societies," spells out an important reason why the family persists as a viable social form in even the most socially differentiated societies: small in scale and inherently flexible, it can address a wide range of tasks in quick succession with "relatively low cost and overhead" because most, if not all, of its members are willing and prepared to exploit themselves. A multipurpose organization par excellence, the family is also the bearer of virtue, "and of its public reflection, reputation" (1966*b*, 7–8).

Yet not all peasant families were the same. Chapter 3 of *Peasants* goes on to disaggregate three familial sets or dyads: the paternal one between father and children, the maternal one between mother and children, and the conjugal one between husband and wife. (*The Hidden Frontier*, 1974, also calls attention to the sibling dyad.) The device suggests ways for sorting out some of the known variability in peasant family forms. More important, it allows for considering differences of gender and generation. Before much attention had been paid to this problem, Wolf noted, for example, that ceremonial and social supports external to the household could shore up the paternal dyad within it, giving the male role "an importance it might not possess on purely utilitarian grounds" (1966*b*, 64). Such insights prefigured and gave methodological inspiration to a generation of scholars who later examined women's and family history.

Peasants' preoccupation with family meant that their wider involvements were necessarily self-limiting. Wolf chose the word "coalition" to describe transfamily sociocultural structures, highlighting their temporariness and contingency. Although such structures brought people together for a common purpose, they could easily disband or release them when other purposes called. Drawing upon a wide range of ethnography, chapter 3 takes

the reader through a series of paths laid out to systematize "modes" of coalition formation. As we might expect, contrasting examples are viewed as
local and creative responses to divergent vectors or forces (paleotechnic
and neotechnic investment; capitalist, mercantile, tributary, or socialist
powerholders; institutions of colonial intrusion). By activating different
pathways, Wolf suggests, such vectors helped to shape the compadrazgo
and fiesta system of Mexican and other Latin American peasantries, the
cross-class *tsu* or clan of pre-Communist Southeastern China, and various
associations for mutual aid, insurance, burial, labor, and other exchanges
familiar to peasants more generally.

Although many forms of peasant coalition are horizontal, bringing
together people of roughly equal status, Wolf was especially interested in
vertical structures, for example the patron-client chains that linked some
peasants with powerful outsiders. Anticipating *Peasant Wars, Peasants* draws
particular attention to the internal stratification of rural communities, their
overt and hidden differences of class, their more or less pronounced processes of differentiation between those with access to land and those without. In the papers of part 1, the reader will revisit these and related
themes: peasants' divided interests, notwithstanding their seemingly cohesive families and communities; their social and cultural resources for inter-
acting with wider forces; and the intellectual origins and limits of the concepts we use to analyze them.

William Roseberry's "The Cultural History of Peasantries" challenges
those who would view *Peasants* as essentially typologizing. Contrasting
Wolf's approach with that of Henry Sumner Maine, it also illuminates his
distinctive use of the concept of "community." James Greenberg likewise
takes aim at any simple notion of peasant typologies. In "Capital, Ritual,
and Boundaries of the Closed Corporate Community," he traces how an
apparently "classic" Mixe (Mexican) village "cracked open" yet did not dis-
solve with the intrusion of commodity relations and money. "Conacre: A
Reevaluation of Irish Custom," presents the "hidden history" of both the
concept and the cultural practice of a form of lease that tied landless Irish
laborers to minuscule potato plots. Analyzed by others as a form of rent or
labor exploitation, Joan Vincent shows, rather, how the conacre lease en-
sured community membership and patronage, even as the British Union
forced the impoverished Irish into seasonal migrations to harvest Scottish
grains.

In "The Prussian Junker and Their Peasants," Hermann Rebel demonstrates that, when the East Elbian Junker of the sixteenth and seventeenth
centuries lowered rents in exchange for an increase in labor dues, they were
intensifying the exploitation of their peasants, not advantaging them, as a
recent cost-benefit analysis has claimed. Sensitive to the peasants' full
round of life as well as to the economics of rent, Rebel also chillingly spec-

ulates that, in celebrating ideals of lineage, house, dynasty, and family, the Junker provided a "cathected speech about lost kin, lost homelands, dispossession and exile" with horrendous reverberations in the twentieth century.

Finally, David Hunt's "Prefigurations of the Vietnamese Revolution" provides an appreciative critique of the Vietnam chapter in *Peasant Wars of the Twentieth Century*. There, Wolf refused the image of peasants as a dying, passive class, calling them, rather, "the party of humanity" for their suffering and aspirations. Admiring above all the chapter's grasp of the complexity of Vietnamese culture and society, Hunt movingly concludes with an update on sociocultural change, based on his own recent research trip to Vietnam.

IN THE MARKET'S WEB: RISK AND RESPONSE

"Some of my insights into how the capitalist mode operates," Wolf tells us in *Europe and the People without History* (1982a, 402), "derive from the experience of growing up among textile workers in the German-Czech borderland of northern Bohemia in the Depression years of the 1930's." The memory, it would seem, formed the central question of his anthropology: how to account for the emergence and persistence of a system whose dynamically unfolding relations can catapult the social and cultural arrangements of everyday life into an abyss of uncertainty as if by an act of nature like an earthquake. To understand his approach to this question, and to the related problematic of how people respond to risk in an ever-transforming world, it helps to return to his groundbreaking research on the peasant predicament. His doctoral dissertation on a coffee-producing region of Puerto Rico, chapter 1 of *Peasants*, and especially *Peasant Wars* all analyze a series of processes through which cultivators became separated from land and turned into "disposable" recruits for expanding labor markets. Deriving from the worldwide expansion of industrial capitalism, these processes foretold that the "new laborers"—as he later called them—would be at once highly differentiated, in possession of a range of cultural resources with which to begin a new life and, key to their vulnerability, in over-abundant supply.

An exceptionally powerful process was the competitive spread of the "neotechnic ecotype," pioneered during the Second Agricultural Revolution in late eighteenth-century England and energized by fossil fuels. Vastly reducing the role of labor in planting and harvesting, neotechnic cultivation also induced environmentally unsound specializations leading in some cases to land abandonment (1966a, 35–36). Yet more telling was the related enlargement of "mercantile domain." By domain Wolf meant the structure of power through which outsiders exert a claim to land that peasants use. Alternative forms—patrimonial and prebendal domain—involved ceremonialized interactions between peasant and lord that expressed the idea of a contractual exchange of tribute for protection. In contrast, under mercantile domain, claims came to be made by powerholders who viewed land as "private property ... an entity to be bought and sold and used to obtain profit for its owner" (1966a, 50–53). Where mercantile domain expanded, landowners converted tribute to money rent that peasants could only obtain through producing for capitalist markets. Landowners also adjusted this rent in relation to changing land values, borrowed against their holdings, which they used as collateral, and otherwise jeopardized (rather than protected) the stability of the peasant communities in their charge.

A third process, encompassing the other two, was the global extension of commercialized "network markets." Having to purchase many things, often including their own food, peasants who produced for these markets were easily trapped by a "price scissors" effect, in which steeply falling returns for their output coincided with an equally steep increase in the costs of what they consumed. "Even quite small changes in pricing," Wolf wrote, "may have astonishing implications for the entire economy of a country" (1966a, 40–45). Larger fluctuations were capable of propelling masses of cultivators into off-farm employment or peripatetic migrations. Meanwhile, a fourth, demographic process added to the volume of the dispossessed. In each case of "peasant war" analyzed by Wolf in 1969, population had tripled or quadrupled during the century and a half preceding armed rebellion, thanks above all to the introduction of crops from other continents— maize, manioc, beans, peanuts, sweet potatoes—in tandem with agricultural commercialization. Furnishing an "existential minimum" for large and hungry families, these crops sustained population growth rates at levels that had not been possible before. Unfortunately, as growth occurred, "many resources, and especially land, were already spoken for ... [and] existing social structures often failed to absorb the added burden of supernumerary claimants" (1969a, 281).

As already noted, Wolf saw peasants managing uncertainty through a wide array of sociocultural structures—the coalitions discussed in part 1. "Sharing of resources within communal organizations and reliance on ties with powerful patrons," as well as any number of "quaint customs," were among their buffers against the curveballs of nature, the wiliness of merchants, the predations of tribute takers and armed bandits, and the exactions of landlords (1969a, 279). *Peasant Wars* describes how these protections crumbled as the "cultural system" of capitalism turned land and labor into free and unencumbered commodities in the areas that it engulfed. (We shall return to this Polanyi-inspired understanding of capitalism in part 4.) Stripping land of social obligations and encouraging the differentiation of peasant classes, the system cut away the "integument of custom" to expose people as economic actors, competing in a labor market (1969a, 279–280).

Turning now to industrial capitalism, it is significant that Wolf rejects Max Weber's definition, revived by world-system theorists: capitalism as production for the market, driven by the entrepreneurial quest for profit. There can be capitalist markets and profit-seeking entrepreneurs without capitalism, which, following Marx, he more narrowly defines in terms of a qualitatively new way of mobilizing social labor. "Capitalists bought machines and hired laborers to set them in motion.... At the same time, capital could halt machines and lay off manpower in regions of low profitability, and recommence production in other regions promising higher returns" (Wolf 1982a, 294–295). Indeed it is "the cyclical alternation of labor mobilization and labor displacement" that distinguishes the capitalist mode: "Each intake of labor power uproots some prior adaptation, while each sloughing off of labor power creates a new cohort of the disemployed" (386).

As a particular system of labor mobilization, capitalism had, for Wolf, specific origins in a conjuncture of elements in late eighteenth-century England. One element was the already noted Second Agricultural Revolution, which accelerated an unusual tendency in English land tenure: separating peasants from secure claims to land (Wolf 1982a, 120–121, 268–269). A second was the development of an export industry in cotton textiles against the formidable competition of the linen-manufacturing United Provinces of the Netherlands and cotton-manufacturing India. This "carrier" industry was launched precisely through the combined application of mechanical invention and newly mobilized wage labor.

Several references to the English state in *Europe and the People without History* (Wolf 1982a, 120–123, 270–271, 309) draw attention to its strategic role in the conjuncture that gave birth to capitalism. Transformed through revolution in 1688 into a unique blend of monarchical, feudal, and republican institutions, this state supported the developmental projects of industrialists and improving landlords, in particular by going abroad for resources, restructuring taxation, centralizing investment and banking, building networks of transportation and communication, legislating enclosures, and disciplining/socializing labor. The state also cradled the cotton textile industry, garnering its main raw materials through colonial expansion and shamelessly deploying credit schemes and gunboats to bolster a favorable balance of trade in cloth. Remarkably, this integument of support continued through the nineteenth century and beyond, even as the new mode of production manifested its inherent tendency to generate crises.

It is above all in connection with this anarchic tendency that Wolf acknowledges his debt to Marx. Having succeeded in its initial "takeoff," capitalist England "upped the ante" in its relations with other European states, so that they, too, gave support to neotechnic agricultural and industrial projects. As the competition intensified, so did the rival quests for raw materials and markets. According to Marx, an important way for capitalists to meet

competition is through technological innovation, but to the extent that machines displace labor, they lower the *rate* of return on investment, in the long
run reducing the component of profit which derives from the difference between labor's value and what it is actually paid. Displacements of labor also
enter into a second explanation for crises considered by Marx—namely,
"over-production," or the inability of consumers to buy more goods either
because their wants have been saturated or because they are disemployed
and lack the means. Wolf concludes that "the form of crises and the manner of their resolution are variable and contingent" (1982*a*, 418), yet the
downturns reproduce a pattern: "capital becomes unproductive and even
subject to destruction. Plants close, credit based on future production collapses, capital depreciates in value. At the same time, growing unemployment drives down wages" (1982*a*, 299).

Already in 1826, and again in the late 1840s, European industries experienced sharp "cyclical" reversals, causing capitalists to regroup around
new industries—railroads, steel, coal mining, shipping. Following Ernst
Mandel (1978), Wolf maps out subsequent "long waves," noting the "hal-
cyon period of machine-made-machines and massive railroad building" between 1848 and 1873, the so-called First Great Depresion of 1873–1894,
the boom of 1894–1913 when rivalrous colonial and imperial initiatives
reached their zenith of audacity, the World Wars and intervening Second
Great Depression, and the new phase of growth after World War II (Wolf
1982*a*, 304–305). His reading obviates the need for Mandel's term, "late
capitalism," to characterize the "space-time compressions" of today (see
Harvey 1989). Capitalists, for Wolf, are by definition restless, investing in
new technologies of production and organization, provoking competitors to
imitate or surpass them, and pushing on when competition threatens. What
mainly distinguishes the post–World War II conjuncture is a set of variations on this theme: technological enhancements to the velocity of capital;
electronically monitored systems spanning continents which allow for coordinating high-skill operations with highly labor-intensive phases of production; the role of credit and advertising in opening up new arenas of consumption; and the centrality of military expenditure in overall development
(1982*a*, 381–383).

The ongoing periodization of capitalism informs Wolf's approach to
working classes, broadly defined. Far from "encompassing the whole world
in a homogeneous field of effects," capitalism is for him the source of "variability and differentiation not only through its combination with other
modes but also in the very course of its own operations" (Wolf 1982*a*,
303). As such it leaves wide spaces for new cultural constructions, responsive to the motion of an accumulation process punctuated by booms and
busts. For proletarians and middle sectors, no less than for peasants, anthropologists need to decipher how social actors, organized into contingent yet

stabilizing groups and coalitions, develop practices for spreading and sharing risk. At stake is culture-building, defined as a series of processes that construct, reconstruct, and dismantle cultural forms and symbols in response to identifiable vectors: "In the rough-and-tumble of social interaction, groups are known to exploit the ambiguities of inherited forms, to impart new evaluations or valences to them, to borrow forms more expressive of their interests, or to create wholly new forms to answer changed circumstances" (Wolf 1982*a*, 387). Responses are specific, creative, and limited because the structural pieces of the larger puzzle within which they emerge are moved around rapidly by forces that, although never inconsequential, are often invisible and beyond control.

Following Wolf, such responses can be revealed through classic sociological methods: participant-observation and interviewing among local groups; historical investigation of shifting social relations; appreciation of small-scale, flexible coalitions through which knowledge is developed and strategies promulgated for enhancing life. Local groups, of course, are often segmented by differences of class, ethnicity, religion, gender, and generational interests, leading to differences of strategy. These points are illustrated in a series of papers on contemporary North America, a corner of the world where, for reasons that could well be delineated using the methods of Wolf, capitalism flourishes as nowhere else, having neutralized any institutionalized opposition, and where it reveals with special clarity the internationalization of the capital-labor relationship since World War II.

In "From Jíbaro to Crack Dealer," Philippe Bourgois examines the impact of declining factory employment and its replacement by entry-level, unskilled jobs on young Puerto Rican men in New York City. The resulting losses include not only job security, but the cultural resources for self-esteem and working-class identity, as witnessed in the life stories of selected drug dealers. Edward Hansen's "The Great Bambi War: Tocquevillians versus Keynesians in an Upstate New York County" compares exurbanites (who commute to often-professional city jobs, seek advanced education for their children, and are mortgaged to the hilt) with "woodchucks" (whose resource packages consist of odd-jobbing in construction, hunting, gardening on land they own, unemployment benefits, and dense social networks). Of the two, the woodchucks' livelihood is more stable, more reproducible, and more recession-proof. Josiah Heyman's "In the Shadow of the Smokestacks" is based on fieldwork in a copper-smelting Arizona town whose recent, tumultuous history reflects the continuous restructuring of capital. Heyman discusses the involvement of union leaders, employed and unemployed workers and their families, ecological activists, and elected politicians in a protracted strike at Phelps-Dodge, only to discover that the more enduring scenario may have been the company's "right" to close the plant and consolidate and modernize its investments in other parts of the region and industry.

"Risky Business: Genetic Counseling in a Shifting World," by Rayna Rapp, examines "risk" as a culturally and historically specific concept, no less for intellectuals and scientific workers than for the populations they investigate. Her analysis highlights the legacies and varied consciousness that people from differing racial, ethnic, and religious backgrounds in the United States bring to the assessment of risk in the unstable world in which decisions regarding pregnancy, genetic testing, and abortion must be made. Finally, Harriet Rosenberg's "From Trash to Treasure: Housewife Activists and the Environmental Justice Movement" tracks local reactions to the ecologically threatening consequences of investment and disinvestment in Canada. Comparing working-class housewives, increasingly desperate over the effects of pollution on their children's health, with middle-class environmentalists, Rosenberg shows how both gender and class influence responses to environmental threat.

NATIONAL INTEGRATION AND DISINTEGRATION

If displaced textile workers of the Depression era left Eric Wolf with a powerful memory of everyday social and cultural routines thrown into disarray, so did Nazi Germany impress upon him the need to understand how nation-states, the presumed managers of such crises, become internally integrated. To apprehend the concentrated violence through which the Nazis sought to define a political community against its imagined enemies meant to think through the range of variation in the historical formation of nation-states. The anthropological tools for doing so in the immediate postwar period were, however, limited by the idea of "national character." In a 1987 essay on nationalism and ethnicity, Wolf laments how this concept had allowed Ruth Benedict to define as characteristically "Japanese" the "idealized and ahistorical statements of the *samurai* elite" (Wolf 1987*d*, 3). Significantly, his own first postdissertation projects were fellowship-supported studies of "nation formation" and the "development of nationalism in Mexico." Both grew out of a 1950 thinkpiece that was published in Spanish in 1953 but never appeared in English. I summarize its contents in order to frame his later writing on integrative processes, which are the focus of part 3.

The essay in question anticipates the well-known "transition debates" that engaged Marxist scholars in the 1960s and 1970s, as well as Wolf's own arguments about the tributary mode of production, appearing in 1982. What were the forms of society and state that incubated the breakthrough to capitalism? How particular were they to Western Europe, or to England? What sorts of state formation processes were called into existence because of Europe's, or England's, subsequent expansion? Establishing that any given organization of power worthy of the designation "state" must equip itself with economic resources, Wolf proposed a distinction in the "ecological basis" of early as opposed to modern nation-states. Early states faced a simple provisioning problem when compared with their modern successors, which appeared in tandem with the possibility of industrial manufacture. Typically, the early states developed in the midst of fertile, nuclear areas, where advanced agricultural technologies guaranteed a substantial surplus to tributary overlords. Seeking advantage from trading networks, and from the towns and cities spawned by trade, the powerholders of these areas also attracted craftsmen and traders into the orbits of their courts. It was not their purpose, however, nor was it necessary, to culturally assimilate or politically integrate these groups. States then "appeared divided into a multitude of small, parochial units which restricted and delimited the loyalties of their members" (Wolf 1950, 8).

For political consolidation to occur, there needed to be "independent sources of wealth brought about [through] the 'marriage' of royal power with the great merchants" (Wolf 1950, 9). In Western Europe, kings became partners in mercantile expansion, whether through trade or, as often happened, through raid and plunder. In exchange for guaranteeing their monopolies, the crown tapped into merchants' wealth, thereby financing a military and judical apparatus independent of the tributary lords. Mercantilist kings also integrated more closely with the court the potentially autonomous activities of manufacturing and commerce. Lords, undercut by these new developments, gravitated toward the court as well. Wolf notes that the word "nation" was sometimes used to refer to such formations, but reminds us that its application to entities as large or culturally complex as "France" was still to come. Although there had occurred "some consolidation of legal codes and some standardization of groups holding similar statuses into statewide 'estates,'" as yet there remained numerous barriers to "internal acculturation among the component groups of the realm" (Wolf 1950, 13).

What changed dramatically, beginning in the eighteenth century, was the ecological basis of European states from one that combined agriculture with overseas commerce to one in which agriculture served new, industrial complexes, located close to sources of power (wood, water, coal, iron) that were usually marginal to the nuclear areas. These complexes, and their attached zones of commercialized agriculture, posed a challenge to integration. The newly emergent industrial bourgeoisie, allied with improving landlords, responded to this challenge with a new concept, the nation-state, which met their need for "decentralization of controls over wealth, over industrial production and over consumption ... for the levelling of differences between localities, between the core (nuclear) area and the margins" (Wolf 1950, 15). Other new groups—industrial workers, specialized agricultural producers, and mediators of all kinds—participated as well in breaking the old mold to create a new state form.

Although highly schematic, Wolf's brief, early essay takes pains to insist on local variation: the characteristics of the nation-state "will depend in large measure on the general type and specific characteristics of the socio-cultural groups involved, as well as on the mode of their cultural interaction; ... the cultural patterns of each group, and the culturally patterned manner in which they relate to each other will play a part in shaping the overall characteristics of the nation to be" (Wolf 1950, 17). From this he envisioned a welcome anthropological contribution to the study of "acculturation"—one that would improve on other disciplines' reifications of the nation-state and presumptions of the creation of a national character. "The members of a nation," he wrote,

> are less characterized by common traits, whether cultural or psychological, than by differential involvement in common historical and functional relationships of ecology, social structure and acculturation. These relations are of course culturally patterned and are "represented" by symbols. Such symbols may either stand for certain ideal norms of relationship between people or they may be "symbolic pantomines" (Veblen) ... they (may) represent the culture pattern of one socio-cultural segment rather than those of another.... It is unlikely that a study of symbolic ideas or symbolic conduct can produce effective results without a study of the things, people or relations to which they refer. (Wolf 1950, 20)

A final, important point was that processes of cultural integration would be affected by timing. The first nation-states, with their seacoasts on the North Atlantic, enjoyed the relative advantage of "rapid, massive and relatively even" ecological change in which the "replacement of older socio-cultural segments tied to the old ecology [was] relatively painless." Rapidly consolidating their industrial potential, these entities became predators on other, still-forming or potential nation-states, both in Europe and in Europe's colonies, "seizing their economic resources ... hindering the development of new socio-cultural groups ... limiting internal acculturation" by enforcing a kind of "medievalism" (Wolf 1950, 18). Social groups outside the North Atlantic core, but adopting its model of nationhood, faced extraordinary difficulties in their attempts at national integration. As we have seen, it has been Wolf's particular concern to analyze the torturous case of Germany.

A key insight, developed in later publications, concerns the strategic role of "interstitial" brokers of power in states that are poorly integrated. Although marginal to formal organizations, such brokers further integration by wielding relationships of kinship, friendship, and patronage at the synapses of local-national interaction. In states highly dependent on mediation, they also promote symbolic forms appropriate to their claims. A prefigurative example was the mestizo brokers of seventeenth-century Mexico for whom there was "no proper place in the social order." In a well-known analysis, Wolf portrayed them as catalysts in spreading the syncretic myth of the

Virgin of Guadalupe—a potent symbol of the "salient social relationships" of Mexican life as against the relationships of metropolitan Spain. "We are not dealing here with an element of a putative national character," he warned, "defined as a common denominator of all Mexican nationals." Rather, nations must possess "cultural forms or mechanisms which groups involved in the same overall web of relationships can use in their formal and informal dealings with each other" (1958).

"Aspects of Group Relations in a Complex Society" (1956*a*) examines the "web" of social relations that emerged in Mexico with the demise of the hacienda system. New cliques of "politician entrepreneurs" surged to fill a vacuum of power, transforming the national revolutionary party into a kind of holding company for local interests. Skilled in manipulation, the brokers or mediators in this arrangement exercised wile and violence to build personal followings, again establishing a symbolic frame that precluded other possibilities. Wolf's essay on friendship and patronage elaborates further on such "upward circulations." It is possible, he wrote, that "complex societies in the modern world differ less in the formal organization of their economic or legal or political systems than in the character of their supplementary interpersonal sets" (1966*b*, 19). In contrast to the "downward circulation" of French aristocratic courtly forms or British public-school manners, in Mexico, the "behavioral grammar" of an interstitial group—its social idiom standardizing interaction between power-seekers and followers—had set the tone, reflecting a new distribution of power in society. Although models of etiquette structuring supplementary interpersonal sets do not define national character, Wolf proposed, they "nevertheless indicate the way in which the parallelogram of social forces in one society differs from that of another" (1966*b*, 20).

In addition to interstitial "manipulators," Wolf has long been interested in the intelligentsia, which participated in each of the revolutions described in *Peasant Wars*. Marginal and powerless under the old regimes that teetered from the impact of European intrusion, members of this group had difficulty finding a secure tenure in the over-staffed bureaucracies of the public sector, even when they were European-educated. Nor could they turn a callous eye to the breakdown going on around them. If anything, a social location that bred frustration, and an education-enhanced tendency to think abstractly about society, predisposed such figures—schoolteachers, petty officials, and professionals—to enter into coalitions with peasant groups, offering expressions of moral outrage, organizational and tactical knowhow, and analyses of social ills (1969*a*, 287–289). They, too, played a role in knitting together emergent nation-states.

On the basis of these two sketches of social elements pivotal to national integration—power brokers with clientelistic followings and educated middle classes—we can see the possibility for tension between competing integrative schemes. An interesting pattern of dispute is explored in David Nugent's paper, "Structuring the Consciousness of Resistance: State Power, Regional Conflict, and Political Culture in Contemporary Peru." Nugent dissects an attempt to challenge Peru's legacy of decentralized, armed elites, wielding large clienteles: namely, the 1975 "moral community" movement in the regional capital of Chachapoyas. In "Notes toward an Ethnography of a Transforming State: Romania, 1991," Katherine Verdery identifies social actors promoting a "law governed" society in opposition to organizations of power in which arbitrariness, fiat, and terror predominate. Calling for a full ethnography of ways to imagine the postsocialist state, Verdery acknowledges Wolf for envisioning public power not as "society essentialized," but as sets of social relations, processes we can analyze.

Pamela Wright's paper, "The Timely Significance of Supernatural Mothers or Exemplary Daughters," concerns the Garifuna minority of Belize, over-represented among schoolteachers. Inspired by Wolf's analysis of the Virgin of Guadalupe, Wright dissects the annual, Garifuna-staged beauty contest to show its concatenous mix of imported models of gender and individual performance with elements drawn from indigenous dances, recitations, and song. Like the Guadalupe figure, the winning queen is shown to transform certain markers of ethnic identity into a claim for national standing.

"Being a Good Swede: National Identity as a Cultural Battleground," by Orvar Löfgren, asks how "the national" is culturally constituted such that the state becomes, in addition to a set of political institutions or organization of power, a focus for moral investment and cultural identity. Arguing for an ethnography of "the national" in the everyday, he concludes with a provocative contrast in the representation of patriotic symbols between Sweden and the United States. In the final paper of part 3, "Cultural Dis-Integration and the Invention of New Peace-Fares," Richard Fox looks at India, where the concept of *satyagraha* or nonviolent resistance spread as a compelling social relation and symbol, furthering not only the struggle for independence, but the imagined coming together of Hindus and Muslims. Interested in how, precisely, Gandhi "invented" this idea of a middle course between passive withdrawal and physical aggression, Fox traces the leader's personal knowledge of the British suffragists, the writings of Thoreau on civil disobedience, the noncompliance of Christian Anabaptists, and the *ahimsa* or nonkilling philosophy of Jainism. The resulting synthesis was, he argues, a dramatic instance of Wolf's definition of culture (Wolf 1982a, 387): "a series of processes that construct, reconstruct, and dismantle cultural materials, in response to identifiable determinants."

As Fox describes elsewhere (1990a), anti-Muslim Hindu nationalists have recently hijacked Gandhian symbolism, even as they resort to violence. We are reminded of Wolf's expectation that histories will take tragic turns. To quote the concluding thought of his essay "Cycles of Violence" (1987*a*, 148), "in this complex world in which many people are walking about among the powder kegs carelessly lighting their matches, we must realize that the enemy is all too often ourselves."

POLITICAL ECONOMY AND CULTURAL IDENTITY

In "Capitalism, Nation-Formation, and Ethnicity," delivered to a panel of the American Anthropological Association in 1987, Wolf noted that "even if we accept *Kapital* as a powerful analysis of the workings of the capitalist mode of production, we will not find in that book much about the culturally marked phenomena we want to comprehend." Because Marx sought to build an abstract model of the interplay of fully mobile capital and labor, he "extrapolate[d] the future of the world from the 'classical ground' of capitalism, England" (1987*d*, 1). Not only did World War I severely test the utopian vision of a united international proletariat; since that watershed, the accelerated accumulation of capital around the globe has been accompanied by a multiplication of "ethnikons." Quoting Ber Borochov's analysis of nationalism, capitalism, and the Jewish Question, Wolf posed the problem "why, on the one hand, the capitalist system appears as international, and destroys all boundaries between tribes and people and uproots all traditions, while on the other hand, it is itself instrumental in the intensification of the international struggle and heightens national self-consciousness" (in 1987*d*, 2).

The problem concerns the cultural dynamics of capitalism which Wolf has approached in two complementary ways, one that highlights responses to the atomizing, individualizing aspects of this mode of production, the other that brings out the ideological aspects of its successive embracing and disgorging of ever more varied diasporas. Regarding the first, there are frequent bows to Karl Polanyi for having discovered in English history the crystallization of an unprecedented model of reality, namely, the "fiction that men, land, and wealth were *nothing but* commodities" (1969*a*, 281–282). For the industrial bourgeoisie of the nineteenth century, this model was a self-evident and morally justified extension of the God-given mission to Improve and Progress, but for others it was a disaster. As Polanyi had observed, it implied disposing of people not only as laborers, but as "physical, psychological, and moral [beings]. Robbed of the protective covering of cultural institutions, human beings would perish from the effects of social exposure" (Polanyi 1957, 73).

Conceived this way, Wolf wrote in *Peasant Wars*, capitalism "entailed its own ruin ... paradoxically, the very spread of the capitalist market-principle also forced men to seek defenses against it ... either by cleaving to their traditional institutions, increasingly subverted by the forces they were trying to neutralize; or they could commit themselves to the search for new social forms" (Wolf 1969*a*, 282). Constructing, reconstructing, and dismantling cultural materials "in response to identifiable determinants," people created, and continue to create, individual and group identities that stabilize their position in relation to an ever-shifting world.

Europe and the People without History considers how the doomed system has lived on, indeed culturally constituted itself, in spite of, *and through,* these paradoxical, contradictory stabilizations. Europeans, the first carriers of capitalist forces, not only provoked the anarchic disruption of sociocultural arrangements, but, Wolf argues, they sought to legitimate their expanding power by installing a dynamic of distinctions. *Some* subordinate groups came to be identified, named, and classified as welcome participants in the wider system (the "manifold" to borrow a favored metaphor, in turn borrowed from Alexander Lesser), whereas other groups were stigmatized—consigned, in the apt phrase of Frederick Cooper and Ann Stoler, to the "dustbin of backwardness" (1989, 619 620). "In the capitalist mode," Wolf writes, "the regnant ideology assumes the equality of all participants in the market, in the face of basic distinctions in political and economic power" (1982*a*, 189). Capitalist ideology links these distinctions to differences of "virtue and merit." To take one example, participation in capitalist culture generally brings with it the "ability to acquire valued commodities"; conversely, "inability to consume signals social defeat." The rhythm of labor mobilization and abandonment "continuously reproduces an opposition between virtuous consumers and the disvalued poor" (1982*a*, 390).

There exists a temptation to account for "divide and conquer" ideologizing in relation to the requirements of the capitalist labor market, as if a hierarchical ordering of divergent groups, played off against one another, and the constant reproduction of a "reserve army" of the disemployed, were brought into being in order to enhance workers' exploitability. Wolf's analysis is different, seeking rather to connect the process of labeling to people's differentiated histories of engagement with capitalist expansion. It is these engagements, not the abstract requirements of capital, that set in motion the continuous production and reproduction of "symbolically marked distinctions." *Europe* invites us to approach the range of histories along a series of pathways through which we encounter forced mobilizations, pogroms, diasporas, and voluntary migrations. At the edges of capitalist expansion were the "commodity frontiers"—of the fur trade, for example—where mercantile action left noncapitalist modes more or less in place, subjecting them to only a gradual erosion. Zones of industrialized plantations and mining drew in squadrons of coerced labor—first as slaves, then under contract as "debt slaves" and indentured servants. Mass migrations supplied workers to growing textile and "heavy" industries, especially in the United States, and so on.

In each case, the history of recruitment to the wider system entered into the process of labeling. To take the most telling instance, stigmatizing racial stereotypes emerged hand in hand with the conquest and enslavement of particular peoples. To many Europeans, Wolf notes, the term "Indian" came to mean conquered New World population; "African" to mean slave and slave-furnishing society. Indians were "forced to labor or to pay tribute"; Africans hewed wood and drew water. They were "obtained in violence and put to work under coercion." The terms draw attention to historic facts of subjugation and servitude for new overlords (1982*a*, 380). Among Europeans, too, historical experiences of degradation flowing from the violent separation of peasants from land, or the ruin of cottage industries, brought, in their wake, a particular vulnerability to stigma. Wolf quotes Marx on Anglo-Saxon stereotyping, which viewed Irish laborers much as "poor whites" viewed Africans in the former American slave states (1982*a*, 277).

Such prejudices surely served the interests of capital—the English-Irish antagonism was "the secret of the impotence of the English working class, despite their organization," according to Marx (1975, 293–294). But Wolf does not rest the case here. Symbolic maneuvers make it possible for those who benefit, however modestly, from their engagement with capitalist markets to live with themselves, in a moral sense, even while knowing of the utter despair of those whose experiences have gone a different way. Like the "fetishism of commodities" that pretends there have been no relations of production, stereotyping naturalizes, and thereby masks, the historical interactions that weakened the stigmatized group. Because the terms "continue to invoke supposed descent from ... subjugated populations," they justify exclusions—from better paid jobs, from information, from political representation. The result is not to undercut the upper segments of the labor market in the interests of capital but, on the contrary, to insulate them "against competition from below" (Wolf 1982*a*, 381).

To the extent that labels refer to interactive processes, glossing over and hiding local experience, they may play a role in aggregating once separate groups. The ethnicities now claimed as authentic in the United States, for example, rarely coincide with "the initial self-identification of the industrial recruits, who first thought of themselves as Hanoverians or Bavarians rather than as Germans, as members of their village or parish rather than as Poles" (Wolf 1982*a*, 381). Such aggregates, when positively defined, embrace their new designations as qualifications for making economic and political claims (382). At the same time, however, the forces of capitalist expansion invariably generate movements of resistance or resentment against the imposed "definitions of virtue and demerit" (390). Thus Southern United States slaves appropriated literacy and with it a discourse of Protestant universalist equality which they turned against their masters.

In the words of the "Cycles of Violence" essay, because political-economic expansion engages "quite diverse populations, brought together either by conquest or by labor migration or both ... the mix of internal competition and resistance is then conjugated by ethnic divergence and conflicts over access to resources" (1987a, 146–147). But outcomes are rarely clear. Wolf has long been attracted to careful, detailed accounts of contradictory encounters. Two examples, presented in the AAA symposia in his honor but published elsewhere, are Gwendolyn Hall's research on race relations in colonial Louisiana (Hall 1992) and Ann Stoler's account of the cultural politics of exclusion in colonial Southeast Asia (Stoler 1992). In the Louisiana case, as analyzed by Hall, frontier conditions united Indians, Africans, and Europeans in mutually supportive ways, enabling a hybridization of race, language, and culture, even as the Spanish crown legally installed its racial categories of white, black, and mulatto. Stoler shows how, in the home country, nineteenth century Europeans experienced an emergent dialectic between "liberal impulses" for social welfare and expanded political representation as against new discriminations based on sexual morality, parenting styles, and domestic arrangements. Translated to the colonies, the dialectic reinforced, on the one hand, a rhetoric of "our civilizing, educative mission," but on the other hand an anxious focus on mixed blood.

The chapters that make up part 4, below, detail encounters of political economy and cultural identity in similarly nuanced ways. Michael Adas's "The Reconstruction of 'Tradition' and the Defense of the Colonial Order" looks at how British colonial administrators in Nigeria sought to nail down a legal and political order in the face of their compatriots' disruptive commercial and missionizing initiatives. Turning to hierarchical arrangements labeled "tribes" as the favored guarantors of social order, they depicted the Northern emirates as "more evolved" than the peoples of the Niger Delta, more like Europe's feudal monarchs, and therefore better suited to participate in rule. Conversely, Western-educated elites and migrants to cities were held up as singularly dangerous sources of disintegration. In "Who Were the Bushmen?" Edwin Wilmsen finds whites in Southern Africa, including white anthropologists, promoting the label "Bushmen" for a congeries of increasingly proletarianized forager-pastoral and forager peoples. This obscured both the fluidity of these peoples' relations with groups differently encoded and the processes that, historically, had produced their marginalization. The term, Wilmsen shows, not only denigrated those who had been relegated to the lower echelons of the labor pool; it served as a "justificatory premise for inequality."

Complementing these papers on the dynamics of distinction are two papers on self-identification. In the first, "Amazonian Windows to the Past: Recovering Women's Histories from the Ecuadorean Upper Amazon," Blanca Muratorio examines how extensively a sixteenth-century Jesuit mission, supplemented by a mission of Josephine nuns in 1922, colonized the minds of Napo Quichua-speaking women. Notwithstanding the mission efforts, and the engagement of Napo Quichua producers with a succession of commodity markets, these women were sufficiently affirming of their own traditions to transform both Eve and the Virgin Mary into local cultural heroes with appropriately indigenous values of femininity.

We conclude with Gustavo Lins Ribeiro's "Ethnic Segmentation of the Labor Market and the 'Work Site Animal.'" Based on fieldwork among highly skilled engineers and construction workers on a mammoth, ten-year project, building a hydroelectric dam near the Argentina-Paraguay border, it examines the self-identifications of what might be called "neo-gypsies"—experts who regularly visit homelands in Italy, France, Germany, or Argentina, but whose social networks, schools, marriage possibilities, and family life are increasingly constructed out of the transnational corporate resources and personnel encountered in permanently "temporary" homes. To Lins Ribeiro, these "work site animals" (*bichos-de-obra*), as they call themselves, exhibit the kind of "homeless mind" that capitalism, in so many of its operations, seems ever more prone to create.

NOTE

This introduction condenses my extended conversations with Rayna Rapp about the "ERW Project" and was further improved through her contribution of many specific phrasings. In preparing this chapter, I also benefited from William Roseberry's suggestion that I reflect on the words of the title—*Articulating Hidden Histories*—and from his own thinking on these concepts. Julia Emberly, Peter Kulchyski, Daniel Nugent, Hermann Rebel, and Derek Sayer gave careful readings to earlier drafts. As always, the most critical editors/questioners of my work have been Shirley Lindenbaum and Peter Schneider.

To the warm gratitude that I owe these colleagues, I would like to add my thanks to Eric R. Wolf, who has been a wonderful teacher and friend since I first attended his peasant seminars in the early 1960s. Declaring a love for facts, Eric Wolf was, even then, prepared to learn from students as well as peers, laypersons as well as professionals, the humble as well as the grand. And, generously attributing credit to even the most marginal and maverick of sources, he encouraged others in the quest for knowledge, too. Rereading his books and papers for the purposes of this volume, I was struck by the consistency with which he has modeled the world over these many years. In addition to ordering, and giving meaning to, his prodigious, beloved facts, his insights have led him to seek out and discover surprising new manifestations of the human condition. I am above all grateful to know that he is still at work.

TWO

Writing a History of Power: An Examination of Eric R. Wolf's Anthropological Quest

Ashraf Ghani

Anthropology, to Eric R. Wolf, is "a cumulative undertaking, as well as a collective quest that moves in ever-expanding circles" (1990*b*, 594). Wolf's anthropological praxis, I will argue, is a cumulative endeavor to analyze the intersection of power and culture in the history of the present. To examine the conceptual unity of his work, I read, and reread, his writings in the chronological order in which they were produced.[1] Theme, not time, however, is the organizing principle of this paper. Being truly cumulative, Wolf's imaginative quest can be best charted in terms of his own image of ever-expanding connective circles.

The conceptual field emerging from the intersection of the circles in his work cannot be mapped within the limits of an essay. I will therefore isolate for attention four nodal points of cross-over among his texts, ignoring other equally important nodal points. These are: (1) the conceptual unity of his texts; (2) the intersection of class, culture, and community in his examination of relations of production as power relations; (3) the processes of articulation of structural and tactical power; and (4) the contextualization of power in ethnographic writing. I will neither discuss Wolf's interlocutors, men and women in response to whose works and lives he has been articulating his own vision of anthropology, nor examine the arguments put forward in *Europe and the People without History*, for an adequate analysis of that book as a text and as a complex of interrelated arguments would require extended discussion. Connections among Wolf's texts, not the author or the changing context of his work,[2] will thus be the major focus of this paper.

I

Wolf's texts, I argue, are not held together by the mere elective affinity derived from being written by the same author. The texts gain their unity from being cumulative contributions to a conceptual space formed around the intersection of power and culture and rendered comprehensible by the engagement of their author in a clearly delineated and systematic attempt to write a history of the present as a history of power.

Wolf has been clear that the "dominant intellectual issue of the present is the nature of public power and its exercise" (1969c, 4). Emphasizing the need for an education in the realities of power, Wolf calls on anthropologists "to engage ourselves in the systematic writing of a history of the modern world in which we spell out the processes of power which created the present-day cultural systems and the linkages between them" (1969c, 10). Returning to an established theme in American anthropology, Wolf situates the issue of interconnection among cultures and societies in an expanded universe of power. Showing that both Alfred Kroeber and Alexander Lesser had conceptualized societies and cultures as "open systems" (1977b, 32; 1981a, 51), Wolf draws on Lesser's metaphors of "weblike, netlike connections" to describe the relations between such open systems (1982a, 19, 385).

Arguing that "architectural metaphors of structure or edifice" are ill suited to grasp overlapping relational fields (1988d, 757), Wolf not only searches for metaphors that are more relational but undertakes a historical examination of one of the most prevalent notions of our time, that of society. Tracing the changes in the historical use of the concept in the Euro-Atlantic region, he convincingly argues that the imagery associated with the concept of society did not fit Confucian China or the Muslim regions. Having revealed the limits of applications of the concept through comparative analysis, Wolf examines the use of the concept of society as a claim, "a claim advanced and enacted in order to construct a state of affairs that previously was not" (Wolf 1988d, 757). When the creation of society in England is examined in terms of a claim, it becomes clear that the morality at the very core of the concept is pivoted upon a state acting as the organ of moral discipline, deployed to expand and enable some actions and, simultaneously, to coerce and proscribe others (Wolf 1988d, 759). A history of the present cannot, therefore, be a history of societies, for to proceed in this manner is to forget that "the concept of Society has a history, a historical function within a determinate context, in a particular part of the world" (1988d, 759).

How then to conceptualize social relations? In *Europe and the People without History*, Wolf answers this question by organizing his narrative around the concept of modes of production. Is this to replace one static metaphor with another? Not if a mode of production is conceived of as "fields of force acting within fields of force" (1977b, 33). Well aware of the dangers of reification, Wolf argues that we

> need a vocabulary which can suggest relations, sets of relations, and forces which shape these relations. We need to turn away from an interest in the form of entities to a concern with vectors—forces of changing direction, ve-

locity, and magnitude, and of vectors of vectors. Once we look at phenomena as points of intersection between multiple vectors, we need to stress opposition as well as convergence, dislocation as well as cohesion, disintegration as well as integration, on the micro-level as well as on the macro-level of analysis ... we must learn how power is exercised and fought over. (1977b, 33–34)

Conceived in these terms, the concept of "social relations of production" is rephrased as the concept of structural power, "as power that structures the political economy" (1990b, 587). A "social game" and a system of signification, however, are central to the relations of governance in modes of structural power, for "each such mode would appear to require characteristic ways of conceptualizing and categorizing people.... Power is thus never external to signification—it inhabits meaning and is its champion in stabilization and defense" (1990b, 593). Stabilization, it should be emphasized, is an ongoing process, for "symbolic work is never done, achieves no final solution. The cultural assertion that the world is shaped in this way and not in some other has to be repeated and enacted, lest it be questioned and denied" (1990b, 593).

Wolf repositions Marx on an anthropological terrain. The result is not a mere importation of Marxist categories into anthropological discourse but the creation of a conceptual space from which to embark on writing the history of the present as a history of power. Having concluded *Europe and the People without History* with the observation that "the human sciences cannot do without a conception of culture" (1982a, 425), Wolf is currently engaged in an investigation of the relations between cultural forms and modes of structural power.

Wolf's agenda for writing a history of the present is clearly anthropological. A listing of some key areas of divergences in the intersecting approaches of Wolf and Michel Foucault, who stated that he was engaged in "writing the history of the present" (1979, 31), should make this clear. Despite the centrality of discourse/practice in his work, Foucault did not explicitly confront the question of culture(s) in the histories of the present. Wolf, by contrast, explicitly focuses on the relation between cultural forms and human maneuvers in these histories. Wolf, like Foucault, is interested in the micro-physics of politics. But whereas Foucault turned to analyze governmentality only toward the end of his life, Wolf has long been engaged in a systematic attempt to explore the articulation between the micro-physics of politics and the macro-politics of the state. Wolf shares Foucault's interest in social space as an arena of power but, unlike Foucault, is interested in the process of production of uneven development of regions or social spaces. Like Foucault, Wolf is interested in the genealogy of modern European practices. But, unlike Foucault, Wolf writes the history of the present as a history of interconnected cultural processes.

The centrality Wolf assigns to power is not the result of mere reflection on the lives of others but flows from his own experience of life, for he has had to grapple with the Holocaust as a marked moment in the history of the present.[3] Born in 1923, Wolf spent the first decade of his life in Vienna. But his Vienna was not Wittgenstein's Vienna, made familiar to us by the writings of Carl Schorske, Allan Janik and Stephen Toulmin, and the exhibition at the Museum of Modern Art. During his childhood, he saw parks turn into arenas of political conflict, where "student groups would come out and beat each other to death, literally" (in Ghani 1987, 346). "Hitler was becoming a presence in the early thirties, and that presence would mark one's life" (Ghani 1987, 348). Moving to Sudetenland in 1933, he stayed five years in a place where not only the "process of proletarianization was an everyday event visible to the naked eye" but where the complex interconnections between class and ethnicity were equally tangible phenomena (Ghani 1987, 349).

When the Nazis absorbed Austria in 1938, Wolf was sent to school in England. But in the summer of 1940, the British government, shaken by the swift German advance in France, decided to incarcerate all aliens from enemy countries residing in or around British cities. He was then sent to the Alien Internment Camp at Huyton, near Liverpool. Most of the detainees were not Nazis, but "Jewish refugees from the Continent; the camp commander was quoted as saying that he never knew so many Jews were Nazis" (Wolf 1977*b*, 28). Prominent in the camp were anti-Fascists, who not only took charge of essential services but organized discussion groups and lectures for and by the inmates. Wolf discovered the social sciences by listening to a lecture by Norbert Elias on social networks and learned "about Marxism by reading C. L. R. James" (1977*b*, 30).

A few months later, Wolf migrated to the United States, one of about one hundred and thirty-two thousand German Jews who were able to secure visas. He attended Queens College but his stay there was brief, for he quickly volunteered to join the United States army. His application was accepted in December 1942, and he spent most of the next three years on the European front with a unit of the mountain troops. Europe had "the feeling of a flood that had poured over people and the flood receding, and actually, physically, that's the way it looked. Italy, when we got there, was a battlefield, and people huddled in half-destroyed houses" (in Ghani 1987, 351). Back from the war, he availed himself of the G.I. Bill of Rights, obtaining first a B.A. in anthropology from Queens College in 1946 and then a Ph.D. in anthropology from Columbia University in 1951. To choose anthropology was not to escape but to confront the problem of power analytically, for "anthropology offered a prospect of studying a 'real' world of 'real people.' One had some hope then that knowledge could be linked to action, and that better knowledge would yield better action" (1978, 17). To insist on studying a "real world of real people" meant developing a research strategy to analyze the intersection of culture and power in the process of control of social labor.

II

Wolf argues that the direct producer is "always someone who stands to others in relation of kinsman, serf, slave, wage laborer. The controllers of production are never neutral technicians but elder kinsmen, lineage heads, chiefs, feudal lords, or capitalists" (1977*b*, 32). How to abstract the characteristic common to all these relations of control of social labor without losing sight of the specificity of each? By building on the insights of political economy. The reason for the choice is that political economy "explicitly emphasized the processes by which an organization of power is equipped with economic resources as central to the organic constellation to be explained" (1969*c*, 7). Taking power as the central problematic, categories of political economy, such as "capital," "rent," or "labor," "do not merely define factors of production, but serve to exhibit classes and the relationships among them" (1983*c*, 48). Focus on relations of power as the unit of analysis thus opens up the possibility of abstraction and generalization. But most of the practitioners of classical political economy who attended to power ignored history and culture—that is, the sources of specificity.[4]

Marx's critique of political economy, Wolf argues, opened up the space for the introduction of history into the discourse of political economy. After Marx's critique, the "classical categories can serve not only to visualize significant relations among classes, but also to illuminate historically different combinations of classes and their changing relationships" (1983*c*, 49). Wolf, the consummate ethnographer and practitioner of comparative analysis, thus produces a reading of classical political economy that is eminently anthropological, for he not only makes the categories of political economy intersect with the categories of culture and community but subjects these categories to the test of space and time through fieldwork: "Cultural form not only dictates the limits of the field for the social play, it also limits the direction in which the play can go in order to change the rules of the game, when it becomes necessary" (1959*a*, 173). To grasp the process of the production of the present as different from, yet based upon, the past is to take account of the dialectical interplay between how cultural forms define fields of human maneuver and how human maneuver always presses "against the inherent limitations of cultural forms" (1959*a*, 173).

To apprehend the tensions of real life is to master the discipline of detail and the discipline of context. Comparison is essential to understand each case (1977*a*, 197). But comparison must focus on processes rather than fetishized and essentialized societies. He argues that "in a majority of cases the entities studied by anthropologists owe their development to processes that originate outside them and reach well beyond them, that they owe their crystallization to these processes, take part in them, are affected by their demands, and affect them in turn" (1982*b*, 9).

Wolf's focus on the intersection of complex relational fields is evident in the very title of one of his papers, "Specific Aspects of Plantation Systems in the New World: Community Sub-cultures and Social Class" (1959*b*/1971, 163–178). He begins by "underlining the fact that the plantation is by definition a class-structured system of organization" (1959*b*/1971, 163). But he immediately moves to conceptualize class in relation to culture: the plantation "enables the laborer to produce more than he needs to satisfy his own culturally prescribed standards of consumption" while allowing the owner to "appropriate that surplus in culturally sanctioned ways" (163). The cultural relation, however, is not given but produced, for

> wherever the plantation has arisen, or wherever it was imported from the outside, it always destroyed antecedent cultural norms and imposed its own dictates, sometimes by persuasion, sometimes by compulsion, yet always in conflict with the cultural definitions of the affected population. The plantation therefore is also an instrument of force, wielded to create and to maintain a class structure of workers and owners, connected hierarchically by a staff-line of overseers and managers. (163–164)

The notion of community is then introduced as the spatial expression of the plantation: "Invariably the plantation creates new communities.... Everywhere these new communities also follow a basic plan which translates into spatial terms the chain of command of owners, managers, overseers, permanent laborers and seasonal workers" (164). To map the social space of the plantation is to render visible the power relations to the naked eye.

An anthropologist's gaze, however, moves to detect differences beneath the seeming unity: "If all plantations are class-structured and conform to a basic spatial plan, they nevertheless differ in the character of this class-structure and in the characteristic sub-cultures of these classes" (1959*b*/ 1971, 165). To grasp these differences, Wolf introduces two more variables: the manner of gearing labor to the enterprise and the manner in which the plantation disposes of its surplus. Focus on the first variable allows Wolf to distinguish old-style plantations, those using bound labor, from new-style plantations, those using free labor (166). Focus on the second variable allows him to draw the following contrast:

> [T]he new-style plantation is single-minded in its pursuit of profit; the fate of its labor-force is of no concern to it as long as enough workers are available to do necessary work. The old-style plantation, on the contrary, has a split personality. It produces goods for a market, but part of its energy goes into self-maintenance and status consumption. (166–167)

Once the field of relations and the terrain of their contestation is identified, Wolf moves to examine the patterning of subcultures in the two kinds of enterprises. He defines a subculture as "those several sets of cultural

forms through which a human group that forms part of a larger society maneuvers—consciously and unconsciously—to maintain or improve its particular balance of life works and life chances" (173–174). Personalized relationships seem to be the hallmark of the subculture of old-style plantations.
But when compared to kin or other face-to-face relationships, it becomes
clear that these relationships only "retain the *form* of personalized relationships, but serve different *functions*" (167). The function served is that of
underlining the dominant position of the owner of the plantation in relationship to the dependent position of the laborers. The social system of the
old-style plantation is mobilized to force the laborer to "adopt this manner
of behavior" (168). Operating on the basis of the cultural fiction that views
labor power apart from the person who carries it, the new-style plantation
"divorces itself from any responsibility to its labor supply" (169), thereby
paving the way for the emergence of a proletarian subculture. The contours
of this subculture, however, cannot be merely assumed on the basis of conditions in one community but need to be demonstrated through careful
comparative analysis.

Rejecting the then prevalent notion of community as a closed system,
Wolf conceptualizes community as a nodal point of intersection among
overlapping relational fields in open systems. In a series of papers published
in the 1950s, he shows how a community can be analyzed as a crosscutting
manifold.[5] Taking peasant to mean "a structural relationship, not a particular cultural content" (1955*b*, 454), Wolf classifies Latin American peasants
into seven relational constructs, called types, carefully distinguishing the relation of each to the market and the state. The closed corporate peasant
community (hereafter CCPC), a type first named in 1955 and elaborated
in 1957, has been the major focus of academic discussion. But to understand Wolf's concept of community, the arguments about CCPC need
to be considered in conjunction with arguments developed in two other
papers written during the same time about Mexico.

Rejecting the notion of community as a closed system, Wolf argues that
communities are best viewed as "the local termini of a web of group relations which extend through intermediate levels from the level of the community to that of the nation. In the community itself, these relations may
be wholly tangential to each other" (1956*a*, 1065). The focus of analysis,
therefore, shifts first to relations among "groups of people" and then to the
"exercise of power by some people over others" (1066). Regardless of "what
combination of cultural forms" a "complex society" may utilize, "it must
also wield power to limit the autonomy of its constituent communities and
to interfere in their affairs ... through the forms of an economic or political
apparatus" (1066).

Power relations among groups are formed and transformed in space and
time, making it necessary to analyze the change or stability of these relations

through historical time and social space. Wolf does not use the concept of social space, but his analyses of "the Mexican Bajio" and the CCPC are superb examples of how the nodal points of intersection among relational fields form distinctive social spaces. Defining the Bajio as an area where development was "subject to violent fluctuation" (1955*a*, 181), Wolf, after analyzing this tortured history, concludes that "the very forces which produced the regional integration of the Bajio seem to have been responsible for the disintegration of the independent nation" (193). To write the history of the present is not to describe a linear development but to come to grips with the complexity of multiple histories taking place simultaneously.

Rejecting arguments couched in terms of "survival" and "cultural lag" (1957, 13), Wolf conceptualized the formation and the possible dissolution of the CCPC in terms of a historical process of relations among groups. The formation of CCPCs was closely related to attempts at incorporation by the Spanish Crown in Latin America and by the Dutch Colonial power in Indonesia (1955*a*, 181; 1955*b*, 456; 1957, 7–8). Wolf argues, moreover, that "the corporate peasant community is not an offspring of conquest as such, but rather of the dualization of society into a dominant entrepreneurial sector and a dominated sector of native peasants" (1957, 8). The process of dualization is then analyzed in terms of social, economic, administrative, and spatial practices (9–15). People in such CCPCs are not, however, mere objects to be acted upon from the outside but active in the production and reproduction of their communities: "Seen from the outside, the community as a whole carries on a series of activities and upholds certain 'collective representations.' Seen from within, it defines the rights and duties of its members and prescribes large segments of their behavior" (1955*b*, 456). Neither power nor class divisions are absent from the CCPC, but the path to power is mediated through the community, and "class structure must find expression within the boundaries set by the community" (458). When the community cannot contain power differentials from becoming enduring, "the corporate organization comes to represent but a hollow shell, or is swept aside entirely" (1957, 14).[6]

Wolf offered his strategy of analysis of group relations in a context when it could be observed that "the peasant is an immemorial figure on the world's social landscape, but anthropology noticed him only recently" (Geertz 1961, 1). Broadening the scope of his inquiry to the world as a whole, he synthesized his findings in his 1966 book, *Peasants*. The guiding threads of his analysis are succinctly stated in a *Current Anthropology* "Comment" six years later:

> I regarded the organization of peasants into states as the chief characteristic distinguishing them from populations of cultivators that do not form parts of states. I therefore regard rent not merely as an economic payment for the use of land, but as a payment made by virtue of relations of power that in the case

of peasants but not in the case of primitives, are guaranteed by the state. For clarification I might add that I here draw on the insight that property is not an economic but a social and political relation, and that the legal and political constitutions exist, among other things, to guarantee property relations. (1972a, 411)

As we have seen, Wolf identifies classical political economy as the general and Marx's critique of that tradition as the particular sources of this insight. But to appropriate Marx's insight, Wolf had to work against the dominant strands of Marxism, characterized by dogmatic insistence on economic determinism and confinement of culture to the realm of the "superstructure" (Colletti 1974, 3–111; Laclau and Mouffe 1985, 7–93). By focusing on the intersection of class, culture, and community, Wolf identifies a conceptual space for anthropological analysis that avoids the ahistorical and reductionist tendencies of classical political economy and Marxism while allowing for the appropriation of their insights. He further expands this conceptual space by differentiating between structural and tactical power.

III

Distinguishing among four modes of power,[7] Wolf singles out structural and tactical power for special attention: "Structural power shapes the social field of action so as to render some kinds of behavior possible, while making others less possible or impossible" (1990b, 587). Tactical power, however, refers to a mode of power where one actor circumscribes "the actions of others within determinate settings" (586). Focus on organization is the key to understanding the intersection of modes of structural and tactical power, for structural power shapes the form of tactical power. And, as we have already seen, to understand the process of production of the history of the present is to analyze the dialectical interplay between cultural forms and human maneuver.

Wolf's writings provide a number of methodological guidelines on how to analyze the organization of power as process. Treating the self-representations of organizations as claims rather than facts, Wolf maps the topography of power relations in terms of regions that are formally strategic and those that are interstitial, supplementary, or parallel to an economic or political system. Sometimes informal organizations merely cling to formal ones, but at other times informal mechanisms play a crucial role in making formal organizations operate: "The anthropologist has a professional license to study such interstitial, supplementary, and parallel structures in complex society and to expose their relation to the major strategic, overarching institutions" (1966b, 2).

With power relations among groups as his unit of analysis, Wolf not only examines the role of kinship, friendship, and patron-client relations in mediating formal and informal organizations but calls for the anthropological study of the role played by "brokers" in this process: "For they stand guard over the crucial junctures or synapses of relationships which connect the local system to the larger whole" (1956*a*, 1075). Brokers derive their power from mediating between individuals operating in a national arena and community-oriented individuals seeking to improve their life chances.[8]

To focus on functions performed by brokers is not to introduce any hidden assumptions about the stability of a system of power relations. Facing, Janus-like, in two directions at once, brokers "must cope with the conflicts raised by the collision" of national and community interests: "They cannot settle them, since by doing so they would abolish their own usefulness to others. Thus they often act as buffers between groups, maintaining the tensions that provide the dynamics of their actions" (1076).

Such tensions could either lead to a dispersal of power of the state or hide its weakness beneath a veneer of strength. Explaining the emergence of the Mexican Bajio as a regional node in the eighteenth century, Wolf argues that "local power in the hands of the entrepreneurs necessarily diminished power in the hands of government officials. The formation of many local nuclei of power necessarily diminished effective state control" (1955*a*, 192). But once these nuclei of power have emerged, the critical variable is whether they could be grouped into a "wide-ranging network of strategic alliances for political purposes" (Wolf and Hansen 1967, 171). Failure to form such networks of strategic alliances could result in the production of Caudillo-like systems of politics, marked by the violent competition of groups of armed men for succession to offices with uncertain periods of tenure (169).

Subjecting his findings from Latin America to the test of comparative analysis in *Peasant Wars of the Twentieth Century*, Wolf formulates a more general conclusion about why seemingly strong states were weak:

> Such a situation of weak contenders, unable to neutralize each other's power, seems to invite the rise or perpetuation of a dominant central executive, attempting to stand "above" the contending parties and interest groups, and to consolidate the state by playing one group against the other.... Yet because the dictatorship is predicated on the relative debility of the class groups and political forces which constitute society, its seeming strength derives from weakness, and its weakness ultimately becomes evident in its impotent struggle against challenges from within, unless it can find allies strong enough to sustain it against the challenge. (1969*a*, 284)

Such an alliance was possible in Germany and Japan but not in Mexico, Russia, China, Vietnam, Algeria, and Cuba. In *Peasant Wars*, Wolf uses the concept of tactical power not only to pinpoint the critical role played by the middle peasantry but also to explain how the formation of a network of strategic alliances allows for the replacement of one form of state by another

(1969*a*, 290–302). To analyze power as process requires not only the conceptualization of community as the "termini of group relations" but also the conceptualization of the state as a site of intersection of strategic networks of alliances among groups. The state is thus a social relation in historical time.

To analyze organization as process, however, one ought not to stop at the temporal dimension but to examine the spatial and cultural dimensions as well.[9] In a series of papers written between 1950 and 1951 but not published, Wolf first explored the "cultural processes involved in the formation of the modern nation-state," drawing a contrast between North Atlantic Europe, where political and ecological changes were continuous, and areas colonized by the nations of North Atlantic Europe, where political and ecological changes were discontinuous (1950, 23). Space, even in this early formulation, is examined as a relational process produced and reproduced in a field of forces, rather than being seen as a structure endowed with fixity. As Wolf wrote with John Cole in 1974, the institutions of state and market are prominent in the field of forces:

> Complex societies are ecologically grounded, but the rise of the state introduces into the ecological set a specifically political element that transforms problems of ecological limitations into decisions of a *political* economy. State development not only entails the subjugation and incorporation of various locally adapted groups. It also aims at the development of an apparatus that recombines ecological resources in new and unforeseen ways.... The market may indeed be seen as a set of mechanisms designed to challenge local adaptations and reallocate resources in ways unique at the local level. (Cole and Wolf 1974, 285)

To examine these processes in concrete terms requires examining property connections in complex societies, "property" understood as a cultural category, as "a battleground of contending forces which utilize jural patterns to maintain or restructure the economic, social and political relations of society" (1972*b*, 202). Culture and power are thus inextricably linked. For example, Wolf insists on interpreting impartible inheritance not merely as an economic strategy but also as a "strategy which creates and maintains a social order, a distribution of rights and disabilities, hence a structure of power" (1970*a*, 111). This means analyzing the multiple processes culminating in the crystallization of impartible inheritance as a cultural form, an approach also evident in his analyses of ritual coparenthood (Wolf and Mintz 1950), the origins of Islam (Wolf 1951), the Virgin of Guadalupe (Wolf 1958), Santa Claus (Wolf 1962*d*), and a number of other such forms. Crystallization of a cultural form does not spell the end of history, however, for "cultural sets—and sets of sets—are continuously in construction, deconstruction, and reconstruction, under the impact of multiple processes operative over wide fields of social and cultural connections. These processes and these connections are ecological, economic, social, political; they also involve thought and communication" (1982c, 11).

To focus on thought and communication in a field of power relations is to focus on ideology, defined as the more "power-laden messages or utterances" in a circuit of communication (1985, 16). The ideological process has three moments: repetition across many social domains, repetition across levels of sociocultural complexity, and the creation and elaboration of rituals (1985, 19–20). Wolf writes:

> The ultimate effect of ritual and its guiding concept lies not in the genesis of particular specifiable meanings, but in the maintenance and elaboration of ideologically charged chains of signification. The ultimate function of these chains of signification is to underwrite, maintain, and enlarge the fund of social power exercised by structurally licensed categories, groups or strata in the domination of society. (1985, 22)

Culture is never external to power, for all modes of power are cultural relationships in space and time. Ethnography is the arena where Wolf contextualizes these manifolds.

IV

Wolf argues that "every society is a battlefield between its own past and its future" (1959a, 106). How does he devise a strategy of presentation to capture the ongoing dialectics of production of society as a claim? Like Karl Marx (1975 [1867], 19) and Bronislaw Malinowski (1984 [1922], xvii, 13, 84), Wolf confronts the question in practice, producing ethnographies that differ not only in content but also in *form* from other ethnographies. To illustrate this contention. I will briefly examine three of his ethnographies.[10]

Sons of the Shaking Earth is described as "an attempt to trace the lifeline of a culture" (1959a, vii). The book consists of eleven chapters, the first four of which are called "The Face of the Land," "Generations of Adam," "Confusion of Tongues," and "Rise of the Seed-Planters." Despite the difference in their content, the form of these four chapters corresponds to divisions found in other monographs of the period. But whereas the dominant tendency in the monographs of the period is to reduce history either to a timeless ethnographic present or to a repetitive structural rhythm, Wolf devotes the bulk of his book to the analysis of historical changes in the modes of structural power in Middle America.

He begins by locating human agency in its spatial setting in Middle America: "where nature pulls toward disunity, men have wrought unity in diversity through human means" (1959a, 18). Prominent among these means have been power relations culminating in the formation of "galactic systems," whereby constellations of villages and towns have been brought within the orbit of an expanding state. The reproduction of a galactic polity, however, is a historical process, for galaxies can break up into solar systems (19–20). The spatial arena is thus clearly delineated. But time provides the dominant narrative structure of the text. It is not just any notion of time but that of historical conjunctures leading to changes in structural modes of power that serve as markers for dividing the book into chapters. In moving from chapter to chapter the reader moves from historical era to historical era. Far from being timeless, the ethnographic present is conceptualized as the battleground between the past and the future. In his concluding paragraph, Wolf argues that "men still remain torn between yesterday and tomorrow; and Middle America remains in travail. There can therefore be no finis to this book, nor any prophecy.... There is still time until the sun rises, but men scan the sky; for their lives are mortgaged to tomorrow" (256).

Wolf deploys his mastery of detail not only to illuminate the specific context but to suggest broader generalizations. Describing the process that allowed Mesoamerican priests to exercise power over people, he states that "the new priesthood controlled the religious calendar which told people when to clear new land for planting, when to plant, when to weed, and when to harvest. Religious ceremonies were held to further the tasks of cultivation" (81). He then goes on to argue that

> all religions are interested in binding time. They gear the life-cycle of the individual to the recurrent rituals of society, and they synchronize this social time with the march of cosmic time. As the individual merges his life-span with that of society, he gains the security of knowing that his life will be lived in a rhythm which was there before he was born and will be there when he is gone. But even societies contemplate the infinite silence of cosmic space with fear and uncertainty. Calendar systems serve to bind this cosmic time, to domesticate it, as religion domesticates other aspects of the universe, and men derive comfort in visualizing the passage of cosmic time reduced to a mere sequence of cycles of social time. (87–88)

He makes an equally striking contribution to the analysis of the process through which a state could rise above classes. By 1492, an aristocratic tendency, emphasizing warfare, and a merchant-entrepreneurial tendency, emphasizing capital accumulation, were heading for collision in Spain. But the conquest of the New World radically changed the rules of the game:

> In the conquest of the New World, the crown saw its opportunity to escape the limitations of internal Spanish politics. Gold from the Indies would enrich not only the eager adventurer; a fifth of all gold and silver mined in the New World would be the king's to finance a new royal army, navy, and officialdom, to build the bases of absolutist power upon institutions wholly indepen-

dent of nobility, middle classes, or peasant cultivators. Wealth from the Indies
would underwrite a state standing above all classes, above the endless quarrels
of contending interest groups. This state would speak with a new voice, with a
new will. It would no longer be bound by precedent; it would set aside solutions which had become traditional, overgrown with the "cake of custom"
and with compromise. The New World would not have to grow, piecemeal,
in the shadows of ancient complexities: it would be a planned world, projected into reality by the royal will and its executioners. Thus utopia would
become law, and law utopia. (1959*a*, 162–163)

The consequences of the failure of this utopia for the history of the present in Mesoamerica and Latin America are discussed not only in *Sons of the
Shaking Earth* but also in *The Human Condition in Latin America* (1972), jointly
written with Edward Hansen. Conceived in the form of a Brechtian drama,
The Human Condition in Latin America is among the early attempts in anthropology to cede to voices other than the voice of the author a central place
in the text. Beginning with the present, the book moves between the past
and the present to make the reader take stock of the history that is present
in Latin America.

Economic dependency is the foremost feature of this history, symbolized
by the prominence of the enclave economy and the dependence of life on
the fluctuations of the world market: "Frequently, in the past, a crop or
product has experienced a boom, only to suffer afterward the consequences
of a sudden slump" (Wolf and Hansen 1972, 10). This dependence on exports is spatially manifested in the pattern of traffic, connecting the interior
to the sea. After describing the traffic pattern, Wolf and Hansen let Juan
Bautista Alberdi, an Argentine, speak on the issue. Writing in 1853, he
argued that Spain

> placed the heads of our states where the feet should be. For the ends of isola-
> tion and monopoly this was a wise system; for our aims of commercial expan-
> sion and freedom it is disastrous. We must bring our capitals to the coast, or
> rather bring the coast into the interior of the continent. The railroad and the
> electric telegraph, the conquerors of space, work this wonder better than all
> the potentates on earth. (Wolf and Hansen 1972, 18)

The authors then conclude that "as a result of past history, the Latin American countries have their face turned toward the oceans rather than toward
the interior of the continent. . . . Rather than effectively locked together on
the same land mass, the countries of Latin America are, in effect, islands
connected by coastwise shipping" (Wolf and Hansen 1972, 19).

The spatial expressions of political economy of Latin America are not
limited to the pattern of traffic, for the enclave economy has carved a series
of distinctive but interrelated social spaces. These social spaces are visible to
the naked eye, for "the enclave and its setting or matrix differ in capitaliza-

tion, in organization, in rhythm of life, in the purposes to which life is de-
voted" (10). These social spaces, ranging from stores to industry, are then
described in detail, allowing the reader to understand the people who
make economic organizations function (118). Recurrent themes in these social spaces are the importance attached to family ties, coparenthood relations, and patron-client relations. The conditions faced by Latin American
people are those of economic scarcity and political uncertainty:

> To defend themselves against such scarcity and uncertainty, in the wider eco-
> nomic and political field, people therefore rely on the more intimate and more
> assured ties of kinship, friendship, and personal acquaintance. If we call this
> set of ties to kin, friends, and personal acquaintances the personal field, then
> we could say that in Latin America people invest much of their effort in con-
> solidating their personal fields. They increase security in the narrow orbit to
> counteract insecurity in the wider orbit. (200)

Relations in the personal field, it is quickly made clear, are relations of
tactical power. Patron-client ties, for instance, "could not occur between
people who are each other's equal; they necessarily imply inequality. They
stem from inequality; but they also serve to soften that inequality, building
ties of mutual support across the gap created by the difference in wealth and
power" (203). Can structural continuity of personal ties be taken as evidence
of political personalism in Latin America? The answer is no, for "when trying to analyze a particular trait in a particular culture, it is imperative to
look at the context in which the trait occurs.... We cannot let the continuity of personalism in the system obscure the fact that it has come to be the
province of the 'classes' at the exclusion of the 'masses,' when once it involved both" (351). The clearest way to deal with issues of continuity and
change in Latin American political structures, Wolf and Hansen argue, "is
to focus on the structural aspects of present power relationships and see how
they compare with past alignments" (351).

A comparison of the Latin American and metropolitan sources of elite
power reveals major changes in the source of elite power and in their relations with the masses:

> Metropolitan intervention in the political organization of Latin America has
> vastly increased in scope and complexity. This intervention has progressively
> entailed a diminution of power wielded by the Latin American elites in their
> own domains, compared to the power wielded by the metropolitan elites. It
> has correspondingly involved increased dependence on the metropolis on the
> part of the elites, coupled with progressive circumscription of their autonomy
> and initiative within their own countries. The increasing interlocking between
> metropolitan and Latin American elites has involved an effort to rationalize
> production, in the capitalist sense of the word (cut costs, enhance profits); as
> this process has been carried out, it has involved a divorce between the masses
> and the elites in every respect. (351)

The Hidden Frontier (1974), a book written jointly with John Cole, focuses on the dialectical relation between village and nation. The relation is dialectical

> because village and total society exist in opposition and often in contradiction. It is dialectical because these two units in opposition interpenetrate each other and act upon one another in social and cultural interchanges. It is dialectical, finally, in that this interaction generates an ongoing transformation over time, which subjects the narrower unit to ever more comprehensive processes of integration, or synthesis. (Cole and Wolf 1974, 3–4)

The bulk of the study focuses on two small adjacent villages in the Italian Tyrol, separated by provincial boundaries. The two villages differ in their systems of inheritance. But research establishes "convergence between the two villages in ecologically grounded practice and divergence in politically grounded ideology" (19). As these convergent practices and divergent ideologies have to be demonstrated, Cole and Wolf marshal an impressive amount of historical and contemporary data to document their contention. Rephrasing their argument in chapter 10, they state that "the two villages converge in social practices that resolve common ecological problems, but diverge in the social ends to which their patterns of behavior are directed" (233). A major difference between the two villages lies in the way power is exercised within the families. In German-speaking St. Felix, adhering to impartible inheritance, "the battle for authority is not only fought between father and heir apparent, it is also fought between older and younger brothers, and among all brothers and all sisters" (243). In Italian-speaking Tret, adhering to partible inheritance,

> authority is not vested exclusively in the male head of household; wife and husband complement each other in its exercise, and each participates in a distinct subset of relations with the daughters and sons of the household. . . . The Tret family may be compared to a severalty, a shareholding corporation, while the Felixers cleave rigidly to the concept of each man a lord on his domain. (244)

This difference, Cole and Wolf argue, "stems from the villages' differential involvement over time with the political systems that have exercised sovereignty in this marginal mountain area" (272). Explication of tactical power is thus inextricably linked with explication of structural power. Both villages were founded as advance posts of two expansionist movements. But organizationally the two movements differed in significant ways from each other:

> While Felixers could link up with a viable political infrastructure already established in the adjacent valleys and piedmont, the Nónes in general and the Trettners in particular found only weak support in a fragmented and impotent political structure, overshadowed by the more dynamic polity to the north.

Thus, the Trettners put their reliance in ties of affinity, weaving and reweaving multiple interpersonal linkages. The Felixers, however, as an advance guard into contested ground, could rely on the Tyrolese apparatus developed first by the Counts of Tyrol and later by the Hapsburgs.... In their local culture, ecological adaptation and commitment to Tyrolese statecraft fused with each other. In turn, participation in statecraft reinforced their cultural antagonisms to other ethnic groups. (278–279)

To indicate how this historical difference is reproduced in the history of the present, Cole and Wolf provide a detailed analysis of the differences in state-sponsored projects in both areas, offering in the process abundant documentation for conceptualizing the state as a social and cultural relation. This is only fitting, for Wolf has been engaged in a systematic effort to write an ethnography of the state.

To face power is to explore the continuous dialectic of culture and power as relations among persons in space and time. Having documented the multiplicity of the histories of the present in his ethnographies, Wolf confronted the challenge of analyzing the intersection of these histories within the framework of a single narrative in *Europe and the People without History*. The narrative is made possible by the premise that the "world of humankind constitutes a manifold, a totality of interconnected processes" (1982*a*, 3). The anthropological task of the moment is "to understand more precisely how cultural forms work to mediate social relations among particular populations" (19). Facing this challenge, Wolf is continuing to write the history of the present as a history of power.

NOTES

I am grateful to Rula Ghani, Sidney Mintz, Rayna Rapp, and Jane Schneider for their comments on an earlier version of this paper.

1. The aim of the first reading was to prepare for a conversation with Eric Wolf about his life and work. A section of this conversation is available in published form (Ghani 1987, 346–366). The aim of the second reading was to prepare for writing this essay.

2. Joan Vincent provides an admirable account of the context. See her *Anthropology and Politics: Visions, Traditions, and Trends* (1990, especially pt. 2).

3. Rayna Rapp and Jane Schneider remind me of the importance of the Holocaust to Wolf.

4. Marx argued that most of the classical political economists regarded bourgeois relations of production as natural. He credits Richard Jones's 1831 essay for recognizing these relations as historical relations (see Marx 1971, 429).

5. Wolf owes the term "manifold" to Lesser (Vincent 1990, 193).

6. For Wolf's review of the CCPC concept, see his 1986*b*.

7. These are: (1) "power as an attribute of the person, as potency or capability";

(2) "as the ability of an ego to impose its will on an alter, in social action, in interpersonal relations"; (3) tactical power; (4) structural power (1990*b*).

8. Clifford Geertz responded to Wolf's call by focusing on the role of cultural brokers in Indonesia (1960).

9. David Harvey convincingly argues that there has been a strong tendency in the social sciences "to give time and history priority over space and geography" (1989, xii).

10. "San Jose: Subcultures of a Traditional Coffee Municipality" (1956*b*, 171–264) is Wolf's first ethnography. As William Roseberry (1978, 26–36) has analyzed this text, I concentrate on Wolf's other ethnographic writings here.

PART TWO

Peasants: Concepts and Histories

THREE

The Cultural History of Peasantries

William Roseberry

Anthropology ... *must* be historical and particular if it aspires to be sociological and generalizing. (Mintz 1982, 187)

Anthropologists normally attempt a task of cross-cultural comparison by first assembling "cases," models of societies or cultures constructed from observed or reported data. These models are then either compared synchronically or seriated with respect to each other, using one or more diagnostic criteria to order the cases in question. On occasion, the synchronic or seriated sequence is given a diachronic interpretation and placed in a frame of elapsed time to arrive at statements of process (e.g., "adaptation" or "development"). We are all familiar with these procedures, and probably have employed them ourselves at some time. We know that it can be done and is done, often with scientifically and aesthetically pleasing results.

I would, however, raise a number of objections to this procedure. First, we often take the data observed or recorded as realities in and of themselves, rather than as more or less tangible results of underlying processes operating in historical time. What we then see and compare are these tangible and observable (and indeed often temporary) precipitates of processes, not the processes themselves. Second, we have known at least since the diffusionists that no society or culture is an island. There are always interchanges and interrelationships with other societies and cultures. What seems less obvious, however, is that these interrelated "cases" appeared in the ken of Europocentric anthropology only because Europeans or Euro-Americans visited them, and these visitors did so because they were propelled by forces that were the outcome of something we call capitalism. Thus, what we explore and observe in the locations anthropologists visit around the world stands in a specific relationship to this process of expansion, which in turn responds to the workings out of a particular structure or relational set. (Wolf 1981*b*, 41, 42)

These statements, published in the early 1980s by two anthropologists whose collaborations began during the late 1940s in their graduate careers and while participating in Julian Steward's Puerto Rico project, seem to call for entirely different anthropological projects. Sidney Mintz's claim might recall a familiar opposition between history and science, the particular and general, or the "idiographic" and the "nomothetic," appearing to restore a Boasian particularism. Eric R. Wolf's statement seems to reject the very foundations of such a particularistic anthropology, drawing our attention to "underlying processes operating in historical time," of which particular social and cultural configurations are "more or less tangible results" or "precipitates." My argument, however, is that both claims emerge from and express a common anthropological vision, one that transcends the very oppositions that Mintz's statement seems to reproduce. In their ethnographic and historical work, both authors have developed approaches to the "particular" that are simultaneously "general," and have shown that "underlying processes" can only be grasped in their historical, particular, and contradictory instantiations—in Jamaican houses and yards, English teas, Mexican reverence for the Virgin of Guadalupe, or Tyrolean inheritance strategies.

To understand this perspective and these anthropological practices, a discussion that first explored the ways in which their work is "historical and particular" and then examined their "sociological and generalizing" features would simply reproduce the opposition. We need instead to concentrate on the distinctive features of this perspective's understanding of the particular and the critical comparative history that it makes possible. I therefore begin with a discussion of Wolf's and Mintz's perspectives on "cultural history," as expressed in *The People of Puerto Rico* (Steward et al. 1956*b*), examine the elaboration of a cultural historical perspective in Wolf's subsequent work, and then contrast this perspective with a well-known and classical attempt to write a critical comparative history.

I

At the beginning of a section on "The Cultural Background of Contemporary Puerto Rico," the authors of *The People of Puerto Rico* outlined what they called a "cultural historical approach." Beginning with the assertion that "the varieties of subcultures which distinguish regional, occupational, and other special groupings within contemporary national societies result from the impact of national and supranational institutions upon the cultural heritage of people living in a particular natural environment," they offered the following observation based on their studies in Puerto Rico:

> From the very beginning of the Spanish colonial period the society became differentiated into socio-cultural segments, or special social groups which cannot be explained solely by the Hispanic tradition. Native Indians of *encomiendas* and *repartimientos*, Indians from Hispaniola and the mainland, plantation slaves

from Africa, unattached laborers, squatter subsistence farmers, large planters, government officials, churchmen, soldiers and army officers all had distinctive statuses, roles, and behavior patterns which must be understood as local responses to and adaptations of colonial institutions. During subsequent centuries wholly new subcultural configurations emerged in response to international historical developments and the resultant changes in institutional forms. Modifications in world markets, trade regulations, labor supply, technology, credit, and legislation reacted upon every subculture in the island.... The lifeways of these ... rural types were so deeply affected both in a developmental and functional sense by the colony and empire of which they were parts that they cannot be properly understood without reference to the larger context. (Steward et al. 1956*a*, 31, 32)

In recent years, it has become common to read this claim, and the subsequent work of its authors, as a kind of world-system theory *avant la lettre*, albeit "less extreme." Although it is true that *The People of Puerto Rico* can be taken as one of the founding texts in an anthropology concerned with the effects of a wider world upon local peoples, the presentist depiction of its authors as Wallersteinians in anthropological disguise misreads their texts and ignores the intellectual challenge they presented. We need to read their claim in the context of the arguments the authors were pursuing in the original text. Here it is important to recognize that *The People of Puerto Rico* contains two levels of argument, which we might call "external" and "internal." At an external level, the authors might be in agreement with Julian Steward, project director and principal author, while making a particular theoretical or methodological point. At an internal level, they might pursue important disagreements with Steward in relation to the same theoretical and methodological points. For example, one of the book's most important goals was to encourage the development of a new kind of anthropology, one that could contribute to the study of "contemporary complex societies and nations" (Steward 1956, 5), for which, in Steward's view, anthropologists of the late 1940s and early 1950s were ill-equipped. Their concept of culture was based on the study of "primitive societies," which were thought to be "small, self-contained, and culturally homogeneous" (Steward 1956, 5). The study of small communities within nation-states required new and more complex concepts and methods, and Steward conceived the Puerto Rico project as an occasion to adapt the community study method to the study of a more complex society, treating the local communities as "subcultures" within a larger "national culture" and studying the "integration" of the local within the national. Confronted by the contemporaneous challenge of the "national character" studies of Ruth Benedict and Margaret Mead, their attention to subcultures and levels of integration, to social and political institutions and classes, was an attempt to grasp a more differentiated whole than envisioned by early national character studies. *The People of Puerto Rico*, then, could be seen as a two-pronged argument, first against an anthropology that would limit its scope to the small primitive society and second against an anthropology that would study larger collectivities—"nations"—as if they were simply larger versions of small communities.

In relation to a primitivist anthropology or one that saw national characters as individual personalities writ large, the authors could present a common and coherent front. When it comes to theoretical perspectives and methodological choices in this new anthropology, however, internal disagreements among the authors emerge. They are most evident in the contrast between Steward's "cultural ecology" and his students' "cultural historical" approach. Steward's approach to complex societies through "levels of sociocultural integration" was one that allowed him to refer to larger social and political institutions while retaining his focus and interest on local, small-scale adaptations to natural environments. Although his more general statements stressed the shaping influence of the higher levels of integration upon the lower and the fact that no one level could be understood without reference to the others, in practice he approached particular levels more conservatively (Steward 1950, 1956). He argued, for example:

> This concept of levels of organization suggests the hypothesis that the higher levels of culture may be changed more rapidly and more readily than the lower ones. When any region or state passes from the sovereignty of one nation to that of another, it has to conform to a new set of national laws, it is integrated in a new economic system, and it may be subject to new religious, military, and social patterns. But it retains a great deal of its original local or community organization and custom, and an even larger proportion of familial behavior. (Steward 1956, 7)

In other words, the "lower" levels of integration were seen as prior to and resistant to a larger history. As is clear from the passage quoted at the beginning of this essay, Steward's students and collaborators envisioned a rather different approach to the study of local "subcultures." Rather than beginning with local adaptations and building up through various levels of integration to a "national" whole while arguing that the local community "retains a great deal of its original local or community organization," they stressed the active force of larger historical currents in the very constitution of family and community "levels of integration." In their words, "wholly new subcultural configurations emerged in response to international historical developments and the resultant changes in institutional forms" (Steward et al. 1956a, 31, 32).

Were this the only internal argument in *The People of Puerto Rico*, there might be ample reason to view Steward's students as early world-systems theorists, and the familiar criticisms of the globalists for their underestimation of local traditions, resources, and histories might apply. But this ignores another internal argument in the text, one that was to become important in the subsequent work of Wolf and Mintz, and one that signals an important intellectual innovation. Paradoxically, the cultural historical emphasis on the role of "national and supranational" forces in the constitution of local communities and "subcultures" was one that required more careful and de-tailed attention to local history and social relations. In contrast, Steward's emphasis on local adaptations and on clearly defined levels of integration (the family, the community, etc.) facilitated the reification of local cultures as "types" within a comparative and evolutionistic anthropological project. In his words:

> Part of the difficulty in readapting methodology stems from anthropology's concept of cultural relativity. As a comparative science, anthropology has tra-ditionally been concerned with contrasts to the extent of placing primary em-phasis upon the uniqueness of each cultural tradition. This emphasis logically negates the possibility of a taxonomy which would put different sociocultural systems or parts of systems in the same category. (Steward 1956, 5)

In practice, this "taxonomic" aspect of Steward's work is muted in *The People of Puerto Rico*. By the time the book appeared, however, Steward's taxonomic interests had become quite significant. He had left Columbia for Illinois and established his project for the "study of cultural regularities," employing two of his former collaborators in the Puerto Rico project (Wolf as research associate at Illinois, and Robert Manners as author of one of the case studies in *Contemporary Change in Traditional Societies* [Steward 1967]).

Taken seriously, a cultural historical approach such as that suggested in *The People of Puerto Rico* undercuts the very foundations of such a taxonomic anthropology—or any anthropology that began with local communities re-moved from history. As we turn again to the description of a "cultural his-torical approach" in *The People of Puerto Rico*, we see a constant emphasis on *local* history. In the passage quoted at the beginning of the essay, the authors stressed the differentiation of the colonial experience, the importance of "local responses to and adaptations of colonial institutions" (Steward et al. 1956*a*, 31). In another passage, they explicitly retreat from the sort of study that a later world-systems sociology and anthropology would take as central, maintaining their focus on the local:

> Although we have presented a fairly rounded, if brief, history of the national aspects of Puerto Rican culture, we have not attempted to "explain" these aspects. Explanations would involve us in complex problems leading far afield from the present inquiry. In order to understand the factors affecting Puerto Rican communities it has not been necessary to concern ourselves with the political and economic history of Europe which saw the rise and fall of the Spanish Empire after the fifteenth century, nor with the growth of industriali-zation, the competition for world markets, the development of the United States as a capitalist democracy, and many other matters that would provide

a more ultimate explanation of Spanish and American policies. But we are concerned with the *effects* of world markets, political history, changing technology, church policies, and other factors upon the lifeways of the Puerto Rican people. (32)

This is not to suggest that the contributors to *The People of Puerto Rico* did not share Steward's interest in comparative work. The conclusion to the Puerto Rico book contains a number of suggested "regularities of cultural change," in which the tensions in the text as a whole are evident and are not satisfactorily resolved. At the same time, Wolf and Mintz were engaged in a series of separate and collaborative typological essays that clearly demonstrate the contrast between their understandings and Steward's taxonomic anthropology. Where Steward's cross-cultural project carried him in search of "regularities"—ways in which culturally distinct peoples experience similar kinds of changes and processes in the course of sociocultural evolution or modernization (as demonstrated, for example, in the principal texts to emerge from the project, the series on contemporary changes in traditional societies; see Steward 1967), the typologies of Wolf and Mintz stressed the *different* ways in which common colonial and postcolonial pressures have been experienced. In Wolf's "Types of Latin American Peasantry" (1955*b*), for example, we encounter an attempt to move beyond the particularistic emphases of an anthropology that could see only a world of cultural difference without succumbing to a taxonomic impulse. The proposed typological distinction between closed and open peasantries rests upon a recognition of local differences and, most important, of different experiences of colonial and postcolonial history. Likewise, Wolf and Mintz's (1957) typology of haciendas and plantations in Mesoamerica and the Antilles was an attempt to grasp a range of local experiences of an unevenly developing world economy.

The typologies remain problematic, however, partly because they pursue a taxonomic approach even as they are undercutting it. The development of a cultural historical anthropology is to be found, then, less in the typological essays than in the ethnographic and historical projects Mintz and Wolf were to undertake—Mintz's subsequent fieldwork in Puerto Rico, Haiti, and Jamaica (1972, 1975) and Wolf's ethnohistorical work in Mexico (1959*a*), his ethnographic work in the Tyrol (Cole and Wolf 1974), and his comparative history of peasant wars (1969*a*). I concentrate here on Wolf's work.

Characteristic of each of these projects was an attempt to understand the constitution of particular anthropological subjects at the confluence of global, regional, and local currents of state making, empire building, market expansion and contraction, migration, and so on. In his study of peasant rebellions, Wolf suggested that "the decisive factor in making a peasant rebellion possible lies in the relation of the peasantry to the field of power which surrounds it" (Wolf 1969*a*, 290). The idea of a "field of power" is one that animates each of Wolf's ethnohistorical and historical works. The notion of "field" seems to draw directly upon Alexander Lesser's (1985 [1960]) use of the concept of social field, itself borrowed from British social anthropology, but applied by Lesser to a criticism of the sociological and social anthropological fixing of artificial boundaries around presumed social and cultural units, levels, segments, and the like.[1]

The concept of social field as "weblike, netlike connections" (Lesser 1985 [1960], 94) undermines *both* a particularistic anthropology that would draw analytical boundaries around villages, regions, and states *and* a generalizing sociology or history that would either turn villages, regions, and states into cases for taxonomic comparison or subsume them within an undifferentiated whole or system. The field places the local within larger networks, and therefore requires a knowledge of those networks and of the sociological and historical concepts (mode of production, class, state, capitalism, etc.) with which we have come to understand them. But the networks (as "webs," "nets") are uniquely configured, socially and historically, in particular places at particular times. The local is global in this view, but the global can only be understood as always and necessarily local. Let us return to Wolf's conclusion to the epigraph quoted above and underline, here, the words "specific" and "particular": "[W]hat we explore and observe in the locations anthropologists visit around the world stands in a *specific* relationship to this process of expansion, which in turn responds to the workings out of a *particular* structure or relational set."

Yet these social fields are fields "of power." In *Peasant Wars of the Twentieth Century*, Wolf elaborates:

> [T]he anthropologist is greatly aware of the importance of groups which mediate between the peasant and the larger society of which he forms a part. The landlord, the merchant, the political boss, the priest stand at the junctures in social, economic, and political relations which connect the village to wider-ranging elites in markets or political networks. In his study of peasant villages he has learned to recognize their crucial role in peasant life, and he is persuaded that they must play a significant role in peasant involvement in political upheaval. To describe such groups, and to locate them in the social field in which they must maneuver, it is useful to speak of them as "classes." Classes are for me quite real clusters of people whose development or decline is predicated on particular historical circumstances, and who act together or against each other in pursuit of particular interests prompted by these circumstances. In this perspective, we may ask—in quite concrete terms—how members of such classes make contact with the peasantry. In our accounts, therefore, we must transcend the usual anthropological account of peasants, and seek information also about the larger society and its constituent class groupings, for the peasant acts in an arena which also contains allies as well as enemies. This arena is characteristically a field of political battle. (Wolf 1969*a*, xii)

Here Wolf's more general list of relevant actors includes "the landlord, the merchant, the political boss, the priest." In *The People of Puerto Rico*, his list had included "Native Indians ..., Indians from Hispaniola and the mainland, plantation slaves from Africa, unattached laborers, squatter subsistence farmers, large planters, government officials, churchmen, soldiers and army officers." In each of the case studies in *Peasant Wars*, the range of actors was equally detailed and specific, and the anthropological project was "to describe such groups, and to locate them in the social field in which they must maneuver."

This can be seen as the central feature of a cultural historical approach. It takes as its point of departure a particular arena—a village in Wolf's study in Puerto Rico (1956*b*), two villages in Cole and Wolf's study in the Tyrol (1974), a country in his study of Mexico (1959*a*) or his studies of Mexico, Russia, China, Vietnam, Algeria, and Cuba (1969*a*). The description of that arena begins with a delineation of the relevant actors—seen as groups, clusters, and classes of people—and their interrelations; the analysis of the actors and their interrelations *necessarily* involves a variety of historical dimensions. The description of a group of merchants requires a study of the expansion and contraction of markets for certain kinds of products in the arena; the description of landlords requires a study of land tenure and the expansion and contraction of particular estates; and so on. Each of the relevant groups may be bearers of distinct historical currents, they may mark different historical "moments," but in their interrelation within a particular arena, a particular field of power, they constitute a unique social and cultural configuration.

In the process, the very definitions and boundaries of local units become situated. Consider, for example, Wolf's (1956*b*) treatment of the definitions and boundaries of peasant communities in Mexico, which sketches distinct boundaries, distinct degrees of openness, distinct relations with power-holders in the colonial period, the nineteenth century, and the twentieth century. Or consider Cole and Wolf's (1974) analysis of partible and impartible inheritance in St. Felix and Tret, which depends upon the placement of each village within different political histories and configurations. Here the classic subject matter of anthropological fieldwork—the analysis of households, kinship, and inheritance—requires knowledge of a wider political and cultural history. Reference to that history is not designed to turn from ethnography to a history of the Habsburg Empire or of German and Italian fascism. The focus remains on the households and householders' inheritance strategies, the understanding of which nonetheless requires reference to and knowledge of Habsburg rule and the more recent effects of fascism. The project, then, is not simply an assertion that local peoples have been affected by a wider world; even less is it an attempt to write a history of that wider world (although such histories remain necessary).

Rather it is one that explores the constitution of anthropological subjects within uniquely configured social and historical "webs" or "nets" of power.

If we return to the taxonomic project of Julian Steward, we see that a cultural historical approach of this sort undermines any search for cross-cultural regularities because it redraws the evolutionary and ethnological map. Particular societies and cultures are no longer available for taxonomy not because each is unique and different but because each has experienced a common world history in specific and particular ways, within uniquely con-figured fields of power. The comparative history that is possible within this kind of perspective is that practiced in *Peasant Wars of the Twentieth Century* (1969*a*)—the careful reconstruction of particular fields, and their place-ment in juxtaposition as part of a reflection on a sociological or historical problem, in this case the participation of peasants in modern revolutions.

II

We may further develop our understanding of this approach's innovative character by contrasting it with a classic use of "comparative history" in anthropological thought—Henry Sumner Maine's *Village Communities in the East and West* (1872). The limitations of this exercise must be stressed. Maine is not the subject of this essay. A good critical essay on Maine's *Village Communities* would need to consider the production of his text; its rela-tion to other texts by Maine; Maine's relation to other legal theorists, histor-ians, and evolutionists of the 1860s and 1870s; the extent to which he did and did not share their basic assumptions; and his service in the colonial administration of India. None of that is attempted here. Instead, I have taken Maine's text out of the context of its creation within an author's life and work and within a set of ongoing intellectual and political arguments. As a text, it emerged from a larger set of historical and sociological assump-tions; it both expressed and transcended the contexts of its creation. In jux-taposing Maine's "historical method" with Wolf's "cultural history," I am not making the absurd claim that Maine should have known in 1872 what Wolf knew in 1972. Rather, I enter into a discussion of *Village Communities* because it gives especially clear expression to a set of historical assumptions and methods, *some* of which are still very much active in the late twentieth century. Wolf's challenge is not simply to the specific assertions and conclu-sions of *Village Communities* but to the assumptions and methods that have informed other texts like it.

Unlike the evolutionists of the nineteenth century, Maine remained skeptical about much that could be known concerning early human society, contending that scholars should pay careful attention to available evidence. A spokesman for what he called the "historical method," he contended that theories, plausible and comprehensive, but absolutely unverified, such as the Law of Nature or the Social Compact, enjoy a universal preference over sober research into the primitive history of society and law; and they obscure the truth not only by diverting attention from the only quarter in which it can be found, but by that most real and important influence which, when once entertained and believed in, they are enabled to exercise on the later stages of jurisprudence. (1986 [1861], 3)

Here his principal opponent was Rousseau, though Maine directed his criticism at all theories of an early "natural state, a social order wholly irrespective of the actual condition of the world and wholly unlike it" (85). Furthermore, his lack of sympathy for the speculative evolutionism of many of his contemporaries is well documented (see Stocking 1987, 117–128). At times, his critical statements come close to something like a "cultural historical" vision. For example, in responding to John Lubbock and J. F. McLennan on the idea of an original matriarchy, Maine suggests that the "early" matriarchal forms they found in India were in truth historical products, the social and cultural results of processes of state and empire building and the displacement of human populations:

> Here I have only to observe that many of the pheonomena of barbarism adverted to by these writers [Lubbock and McLennan] are found in India. The usages appealed to are the usages of certain tribes or races, sometimes called aboriginal, which have been driven into the inaccessible recesses of the widely extending mountain country on the north-east of India by the double pressure of Indian and Chinese civilisation, or which took refuge in the hilly regions of Central and Southern India from the conquest of Brahminical invaders, whether or not of Aryan descent.... Much which I have personally heard in India bears out the caution which I gave as to the reserve with which all speculations on the antiquity of human usage should be received. Practices represented as of immemorial antiquity, and universally characteristic of the infancy of mankind, have been described to me as having been for the first time resorted to in our own days through the mere pressure of external circumstances or novel temptations. (Maine 1872, 16, 17)

In practice, however, Maine's historical skepticism was selective. His own favored historical sources, Roman law and the Bible, were not subject to critical scrutiny, and he remained confident that one could construct ancient, aboriginal social forms on the basis of such sources. He remained convinced, for example, that a universal history could be written, that the early experiences of people in Europe, the Near East, and South Asia had been similar, and that the basic social form in early societies was the patriarchal family within village communities. The criticisms of Lubbock and McLennan did not lead him to a "cultural historical" conclusion that *all* human populations are located in socially and politically configured fields of power and therefore cannot be taken as "our contemporary ancestors." Lubbock and McLennan simply picked the wrong contemporary ancestors—refuge populations that had an unfortunate and recent history. Maine remained confident that other populations and groups could be taken as more authentic representatives of a universal, primordial past. For Maine, these representatives could be found in the more centrally located Indian village communities incorporated within the British Empire.

His criticisms of "speculative" historians, then, did not entail a rejection of an evolutionary project; Maine was simply more circumspect and skeptical about method. When he encountered new bodies of evidence that seemed to illuminate the conditions of early society, then, he was willing to use that evidence in addition to and in comparison with the other sources he had earlier used. *Village Communities in the East and West* represents one such comparative exercise. Written as a lecture series after his service in the colonial administration of India, the essays present two forms of evidence to supplement his earlier use of Roman law and biblical sources. From the colonial records of India, he took the Records of Rights written by Settlement Officers as new territories were included under British administration (records that attempted to detail prevailing claims on land and other resources, customary usages and rights to land and the like), along with the records and decisions of colonial courts regarding land use. He also took the occasion of the lecture series to introduce to an English audience the then-recent work of Georg von Maurer and other German writers on the Mark communities of Germany. One object of his studies was to suggest that the ancient village communities described by German writers had characterized the English countryside as well, that they formed a prefeudal basis for village agriculture and social life, developing a series of customary usages and rights that preceded feudal charters. Another was to take the evidence from both the German writers and from the land records of British administration in India to reconstruct an ancient village community of more general, universal occurrence. That is, village communities had once been the basis for English social life, but they had disappeared. We could look for evidence of what they must have been like in the reconstruction of German writers, but especially in India, where these ancient forms survived and could still be examined. "In India these dry bones live" (Maine 1872, 148).

Maine's "historical method" and careful use of evidence therefore depended on one of the most well known features of the more speculative forms of evolutionism—the comparative method.[2] In his examination of German literature and Indian records and materials, Maine showed himself to be a sophisticated and sensitive reader on a number of points. He had a remarkable appreciation of the social and cultural effects of open field agriculture and three field rotation schemes, and of the importance of the commons, and his attempt to find in the commons earlier, prefeudal rights and usages that had been ignored in English jurisprudence is noteworthy. Likewise, he offered an insightful discussion of the complex of rights and claims associated with property in European feudalism and in precolonial India and of the legal revolutions that resulted in the recognition of exclusive claims to land. Here and in his discussion of the emergence of feudalism, he demonstrated a good understanding of power-in-formation. When he turned from these discussions toward more general historical or evolutionary questions concerning the emergence of markets, prices, rent, and the like, he was again insightful, undermining the rationalist assumptions of the political economists of his day (see, e.g., 1872, 191).[3]

Nonetheless, Maine's understanding of power relations never affected his evaluation of the evidence available to him for a universal history. Evidence of village communities in England, Germany, or India was assumed to be *pre*historical, in a sense, evidence of social forms that existed before the emerging power relations associated with feudalism in the West and what he called an incomplete feudalization in India. Evidence gained from observation of village communities in India, then, was used to illuminate those aspects of English village communities that must have been present in a now irrecoverable past. Here, the comparative method supported a universal history. Rather than serving a comparative history in which the emergence of village communities in Germany or England was examined within specific social and political relations and then compared with the emergence of village communities in India within another set of social and political relations, English, German, and Indian communities became examples of a not-uniquely-English-or-Indian history, a human history that people in both England and India had lived. Thus, actual societies were removed from historical time and social space and reconfigured in evolutionary time and ethnological space.

This decontextualization/recontextualization is hardly limited to Maine. It can be seen to characterize, in different registers, whole traditions in anthropological thought, in, for example, an evolutionist recontextualization within evolutionary time or a cross-cultural recontextualization within ethnographic atlas space. In contrast, the cultural historical emphasis on specific conjunctures and historically configured fields of power provides the basis for a comparative history that avoids both the evolutionist and the taxonomic decontextualizations.

How might Maine's account have differed had he not removed Indian, English, and German communities from historical time and social space? What if he had placed them within Indian, English, and German fields of power rather than taking them as markers in a universal history? What, in short, if he had approached his own materials with the historical skepticism with which he approached the materials of Lubbock and McLennan, seeing them not as "practices ... of immemorial antiquity and universally characteristic of the infancy of mankind" but as practices "resorted to in our own days through the mere pressure of external circumstances" (Maine 1872, 17)? Here the fact that the Indian documents Maine took as evidence were gathered in the most contentious of colonial circumstances, were the products of a colonial encounter and the means by which a colonial field of power was to be instituted, would require more attention. It is not surprising that all of the parties to such colonial enquiries—from the British officers inquiring into precedents, to the various villagers and overlords attempting to establish and legitimize claims—would express their findings and claims in *historical* terms. British officers posed their questions in such terms, and Indian claimants almost certainly learned to oblige them. One way of using the resulting documents is to read them as presenting a kind of history; another is to read them as sociology and politics.

Using recent historical work (*not* available to Maine, of course), we can pose similar questions of the village communities of England and Germany. Using von Maurer's work on the Mark community in Germany, Maine suggested that England also had an ancient village constitution—a constitution that could still be read in the land, in the ridges and troughs beneath the midland pastures that give evidence of old plow lands and ancient three field rotation schemes. In both areas, however, the antiquity of such communities may be questioned. In both cases, the revisionist literature depends on the observation that the documents outlining the rights, privileges, and duties of village communities only begin to appear in the twelfth and thirteenth centuries. By exploring the general and specific conditions that produced such documents, a new set of historical questions can be posed.

It has been suggested, for example, that the Mark communities of Germany and northern France resulted from the demographic expansion and colonization of the twelfth and thirteenth centuries. For villagers holding full rights to common lands, increased cultivation of waste lands intensified conflicts with overlords and with cottagers encroaching on the commons. Documents outlining the rights of Mark communities resulted when commoners banded together against both lord and cottagers to defend their rights. The dispute might result in a division of the commons between lord and commoners, with the lord retaining control of one-third of the waste. More important, it resulted in an agreement that served as a charter for the community, the basis for its claims and forms of self-governance. The chartered community was a community of privileged tenants, defined in opposition to a lord and in opposition to a population of cottagers, denied membership in the community (Slicher van Bath 1963*a*, 158, 159).

In England, debate has concentrated on the antiquity of the open or common fields, including the well-known three field rotation schemes and division between arable and common. Joan Thirsk (1964) suggested that documents outlining such schemes only began appearing in the twelfth and thirteenth centuries and that our stereotypic images of agrarian villages and three field systems come from the early modern period. Her argument is tied to a reconstruction that proposes an original noncommunitarian, household-based peasantry that moved toward strong villages only under population pressure and the institution of impartible inheritance.

This argument, and the debate that it provoked, need not concern us here (see Dodgshon 1975; Hoffman 1975; Thirsk 1964, 1966; Titow 1965). I simply want to emphasize the range of questions that emerges when we remove villages from evolutionary time and place them in historical time and social space. Marc Bloch's observation concerning French villages that "the word 'community' is rarely found in any document prior to the thirteenth century" (1966 [1931], 167) can then serve as an important point of departure for a different sort of analysis. One would not conclude from this that communities did not exist prior to the thirteenth century, either on the Continent or in England. Rather, one would pay special attention to the thirteenth-century field of power that began to produce documents outlining communities and specifying agricultural practices as well as social rights and obligations. The rights and obligations would be claimed as *historical*: they date from "time immemorial"; they represent "the custom of the manor." Claims were expressed in terms of a distant and irrecoverable past, but the documents themselves were the products of contemporary struggles that defined both manors and villages: "the manor could be strong only where the village community was strong" (Homans 1953, 40). It is inappropriate to read these documents solely in terms of their historical claims, to sort out the elements that appear more ancient and those that appear more recent. They speak *of* the past, but they speak *to* (and can be used as evidence for) the period in which they were inscribed.

Let us return to Maine and *Village Communities*. I have suggested that in his exploration of Indian, English, and German communities he used documents (or the work of other historians who used documents) that had emerged in a particular arena of contestation or struggle. Ignoring the arena of struggle, he took the historical arguments presented in the documents as evidence of a past that he assumed to be universal. In contrast, a cultural historical approach would begin with the arena of struggle, in historical time and social space. These arenas might then be available for a comparative history, but not one that takes them as markers in an evolutionary progression. As with the villages appropriated by Lubbock and McLennan, so with those appropriated by Maine: they are historical products that stand in "specific relationship" to wider fields of power and represent "the workings out of a particular structure or relational set" (Wolf 1981*b*, 42). The only comparative history that is possible is one that refuses to remove its subjects and problems from their specific relationships and particular structures and relational sets.

III

If we return to Wolf and the cultural historical approach outlined above, we encounter a radically different understanding of social evolution and comparative history. It is an approach that is rooted in the particular, neither as case or type for comparative taxonomy nor as unique example of human cultural diversity. Rather, particular villages, regions, or states are social sites from which and through which one can examine "social aggregates not as isolated, separated by some kind of wall, from others, but as inextricably involved with other aggregates, near and far, in weblike, netlike connections" (Lesser 1985 [1960], 94). Although one begins with the particular, then, local situations are placed within wider social fields, understood as "webs" or "nets." The emphasis remains on the connections that make it possible to understand and appreciate social and cultural diversity within a common history.

NOTES

1. Lesser expressed it:

> I propose to ask what difference it makes if we adopt as a working hypothesis the universality of human contact and influence—as a fundamental feature of the socio-historical process; if we conceive of human societies—prehistoric, primitive, or modern—not as closed systems, but as open systems; if we think of any social aggregates not as isolated, separated by some kind of wall, from others, but as inextricably involved with other aggregates, near and far, in weblike, netlike connections....
>
> The concept of social field has a fundamental implication: social relations within the field are patterned, not unstructured, adventitious, or incidental....
>
> Thus, within a field of social relations interpersonal relations are structured and patterned. Conversely, when structured or patterned relations are found—or are implied by other evidence—a field of social relations is involved, embracing more than one social aggregate and usually a considerable number. (Lesser 1985 [1961], 94–96)

Compare this claim with the well-known opening passage of *Europe and the People without History*:

> The central assertion of this book is that the world of humankind constitutes a manifold, a totality of interconnected processes, and inquiries that disassemble this totality into bits and then fail to reassemble it falsify reality. Concepts like "nation," "society," and "culture" name bits and threaten to turn names into things. Only by understanding these names as bundles of relationships, and by placing them back into the field from which they were abstracted, can we hope to avoid misleading inferences and increase our share of understanding. (Wolf 1982a, 3)

2. Indeed, in the first essay of *Village Communities* we can find an especially lucid statement of that method, one that illuminates its underlying assumptions:

> I think I may venture to affirm that the Comparative Method, which has already been fruitful of such wonderful results, is not distinguishable in some of its applications from the Historical Method. We take a number of contemporary facts, ideas, and customs, and we infer the past form of these facts, ideas, and customs, not only from historical records of that past form, but from examples of it which have not yet died out of the

world, and are still to be found in it. When in truth we have to some extent succeeded in freeing ourselves from that limited conception of the world and mankind, beyond which the most civilised societies and (I will add) some of the greatest thinkers do not always rise; when we gain something of an adequate idea of the vastness and variety of the phenomena of human society; when in particular we have learned not to exclude from our view of earth and man those great and unexplored regions which we vaguely term the East, we find it to be not wholly a conceit or a paradox to say that the distinction between the Present and the Past disappears. Sometimes the Past *is* the Present; much more often it is removed from it by varying distances, which, however, cannot be estimated or expressed chronologically. Direct observation comes thus to the aid of historical enquiry, and historical enquiry to the help of direct observation. (Maine 1872, 6, 7)

3. That his insights were wedded to a series of conservative proposals on Indian land settlements, and that he continually engaged in apologetics for empire should also be noted. Were anthropology and colonialism the subject of this essay, I would explore these passages in some detail. This is not the purpose here, however.

FOUR

Capital, Ritual, and Boundaries of the Closed Corporate Community

James B. Greenberg

Few articles in anthropology have had the impact of those by Eric R. Wolf (1955*b*, 1957) in which he set forth a schemata of peasant communities in Latin America and elaborated the model of the closed corporate peasant community.[1] These works were path-blazing. Wolf not only delineated the structural features that demand inclusion within an outline of peasant communities, but he argued that their structures were historical responses to certain kinds of economic and political environments created by the wider society. Specifically, he argued that closed corporate peasant communities were the creations of particular colonial policies that erected a series of barriers around native communities not only to limit their access to the sources of power and wealth in the wider society, but also to ensure that native communities would both provide the labor needed by colonial enterprises and produce the cash crops their mercantile empires required. To avoid the costs of direct administration, colonial powers granted native communities a relative measure of autonomy over their internal affairs. Although this policy of indirect rule saddled peasant communities with the costs of their own administration, it also provided them the cultural space needed to evolve defensive mechanisms—often by reworking the very institutions imposed on them—to cope with the new forms of exploitation that integration into a market economy entailed.

In Mesoamerica, for example, Wolf argued that the institutions imposed on native communities for their civil administration and religious instruction came to be principal elements in the defense of the community's economic well-being, lands, and even systems of belief. Since all men were required to participate in the community's civil-religious hierarchy, Wolf argued it not only distinguished community members from outsiders, but also delimited those who had legitimate rights to the communal resources. For example, Wolf argued because men during their lifetimes must repeatedly serve in a hierarchy of expensive civil and religious cargos, the fiesta system organized a prestige economy that not only redistributed wealth within the community but, more important, acted as a leveling mechanism to inhibit those forms of accumulation and capitalist investment that might intensify class divisions within it. Lamentably, generations of ethnographers since have fixated on the structural and economic aspects of civil-religious hierarchies and religion in Mesoamerican communities.[2] Although debate has raged about the "leveling" or "stratifying" consequences of the cargo system, or to what extent it siphoned wealth out of the community or redistributed it, other aspects of Wolf's model have remained relatively unexplored.

Two related dimensions of Wolf's model have received particularly short shrift: one, the Kroeberian notion that peasant communities are part-societies and part-cultures (Wolf 1955*b*, 452); two, the problematic nature of the cultural boundaries that define closed corporate peasant communities as distinctive social formations within a wider capitalist world. The failure of ethnographers fully to explore the nature of these communities as part-societies and part-cultures probably stems from a certain romantic fascination with native cultures. As a result, the character of the cultural boundaries that define these communities and the implications of the parts of their culture that are interwoven with threads of the wider society have been ignored.

In this paper, I want to reexamine the cultural dimensions of the closed corporate community. In doing so, I shall use the Mixe of Oaxaca to explore how elements of capitalist and noncapitalist modes of production are culturally integrated to define a syncretic social formation.[3] My concern here is to show how elements of the capitalist mode—such as money, credit, wealth, contracts, and property—are reinterpreted and reworked as they pass through the prism of Mixe culture. Limited space, however, forces me to focus on the cultural meanings attached to money and wealth. Essentially, I argue that Mixe notions of "good" and "evil" money and the rituals associated with Mixe businesses influence how capital and wealth are deployed within the community. Moreover, these ideas and rituals are among the cultural means Mixe communities use to mediate their relationships with the larger capitalist world.[4]

MIXE COMMUNITY

Tamazulapam survived well into the twentieth century as a virtually monolingual Mixe community (Nahmad 1965, 35) and had the reputation of being among the most conservative Mixe communities in the highlands (Beals 1942, 84). Even when I first visited Tamazulapam in 1973, just after the opening of the first road to the village, the community still retained all the classic earmarks of a closed corporate peasant community. All the permanent residents of the town were Mixe. There existed an elaborate civil-religious hierarchy and fiesta system in which all men in the *municipio* served. Villagers grew subsistence crops on communal lands, produced crafts for the local market, and, to earn needed cash, migrated seasonally to pick coffee in the temperate zone and lowlands. The town showed little visible evidence of stratification: houses were of adobe or wattle-and-daub. Although there was a small periodic market, there were no stores in the village.

The Tamazulapam I returned to in 1990 was almost unrecognizable. Nearly everyone was bilingual. The adobe and wattle-and-daub houses had been largely replaced by brick and concrete structures, many of which were two stories. Many villagers owned trucks. A thriving set of small businesses and stores was in the center of town, in its new market, and scattered through the community. Tamazulapam was clearly no longer a simple peasant community, but a much more stratified town. Besides a commercial class of store owners and merchants, the town contained a variety of tradespeople—mechanics, carpenters, masons, and electricians—making their living in the market economy. Moreover, a new class of Mixe professionals with university educations had emerged, including at least seven men who have or are taking degrees in anthropology.

Several internal and external factors combined to erode Tamazulapam's closed corporate boundaries and produce this transformation. To begin, the municipio is land poor—only 63.79 square kilometres, much of which is too steep or too rocky to cultivate. To make matters worse, its population exploded from 2,041 in 1950 to 6,379 inhabitants in 1990. Because of this, although most households grow some subsistence crops, few have enough land to meet more than 30 to 50 percent of their needs and must engage in other activities that inevitably involve them in the market economy.

State policies too have played a major role in reshaping Tamazulapam. For example, Indian policy in Mexico has been aggressively assimilationist, seeking to break down what it defines as the colonial and cultural barriers that keep Indians from participating in the national culture (Aguirre 1973; Nahmad 1965, 132–133; Nolasco 1972). In 1971, the Instituto Nacional Indigenista established a center in Ayutla to coordinate its development efforts. Because these programs needed bilingual teachers or cultural promoters, in 1973 the first technical and agricultural secondary school in the region was built in Tamazulapam. Since then the town has turned out some two hundred teachers, not to mention other professionals. Economically, state investment in infrastructure has also reshaped the region; since 1970, over five hundred kilometers of roads have been built (Ledesma Ruiz and Rebollar Dominguez 1988, 199–200). Roads not only opened up new markets for perishable produce like avocados, peaches, potatoes, and oranges that once had only very local distribution, but also allowed petty traders to increase the scale of their operations and the pace of capital accumulation. Business flourished not just in Tamazulapam, but its merchants also played prominent roles in every Mixe village.

Despite these marked changes, Tamazulapam's "closed corporate" character, although changed, has not disappeared entirely. Rather many noncapitalist elements remain—communal lands, closed membership defined by service in the civil-religious hierarchy, a fiesta system that organizes redistributive forms of exchange, and systems of communal labor. It should be noted, however, that although some of these features may have pre-Hispanic roots, they are as much a product of five centuries of integration into the world economy and domination by the larger society. Nevertheless, such noncapitalist elements continue to define a distinctive set of moral values and codes that influence how money may be legitimately made, used, and invested within the community. Consequently, Tamazulapam's systems of production, forms of exchange, and ideological constructs do not conform to a purely capitalist logic, at least not yet. Instead, such noncapitalist forms and the ideological constructs behind them persist and continue to be part of the instrumentality through which the community negotiates and renegotiates its relationship with the dominant society.

CONCEPTIONS OF CAPITAL:
MIXE INTERPRETATIONS OF MONEY

Capitalist forms of exchange present a dilemma for noncapitalist social formations. On the one hand, market exchange offers access to a world of wealth and goods beyond the community. On the other hand, money tends to transform all things into commodities. Indeed, capitalist ideology—as Marx (1959 [1894]) observed—fetishizes money and endows it with lifelike power and fecundity that make it appear that money rather than labor produces wealth. Through its sleight of hand, profits become an intrinsic quality of a commodity, and relations between people masquerade in a magical matrix as relations among things (Taussig 1980, 23–26). Through its necromancy, not only are things that people make or grow turned into goods, but even nature and time may become commodities that may be alienated from the community and sold as property and labor power. It is hardly surprising that peasant communities often "represent money as a dark satanic force tearing at the very fabric of society" (Parry and Bloch 1989, 6).

In reaction to the ideology of capitalism, the Mixe, like many other peasants, have cast the competing native and capitalist paradigms of wealth into a moral framework, weaving into their worldview a complex set of ideas about "good" and "evil" money. Nevertheless, in other modes of production, as Maurice Bloch (1989, 176) has shown, other things besides money or commodities may be the central fetishes around which economic life is organized. Among the Mixe, it is nature that is the magical fetish that provides all good things. For the Mixe, nature is not just so much raw material to be used by man, but a living force, whose pantheon of gods takes many forms. Rocks, trees, mountains, streams, rain, wind, and lightning are sentient beings that provide people with the things they need and to which they must make offerings to perpetuate order and balance in the world. Because the Mixe fetishize nature, all money is seen to derive from supernaturals.

In very broad terms, "good" money has two basic characteristics: it depends on forming and sustaining the proper relations of reciprocity with the gods and nature, and like growing corn, it must be earned through hard work. In other words, "good" money is earned in a relationship with nature. Although the gods provide the resources, wealth comes from the sweat equity of men.

"Evil" money, by contrast, derives from certain kinds of capitalist forms of exchange. "Evil" money, "money of the wind," comes to people without their working for it. It is acquired by making contracts with the earth lord or devil who is depicted as a fat, greedy Ladino in constant need of workers for his vast cattle ranches inside the mountains. Such contracts are considered witchcraft and entail selling one's soul or promising to deliver others to the devil in return for riches. People who become rich quickly are said to have made pacts with the devil. Such money is dangerous, and it often leads to bankruptcy, illness, or death for those who take it. Although it may provide temporary benefits, these are shortlived. Unlike "good" money, "evil" money, they say, blows away, fails to reproduce itself, and is ultimately sterile.

Although the categories of "good" and "evil" money would seem to contrast different "essences," this distinction is not as much a clash between use-value or exchange-value orientations, as Michael Taussig (1980, 18–22, 126–139) argues, as it is an evaluation of different sorts of capitalist transactions. It is not the money per se that is "good" or "evil"; rather, these labels place all such transactions into a moral framework. Because money is the coin of capitalist forms of exchange, it is morally ambiguous at best. Like other things in the world, money is infused with both good and evil. Whether it is good or evil depends on how it is obtained and used. Money earned in harmful ways—such as selling lands to outsiders, cheating, stealing, gambling, or charging exorbitant interest rates on loans—is likely to be seen as evil.

This complex of ideas associated with evil money marks the forms of exchange and kinds of relationships in a capitalist world that are dangerous. For example, contracts are viewed with deep suspicion, as are dealings with more powerful people beyond the community. Such people are not to be trusted. They make demands that are often nearly impossible to meet, they fail to keep their word, and when they act in capricious ways there is little recourse. Certain ways of earning money are fraught with danger; even receiving money may cause harm. Money may incite jealousy, may cause conflicts, and even the things it buys may be hazardous. Since the money one receives may be tainted, unless the gods are propitiated and offerings are made to remove its dangerous qualities, little good can be expected to come of it. Its dangerous qualities are removed by treating money like any other good that stems from one's relationship with the gods and making offerings to them in gratitude for it. Such rituals not only purify money but provide a moral model for its use in socially approved ways.

This cosmological model reflects the values of a preexisting tributary mode which, although substantially transformed through interactions with the dominant society, continues to provide the ideological underpinning for reciprocity and ritual redistribution. This model starts from the premise that all good things flow from the supernatural guardians who are identified with mountain peaks and other features of the landscape. So to protect the stability of the universe and meet their needs, each family must pay tribute to the gods (Martinez 1987, 28). Such relations are sustained through the rituals that link the beings inhabiting a series of ever-larger symbolic "worlds" to one another, extending from the house, to the church, to the cemetery, to fields, sacred caves, and mountains. In each of these "worlds" (defined by its center and four corners representing the cardinal directions) candles are lit and offerings are made to the gods. Though these offerings are symbolically given as tribute to the gods, most of the food and drink required for these rituals is redistributed at festive meals to which family and friends are invited. In essence, this tributary model proposes that just as the gods return one's offerings manyfold, money and wealth invested in reciprocity and redistributive exchange are similarly multiplied. Failure to make such offerings, of course, invites supernatural sanctions.[5] If these ceremonies are not done, the gods become angry and show their vexation through any number of means—illness, injuries, poor harvests, financial troubles, and even death (Martinez 1987, 90).

Although the assumptions behind Mixe notions of "good" money differ markedly from capitalist ones that make fetishized money productive, because they participate in a market economy their ideas about the use of "good" money converge with—although are not identical to—the rational calculations for productive investments in the wider society. Despite their notions that reciprocity between the gods and man makes money productive, "good" money or capital, like corn, must be treated with respect and valued. Such respect entails its adequate and productive use. Money should be invested in productive things—animals, tools, inventory—to create wealth. Respect, also, entails self-confidence and having a positive attitude toward money not just in ritual petitions and offerings to the gods, but in one's dealings. For money to be productive, people must believe in themselves and that they will come out ahead in any endeavor, then not betray that belief. As one woman put it: "To do so is to betray not only oneself, but the gods and nature. If one thinks bad thoughts, it creates a disequilibrium with the gods and nature. Without 'faith,' money is unproductive and will disappear. If the people lack faith that their money will turn a profit, then such money will not be productive. The proper attitude—when one goes out to buy merchandise—is not I'm going to see if I can buy something, but I'm going to buy it, and do so."

XÏMAAPY AND DIVINATIONS FOR COMMERCIAL ENTERPRISES

Because the Mixe believe that all good things come from the gods and nature, Mixe merchants hold a set of ceremonies when they begin a new enterprise,[6] perform an annual cycle of rituals to maintain the favor of the gods, and, should their businesses decline, effect curing ceremonies for them.

Although rituals for money or commercial undertakings universally require that offerings be made at sacred sites in the mountains surrounding the village and in the church, for each business the details of these rituals are determined by a *xïmaapy*, or calendar priest who functions as a curer and ritual specialist. Before beginning a new enterprise, a xïmaapy is consulted for ritual instructions and advice. He performs divinations based on the Mixe calendar (see Lipp 1982) and then prescribes which sacred sites must be visited and how rituals must be done for a specific enterprise. Because each undertaking and each person's situation is different, the details and content of the rituals the xïmaapy prescribes vary. For instance, each aspect of a business requires that offerings and petitions be made to the gods to maintain its equilibrium. So where coffee buyers' rituals entail offerings and prayers for the coffee, capital, and transportation, those for grocery stores include only the merchandise and capital. Besides prescribing which rituals to perform, the xïmaapy instructs the owners when to do these rituals according to the Mixe calendar and what offerings to make.

If large sums of money must be borrowed for a business, the gods also must authorize it. In such cases, the xïmaapy also does divinations and dictates which rituals must be done. Again, because each family, each couple, has characteristics of its own, the xïmaapy prescribes which rituals they must do and where. Nevertheless, customarily, borrowing money requires sexual abstinence for a fixed period: "It's not a matter of thinking, I'm going to borrow money, but I just got out of bed. One must plan such things ahead of time." Because these rituals establish a sacred covenant between the lender and the borrower, often both parties are involved in making offerings to the gods. If it is a long-term loan, these rituals are repeated each New Year's Day. The xïmaapy's ritual prescriptions and interventions help ensure that both parties have the right attitudes toward the transaction. Because of their complexity, such rituals help guarantee that money is not borrowed for frivolous reasons and that time is taken to consider the transaction and other aspects of business affairs that have made it necessary.

Ritual divinations for business transactions take other forms as well. For instance, one ritual divination connected with establishing a new enterprise consists of killing a chick by throwing it onto the rocks in the arroyo by the road into the village. The way its beak points shows the path where one's luck lies. If its beak points toward town, that is where to do business; if it points toward Ayutla, then one must go in that direction, and so on. When followed, this procedure distributes merchants randomly over the landscape and prevents villagers from concentrating and competing in the same markets. Indeed, Tamazulapam's merchants are to be found in every Mixe village, and although Tamazulapam produces no coffee, its buyers now dominate the coffee trade within the region.

MIXE RITUALS FOR COMMERCIAL ENTERPRISES

The rituals for a business are variants of those done by agriculturalists for their fields, animals, and the economic well-being of their family. Although originally, the Mixe explain, such rituals were appeals for a good harvest or for cattle herds to prosper, merchants and other new professionals have adopted and elaborated this form as a prayer for success in their chosen ventures, adding money to their petitions to the gods and nature. The symbolic equation here is that, like the cornfield, a business grows because there is a basic contract between man and the gods. Men make nature productive through their work, and in return for sharing in its bounty, they must respect nature and pay tribute to it. Since the accumulation of wealth depends on maintaining the favor of the gods, it not only requires showing them the proper respect and hard work, but also entails its moral use. Accumulated wealth should be shared with friends and neighbors and be used for the good of the community. If one fails to pay proper ritual tribute to the gods and nature, uses wealth in immoral ways, or lacks the proper respect for money that endows it with its value, then one's business may begin to fail.

Because the rituals merchants perform for money are variants of those done for the well-being of the family, they follow the same ritual sequence: three times a year offerings are made in the house, cemetery, church, and sacred places surrounding the village. Offerings are first made in the house for death and *naaxwi'iny*, the immense-earth or nature, which is equated with the Santísima Trinidad, the Holy Trinity. These offerings include candles, eggs, cornmeal, mescal, and four tamales that represent the four aspects of life, which together maintain the universe in equilibrium through their reciprocities with human beings: *ap teety* or ancestors, naaxwi'iny, *ïnaa*

or gods, and *tso'ok* or a person's *tonas* or animal spirit-companions. The offerings made in the house are then taken to the cemetery and left for the
ancestors. Mixe merchants then perform a series of rituals in the church
for money and the economic well-being of enterprises. Behind the pulpit,
at the foot of the steps that ascend to the altar, merchants light candles and
leave four tamales and offerings that represent the products they sell. This
spot has special power. It is conceptually the "heart" of the church and represents the ap teety. They also light candles and leave four tamales before
the images of Santísima Trinidad and Espíritu Santo. Santísima Trinidad
represents naaxwi'iny or nature. The Mixe use "nature" as a cover term to
refer to the gods. Because it is "nature" that provides for the family's well-
being, prayers and offerings to Santísima Trinidad come first. In making
offerings to Santísima Trinidad, it is important for merchants to remember
the important events and struggles in their lives and how others have helped
them through these. The image of Espíritu Santo, or the Holy Spirit, is the
patron saint, tona, and protector of the village. Because each being—gods,
people, and saints—has tonas whose fates are intimately conjoined with
their own, merchants make offerings to the image of Espíritu Santo for
their well-being and protection.

After performing their rituals in the house, cemetery, and church, the
merchants visit the sacred sites in the mountains surrounding the village.
Like agricultural rituals, these rites follow an annual cycle. They have three
stages, each spaced at three- to four-month intervals, beginning on January
1st.[7] The first stage happens to coincide with the ceremonies for changing
civil and religious officials. It begins by their going to Nïweyopk, a sacred
site to the west where change of office ceremonies are held. It ends by their
climbing Zempoaltépetl, the highest mountain in the region, which the
Mixe consider the "supreme being who teaches the Mixe the cosmic order
that is maintained by sacrifice and offerings" (Kuroda 1984, 71). Merchants
consider this peak the most important of the places they visit and have their
altars there. The second stage of rituals ends atop a mountain at a sacred
place called Matskatsp. For the third stage, after visiting a series of sacred
places, they climb Cerro Grande, Nkatyjïmp.

At each of these sites, as a petition to the gods for the fertility and vigor of
their family and business, Mixe entrepreneurs light candles, sacrifice chickens or turkeys, and sprinkle drops of bird's blood over offerings of flowers,
tobacco, cornmeal, tamales, eggs, and mescal (Martinez 1987, 109). On
these mountain peaks, their petitions to the gods take the form of small rep-
licas—houses, fields, cattle—of the things they want, and small coins are left
as tokens for money.

Each stage of these rituals for commercial undertakings includes a two-
day fiesta in the sponsor's home that is like a miniature *mayordomia*. The merchant invites friends, relatives, clients, and neighbors to partake in ritual

meals of tamales and soup prepared from the sacrificial birds. The size and expense of this fiesta depend largely on the xïmaapy's instructions about what offerings must be made. In giving ritual directions, however, the xïmaapy takes the family's economic situation into account. Here there are three levels of ritual prescriptions: those for the well-off, those for people of moderate means, and those for the poor. For example, each aspect of a business requires the sacrifice of thirteen domestic birds. Thus, three times a year, a coffee buyer must sacrifice thirty-nine birds for the three aspects of his business—his capital, product, and transportation. Because of the high ritual demand for domestic fowl, even a chicken may cost as much as $10 (U.S.)! So although the xïmaapy may instruct those who are well-off to follow rigidly the religious calendar and ritual prescriptions in making offerings, he may tell others of lesser means also to go to the same sacred places, but complete their offerings with other ceremonial materials. Instead of sacrificing thirteen turkeys for each aspect of a business, a poor man may be told to offer three chickens and use bird eggs to represent the other ten birds. The concern here is to strike a balance between the demands of ritual redistribution and the need for capital as an instrument of production. For instance, although a poor grocery store owner may spend some $180 a year for domestic fowl to sacrifice for the two aspects of his business, a rich coffee buyer might conservatively spend $1,170.

Although this may seem an excessive figure, to put such ritual expenditures in perspective, let us examine the business of one medium-sized coffee buyer. In 1990, this buyer made about $4.44 (U.S.) on each 46-kilogram sack of coffee he bought, and he purchased some two thousands sacks, making the equivalent of some $8,880. If he spent $1,170 on rituals, these expenditures would make up about 13 percent of his earnings. In actuality, ritual expenditures require more than just fowl, but the point is that although such expenses may slow the rate of capital accumulation, they do not prevent it. In fact, this coffee merchant had more than $100,000 in working capital. Moreover, although sponsors face immediate costs, their outlays are largely repaid, because guests are obligated by norms of reciprocity to invite them to the ritual meals they hold. All this said, because Mixe businesses are infused with ritual import, they have a different dynamic—and their use of capital and decisions concerning business are not made simply in response to market factors.

CURING RITUALS FOR BUSINESS

When a business venture is plagued by problems, loses money, or fails, it is a sign that the gods are unhappy. These problems indicate an imbalance that comes from the neglect of rituals or lack of respect for gods and nature. When this happens, the merchant consults a xïmaapy about why this has occurred and what needs to be done to normalize ritual activities and re-store the equilibrium with the gods and nature. As the following account of the problems that plagued a Mixe merchant show, the xïmaapy's diagnosis and prescriptions may be complex.

> When his mother died, he began to despair. He felt hurt and troubled and sought to forget his problems by drinking, but this enveloped him with count-less difficulties. He lost his sense of self-assuredness and went about his daily activities without any enthusiasm. Because of his business problems, he began to be careless about doing rituals. His problems also had another moral aspect. He hadn't married according to Mixe ritual. It was as if there was a barrier that prevented him from doing the rituals. So his business soon failed. He went to Oaxaca and lost all his money. They stripped him of it, and left him in economic plight. So he consulted a xïmaapy about why this happened and what he needed to do. Simply put, the xïmaapy told him this happened be-cause he was betraying his own principles of work, betraying his own strat-egies. "Look, you aren't respecting Mixe rituals or marriage rites. You are fail-ing because you aren't sure of yourself; you need to be ritually cleansed; your soul needs to be ritually purified. All the troubles you have inside must be re-moved so that you will regain your self-confidence. This is the reason for your problems. You need to show your respect for the gods and nature by returning to the sacred centers to perform the proper rituals." (Greenberg interview 1990)

Maintaining a successful business anywhere requires a delicate balancing act. Yet as the above account illustrates, the Mixe frame their success or failure not in terms of market factors or business acumen, but in the moral language of faith, reciprocity with the gods and nature, and personal sins. The underlying premise is that their faith in the gods makes money pro-ductive. As one Mixe put it, "People who have wealth think they are rich because they have won the gods' favor. Those who are poor, well, they have done something to displease them." Oddly, what emerges from this ritual and cosmological framework is a set of values that has overtones of the Protestant work ethic.

MIXE BUSINESS ETHICS AND PRACTICES

Mixe business ethics and practices present a curious blend of market values and the values rooted in an older tributary mode of production in which reciprocity is the basis of exchange. On the one hand, like their capitalist counterparts, Mixe merchants value money and place great store on hard work, sobriety, self-confidence, and positive attitudes. On the other hand, because Mixe religious beliefs and rituals encapsulate their commercial en-terprises, the ethics of reciprocity permeate their treatment of clients. In contrast to an anonymous market economy in which merchants may charge whatever the market will bear, the Mixe merchant is constrained by the norms of reciprocity to respond to his clients in the same way they treat him, that is, with respect, fairness, and even generosity. These principles are clearly enunciated by Mixe merchants: "There are two things that maintain one's business, one's clients and the gods. If your clients are unhappy, it is a manifestation that the gods are unhappy. You must respect your clients the way you would your father, and not turn your back on them, because they are the ones who give you your daily bread." Fairness and just price, thus, are moral questions. The Mixe merchant cannot afford to be seen to be greedy. If he buys or sells at prices that hurt his clients, they will not forget it. "You reap what you sow," as another Mixe merchant biblically put it. "If you cheat your clients, or treat them badly, you won't have them. If you treat them well, generously, then they will come back."

Generosity, whatever its historical foundations, is good business. For example, grocery store owners often give away the produce they cannot sell before it spoils to customers who really need it. These acts not only win loyal clients, they reinforce relations of reciprocity within the community. So even if merchants give goods away, doing so is not a real loss. These gifts place a future obligation on their clients to reciprocate with the things they grow—potatoes, beans, corn, or squash. Store owners may either consume this produce or sell it to recoup their capital. In short, because of reciprocities, merchants need not make profits on every transaction. Nevertheless, because Mixe merchants operate in a market economy, they must carefully calculate what they must earn to maintain their families and keep their businesses going. If they are not to lose money, they must be careful not to be too generous or give too much away. This balancing act is a difficult one, as one store owner complained, "It is very difficult to get ahead—people won't let you. If you refuse peoples' requests, you open the doors to criticism and worse." Because running a business is seen as a service to the community, as long as merchants roughly conform to the norms of reciprocity, they may accumulate wealth. However, if these norms are blatantly violated, their businesses may suffer, their clients go elsewhere, and they may be accused of engaging in witchcraft or of having made a contract with the devil.

CONCLUSION

Among the most challenging problems the social sciences face is how to link our macro models of modes of production and world economies to the societies and micro populations we so often study without reducing one to the other. This is more than a problem of trees and the forest, but one of how cultural differences shade and color both. Even this metaphor is not fully adequate: it understates the dynamic quality of these constellations, overstates the independence of its objects, and omits the dimensions of power.

Yet, if we are to understand cultural evolution or cultural change, we must understand that societies are always parts of interconnected systems that are "variously linked within wider social fields" (Wolf 1982a, 76). The problem has been that in our attempts to link macro and micro models, too often either cultural differences drop out of the macro model or, at the other extreme, the dimensions of the political economy disappear into micro worlds of texts and interpretations. One way to understand the linkages between local populations and world systems is to examine the institutions that tie local communities as part-societies and part-cultures to larger wholes. In this paper, I have examined one of these—the money issued by the state that circulates as part of a capitalist economy. This is not to say that local social formations are necessarily capitalist. Here Wolf's work has been fundamental in shaping our understandings of these linkages.

Unlike the monolithic vision of a world capitalist system of Andre Gunder Frank (1966, 1978) and Immanuel Wallerstein (1974), Wolf (1982a) recognized that although the spread of the capitalist mode of production has been global, its effects have been uneven. Although capitalism brought some areas under its direct control, in the dependent social formations in other regions the capitalist mode is combined with other modes. So although capitalism profoundly transformed all societies, this does not make all societies within its orbit capitalist, nor does it mean that their forms of production or exchange necessarily will conform completely to its logic. Rather, because such societies are embedded as part-societies and part-cultures in the wider capitalist world, as part of their means of coping with their subjugation and penetration, local social formations often syncretically combine elements of capitalist and noncapitalist forms of production and exchange. Ultimately, since local social formations, such as closed corporate communities, face both internal and external pressures, their continued distinctiveness depends on the maintenance or imposition of social, political, economic, and cultural boundaries. Such boundaries are under constant negotiation and renegotiation.

In making his argument that closed corporate communities attempt to mediate capitalist encroachments through leveling mechanisms that impede the mobilization of wealth within the community in capitalistic ways, Wolf (1955b, 1957) deliberately downplayed the ideological and cultural dimensions of this defense because he did not want to limit his typology to particular ethnic communities. Yet, if such communities are to resist the pressures that would turn their lands and labor into commodities for sale in the capitalist markets, they also must resist the ideologies that underwrite capitalist forms of production and exchange.

The Mixe materials make it clear that the cultural meanings attached to "good" and "evil" money and the encapsulation of Mixe commercial undertakings within the ritual system are parts of such resistance. As in religion, these syncretic cultural and ideological forms are part of the means through which such communities have come to terms with the market economy, and so continue to play an important role in negotiating and maintaining their boundaries within the larger world.[8] Yet these are the weapons of the weak. Although such forms may mediate, at least partially, how capital is used within the community, they accommodate it as well. So although I have argued that Mixe ideology has roots in a tributary mode that fetishizes nature rather than money, that it contains a critique of capitalist forms of exchange, and that its rituals provide a blueprint for redistributive exchange and reciprocity, I am not arguing that these features are unaltered survivals of a precapitalist past. Instead, like the civil-religious hierarchy and fiesta systems within these communities, these cultural and ideological forms are the products of a long history of interactions with the wider society. So despite their very different premises, such forms have come to contain many values and practices that, although not identical, converge with those of the wider capitalist world. As a result, such forms have a double character. They are both forms of resistance and means of accommodation. It is this dual character that allows such forms to mediate between the community and the surrounding society.

NOTES

1. The fieldwork on which the present article is based was carried out during two seasons, the summer of 1989 and from June to December 1990. In June of 1991, I returned to Tamazulapam for three months with a draft of this article in hand to check ethnographic details and points of interpretation. This work was done in collaboration with Mixe investigators from the Centro de Investigación Ayuuk Jujkay-jitin Jinma'amy, and the Equipo Ayuuk, Centro de Investigaciones y Estudios Superiores en Antropología Social de Oaxaca, and was sponsored by a Fulbright Fellowship and by the Bureau of Applied Research in Anthropology at the University of Arizona. I am particularly indebted to the Mixe ethnolinguists Daniel Martinez, Candido Canseco, Marcelino Dominguez, and Margarita Cortez. As well, this work would not have been possible without the insights offered by Ernesto Martinez, Gerardo Martinez, Victor Martinez, Genaro Rojas, Gena Martinez, Norma Martinez, and the many others in Tamazulapam.

2. See Brandes 1988; Cancian 1965; Chance 1990; Chance and Taylor 1985; DeWalt 1975; Dow 1974; Greenberg 1981; Harris 1964; Mathews 1985; Monaghan 1990; Russ and Wasserstrom 1980; Smith 1977; Stephen 1990; and Wolf 1986*b* for discussions of the civil-religious hierarchy and fiesta systems in Mesoamerican communities.

3. In this work I use Wolf's definitions of capitalist and tributary modes of production. I also follow his method and distinguish abstract modes of production from the concrete social formations in which they may be differentially present: "The two concepts—mode of production and society—pertain to different levels of abstraction. The concept of society takes its departure from real or imputed interactions

among people. The concept of mode of production aims, rather, at revealing the political-economic relationships that underlie, orient, and constrain interaction. Such key relationships may characterize only a part of the total range of interactions in a society; they may comprehend all of a society; or they may transcend particular, historically constituted systems of social interaction" (Wolf 1982a, 76–77).

4. Since the present work can only sketch the complex terrain of Mixe culture, ritual, and cosmology, I refer the reader to Andrade 1986; Dominguez 1987; González Villanueva1989; Kuroda 1984; Lipp 1982; and Martinez 1987 for details.

5. The *inaa* (literally, thunder) is the term the Mixe use to refer to the gods generally as well as specifically to the rain god who is not only the deity who brings the rains but is also the lord of "maize and all other crops.... Each year the *inaa* sends out his 'cowboy' mounted on a jaguar, leading hordes of badgers, peccary, and other wild animals, to destroy the fields of those who have not given him offerings" (Lipp 1982, 104).

6. When a new business is started, elaborate rituals are performed. The owners may go to more than one hundred sacred places in the mountains surrounding the village to make offerings to the gods and nature. If the business is a store, the merchant sacrifices chickens or turkeys and buries them in its center and its four corners as he would for a new house.

7. In Tamazulapam the first twelve days of the year are said to prognosticate how business will fare during the year much as they predict the weather for the year. For example, January 5th represents the month of May. The last six days of January, January 7th through 12th, are divided into the morning and afternoon, with each part of a day representing a month. Thus the first twelve days also prognosticate the eighteen months of the Mixe calendar.

8. "Good" and "evil" money is reported widely in the literature. Such cultural interpretations appear to be part of the means through which societies negotiate their boundaries and come to terms with the wider market and capitalist economies in which they are variously embedded. For discussions, see Parry and Bloch 1989; Shipton 1989; and Taussig 1980.

FIVE

Conacre: A Reevaluation of Irish Custom

Joan Vincent

An Irish custom, conacre, which is part of a "hidden history" through which local moral and customary relations became articulated with a wider political economy, including the discourses about it, is reevaluated in this essay. Conacre was, in nineteenth-century Ireland, an agricultural custom in which labor was exchanged for the use of a plot of land on which was grown a crop of potatoes sufficient for a family's annual subsistence. I began to inquire into the nature and practice of conacre in order to understand the lives of 351 men, women, and children in county Fermanagh in May 1847. They had stormed into the council chamber of the Enniskillen Poor Law Union demanding that they be admitted to the workhouse. What had driven them there? My analysis of this event suggested it marked a phase in a faminization process that had begun with the incorporation of Ireland into the British imperial economy in 1800. In line with research I had already conducted into the political orchestration of the Irish famine I anticipated going to the bureaucratic record to contextualize the lives of the paupers. This mode of surveillance had, after all, been chosen by the State for exactly such a purpose. As it was, I found the paupers to be a population "beyond history." The only time their names entered the bureaucratic record of the expanding state was when the workhouse clerk entered them into his admissions register, and this was on the verge of their extinction. This essay deals with the condition of their marginalization.

The "hidden economy" of conacre—a form of social contract not written into any law—was critical to reconstructing how Fermanagh's rural poor—landless and laborless—came to exist and continued to exist, at least until the famine of 1847. It, too, had to be reconstructed from sources that barely acknowledged its existence or, if they did, misrepresented it through the testimony of men (and only men) who had never engaged in it. Neither subsistence cultivation nor monetized labor customs were addressed by classical political economy (Perelman 1984), hegemonic in parliamentary and administrative circles. Nor were they prominent in popular political economy (Thompson 1984), although its alternative analysis of the agrarian economy centered on laborers and wages rather than on landowners and rent. Both these bodies of high theory were directed toward explaining changes coming about with industrialization and agricultural improvement in England; neither addressed a postwar rural economy (such as that of Ireland) in which the very circulation of money, let alone capitalist expansion, was virtually moribund.

My discovery of sources more obscure than the publications of political economists; my scrutiny of the reports of local and national commissions of inquiry, published and unpublished; my reconstruction of genealogies and family histories; and my growing acquaintance with the topography and social landscape of the localities from which the destitute had fled provided a starting point. Walking the fields and talking to today's farmers about past agricultural techniques, I moved toward envisaging conacre both as a custom that had failed for the famine victims of 1847 and as a dynamic, paradoxical feature of a parallel "hidden economy" that, for others, had actually furthered their embrace of capitalism.

This essay is divided into four parts. First, I discuss conacre as political economy: both as rent and as labor. Second, I suggest that conacre also be viewed as custom. This leads me to address the importance of place in the lives of the rural poor, providing for stability and continuity, and then to analyze conacre paradoxically as customary law operating to further change. The near invisible local custom was part of a very visible—and disturbing—national economy. I then document the underlying rationale for conacre—a lack of money in rural circulation—that shaped both the hidden economy and customary law. Finally, I suggest that local forms of conacre represented outcomes of struggle between capital and custom in these critical years leading up to the Great Famine.

CONACRE AS POLITICAL ECONOMY

Classical Political Economic Discourse

Most views of conacre have been shaped by a school of classical political economy dominant at the end of the eighteeth century; the writings of Adam Smith, the Rev. Thomas Malthus, and Nassau Senior were most influential in Ireland. Conacre was seen as a relationship between landholder and tenant, a form of rent: a potato plot rented out for money or labor or both. Thus Cormac O'Grada, statutory lecturer in political economy and the national economics of Ireland at University College, Dublin, defines conacre as "a form of annual subletting of small sometimes well fertilised plots of land" (1989*a*, 115).

Although the political economists generated the view that conacre was a form of rent, their rare and often somewhat puzzled references to it were usually incidental to their interest in more important matters, such as the responsibility of absentee landlords toward the poor or sponsored emigration as a solution to Ireland's miseries. Focusing on structured relationships within *a system* of man–land relationships, political economists then and historians now describe conacre as property relations and subsistence cultivation involving land and the potato. The farmer gains four assured entitlements. First he receives rent and this elevates him above the cottiers and landless masses on the landholding, rack-renting ladder. Second, he acquires casual labor when and as he requires it. Given most small farmers' lack of capital and ready money such a contingent arrangement was preferable to the hiring of full-time outdoor laborers. Through conacre, farmers were able to quarter casual laborers close by—an important consideration, I suggest, in a country where inclement weather often rendered field labor intermittent and the employment of "tied" workers unprofitable. Third, the renting out of conacre plots for the growing of potatoes provided the farmer with an inexpensive form of crop rotation. Those with under twenty acres of land—and it was they predominantly who let out conacre—were spared the cost of fallowing. Potatoes cleanse the land of pests and diseases and thus were grown prior to planting a grain crop for market. Good soil management required that potatoes should never be planted in the same plot twice lest disease set in. It is significant, therefore, that although a conacre taker might, indeed, acquire annually from a farmer a plot on which to grow potatoes, it was not the same plot year after year. Finally, of course, conacre provided the farmer with an *army* of spade labor amassed through a multitude of conacre contracts each for minute plots of land, each exclusive of wages. In turn the conacre taker gained one particular entitlement. Landless, he was able to grow a subsistence crop, vital in an economy in which he lacked money to buy food.

This construction, centering on land and the potato, implies conacre works to the advantage of tenant farmer and laborers alike. Indeed, such a perception of a *system* working to the advantage of all contracting parties is a quintessential feature of classical political economy's "intellectual armamentarium," to use Eric Wolf's (1988d) memorable phrase. In documenting the hegemony of certain intellectual ideas over others, this essay stresses the linkage of cultural hegemony and political economic power. In an era of unbridled capitalism, utilitarian system building dominated the academy, shaped the views of parliamentarians and planners, and guided the practices of bureaucrats (Black 1960).

Yet classical political economy was not alone in the field. Partly in opposition to its overriding concern with property, the market, and the interest of the State, a so-called popular political economy had come into being by the end of the Napoleonic wars. It addressed two main issues: first, labor and its exploitation and, second, the extent to which crisis was inherent in any capitalist economic system. Although classical political economy was hegemonic in the early nineteenth century it is important to recognize that this alternative discourse did, in fact, exist. The texts of classical political economy were well known at the time and are well known now. Those of popular political economy have been neglected.

Popular Political Economic Discourse

A focus on labor rather than property, on wages rather than rent, encourages a reevaluation of the established view of conacre. Yet certain difficulties frustrate a reconstruction of the part played by conacre in the working lives of the poor. Conacre turns out not to be as clear or definitive a practice as rule-centered system building assumed. Thus, for example, when in the 1830s an inquiry was made into the condition of "the poorer classes" in Ireland, questions were, indeed, put about laborers and the terms of their employment. The inquiry was conducted in parishes throughout Ireland, a cluster of clergymen, tenant farmers, and, in rare cases, their (presumably tied, waged) laborers being brought together to respond to a formal questionnaire. One question asked "Are wages for labour usually paid in money, or provisions, or by con acres? or in what other way?" Rather like early anthropological inquiries into polygamy in exotic societies, once a formal label was supplied by the questioner its categorical set (i.e., wages) was imposed on the respondent who might have described conacre differently. Its existence acknowledged, conacre could then be taken to characterize a local economy without any further inquiry being made as to whether it was practiced by all persons, several, or only a few (again, rather like early ethnological inquiries into polygamy). Categorization, codification, rule articulation, and system building thus constrained any popular discourse positioning labor.

There is a second problem. So pervasive was the hegemony of utilitarian thought that even Irish eyewitnesses of conacre at work (such as the pamphleteers on whom I draw in this essay) framed their observations within the classical mode. Thus they considered conacre an institution of the lower orders—at best an anomalous, at worst an alien, practice within the progressive, modern, economic system developing all around them. But, as John Lucas reminds us (1992, 155), " 'Speed the plough' was the farmer's and the squire's exuberant, exhortatory cliche.... Change the angle of vision [to that of spade laborers, for example] and the 'never weary plough' provides not wealth but devastation." Only by attending not merely to what such eyewitnesses say but to what they are ill situated to say, can we attempt a popular understanding of conacre.

By the 1830s the Irish poor had been successfully marginalized for so long that they had become nothing more than a contingent problem for the English. Only when Irish harvesters flooded England and Scotland looking for work and worked for less than the English farm laborer did the State demand that inquiries be instigated and relief measures introduced. In this climate John Revans wrote a pamphlet advocating the extension of the English Poor Law to Ireland in order to ease the pain of both the English worker threatened by Irish competition and their masters faced with civil unrest.

Revans described as "the most wretched class in Ireland"

> those who hold barely sufficient land to produce the food of their families, and who are not employed by the persons under whom they occupy. The situation of this class is extremely painful, as they depend for the means of paying their rents upon the casual employment, and upon the extra demand for labour which arises at seed time, turf-cutting, at harvest, and during other busy seasons. They migrate to England annually, for the purpose of making, during the harvest, something toward the rent of their con-acre; and their wives and children in the meantime beg about the country. This class, who may be called *"casual labourers,"* are sometimes termed "labourers," and sometimes "con-acre men." (n.d., 7)

Revans's falling-away phrase distances "con-acre men" from systemic economic theory, evoking rather the impoverished countryman's efforts to put together a livelihood by any means at hand.

Conacre, I suggest, raised problems for the political economist not only because it played an important, though unacknowledged, role in the formal economy of agrarian capitalism but, more important, because it provided the fundaments of a "hidden" or informal economy that nurtured seeds of opposition to it. Its analysis requires concepts other than those of classical and popular political economy alone.

CONACRE AS CUSTOMARY LAW

In spite of the simplicity of its definition as an economic institution—a form of subletting of small plots of land—conacre had several peculiar features. These alert us to its paraeconomic character. First, it was a *minimal* holding (usually less than an acre) of potato ground incapable alone of supporting a family. At that time the daily consumption of potatoes per adult male was 12 to 14 pounds (or 5 to 6 kilograms) and the rest of his family in proportion. Potatoes accounted for one-third of all tilled land in Ireland (O'Grada 1989*b*). A second peculiar feature of conacre was that the potato land could be rented for only eleven months of the year. Since its use was accompanied by the right to "throw up a habitation" (of which more anon) such restrictions served to deter any conacre taker from making long-standing claims: he acquired no more than "squatting" rights. These limitations on the size of a conacre plot and the duration of its use provided the small farmer with something of a bulwark against communal pressures toward benevolence and charity. In the new capitalist order that privileged money making, this moral insurance was no small matter. He also retained a fair degree of "social control" (i.e., structured power).

The existence and operation of conacre as a "peculiar" economic institution reflected, I suggest, its articulation with the invisible realities of Irish customary law. The concept of "invisible realities" is Bronislaw Malinowski's (1935, 317). In Irish customary law some customs were more "invisible" than others. Economists were intrigued, for example, by "Ulster Custom" governing informal contractual relations between landlords and tenants over fixity of tenure, outhouse improvements, and the like. Although not spelled out in law, "Ulster Custom" was clearly recognized if variously honored (Vincent 1977). Yet I know of no instance in which conacre (also a contractual arrangement) has been viewed as custom operating outside the law of the centralizing state.

The analysis of particular conacre practices in a particular place (county Fermanagh in the northern province of Ulster) at a particular time (1834–1847) permits a reevaluation of conacre not simply as an economic institution based on land and rent (as in classical political economy), nor simply as a labor contract between employer and casual laborer (as in popular political economy) but, further, as a moral and legal institution intimately related to change. Unregulated by the hegemonic principles of classical political economy it operated outside the centralizing legal system imposed by the State. Conacre marshaled contractual relationships that were, I suggest, at one and the same time customary structures of feeling within a moral economy and vehicles for the march of capital.

Conacre as Custom Ensuring Continuity

As customary law, conacre addressed those *domestic* dimensions of property and labor relations that classical and popular political economy ignored. It embraced not simply the "con-acre man" but an interdependent family practicing a division of labor. We gained our first inkling of this in the pamphlet quoted earlier and confirmation is to be found in the letters and journals of virtually every traveler in early nineteenth-century Ireland, whatever his route. We are assailed, as the traveler was assailed, not by cold statistics and social categorizations but by "hordes" of beggars—the wives and children of conacre men. Hence my emphasis on the "conacre-family" (Vincent 1992).

The need to grow potatoes for the family's year-long subsistence was critical but, I suggest, not as critical as the need to be attached to a *place*, to a locality where a man and his wife and children were known. To be sure, the small farmer mobilized the labor power of a man's wife and children as

well as that of the laborer himself for specific tasks, but these obligations
were surely outweighed by the advantages that accrued to being identified
with a *place*. Works in classical political economy linked the desire of the
landed classes for "Improvement" with the primordial need of the poor for
"Habitation." In a strict legal sense this meant the right of a man with his
family to occupy the residential property of another as a home and, as the
nineteenth century proceeded, the two interests—Improvement and Habitation—were seen to be more and more in conflict. No small matter, then,
that the customary law of conacre involved the right to "throw up" (the
contemporary term) a habitation. Rights of habitation conveyed entitlements to turbary and gleaning as well as access to charitable neighbors, possibly to kin and patron, assuredly to "friends" (Wolf 1966*b*). The value of a
family's conacre plot was increased by the social and moral contingencies
surrounding it.

Place mattered to none more critically than the family of the conacre-
man obliged to migrate in search of work. Belonging to a locality alone
made his family credit-worthy. Indeed, one Irish landlord was moved to observe of the rural poor:

> [W]hat may be called their permanent industrial residence [is] preserved with
> greater tenacity ... than any privilege which the mere written law can give. As
> soon as the harvest is over, they return, not only to the parish, but to the same
> corner of the parish, and the very townland which they have left [because] as
> long as they are candidates for support from agriculture in Ireland, their only
> chance of obtaining it is in the immediate neighbourhood where they are
> known. Arrangements for hiring, and labour, are generally made only among
> parties who are perfectly well acquainted, and who are probably born in
> the same corner of the parish.... [A] man would not leave his "friends" if
> he could avoid it ... and those who do are looked upon with distrust and dis-
> like, and find it particularly difficult to obtain any regular work elsewhere.
> (Clements 1838, 126–129)

Conacre as Custom Accommodating Change

But it is important to recognize that conacre made possible not only survival
but change. This was a critical period in British imperial history when England faced financial crises at home; imperial markets took on new forms;
and expansive industrial capitalism moved to harness the workforce and
suppress political opposition. All three crises affected Ireland. Fifteen years
after purportedly making "the sister kingdom" a full member of the new
centralizing state, Irish industry was in advanced decline. Having created a
breadbasket for its own urbanizing labor force, England then repealed the
corn laws protective of Irish agriculture, casting the impoverished and demoralized island into full market competition with Europe and America.

It was under these circumstances, I argue, that conacre was transformed.

The importance of access to place for the conacre-family was heightened by the equal importance of periodic movement away from it. In short, conacre operated in tandem: the conacre-family's domestic economy articulated with casual work not only in the locality but also, as we shall see, overseas.

The agricultural calendar varied little throughout Ireland. Seed potatoes were planted customarily (and a lot of custom and ritual accrued to the potato) by St. Patrick's Day, 17 March. An early crop was lifted in late July or August. These potatoes were small and did not keep well; they had to be eaten quickly; if many appeared on the market, prices fell. The main harvest occurred in November. The "hungry months" of the year were June and July and the more severe they were the earlier the hidden conacre economy geared itself up, the menfolk embarking on harvest migrations to England or Scotland. So great was their immiseration that they begged their fare in the parishes through which they passed (O'Dowd 1991, 15).

The seasonal round was an integral part of the Fermanagh conacre-family's hidden economy, the laboring poor growing a root crop (potatoes) on rented land in one country (Ireland) and selling their labor power seasonally to harvest grain crops (oats and corn) in another (Scotland). In its nineteenth-century form, conacre permitted the potato-fed rural Irish poor to harvest the fields that supplied the grain-fed urban industrial Scottish poor. Conacre, an institution in Ireland that was so poorly understood and misrepresented by political economists, was instrumental in advancing the industrialization of the southern lowlands of Scotland, the fertile crescent of their classical political thought.

Spalpeens (literally, short spell workers) from the north of Ireland made their rounds of the Scottish cornlands, crossing for the early harvest in July or August, making their way northwestward across the country as the corn ripened in Stirling and along the Forth valley, and finally homeward by way of the granaries of the southern borders of Fifeshire and Perthshire (Handley 1945, 44), a seasonal peripatetic migration of some four hundred miles. The wages Fermanagh's spalpeens received were likely to be the only money they saw in the course of the year.

At war's end the number of Irish seasonal harvesters in Scotland began to increase (Collins 1976, 49). By the 1820s some six to eight thousand crossed each year; by the 1840s their number had risen to six to eight thousand *each week*. One-third came from Ulster (Fitzpatrick 1989, 631). Contemporaries began to refer to the steamships that carried them across the Irish channel as "floating bridges." Of the 19,312 from Ulster, only around 6 percent did not return home. Most, I suggest, were family men and of these, if one can generalize from the Fermanagh data, most held conacre. Whether women and children also engaged in seasonal labor migration is not clear; certainly males predominated. This "gave an advantage to the Irish worker whenever he came into competition with female Highland harvesters [who] formed the major part of the bands of itinerant Highland workers who wielded the reaping-hook on the farms of the Lowlands " (Handley 1945, 40).

The driving force behind the seasonal migration was a lack of money circulating in Ireland itself. The Rev. Jasper Rogers writes (1847, 1–2) of a "potato coin" throughout Ireland. Knowledgeable about Caribbean slave plantations, he deplores the "evil aspects" of what he sees as a similar "truck system" in Ireland. He describes the potato truck system as follows:

> [Agricultural laborers] are paid for their labour by the potato, or by the land to raise it. The operation between them and the farmer is simply thus: the farmer engages his labourers from year to year, giving them land to produce their potato crop, and seed when necessary, charging, in almost every instance, a rent much beyond his own; and if a cottage be included, frequently in a similar ratio. Against this, he credits the labourer's work, keeping strict account of *days* and *halfdays*, as the weather permits labour; and once a year—perhaps, in some instances, twice—the account is settled, and the balance, either way, struck. [Thus] the "truck system" in its worst form exists in Ireland, and has so existed for ages.

At the heart of the potato truck system lies the potato coin. Little money changed hands among the laboring class. Writer after writer, novelist, traveler, and political economist alike testified year after year that Ireland's fundamental problem was a lack of money in circulation. Rogers's observation that potatoes *were* money may be a proposition more familiar to anthropologists than to his contemporaries. Today's anthropologically informed critiques of classical political economy (Reddy 1987; Spivak 1987) emphasize that monetary exchange conceals a *social* relationship. Asymmetries rest on the differential use value of given commodities to each party. Money is never a politically free form of relationship. Money is primarily an instrument not of accounting but of discipline.

Such a "deconstruction" suggests how critical nonmonetized conacre was to the rural Irish. At the beginning of the nineteenth century, three forms of money were to be found in Ireland, each with a relatively distinct sphere of circulation. Bank deposits were used only by the wealthy or for commercial payments. Gold was used, first, for external payments when exchanges were adverse (i.e., by landlords and merchants) and, second, for emigration. Among small farmers, silver coin predominated. Banknotes of less than £5 also circulated. Fearing armed robbery, weavers who were paid in gold at Ulster linen markets changed it for notes before going home (Barrow 1970).

How then did money circulate in prefamine Ireland? Most entered the country from England in the form of bills paid to export merchants. These were presented at banks in the large towns and either credited to accounts or exchanged for notes and coin. This was then used to buy produce from farmers in the markets. The farmers used the money primarily to pay rent to their landlords' estate agents. They needed little for wages since most farm work was done by family members, servants in husbandry (meager wages plus keep), and laboring cottiers with conacre. Rural traders accepted commodities and even labor for their wares. Neither small farmer nor laborer handled much money over the course of a year. Money flowed back to absentee English landlords through rents, and money fed into circulation to pay for exports was withdrawn again to pay for imports. Typical of a colonial economy, this situation actually worsened after the Act of Union of 1800. To survive within this circulatory system, conacre-men were obliged to seek access to money away from their home turf.

Distinctive about conacre, I suggest, was not its economic, but its social and moral characteristics—its attributes as custom. As such, its *changing* nature (as contrasted with the unchanging nature of written law) allowed it continually to articulate in different ways with the formal economy of industrial capitalism. This explains why elements of the conacre contract varied from place to place, and why accounts of it were so diverse, frustrating any effort to frame it within a principled system. In some places the farmer provided manure for the potato crop; in other places he did not. In most places conacre was held for less than a year; in a few places it was not. In most places conacre rent was paid in labor, certainly initially; in a few places the farmer seized his portion of the potato crop as soon as it was harvested; in even fewer cases the rent was paid partly or entirely in money. In most places only men held conacre; in a few instances women (widows?) did.

By the 1830s disparate conacre practice reflected differential involvement in the English and Scottish home markets. Developments in agrarian capitalism had resulted in (1) an advanced eastern zone closest to English and Scottish markets; (2) a peripheral commodity-producing zone; and (3) a marginal, underdeveloped zone in the west (Freeman 1957). Fermanagh east of Lough Erne was clearly a peripheral commodity-producing region whereas western Fermanagh was marginal to the market economy. Eastern Fermanagh experienced monetized conacre (as I will call it); the emigration of small farmers; estate improvement; rural crime; and, subsequently, gentry responsibility for famine relief. Western Fermanagh was characterized by customary conacre (land for labor); seasonal migration; the pauperization of small farmers; movement to towns; landlords indifferent to estate improvement; and, ultimately, large-scale mortality during the famine.

By the eve of the famine, conacre contributed at one and the same time to both interclass harmony (as customary law) and intraclass conflict (as political economy). On the one hand, it reflected a contractual working relationship between small tenant farmers and poor families that allowed both to distance themselves from the landlord class. It was a flexible adaptation, as customary law often is, to changing economic circumstances because it operated within the bounds of moral community. It permitted the unbound casual laborer some control over his own subsistence and some degree of autonomy and escape from exploitation, even while it served the needs of the undercapitalized small farmer. Conacre allowed the worker's family to feed itself and so to reproduce—in the Irish setting, very much a *reserve* army of labor.

On the other hand, as capitalist agriculture introduced differently formulated relations between tenant farmer and laborer and among laborers themselves, so the context of its operation changed and conacre became an expression of intraclass conflict. After the end of the war, increasing population pressure on meager resources led to marked differentiation within the small farmer class, most becoming poorer, many who could afford to emigrating. Many who remained joined the landed proprietor in maximizing his income from rent rather than from production, auctioning conacre plots for money. At the same time enterprising small-time rural capitalists living near towns (some of them returning veterans and servants in husbandry) began to purchase conacre plots to grow potatoes for the market. This conversion process reflected both the penetration of capital and the relative strengths and weaknesses of particular localized communities within the transformed agrarian economy.

CONCLUSION

Several related themes have been addressed in this essay. First, in showing how conacre was variously viewed as a concept, I have taken up Eric Wolf's suggestion that we should scrutinize critically the intellectual armamentarium of the historical and social sciences. I have attempted to show that both contemporary and current understandings of conacre have been shaped by the biases and preconceptions of classical political economy. By exploring some rather obscure publications more or less in accord with the principles of popular political economy, a concurrent development in nineteenth-century British intellectual history, I have attempted to change the angle of vision on conacre.

Conacre was, in the first instance, I have suggested, an institution that embedded a family within a locality. With conacre went habitation and with habitation contiguity, neighborhood, and friendship. Family and kinship, gendered work, and the integrity, seasonally, of female-headed households—all formed the sheet anchor of a conacre-man's working existence. Viewed not from the systemic perspective of classical political economy, with its centralizing focus on landed property and rent, but from an alternative perspective that focuses on getting work and the ability to ride out the recurrent crises of capitalism, conacre takes on a very different appearance.

As local economies throughout Ireland became more and more vulnerable to contending market forces so conacre took on different forms. Some elements furthered the seasonal migration that increasingly became a necessary feature of survival for the Irish poor. Other elements were disregarded and set aside, by those who could profit from the postwar economy. Conacre became the site of confrontation and violence, a topic so important that it must be addressed on another occasion. In this essay "property and rent" and "labor power and crisis" were engaged as two aspects of the same problematic. My analysis of conacre drew attention to their changing dialectical relationship over time and the relationship of these changes to phases in the development of agrarian capitalism. The imperial State's claims on classical political economy's scientific legitimization and its manipulation of legal relations between England, Scotland, and Ireland could only be suggested in this essay, but are fully documented in the historical ethnography of county Fermanagh from which this essay derives.

NOTE

Fieldwork and archival research carried out in Fermanagh, Belfast, and Dublin was initiated with a Guggenheim fellowship in 1973 and by private funding during a sabbatical leave from Barnard College. The National Endowment for the Humanities supported fellowships at the Institute for Advanced Study (1985–1986) and the National Humanities Center (1986–1987).

SIX

The Prussian Junker and Their Peasants: Articulations with Kinship of a Tribute-taking Class

Hermann Rebel

Eric R. Wolf's wide-ranging work on peasants has so far culminated in a powerfully sustained critique of what he sees as a misleading modernization paradigm based on a market calculus that elevates "our" benefits over "their" costs; further, this market-based paradigm disconnects socio-cultural forms from each other, and the experiences of what he (ironically) terms "people without history" from the broad historical processes that are allegedly all that matter. His arguments make a compelling social-scientific contribution by contradicting the full spectrum of developmentalist-technocratic perspectives, including those aspects of "world-systems" theory which reduce specific and individual cultural-historical experiences and agency to historical insignificance (Wolf 1982a, 12–13, 23, 401; cf. Elliott 1987, 165–166). Wolf, as much historian as anthropologist, explores the interplay during the *longue durée* of economic, social, and cultural formations on all levels and on a global scale.

His work is of particular interest to historians concerned with the long-term articulations and disarticulations of unevenly matched ways of life whose exploitative and oppressive features some analysts are currently covering over with euphemistic formulas about necessary costs that have to be suffered for the general benefits of economic development (e.g., Komlos 1989). Rather than accepting the simpleminded visions of civilizational choices posited in such work, Wolf requires us simultaneously to focus our gaze more rigorously on and to disentangle creative and destructive historical encounters that are so complicated that we have to abandon any kind of simplistic cost-benefit analyses that ascribe necessary power to those who "have" history and necessary victimization to those who experience but do not have it—with the latter's acceptance of the reasonableness of their suffering as their price of admission to an often fraudulently constructed historical memory.

Wolf offers powerful new conceptual tools for challenging the momentarily fashionable denial of exploitation as a significant dimension of historical experience. He acknowledges the Althusserians' achievement in releasing the mode of production concept from the Eurocentric "real" types on which Marx had grounded his "ideal" formulations, but he retains the concept itself (1982a, 400–404, passim) to posit, alternatively, three modes of social production and surplus appropriation (kin, tribute, and capital—themselves theoretical products of cosmopolitan social and cultural investigations) as ideal types with which to grasp analytically the global variety of historical real types. It is a move that opens up a number of new cultural-historical analytical paths that remain closed not only to the cost accounters but to much of that brand of the "new cultural history" that is trying to displace social analysis with a courtly pursuit of the "perpetual romance" of an endlessly refinable historical aestheticism (Hunt 1989).

Wolf's first step toward retaining a strong social dimension in the framing of a new cultural history is to avoid any kind of essentializing closure in his mode of production formulations. When he speaks of following up Marx's "philosophy of internal relations" (1982a, 401), Wolf does not mean analyses of the inner workings of closed kin or tribute systems as such, or of essentialized mechanisms of articulation among such systems, but rather points toward a disentangling of kin, tribute, and capitalist relations—and of the languages of connectedness, justice, and valuation in which they "speak"—as they are knotted together in any given historical sociocultural formation. By tracing the connections among relations of production and appropriation across historically (and not only "systematically") articulating modal relationships, we are able to explore specific patterns of power and hegemony and to recalculate exploitation both "arithmetically" and culturally (Althusser 1979, 233–234) in new ways. This helps generate a critical social and economic analysis that dovetails with the narrative turn away from analytical linearity and toward a sense of "tropological" displacements to crack open the hypostatized and frozen dualisms of modernist discourse. Finally, since Wolf's categories look toward the provisional universality of ideal types we can redeploy them toward an analysis of the European historical experience where they release us from such general concepts as "feudalism," the "second serfdom," "bureaucratic capitalism," and so forth, whose limits and increasingly tortured applications have long been known. They lend themselves well to contesting the linear and modernist constructions of the neoclassical and social romantic arguments that continue to claim attention in the debate.

To illustrate the point, we put his concepts to use on a question that has resurfaced recently in German history concerning the contribution of the East Elbian aristocrats, the so-called Junker, during the formation of the early modern Prussian state. The "new" historical view of the Prussian aristocracy follows a general trend toward a positive revaluation of the services rendered by ancien régime elites toward so-called modernization. Although there has been some dissent against this trend in the case of the French aristocracy (McPhee 1989), the historical performance of the Junker is once again perceived as it was over a century ago by both conservative and nationalist–liberal traditions (Carsten 1947, 145; Hintze 1975) as an unequivocally positive contribution to Germany's development.

Writing as witness to the fall of the Prussian-based German empire, the great liberal institutional historian Otto Hintze accused the socialist historians of being the only opponents of a positive valuation of the Junker. However, there was also a strong scholarly critique of the Prussian aristocracy from another liberal source in the historical sociology of Max Weber and, more recently, in the work of historians Hans Rosenberg, Otto Büsch, and others. This view also represents an early and negative cost-benefit perspective on the Junker's "modernizing" contributions. Weber's fundamental observation was that the Prussian aristocracy's drive as a class for economic supremacy destroyed the possibility for East Elbian peasants and townsmen to exercise any seriously competitive market rationality (Weber 1958, 365–366). It was a considerable part of Hans Rosenberg's life work to convert Weber's historical sociology into a more detailed, long-term narrative in which the Junker's "career success" as a group is shown to have imposed on their subject populations such costs of "legal and social degradation, political emasculation and crippling of [their] moral backbone" that it destroyed "the chances for self-determination of the rural estates' subjects." The deep wedge between town and country whose centuries-long history created a culturally imbedded, thus far irreversible structural dichotomy between eastern and western Germany was also a result (Rosenberg 1978, 81–82).

In what follows I shall pursue two objectives. The first is to take on the cost-benefit argument directly and to render more clearly (by rethinking a recent noteworthy investigation by William Hagen that argues against them) the positions of Weber and Rosenberg about the quality of rationality that was possible in Prussian rural society under Junker rule. With this critically reworked perception of how a "positive" cost-benefit argument may be calculated "negatively," we may then, secondly, propose for the Weber-Rosenberg thesis an alternative conceptual context to the one about modernization by availing ourselves of the cultural-analytical innovations contained in Eric Wolf's reformulation of the nature of and the relationships among historically formed modes of production. Rather than propose Wolf's concepts as an alternative to cost-benefit arguments, my intent is to show how they allow us to appropriate and reformulate perceptions of gains and losses and to solidify a historical narrative about exploitation, particularly about its long-term cumulative weight in shaping the cultural-historical outcomes of legal and institutional changes.

PEASANT LABOR AND CHOICE
UNDER JUNKER MANAGEMENT

The system-theoretic assertion that one indicator of modernization is a peasantry's progressive admission to and integration with larger political processes has found many adherents among historians of early modern German rural society. Beginning perhaps with Peter Blickle's substantial study of the so-called common man's place and activities in the village and territorial corporations of southern Germany since the sixteenth century (1973), there has grown a major industry of German peasant studies stressing the communal, participatory, negotiative, and positively consensual dimensions of peasant politics under the absolute state. This work often has been expressly opposed to viewing communal experience in terms of the social relations of production and, for the Central European context, in terms of the dominant tribute-extracting mode of production. It is a story that so far has largely turned a deaf ear to other voices in the historical-anthropological literature which suggest that German peasant communities under the authorities' tribute pressure were torn apart socially and manifested such severe social pathologies that any sense of a progressive historical process of integration becomes altogether questionable (Sabean 1984). Early modern European peasant or urban-communal populations may indeed have developed subtle and even successful traditions for political resistance and negotiation but, as Harriet Rosenberg's (1988) historical ethnography of a peasant community in the French Alps or Robert Scribner's (1975) sophisticated history of the sixteenth-century politics of the city of Erfurt both show, such skills tend to appear and develop when alternating tribute-taking authorities repeatedly compete for the loyalties of the same tribute-rendering populations. Andreas Suter (1985), finally, has recently been able to demonstrate that for the south German peasant communities under the ecclesiastical princes of Basel during the first half of the eighteenth century the legal, economic, and social policies of the authorities intentionally undermined and hollowed out the legal and cultural institutions of rural communal life and very rapidly reduced members of the peasants' communities to vigilantism and violent demonstrations against each other. Among the Basel peasants, some had been integrated and "modernized" at the expense of others and the result was a regressive and embittering communal civil war (Berger 1972). The political integration paradigm, however, undeterred by the accumulation of these and other anomalies, remains strong and is consolidating its hold over historical analysis where languages about costs and benefits and "community" all too easily serve the game and choice-theoretic formulas that are still the neoclassicist core of certain repressive modern states.

Currently the most visible exponent of such ideas for the history of Brandenburg-Prussia has been William Hagen, whose research into the archives of Stavenow, a medium-to-large noble estate in the Prignitz area of Brandenburg, has sought to challenge Weber's and Rosenberg's largely negative accounting of the Junker's role (1985, 1986a, 1986b, 1989). Hagen is concerned to present a "new balance sheet" about "the social costs and benefits of early absolutism in Brandenburg" (1989, 303). To achieve a new calculation of the balance of benefits between lords and peasants he rules out as not relevant to the debate the extensive—in some areas absolute—legal and political power the Junker could wield. He argues that "however great the landlords' formal coercive powers and however weak the villagers' legal status, *the measure of Junker gains and peasant losses during the sixteenth century lies in the movement of the seigneurial rents* levied on the peasant farm and on the actual profitability to the manor of servile labor" (1985, 83; emphasis added). Hagen proposes that the rent reductions the lords granted their subjects in the late fifteenth and early sixteenth centuries gave peasant farms a sufficiently increased margin of return to balance out the imposition of substantial, on the face of it even extortionate, increases in the peasants' labor services for the lords' own productive, marketing, and managerial operations.

To the figures Hagen's research has produced, one could simply say that since rent reductions amounting to from 30 to 50 percent were balanced by increases in labor services that went from between 4 to 12 days *a year* to 2 to 3 days *a week* (i.e., an average increase of 23,000 percent), then there would seem to be no sensibly commensurable cost-benefit accounting possible and we could simply walk away from Hagen's arguments with enough said. My interest in pursuing Hagen's overall argument is, however, not to mount a factual-objectivist refutation as the professional tradition would require. Instead, I want to point to Hagen's *narrative* sleights of hand, even as they occur at the heart of his most objectively quantitative arguments. I also want to stay with these arguments in a way that allows us to recast Hagen's materials so that they not only favor and reinforce the Weber-Rosenberg position, but also finally open new windows on a possible cultural-historical reworking of the Junker/peasant relationship.

The figures in the table present the gist of Hagen's cost-benefit calculus by summarizing the productivity data from the "typical" Prignitz "full peasant" holding of about 80 acres and by drawing together and averaging the rental figures scattered throughout Hagen's initial essay (1985). Fixing on an average yield ratio for all grains at 1:3, which he presumes appropriate for the period under investigation, he calculates that a typical farm, with 65 acres arable and the 3-year fallow accounted for, could, if it planted 60 Scheffel of grain yearly hope to produce 180 Scheffel of which it would keep 60 for seed, pay out 53 in rents and dues (i.e., at the medieval rates of 24 Scheffel per Hufe plus a 10 percent royal tax) and have 67 left for human and animal consumption and for the market. The rent reductions the land-

TABLE 6.1   Family Farm (2 *Hufen*): Marginal Benefit from Rent Reduction

Yield Ratio	1:3	1:4
Planting	60 Scheffel	60 Scheffel
Product	180 Sch.	240 Sch.
Rent/Taxes (before 1450)	53 Sch.	53 Sch.
Consumption/Market Surplus (before 1450)	67 Sch.	127 Sch.
Percent of Product	37	53
Rent/Taxes (after 1450)	29 Sch.	29 Sch.
Consumption/Market Surplus (after 1450)	91 Sch.	151 Sch.
Percent of Product	51	63
Marginal Increase in Surplus (before 1450: after 1450)	36%	19%

NOTE: 1 *Hufe* = approximately 40 acres; 1 *Scheffel* = 1.5 bushels.

lords granted by the late fifteenth century varied considerably from place to place but if we average the figures Hagen gives we get a post-1450 rent average for 2 Hufen of about 29 Scheffel, a rate that lasted into the early seventeenth century. In other words, if we apply this reduction to his model farm, then the 120 Scheffel of surplus rye would have to give up only about 29 Scheffel for rent and taxes leaving the farm with an additional 24 Scheffel (for a total of 91) to dispose of. This marginal increase in surplus is substantial at 36 percent; another way of representing this improved benefit is to say that the surplus share of the gross product increased from 37 percent to 51 percent.

The narrative weakness here is in the choice of an extremely low 1:3 yield ratio. Hagen's eighteenth-century sources tell him that the Brandenburg yield ratios for all grains were 1:4 and from this he argues that for the earlier period "the ratio stood more modestly at 1:3." He makes no statement about this or another ratio for any time in the sixteenth century, which is the time in his narrative, but assumes the 1:3 ratio once more to make calculations from a 1649 inventory (1985, 86, 107). When there is no reason other than "modesty" to believe that the yield ratio and the quantitative-explanatory edifice constructed on it represent the only, let alone the best, foundation for the story that can be told about sixteenth-century Prussia, then we are free to experiment with other figures and other stories.

Carlo Cipolla's summary of work on early modern yield ratios suggests strongly, to begin with, that the increased yields associated with the medieval agricultural revolution were felt throughout Europe after the fourteenth century and produced a leap in yield ratios to a plateau that lasted until the fertilizer and mechanization revolutions of the late 1800s (Cipolla 1976, 118–122; also Abel 1964, 40–49, 103–105; Gimpel 1977, 43; Huggett 1975, 126–127; cf. Wrigley 1989, 251–252). For sixteenth-century Germany as a whole the grain yield ratio was just above 1:4 (Slicher van Bath 1963*b*). Michael North's investigations into even less favored areas of sixteenth-century East Prussia find a 1:4 ratio in the agricultural accounts (1983, 9, n. 4). Especially compelling is a statistical-topographical description of Brandenburg (not consulted by Hagen for yield ratio calculations; see 1986*a*) in which figures for the Prignitz in the bad harvest year 1801 were indeed 1:4, with wheat possible at 1:5, rye at 1:4, and barley and oats, the foods of the hired help and the horses, respectively, at 1:3 (Bratring 1968, 397–402). Given such figures, there can be no harm in overthrowing modesty and seeing what results. Based on the returns for a 1:4 yield ratio, the marginal increase after the post-1450 rent reductions was much smaller, being only about half of Hagen's figure. In other words, the benefits of rent reductions would not be nearly as favorable to the peasants as he would have us believe. It would appear that what purports to be a quantitative, and therefore "scientific," cost-benefit analysis has at its heart a disingenuously coy narrative move, one that serves us now as an entry point for unraveling this argument even further.

In calculating the other side of the equation, namely the relative value to the lords of the increased labor services that the peasants had allegedly bargained away for rent reductions (with language about the peasants' "bowing" to their lords striking an odd note in a discussion about bargaining; 1985, 83, 105), Hagen makes it rather easy for himself. Where, for the peasant, he sees a simple substitution of a labor for a cash "rent" with the former absorbed by individual farms without additional costs (1985, 87, 96), he posits for the lords only a small marginal benefit that he derives from the low values placed on labor services in the lords' commercial valuations of their estates (96–97). One has to disagree: where labor is free it has little cash market value. Moreover, simply equating a cash with a labor rent where the latter is priced according to the market in labor opens a question of incommensurability. R. Rosdolsky, in his famous effort to work out a "rate of exploitation" for seigneurial enterprises, finds this equation inaccurate because it cannot "represent the full values that the peasants' labor created for the landlord." In the end, Rosdolsky himself resorts to that measure and even calls labor services a "rent" once or twice, but he does so with the (for us) significant caveat "that the results of . . . computations, based on such appraisal of the labor services, will necessarily lead to underestimating the real exploitation of the serfs" (1951, 261–262; cf. Abel 1980, 215–216 for an unfair dismissal of Rosdolsky's work).

Rosdolsky's substantive contribution allows us to redefine the East Elbian peasants' relationship to "their" farms by showing that the lords were in effect substituting for a portion of a rent (that was in any case losing value for them) an extraction of labor whose productivity for the market was, for the lords, far greater than its rental equivalent value. In this sense, we may consider the new labor services a form of tribute (cf. Lane 1975, 12). Following the prescription of the early nineteenth-century English economist, the Reverend Richard Jones, Rosdolsky saw the peasants' farms not as something they controlled for themselves and for which they had to pay a use rent, as it happened, in labor; rather, he allows us to see that the farms were put at the peasants' disposal as the source of their livelihood. On this basis they were then able to work three to four days a week with horses, wagons, and manual labor in the lords' fields. This led to a paradoxical and conflicted condition: their wage was raised or lowered inversely to the amount of labor time required by the lord. That is to say, the more labor the peasant had to furnish for the lord, the less time he had for producing his wage—in effect, the lower his wage. To draw a further connection to a tribute characterization one can restate the inverse relationship between wage and labor as one where labor is in effect extracted from income. Simply to call this change a shift from one kind of rent to another misses an important historical moment of primary accumulation in which kin-ordered peasant household labor is captured as a tribute for sustaining the early formation of the Prussian dynastic-aristocratic state.

Hagen's data do not allow us to construct the kind of "rate of exploitation" ratios Rosdolsky's analysis tries to achieve (more or less successfully), but there are a number of arguments that one can make with those data to develop an alternative story to the one he tells about a pareto optimum at the rural heart of the emerging Hohenzollern empire. The wage that was the peasant farms' own surplus served to reproduce not only the laborers that were available for the lords' work services but also the "labor fund" consisting of various draft animals, of large implements and tools, and of the calories to feed the animal and human labor expended for the lords' production and transport-marketing needs (Marx 1967 [1867], 593–594). By exploring such structural dimensions of cost-benefit calculations we can argue further that the enormous cost increase to the peasants in the application of their tribute labor to the lords' fields more than wiped out their marginal gains from the rent reductions and resulted in an enormous windfall in capital accumulation for the lords.

Returning to the table, it is apparent that the rent reductions after about 1450 yielded an additional 24 Scheffel (about 38 bushels) of grain. These could not hope to cover the additional caloric needs of the farm's greatly increased labor output. Moreover, the marginal improvement in rents could not improve any single farmer's competitive position since the same or similar improvements were shared by most of the neighbors in the region. The farmers' increased grain surpluses, if they reached the market at all, can only have helped to keep the price of grain low in oversupplied local markets relative to the higher price at more distant export venues to which only the nobility retained access (cf. Hoszowski 1972). It is, finally, from

Michael North's (1983) investigations into sixteenth-century peasant-lord relationships in East Prussia that we can develop a perspective to rework along these more structural-analytical lines the cost-benefit equation as it was experienced in East Elbian rural society generally.

North allows, first, a sharper focus on such "labor fund" costs as maintaining draft animals for labor services. In his analysis of the inventories of the noble estate owners' domain farms in 1585 and 1590, he finds that in the case of one 840-acre domain farm whose acreage ratio to the surrounding peasant land was 2:1 and where relatively few peasant farms served the domain farm with labor, the lords had to maintain thirty-three to forty-five horses; in those more prevalent areas represented by a domain farm of over 1,500 acres with a 1:4 acreage ratio to the surrounding peasant farms and where much more peasant service labor was available, the lord's stock in horses varied between four and twelve (North 1983, 5, 7, 10–13). Whether these latter were workhorses or, as I think far more likely, luxury goods in the form of hunting, carriage, show, and breeding horses, North does not say. The point to be made, however, is that not only were horses the most expensive and highest grain-consuming capital good in rural society (Wrigley 1989, 240), but (with a yield ratio of about 1:2.5 or 3) the oats they consumed to perform work required more land per bushel of yield than the wheat and rye (with yield ratios of 1:5 and 1:4, respectively) that were destined for the market for urban consumption. To the extent that the peasants' labor obligations included supplying draft animals to the lord, the increased labor dues were crushing.

One of the Osterode domain farms examined by North was planted in 1597–1598 with about 30 percent rye, 19 percent barley, and 51 percent oats; it was harvested in the proportions of 59 percent rye, 25 percent barley, and 17 percent oats. To take advantage of peak market conjunctures in rye in the decades between 1590 and 1609, the farm's managers squeezed out their oat planting whenever they could to the point of being unable to feed their own few horses (North 1983, 8–9). At such times, the subject farmers who had to supply the domain farms with horses clearly had to take land out of higher-yield rye and wheat production to feed the labor service horses with additional amounts of homegrown, low-yield oats. The results were twofold: first, looking at the table one last time, we can see that if the subject peasants during the sixteenth century were thus pushed out of growing the higher-yield food grains with an average yield ratio of at least 1:4 and into growing the necessary oats and barley, yielding about 1:3, then it is possible to argue that despite the rent reduction and because of the structure of the rent-labor tradeoff, they in fact took a net loss in this period, going from a 127 Scheffel (or a possible 151 Scheffel) surplus to 91 Scheffel (cf. Baumgart 1966, 68). Second, if we recast this in terms of what E. A. Wrigley calls "risk spreading" (1989, 253–257) we can see that the

peasant farmers were not free to calculate their own plantings in an immediate relation to actual and projected grain supplies and to corresponding
movements of the market but could do so only as the logic of the market
was mediated, and for them actually reversed, by the grain marketing (and
labor demand) strategies of the domain owners and their managers. The
subject farmers had to plant more oats on the land they occupied (in effect
a further wage reduction) to make up the deficit when the domain farms
shifted exclusively to producing and capturing the greatest local market
share in rye and wheat. It would appear, moreover, from the considerable
proportion of domain-produced rye (13–20 percent of the total rye harvest) that was sold in Osterode and Soldau in the decades between 1570
and 1599 (in addition to 22–32 percent destined for sale in outside markets; North 1983, 9) that the domain farms sold rye in turn to the farmers
to make up for the latter's necessary deficits in rye production.

Finally, the risks of miscalculating the optimal draft animal and labor in-
puts were no longer carried by the domain farms but were dumped entirely
on the peasant farms. There may have been individual peasant success
stories, but on the whole, the peasants' absorption of risk and of the structurally determined chances for individual failure were much greater under
the new system of labor tribute because their capacity for exercising any
kind of market rationality was subsumed under their lords' prior market
choices. Parenthetically, one can draw attention to the suggestive case that
has recently been made (Beck 1986) that we are on the threshold of yet
"another modernity" whose central concern will be to displace a traditional notion of economic and social justice calculated in terms of the distribution of surplus with one that focuses on the distribution of risk. The
sixteenth- and seventeenth-century Prussian experience suggests, however,
that not only are *both* kinds of calculus compatible with and even necessary
to analyses of the structures determining costs and benefits, but that they
may be read into historical tropes for which the "modern" discovery of
risk "management" becomes merely another replay, another repetition
without change.

For the Prussian case, once we begin to dismantle the structure of the
distribution of costs and benefits, any consideration of a simply rent/labor
service tradeoff becomes untenable. Obviously the landlords did not everywhere achieve a uniform optimum balance of subject farms and domains
and certain peasants did not become wholly absorbed in their lords' calculations; but it is clear that the great majority of tenant subjects who were a
part of the new order could not have willingly struck such a bad bargain,
that only the elements of judicial and police power at the landlords' disposal can account for the almost completely one-sided restructuring of the
local rural economy in the landlords' favor. Hagen's own evidence belies
his attempts to put on these arrangements the face of a rational and mutu-

ally satisfactory agreement between negotiating partners bargaining from their respective positions of strength. In none of the examples of rent reduction and labor service increase that he cites can he point to such proceedings, and indeed he has to admit that the actual processes of change either appear to remain unknown or were imposed in the estate courts of the landlord. He waves vaguely in the direction of the royal treasury court (*Kammergericht*) in Berlin as a possible court of appeal but he does not say how this might have worked as a basis for equal negotiations between lords and subjects in matters of private estate administration. The one instance he gives us in which peasants apparently spoke up to seek redress was in a legal quarrel between two lords *about* an exchange of farms and subjects in which the affected subject farmers were called on to testify and whose outcome was in the end only a settlement of the lords' dispute. One of the subject farmers gave this testimony about working for his new master: he now serves "two days each week with the horses or three days with the neck. He gives 24 bushels but he would rather stay with his previous manorial service [a half day a week with horses or one day manual labor] and pay the full 36 bushels" (Hagen 1985, 105–106).

The peasants did have a desire for negotiated economic or political relations. When both the free and subject farmers of the East Prussian Samland took political action in 1525 against the lords' innovations in estate management practices and the imposition of heavy labor services, the village notables leading the uprising induced their followers to lay down their arms in the hope of a negotiated settlement to be refereed by the Duke. The latter, however, returned to side with the nobility and ended the uprising with an act of judicial terror by having fifty of the peasants' representatives and leaders executed. Heide Wunder concludes her excellent account of these events with the dry observation that the experience did not contribute toward "a durable new self-understanding of the peasants" (1975, 37).

REARTICULATIONS OF KIN AND TRIBUTE IN THE PRUSSIAN DYNASTIC STATE

Hagen's modernist fiction about a peasantry achieving a balanced and rationally negotiated relationship with the nobility has, paradoxically, prompted a discovery of an enforced rational dualism at the core of Prussian rural society. This allows us to refocus attention on and reaffirm the critical stance of Max Weber and Hans Rosenberg who understood that the gains made toward Prussian economic development by the lords' personally profitable estate management incurred costs both in terms of the destruction of an infrastructure in commercial towns (Rosenberg 1978, 76–77) and of the derationalization of the rural population's position in the market. We need not stop, however, at the point where the Weber-Rosenberg paradigm can serve, at worst, to reinforce national "character" or culture and personality statements about German irrationalism and authoritarianism or, at best, to place a flawed or even failed transition to modernity at the base of Germany's conflicted and horrendous history in the twentieth century. A more positive and creative way of reworking the Weber-Rosenberg view is to turn it away from a modernization paradigm altogether and toward Eric Wolf's model of historical social relations. This opens up a more subtle and interesting story, one that will, without question, eventually make possible a more satisfying reintegration of Germany's history into other world-historical processes.

The literature, again with Max Weber (1958) in the lead, has mainly focused on the East Elbian aristocrats' essential differences from their counterparts in the western German states and points now toward a view of Germany's ancien régime aristocrats generally becoming tribute-squeezing colonial agents vis-à-vis their peasants to pay off their enormous consumption, investment, and gambling debts to the centers of capitalism in southern and northwestern Germany, Italy, Holland, and, eventually, London. It goes beyond the scope of this paper to elaborate on this still to be written history of German tribute's disadvantageous "foreign political" relationship to capital, and we focus finally only on the domestic relationships between Prussia's tribute-taking aristocrats and tribute-producing peasants to see what contribution the preceding critical discussion about labor services can make in the context of Wolf's social analytical concepts.

It would be a mistake to assume that a kin-ordered mode of production refers only to primary small-scale producers in agriculture or household industry. Eric Wolf refers as well, perhaps even more significantly, to what the aristocrats are doing and to the legally and economically mediated relationship between their family management and that of the subaltern classes. The key is to learn to see the Prussian nobility not merely as tribute-takers as such but also as dynasts in an absolute state; that is, as legally empowered managers of family personnel and property, or, putting it yet another way, as kin-ordering producers adjusting their dynastic management by means of a new tribute-collecting state to the changing necessities of the world market. This raises questions about how and to what ends aristocratic labor was organized. With a phrase that conjures up Norbert Elias's aristocrats laboring at court, Hans Rosenberg at one point refers to the Prussian nobility as "this aristocratic working class" (1958, 29–30). We can put together a brief narrative to illuminate Rosenberg's pregnant characterization by showing how well the course of the Junker's emergence as a dynastic-corporate ruling class provides a historical instance to match Wolf's perception about how "kinship on the jural-political level subsumes and organizes kinship on the familial-domestic level, making interpersonal relations subject to char-

ters for categorical inclusion or exclusion" (1982a, 92; see also Weber 1980
[1925], 226–228).

The sixteenth-century Reformation coincided in Germany with that aristocratic dynastic crisis conceptualized by Wolf (1982a, 96–99) in which an
increasingly violent competition among lineages for inheritance and the
emergence of competing leaderships and alliances all threaten to destroy
the social organization of aristocratic lineage itself. The solution that
emerged in Prussia and, analogically, everywhere else in Germany (of
course, with an enormous range of timing and institutional and other variants) involved three levels of social organization. At the top, the heads of
aristocratic families reorganized themselves corporatively in the so-called
Estates and, together with the royal authorities, agreed to enforce the ruling dynasty's family compacts and charters and to raise tribute to underwrite the quasi-public but primarily private debts of both the ruling houses
and of their own territorial-aristocratic corporations (Carsten 1959; Vann
1984). The proliferating institutions of this reorganized dynastic tribute
state not only solved cash flow and labor problems for the aristocracies
but, more important, also employed and organized, in the middle, the
labor capacities and welfare needs of those dynastic claimants, collaterals,
and affines who could not be accommodated by the more formalized and
tougher regulation of aristocratic inheritance. Rather than furnish the manpower for family and factional intrigues and for dynastic wars, the latter
now became a dynastic proletariat laboring alongside non-noble career
bureaucrats to reproduce the institutions and daily operations of the tribute
state. At the bottom, the tribute state's institutions invaded and reorganized
the peasants' own processes of labor, family reproduction, and inheritance
management to serve the dynastic hegemony of the aristocracies. In the
East Elbian provinces it was precisely in the shift from peasant rent to
tribute labor that we see this invasion of one sector of kin-ordered social
reproduction by another (Plakans 1975, 641; Rosenberg 1978, 71).

The aristocratic lines occupying the Prignitz estate of Stavenow that
Hagen presents to us did very well between the sixteenth and eighteenth
centuries. The price of the estate increased by only 17 percent, going from
6,000 to 7,000 fl. in the period 1405 to 1533. Hagen, correcting for money
devaluation, actually sees an 84 percent decline. However, between 1533
and 1601, when the new tribute labor was put to work toward capital formation in the form of construction, land reclamation, and the creation of
new domain farms, the value of the estate went up by 500 percent. During
the eighteenth century, Hagen sees further valuation increases of 136 percent between 1717 and 1763 and of 120 percent from then until 1801
(1985, 1986a; see also Carsten 1989, 66–67). Although these numbers by
themselves put an unacknowledged final accounting to Hagen's previous
cost-benefit story, their importance for us now lies rather in their mode-of-

production context which, on the aristocratic side, demonstrates a revivified, reempowered kin mode managing property, inheritance, and peasant tribute labor with an eye toward the long-term accumulation of dynastic wealth (Hagen 1985, 1986a passim).

The reinvention of the aristocratic patrimonial house whose successive incumbents could enter the market as legally privileged and economically rational actors stands in sharp contrast to the simultaneous reinvention of the peasant householder as someone encouraged, perhaps by falling rents and by the illusion of dynastic opportunity contained in the heritable lease to a farm, to labor for the lords' domain farms. As we saw, however, peasants' inversely rational relationships to both the commodity and labor markets, their absorption of the costs of reproducing draft animal and human labor for the labor fund, and their almost complete assumption of the risks of labor and personnel calculations all combined to program for failure most efforts by rural householders to achieve the hegemonic family ideal represented by the aristocratic dynasties.

Both aristocrats and peasants shared the desire for "house" and lineage and saw a basis for mutual comparison in the well-managed dynastic house, but only the former, by reorganizing both their own and the peasants' kin relations around the tribute state, were able to sustain a long-term drive for dynastic self-management. Whatever the subsequent circulation of noble families and the tightening structural conditions affecting such dynastic hegemony (Reif 1979; see also Rosenberg 1978, 83–101), their chance for dynastic success was purchased throughout at the cost of forcing peasant families to constitute themselves in ad hoc kindreds and pseudo-kin mobilized for both tribute and family labor and to make unending choices about the exclusion, expulsion, and dispossession of "uneconomical" and marginal family members and all so that the families of the aristocracy did not have to do so. At the heart of German social life we find a hidden war between those who capture tribute to develop dynastic families and those who produce tribute and cannot form families that last. Between aristocrats and their subjects and, indeed, *within* those classes, we find a pervasive cultural war between classes of lineage, that is, classes of race and, in the domestic sphere, between classes of gender and inheritance. When we wonder about the historical weight we should assign to such centuries-long, brutalizing tropes of necessary difference and "selection" in the intimate and emotionally charged spheres of family life, then we have to recall those populists who, in the worst moments during the long period of Germany's social collapse from the 1870s through the 1940s, rose to power with repetitiously cathected speech about lost kin, lost homelands, dispossession, and exile, becoming in turn a language of practice about ancestral passports, bloodlines, and miscegenation, all ending finally in insane acts of mass murder intended to effect social reconnection by means of racial repossession.

SEVEN

Prefigurations of the Vietnamese Revolution

David Hunt

"Viet Nam constitutes the overriding issue of the moment," Eric R. Wolf wrote in the preface to *Peasant Wars of the Twentieth Century*, a text to be counted among the great monuments of peasant studies and of the antiwar movement (Wolf 1969*a*, x). Throughout the war, journalists, activists, scholars, and government officials for the most part ignored the agrarian character of the world into which the Pentagon was intruding, a lack of specificity that lessened the value of their recommendations on behalf of the Vietnamese people. By showing that Vietnam's history had been shaped by the desires and capabilities of peasants, Wolf achieved a scholarly breakthrough and underscored the futility of U.S. intervention.

But it was not alone a focus on the countryside that made Wolf's work original. Many voices, from Eric Hobsbawm to James Scott, from Teodor Shanin to Barrington Moore, helped to shape peasant studies in the 1960s, and Moore was not speaking for everyone when he called on scholars to heed before it is too late the "dying wail of a class over whom the wave of progress is about to roll" (Moore 1966, 505). Nonetheless, this sentiment came to characterize much work in the new field. For Moore and others, the sympathy elicited by country people tends to collapse into pathos.

At times Wolf appears to share this pessimism. "The peasant's role is ... essentially tragic," he writes in the conclusion of *Peasant Wars*; "his efforts to undo a grievous present only usher in a vaster, more uncertain future." But the tone quickly changes when he adds:

For the first time in millennia, humankind is moving toward a solution of the age-old problem of hunger and disease, and everywhere ancient monopolies of power and received wisdom are yielding to human effort to widen participation and knowledge. In such efforts—however uncertain, however beset with difficulties, however ill-understood—there lies the prospect for increased life, for increased humanity. If the peasant rebels partake of tragedy, they also partake of hope, and to that extent theirs is the party of humanity. (Wolf 1969a, 301–302)

Coming at a moment when many Americans saw the Vietnamese as scarcely human, this affirmation was an extraordinary act of political courage and human sympathy. Previously regarded as faraway indigenes prowling the jungle like wild animals, peasants in Vietnam were the heirs to Voltaire and Mozart. Dressed in rags and speaking an indecipherable patois, they and not their smooth-talking adversaries represented enlightenment and progress. There was both grandeur and humility in Wolf's demonstration that a new language, a new science, was needed to understand these rural revolutionaries.

The present essay begins with an analysis of Eric Wolf, it reviews the contribution of scholars who took up the issues he defined, and it concludes with a comment on Vietnam today. In the 1970s, a number of important studies appeared on Vietnam's peasant revolution. However, for all their many merits, these texts failed to go beyond Wolf, and in the 1980s, too hastily concluding that the topic had been exhausted, scholars moved to other concerns. As Vietnamese peasants and peasants elsewhere continue their struggle for a better life, Wolf's work remains a precious resource, its promise yet to be realized.

I

Peasant Wars was part of a broader scholarly movement gathering momentum in the 1960s and demonstrating that collective action is grounded in popular culture, that mass movements are prefigured in social experience. By explaining how political commitments derive from sociability broadly conceived and not just from exploitation at the point of production, Wolf and others revealed the inadequacy of narrowly materialist analysis. Their insistence that all relations articulate differences in power deinstitutionalized and enriched the study of politics. Their move beyond elite definitions of culture opened the way to a realization that even the most humble groups create meaning, articulated in the frameworks and dynamics of daily life, and that the comportments of anonymous people are expressions of historical agency.

Wolf saw peasants as capable of reflection and change. In a memorable passage, he calls on readers to think

> not in terms of abstract categories—such as the retention of "tradition" or the advent of "modernity"—but in terms of a concrete historical experience which lives on in the present and continues to determine its shape and meaning. Everywhere, this historical experience bears the stigmata of trauma and strife, of interference and rupture with the past, as well as the boon of continu-

ity, of successful adaptation and adjustment—engrams of events not easily erased and often only latent in the cultural memory until some greater event serves to draw them forth again. (Wolf 1969a, 276)

The literature Wolf sought to enlarge had dwelt on the first theme in this passage, concerning peasants who bore the scars of victimization and who pined for a lost heritage, but it had less to say about peasants as innovators. Often informed by the past, their story is primarily one of "adaptation and adjustment." Attached to a received culture, they are not prisoners of routine. On the contrary, Wolf insists, even when the peasants in his case studies remain loyal to tradition, they also strive to build new communal arrangements.

Wolf's Proustian fascination with memory prompts an inquiry that vacillates between the scientific and the poetic. Borrowing from biology, he draws attention to "engrams of events not easily erased and often only latent in the cultural memory until some greater event serves to draw them forth again." An "engram" is not just a memory, but a term of process, an alteration of neural tissue occasioning the return of a buried image from the past. The hypothesis addresses the way people lose and find ways to recover and employ fragments of their experience. Stretching for words to describe a neglected human potential, Wolf suggests that attachment to custom may help embattled populations find the strength to remake themselves.[1]

Wolf does not claim that the revolutionary vocation of Vietnamese peasants was informed by utopian memories. On the contrary, he declares, agrarian populations in the precolonial era were "dispossessed and downtrodden" and their villages were ruled by oligarchies of local notables (Wolf 1969a, 162, 171). At the same time, these circumstances did not prevent them from affirming themselves. A legacy of struggle more than some vision of an idealized past enabled them to make their presence felt in the twentieth century.

Informed by these insights, Wolf offers a brilliant but not fully realized analysis of Vietnam's rural revolution. Attuned to spatial variables limiting the prospect for collective action, he begins by asking what "the Vietnamese may have been like before their Sinicization," an inquiry that demonstrates how fissures between an imperial/Confucian model derived from China and a more decentralized indigenous political conception left room both for local gentry and for the peasantry to form their own destinies. His pathbreaking stress on the role of the peasants, middle or other, with some "tactical freedom" to act also postulates space as a social rather than a merely topographical phenomenon (Wolf 1969a, 159, 202–203, 291).

Elsewhere, Wolf's treatment does not succeed in emancipating itself from a conventional way of understanding space, one that turns physical attributes of the terrain into metaphors for social and political relations. According to a common image, the village is juxtaposed to the real world of the state and civil society, a notion that assigns peasants to a hinterland, remote from urban centers where real history is made. Wolf's reference to the often quoted and misleading proverb, "the power of the state stops at the bamboo hedge of the village," evokes this view, though in characteristic fashion he employs the hedge not to establish the parochialism of the village, but to illustrate why peasants were able to act autonomously (Wolf 1969a, 172).

Popular power in the countryside is the most important theme in Wolf's work. Vietnamese peasants created a distinctive civilization, he suggests, in which household and collective labor were combined in an original fashion, voluntary associations proliferated, and the majority joined in worshipping the village "guardian spirit" (Wolf 1969a, 172–174). The imprint of country people was also evident as the struggle for national independence gained momentum and took on an increasingly revolutionary tenor. The linking of these two realities, suggesting that the activism of the peasants was anticipated in their communal existence, is an expression of Wolf's belief that they had always participated in the making of society and history in Vietnam.

Today, its emphatic statement of agrarian autonomy dates *Peasant Wars*. In the text, the horizontal vector among peasants is portrayed as far more powerful than the vertical vector, derived from interchanges between country people and the dominant classes. Saying nothing about mental space, the play of hegemonic and counterhegemonic themes within peasant consciousness, Wolf does not provide a rigorous demonstration of grassroots independence. Still, in its context, his emphasis was fruitful. A patron-client framework, a preoccupation with landlord paternalism and peasant deference, had previously obscured and was later to obscure the insight Wolf achieved through an insistence on popular initiative. For him, culture is an artifact that even the most oppressed groupings are always shaping.

The merits and flaws of his approach are evident as Wolf hones in on the Vietnamese Revolution. Searching for prefigurations, he notes that "manifold village associations ... came to serve as a template for welding" the guerrilla army and the peasantry "into a common body" (Wolf 1969a, 298). *Peasant Wars* deserves credit for this affirmation, which properly accords a historical legitimacy to the guerrilla movement, but, once stated, the point is not much developed. The reader especially misses a treatment of plasticity in peasant thinking, as the text switches from a language of movement ("engrams") to a static representation of the revolutionary process ("templates").

The problem is compounded as Wolf strives to incorporate all of the regions of Vietnam into his analysis. The Viet Minh flourished especially in the northern and central sections of the country, he declares, where villages were more established and better organized than in the South. During the

First Indochina War, the foothold of the movement in "the South remained more tenuous than in the North. This was in part due to the more atomized social structure; village level organization was much less cohesive than in the North" (Wolf 1969*a*, 192–193).

The insurgency after 1960 among "the more individualized and less solidary peasantry of the southern frontier zone" appears as an anomaly within *Peasant Wars*. Wolf tries to salvage the rudiments of a prefigurative explanation by affirming that middle peasants with something to lose were the most ready to join the guerrilla movement. But in the end, he takes refuge in an institutional conception, according to which "the NLF alone, among other organizations in the South, offered a viable organizational framework and ideology for an atomized society striving to attain greater social cohesion." The accompanying citations are almost all from the work of Douglas Pike, who was close to U.S. counterinsurgency efforts in Vietnam and who sees the NLF as a cleverly constructed organizational grid rather than as a social movement (Pike 1966; Wolf 1969*a*, 193, 202–203, 207).[2]

In short, the prefigurative approach adopted by Eric Wolf makes more sense of the northern than of the southern revolution and leaves the impression that it was more grounded in the Vietnamese reality. Here again extrapolating too readily from a geographic datum, he exaggerates the South's "frontier" anomie, thereby missing an opportunity to find the "boon of continuity" that oriented peasants of this region toward the left. At least one study of the region, conducted with *Peasant Wars* very much in mind, reveals that National Liberation Front cadres both criticized and took their cues from a dense, vital popular culture. Wolf was more right than he knew (Hunt 1974, 1982).

Though incomplete, Wolf's analysis broke new ground and established a standard against which to measure later efforts to explain the Vietnamese Revolution. Popular movements do not come ex nihilo; it is not plausible that an inert, scattered peasantry could have been endowed by an external leadership with the cohesion to become a political force. Only people with a culture, an experience of self-organization, will be properly situated to take advantage of a crisis. By contrast, demoralized or defeated populations may not have the will to fight even when guided by organizers coming from outside. Whatever else may be said about the Vietnamese Revolution, after Eric Wolf it is difficult to deny that a history-making peasantry occupies a central position in the drama.

II

Wolf was soon taken to task in Jeffery Paige's *Agrarian Revolution*. Reversing the emphasis found in *Peasant Wars*, Paige denies the reality of a horizontal axis and affirms that the seeming cohesion of rural communities in North and central Vietnam was due to the "tyrannical rule of the council of notables." "Rugged individualism" was the dominant ethos in the countryside, and a collective experience "imposed from above" and rent by internecine quarrels stifled popular initiative. For Paige, Vietnamese peasants were defenseless within a grid controlled by their exploiters and made no autonomous choices (Paige 1975, 315, 295, 299).

Whereas Wolf portrays the absence of culture as a deficit, even a spiritual death, Paige sees it as an advantage. In the northern and central regions, the traditional order, with its hierarchical villages and isolated, competitive households, lacked a prefigurative potential, but in Cochinchina, there were no strong communal structures to confine the inhabitants. There, an internationally based rice economy fueled class struggle, with a mass of tenants on one side and a tiny coterie of landlords on the other. Communist party success in the region followed from the fact that peasants had nothing—no land, no community—to lose.[3]

Paige's conviction that "economic conditions" alone "create strong peasant political solidarity" does not yield an explanation of how southern villagers organized themselves and intervened in the revolutionary process (Paige 1975, 318). Persuaded that shared interests lead to concerted action, he accords no autonomy to the political sphere. Scattered in their social experience, peasants were transformed into a unified movement by a common sharecropper status. Community counts for little in his analysis whereas class is endowed with a magic power.

Interested in landlord as well as in peasant capabilities, Paige goes beyond Wolf in exploring the relational, class-struggle determinants of the space occupied by agrarian populations. His effort to prove that middle peasants were not backbone elements in the NLF is no more successful than Wolf's claim that they were crucial to the Front's success. But it can be said that he more thoroughly explores the question of "tactical mobility" broached earlier (Paige 1975, 326ff.).

In other respects, Paige's effort constitutes a step back from the standard established in *Peasant Wars*. In citing that text, he pays slight attention to the theme of prefiguration, and his dismissive reference to scholars who idealize "the tranquil communal village of the past" may put others in their place, but does no damage to the argument presented by Wolf (Paige 1975, 319). There is an appreciable loss of credibility as one moves from Wolf's treatment of popular culture and political engagements emerging from the total experience of the peasantry to Paige's economism, according to which peasants (and landlords) do not make their own culture, but are assigned a political role by the economy.

Wolf seemed to gain an ally when James Scott published *The Moral Economy of the Peasant* in 1976, and, as will emerge below, the two were grouped together by later commentators. But Scott's occasional references to *Peasant*

Wars are tangential and sometimes misleading. See, for example, the claim that Wolf analyzes the "detonation" of "social dynamite," a "spasmodic" formulation at odds with the spirit of his work; or that he attributes a "last gasp quality" to "peasant innovation" (Scott 1976, 4, 26).[4] A careful reading shows that Scott owes little to Wolf and in key respects adopts an approach at variance with the method employed by his predecessor.

Scott's analysis of agrarian life quickly moves from communal solidarity to patterns of deference, from millennial dreams to a fear of dearth, from the horizontal to the vertical axis. It does not yield an impression of a dense village culture, created by peasants. The author focuses attention on tenants rather than smallholders, an approach that conjures up a weak peasantry, not able to act in its own name. And he argues that a strongly held paternalist climate of opinion is necessary to motivate rural insurgency, that peasants "take up arms less often to destroy elites than to compel them to meet their moral obligations" (Scott 1976, 192). The plasticity that fascinated Wolf is also missing.

> The vast majority of peasant risings with which I am familiar are without doubt largely *defensive* efforts to protect sources of subsistence that are threatened or to restore them once they have been lost. Far from hoping to improve their relative position in the social stratification, peasant rebellions are typically desperate efforts to maintain subsistence arrangements that are under assault. (Scott 1976, 187; emphasis in original)

No "engrams" here, no sense of fluidity in comportments and states of mind within agrarian communities. Scott does not join Wolf in stressing movement over stasis in the countryside.

Scott's ambitious, powerful work is comparable in stature to Wolf's, but scholars who couple the two overlook differences between the "dying wail" minimalism expressed in *Moral Economy* (Scott 1976, 192) and Wolf's confidence in peasants as "the party of humanity." Scott's later treatment of "everyday resistance" brought an unparalleled specificity to the literature on peasant struggles. But it also reaffirmed his doubts about the revolutionary vocation of the peasantry, which Wolf had taken such pains to celebrate (Scott 1985).

In light of this contrast, Samuel Popkin's insistence, in *The Rational Peasant*, on associating his two predecessors sows confusion, and the situation is not improved by the highly schematic summary he offers of the "moral economy" position. Wolf did not believe that precolonial villages in Vietnam were "organic" and "harmonious" and cannot be said to argue that "the norms and procedures of villages and of patron-client exchanges are fixed and culturally determined." When Popkin embarks on a discussion of changes wrought by French colonialism, he makes no mention of Wolf, preferring to aim his critique at Paul Mus, John McAlister, and Frances Fitzgerald, who might more properly be taxed for exaggerating the integration of Vietnamese society. And Wolf, whose peasants were driven by revolutionary as well as patriotic motives, would not be shocked, as Popkin implies, by the notion that rural movements in Vietnam benefited from an "antifeudal" impetus (Popkin 1979, xi, 22, 245).

Popkin also wrongly situates Wolf as a believer in the immobility of agrarian values. "To moral economists, peasant protests and movements are 'defensive reactions' against massive threats to their traditional institutions," he declares, with a footnote to *Peasant Wars* (Popkin 1979, 245). In the cited passage, Wolf states that peasants could deal with crisis

> either by cleaving to their traditional institutions, increasingly subverted by the forces which they were trying to neutralize; or they could commit themselves to the search for new social forms which would grant them shelter. In a sense all our six cases can be seen as the outcome of such defensive reactions, coupled with a search for a new and more humane social order. (Wolf 1969*a*, 282)

Popkin sees one-half of the argument, but not the other. He misses Wolf's insistence on peasant impetus toward "a new and more humane social order."

After the poetry in *Peasant Wars*, with its reflections on memory, on the link between suffering and insight, Popkin's treatment of changes in peasant consciousness is disappointing in its flatness. He believes that the "moral economists" complicate the task of explaining rural political engagements, that "investment logic" can generate a history of the Vietnamese Revolution (Popkin 1979, 18).[5] When the Communist party offered peasants a better deal than the one they were receiving from the landlords and the French, a rapid shift in political allegiance naturally followed. What separates Popkin from Wolf is not the notion that peasants were capable of changing their minds and affiliations. Whereas Wolf might be scored for the romanticism of his 1960s-style confidence in peasant agency, Popkin raises optimism to an even more unreal level, where peasant actors are free to follow whatever path calculation dictates.

Popkin discounts the vertical or paternalist vector underscored by Scott and others, arguing that in the harsh, backward conditions of the old regime, landlords held power, but no legitimacy. At the same time, his individualist paradigm also discourages attention to the horizontal vector, which accounts for links among peasants. Interested in voluntary associations and communal property, he does not effectively incorporate these topics into the text.[6] His tendency to interpret relations in society as contracts among individuals precludes the treatment of social realities that Wolf teaches us to require.

To sum up, this complex discussion, in which each participant operates on his own level and no one fully engages with anyone else, leaves many questions unresolved. Vietnam's national revolution drew support from very different social formations in the northern, central, and southern regions, and results in *Peasant Wars* would have been more persuasive if Wolf's guiding assumptions had been applied to the South as they were elsewhere. But his partial emphasis on multiple institutions and fervent sociability in the countryside at least has the merit of pointing the way forward. So much remains to be done on relations between men and women and between youth and their elders; on patterns in recreation and sociability; on grassroots religious practice; and on the meanings expressed in language, dress, and gesture. And sooner or later, this endeavor will require a parallel investigation into the changing organization and consciousness of landlords, so that an accurate charting of the horizontal and vertical vectors can be assayed.

The social history of Vietnam's peasant revolution has yet to be written. When a recent text expresses impatience with "the well-worn conceptual framework of 'tradition and revolution,'" it prematurely closes a debate that was never properly engaged (Marr and White 1988).[7] Far from being "well-worn," the route opened by Eric Wolf is still unexplored.

III

As revolutionary expectations wane all over the world and cynicism mounts, does *Peasant Wars* still have something to teach us? Does Wolf's chapter on the "peasant war" waged against the French and the Americans provide any purchase on life in Vietnam today? Studies of the war's last years and of the postwar period suggest that Vietnamese society has been substantially reworked, by socialism in the North, by capitalism in the South, by the destruction of ecosystems and the forced movements of peoples, the withering of old values, and the shuffling of class, age, and gender roles during the war. Is it still possible to speak of a Vietnamese peasantry?[8]

On a 1988 journey to Vietnam, the group with which I was traveling visited the Citadel in Hue. Crumbling and full of holes, its walls still show the effects of fighting during the Tet Offensive, when most of the old buildings that once housed the royal court were destroyed. As our guide did her best to evoke now invisible imperial splendors, I noticed a nearby vegetable garden and asked who was responsible for maintaining it. "In reality, it is not allowed," she answered, then, as we frowned in puzzlement, explained that cultivators from the environs had been illegally coming through the walls to till the soil. Listening to her, we became aware of many previously unremarked people hoeing and weeding in various corners of the enclosure, which on second glance seemed more like a giant domestic garden than an imperial city.

"In reality, it is not allowed," the guide affirmed again, as if to overcome the uncertainty she still detected in our faces. By "reality," she meant the laws and proprieties of urban society, where one simply does not turn a major tourist site into a truck garden. Absorbed in their tasks, the peasants paid no attention to us.

During my trips to Vietnam in 1990 and 1991, this sense of an agrarian people who stubbornly refuse to vacate the terrain was even more marked and nowhere more strikingly than in the revival of the festival. Interrupted by the war and discouraged by the authorities, many of whom regarded them as vestiges of feudalism, rural celebrations of all sorts, pegged to the agrarian cycle, in honor of village heroes, on the occasion of a marriage, or for religious observances, are coming back in Vietnam.

Everywhere, the scholars and government officials who comment on this phenomenon express approval of it. Collectivism was once assumed to be the answer in the economic sphere and materialism in the cultural sphere, they declare, with no room for religious beliefs and practices. State ownership of the means of production and an elitism that condemns popular "superstitions" are now both discredited. Employing one of the buzzwords of *doi moi* or "renovation," which has guided state policy since 1986, my informants asserted that revival of the festival is a "joint venture" based on cooperation between the government and the people.

These urban intellectuals voice none of the scorn for peasants that one might expect from a stratum identified with modernization, yet surrounded by a vast, still partially archaic rural world. Understanding that they are separated from the farming population, they adopt a conciliatory, respectful posture. Urban dwellers regard January 1 as a holiday and celebrate Tet as well, but in the countryside "New Year's" is Tet, and everyone works on the first day of the Christian year as they do on any other day. "The peasants have their holidays, we have ours," one friend remarked to me, with seeming confidence that the coexistence of two time disciplines, two views of the cosmos, posed no problem. Another argued that freedom of religion was already in Ho's Declaration of Independence and that village rituals therefore deserved constitutional protection. In hoping for a reconciliation between science and the spiritual values of the common people, yet another cited research showing that the human body undergoes a slight loss in weight at the moment of death, as if providing a material proof for the departure of the soul.

I was both moved and troubled by these accounts. Vietnamese commentators reject materialist and other reductionisms, but their interpretation of festivals as a narrowly "religious," rather than a social, phenomenon is subject to the same charge. They rebuke "educated" people who criticize the backward character of festivals, but then affirm that reviving festivals is now feasible because a "better educated" population is less likely to imbue them with feudal values. Evoking a preoccupation with "renovation," they point out that festivals often center on markets and therefore stimulate economic activity. The "water buffalo fighting festival" in the Haiphong region does not squander the "means of production," a member of the local administration assured me, because the peasants use the competitions to select the best animals for stock breeding purposes. But this notion raised eyebrows among other Vietnamese I questioned, who testify that the contest results in the slaughter of many animals and leaves the victors unfit for any productive purpose.

Time will tell if there is room in a "renovated" Vietnam for multiple calendars, multiple cultures, but this coexistence may not come in a form so simple as a constitutional guarantee of the freedom of religion. The folklore surrounding festive events constitutes a language charged with ideological significance, one that molds human behavior to various, perhaps contradictory ends. Festive space and time are distinctive. Village celebrations reinforce local patriotism and eventuate in a map of Vietnam that may not coincide with the administrative boundaries defined by the state. The agrarian calendar, punctuated by festivals, imposes its own rhythm of work and relaxation, consumption and self-denial, potentially at odds with government norms.[9]

The tolerant but uneasy urban discourse on festivals overlaps somewhat, but does not coincide with the way in which such issues were once debated within the peasantry. Cultural revolutionaries of the NLF would have condemned the bloodletting occasioned by water buffalo fighting contests and would have waved off attempts to prove that the human soul has a corporeal reality. But although they were less patient than my recent interlocutors with wasteful, hierarchical, obscurantist tendencies in the received culture, they also loved and had confidence in their communities. According to Wolf, vigorous folkways signify that working people retain a degree of autonomy and therefore a potential to contribute to the future of their country. In this sense, the return of the festival is a positive sign: it suggests the possibility that village culture remains "a common amenity, a common instrument" in the hands of Vietnam's peasants (Hunt 1982, 157).

My most recent inquiry concerning festivals, in August 1991, ended in the Mekong delta city of My Tho. In Hanoi, I had been told that agrarian festivals remain "deep in people's minds and thoughts," but in the southern region, local informants said they had disappeared. With new technology, new seeds, new techniques, the peasants do not believe in gods anymore. Feudal practices were concentrated in the central region, and Chinese customs dominated the North, but in the South, the European influence is more pronounced, the area is more in touch with the world, more open-minded. "The South is a new land," a provincial official concluded proudly.

I was about to change the subject when my hosts went on to say that it was a different story with nonagrarian festivals. Jumping from one calendar to the other, they informed me that the "August" or "Seventh Month Full Moon" festival was taking place the very day of my visit. That evening throngs of young people, hand in hand, including many from the rural communes of the environs, filled the streets. A current of excitement ran through the crowds in the dark gardens and the interior of the temple, with their nooks and secret places. The atmosphere was unmistakably romantic (dance music from a nearby cafe heightened this impression), and I could see why so many teenagers were drawn to the event. A monk later told me that older people had come earlier in the day.

This festival is intended to honor soldiers in unmarked graves, solitary people who die with no one to attend them, and all the other lost spirits of the dead, and, the monk explained, it encourages communicants to ask forgiveness for their sins. But the atmosphere that evening was more joyous than penitential. People removed their sandals and stepped onto a bamboo mat before the altar, they bowed and with much fervor made a wish. Standing amidst clouds of incense and with hundreds of Vietnamese, vibrant and peaceful, all around, I remembered how in the 1960s, as the war escalated and the revolutionaries affirmed with an insistence far beyond the ordinary their right to be happy, as they imposed bit by bit their will on circumstances, I and my friends felt ourselves in the presence of events charged with a sacred meaning. The celebrants making a wish in My Tho radiated that same passion for happiness.

Perhaps it will not seem far-fetched to readers who know his work if I affirm that the Full Moon Festival made me think of Eric Wolf. Wolf would have been intrigued by the paradoxical commentary the celebration offered on southern Vietnam, a "new land," yet one in which customs demonstrate an unmistakable vitality. He would have appreciated the way in which a rich, adaptable popular culture, centered on the festival and with the power to move young and old, continues to provide a vehicle for people to express their aspirations. And he would not have been surprised by the energy of the peasants on their bikes and motor scooters and on foot flocking to the pagoda from all over the delta. Having won the war, yet still seeking a better life, they retain their affiliation with "the party of humanity."

NOTES

This article could not have been completed without the generous support of the Provost's Office and the William Joiner Center at the University of Massachusetts at Boston.

1. I owe thanks to Ruth Bennett of the Biology Department at the University of Massachusetts/Boston who helped me make sense of Wolf's reference to "engrams."

2. Wolf's treatment of the middle peasants is based on a much questioned study by Edward Mitchell (1968).

3. The revolutionary contribution of the North and the Center, for example, in the First Indochina War remains something of a mystery in Paige's account; see Paige 1975, 300–301.

4. For more on "spasmodic" metaphors of revolt and for a discussion of Scott's work, see Hunt 1988a.

5. Popkin notes "the importance of contributions, some of which were not stimulated by any expectation of future selective payoff" and he emphasizes "how important internalized feelings of duty or ethic can be" (Popkin 1979, 223). But these affirmations come in the form of an aside and have little to do with his overall interpretations. Pentagon leaders also employed a rational choice model when they tried to punish the guerrillas into submission (I thank Peter Weiler for reminding me of this similarity in assumptions). Policy makers expected the Viet Cong guerrilla to "be reasonable, i.e., to compromise or even capitulate, because we assume he wants to avoid pain, death, and material destruction" (Hoopes 1971, 128). But events showed that a simple pleasure/pain calculus could not account for the behavior of village militants, whose conception of self-interest and self-sacrifice was complex. As one participant put it, "All of us thought that we would have to die and the cadres also said that we ought to expect to be killed if we were decided to fight for the revolution. They added that our death would serve our children's interests and therefore would be of value" (Rand Corporation 1971, 47, interview 121).

6. On village festive life, see Popkin 1979, 60; on voluntary associations, Paige 1979, 97 and 230. Popkin cannot let go of communal property and cannot get it to fit. He wants the peasants to embrace a private property conception, yet recognizes that they remained attached to common lands. The most he feels authorized to declare is that villagers "may have preferred permanent control of a mediocre plot to rotating access to good, bad, and average public plots." When local notables seized joint property, he gratuitously suggests that these usurpations "may have had support among many villagers." See discussion in Popkin 1979, 102ff. Later on, he notes the continuing importance of communal property in the 1940s and the Viet Minh promise to distribute parcels to all villagers. "It is not unreasonable to assume that there might have been serious resistance" to this radical egalitarianism, Popkin remarks. "It is hoped that further research will supply details" (1979, 226ff.). For more on the topic, see Ngo Vinh Long 1990; and for a comparative treatment, Hunt 1988b.

7. As if bored by the topic, which had not been treated since Wolf, one otherwise astute observer notes that Paige "pays little or no attention to ideology, values, religion, clan, family, or tradition. Perhaps that is why I find the book so original and refreshing" (Cumings 1981, 479). For an addition to the social history of the Vietnamese Revolution, especially with respect to gender, see Wiegersma 1988. This important text is omitted here because it makes no mention of *Peasant Wars* and does not appear to have been influenced by Wolf's approach.

8. On social consequences during the last years of the war, see Kolko 1985; on the postwar situation, Beresford 1988.

9. "During the movement of agricultural cooperativization from the late 1950s

to the late 1970s, most agricultural co-ops in the North were organized on a communal scale, depriving villages of their self-administrating power, and as a result, village festivals were neglected," writes one contemporary observer. "Of late, alongside renovation work in agricultural management, the role of villages has been restored. So has the community consciousness among the inhabitants of each village" (Dao Hung 1991, 12). A fascinating discussion of the revival of the festival is contained in Hy Van Luong's unpublished "Economic Reforms and the Resurgence of Local Tradition in a North Vietnamese Village (1980–1990)" (inquiries to the author, care of the Department of Anthropology, University of Toronto).

PART THREE

In the Market's Web: Risk and Response

EIGHT

From Jíbaro to Crack Dealer: Confronting the Restructuring of Capitalism in El Barrio

Philippe Bourgois

Following his year and a half of fieldwork in a rural coffee-growing county in the central highlands of Puerto Rico from 1948 through 1949, Eric R. Wolf warned that even the small farmers and coffee pickers in the most isolated and traditional rural barrio that he was studying "in the future will supply many hundreds of hands to the coast, to the towns, and to the United States" (Wolf 1956*b*, 231). Macroeconomic and political forces proved Wolf's warning to be an understatement. American industrial capital was provided with extraordinary incentives and local agricultural development in Puerto Rico atrophied at the same time that emigration to the factories of New York City was actively promoted. The ensuing exodus over the next three and a half decades of almost a third of Puerto Rico's total population resulted proportionally in one of the larger labor migrations in modern history.

STRUCTURAL CONSTRAINTS OF THE NUYORICAN EXPERIENCE

The majority of the immigrants found employment in New York City's most vulnerable subsector of light manufacturing. They arrived precisely on the eve of the structural decimation of factory production in urban North America. Indeed, the post-World War II Puerto Rican experience provides almost a textbook illustration of what Wolf in his later work refers to as "the growth of ever more diverse proletarian diasporas" that "capitalist accumulation ... continues to engender" as it spreads across the globe (1982*a*, 383). Perhaps most interesting and relevant for understanding Nuyorican ethnicity—that is, the experience of New York City-born and raised Puerto Ricans—are the contradictory ways that the "changing needs of capital ... continuously produce and recreate symbolically marked 'cultural' dis-

tinctions" among "the new working classes" who have crisscrossed oceans
and continents in their struggle for survival and dignity (Wolf 1982*a*, 379–
380).

Depending upon one's formal definition, over the past three or four generations, the Puerto Rican people—especially those living in New York—
have passed through almost a half dozen distinct modes of production: (1)
from small landowning semisubsistence peasantry or hacienda peons; (2) to
export agricultural laborers on foreign-owned, capital-intensive plantations;
(3) to factory workers in urban shantytowns; (4) to sweatshop workers in
ghetto tenements; (5) to service sector employees in high-rise inner-city
housing projects; (6) to underground economy entrepreneurs homeless on
the street.

This marathon sprint through economic history onto New York City's
streets has been compounded ideologically by an overtly racist "cultural
assault." Literally overnight the new immigrants—many of whom were en-
veloped in a *jíbaro* (hillbilly)-dominated culture emphasizing interpersonal
webs of patriarchal *respeto*—found themselves transformed into "racially"
inferior cultural pariahs. Ever since their arrival they have been despised
and humiliated with that virulence so characteristic of America's history of
polarized race relations in the context of massive labor migrations. Even
though the Puerto Rican experience is extreme, it is by no means unique.
On the contrary, peoples all through the world and throughout history
have been forced to traverse multiple modes of production and have suffered social dislocation.

The historic structural transformations imposed upon the Puerto Rican
jíbaro translate statistically into a tragic profile of unemployment, substance abuse, broken families, and devastated health in U.S. inner cities.
No other ethnic group except perhaps Native Americans fares more poorly
in the official statistics than do mainland U.S. Puerto Ricans. This is most
pronounced for the majority cohort living in New York City where Puerto
Ricans have the highest welfare dependency and poverty rates, the lowest
labor force participation rates, and the fastest growing HIV infection rates
of any group (Falcon 1992; Lambert 1990).

THE ETHNOGRAPHIC SETTING

These contemporary expressions of historical dislocation formed the backdrop for my five years of participant-observation fieldwork on street culture
in the "crack economy" during the late 1980s and early 1990s. For a total of
approximately three and a half years I lived with my wife and young son in
an irregularly heated, rat-filled tenement in East Harlem, better known locally as El Barrio or Spanish Harlem. This two hundred-square-block neighborhood is visibly impoverished yet it is located in the heart of the richest
city in the western hemisphere. Its vacant lots and crumbling abandoned

tenements are literally a stone's throw from multimillion-dollar condominiums. Although one in three families survives on public assistance, the majority of El Barrio's 130,000 Puerto Rican and African-American residents comprise the ranks of the "working poor." They eke out an uneasy subsistence in entry-level service and manufacturing jobs in a city with one of the highest costs of living in the world.

In my ethnographic research, I explored the ideologies (i.e., the power-charged belief systems) that organize "common sense" on the street—what I call "street culture." Consequently, over the years, I interacted with and befriended the addicts, thieves, dealers, and con artists who comprise a minority proportion of El Barrio residents but who exercise hegemony over its public space. Specifically, I focused on a network of some twenty-five street-level crack dealers who operated on and around my block.

On the one hand, such an intensive examination of street participants risks exoticizing the neighborhood and may be interpreted as reinforcing violent stereotypes against Puerto Ricans. On the other hand, case studies of the "worthy poor" risk "normalizing" the experience of class and racial segregation and can mask the depths of human suffering that accompanies rapid economic restructuring. Furthermore, the legally employed majority of El Barrio residents has lost control of the streets and has retreated from daily life in the neighborhood. To understand the experience of living in the community, the ideologies of violence, opposition, and material pursuit which have established hegemony over street life—much to the dismay of most residents—have to be addressed systematically. Furthermore, on a subtle theoretical level, the "caricatural" responses to poverty and marginalization that the dealers and addicts represent provide privileged insight into processes that may be experienced in one form or another by major sectors of any vulnerable working-class population experiencing rapid structural change anywhere in the world and at any point in history. Once again, there is nothing structurally exceptional about the Puerto Rican experience except that the human costs involved are more clearly visible given the extent and rapidity with which Puerto Rican society has been absorbed by the United States and the particularly persistent virulence of American ideologies around "race" and culture.

My central concern is the relationship of the street dealers to the worlds of work—that is, the legal and illegal labor markets—that employ them and give meaning to their lives. The long-term structural transformation of New York from a manufacturing to a service economy is crucial to understanding this experience. Although economists, sociologists, and political scientists have argued extensively over the details of the statistics, most recognize that the dislocations caused by the erosion of the manufacturing sector are a driving force behind the economic polarization of urban America (Wilson 1987). They also specifically recognize that Puerto Ricans are the most vulnerable group in New York's structural adjustment because of their over-concentration in the least dynamic subsector within light manufacturing and because of their fragile incipient foothold in public sector and service employment (Rodriguez 1989).

Through my ethnographic data I hope to show the local-level implications of the global-level restructuring of capital and, in the process, give voice to some unrepentant victims. In a nutshell, I am arguing that the transformation from manufacturing to service employment—especially in the professional office work setting—is much more culturally disruptive than the already revealing statistics on reductions in income, employment, unionization, and worker's benefits would indicate. Low-level service sector employment engenders a humiliating ideological—or cultural—confrontation between a powerful corps of white office executives and their assistants versus a mass of poorly educated, alienated, "colored" workers.

SHATTERED WORKING-CLASS DREAMS

All the crack dealers and addicts whom I have interviewed worked at one or more legal jobs in their early youth. In fact, most entered the labor market at a younger age than the typical American. Before they were twelve years old they were bagging groceries at the supermarket for tips, stocking beer off-the-books in local *bodegas*, or shining shoes. For example, Julio, the night manager at a video games arcade that sells five-dollar vials of crack on the block where I lived, pursued a traditional working-class dream in his early adolescence. With the support of his extended kin who were all immersed in a working-class "common sense," he dropped out of junior high school to work in a local garment factory:

> I was like fourteen or fifteen playing hooky and pressing dresses and whatever they were making on the steamer. They was cheap, cheap clothes.
>
> My mother's sister was working there first and then her son, my cousin Hector—the one who's in jail now—was the one they hired first, because his mother agreed: "If you don't want to go school, you gotta work."
>
> So I started hanging out with him. I wasn't planning on working in the factory. I was supposed to be in school; but it just sort of happened.

Ironically, little Julio actually became the agent who physically moved the factory out of the inner city. In the process, he became merely one more of the 445,900 manufacturing workers in New York City to lose their jobs as factory employment dropped 50 percent from 1963 to 1983 (Romo and Schwartz 1993). Of course, instead of understanding himself as the victim of a structural transformation, Julio remembers with pleasure and even pride the extra income he earned for clearing the machines out of the factory space:

Them people had money, man. Because we helped them move out of the
neighborhood. It took us two days—only me and my cousin, Hector. Wow! It
was work. They gave us seventy bucks each.

Almost all the crack dealers had similar tales of former factory jobs. For
poor adolescents, the decision to drop out of school and become a marginal
factory worker is attractive. It provides the employed youth with access to
the childhood "necessities"—sneakers, basketballs, store-bought snacks—
that sixteen-year-olds who stay in school cannot afford. In the descriptions
of their first forays into legal factory-based employment, one hears clearly
the extent to which they and their families subscribed to mainstream
working-class ideologies about the dignity of engaging in "hard work"
versus education.

Had these enterprising, early-adolescent workers from El Barrio not been
confined to the weakest sector of manufacturing in a period of rapid job loss
their teenage working-class dream might have stabilized. Instead, upon
reaching their mid-twenties they discovered themselves to be unemployable
high school dropouts. This painful realization of social marginalization expresses itself generationally as the working-class values of their families conflict violently with the reality of their hard-core lumpenization. They are
constantly accused of slothfulness by their mothers and even by friends
who have managed to maintain legal jobs. They do not have a regional perspective on the dearth of adequate entry-level jobs available to "functional
illiterates" in New York City and they begin to suspect that they might
indeed be "vago bons" (lazy bums) who do not *want* to work hard and help
themselves. Confused, they take refuge in an alternate search for career,
meaning, and ecstasy in substance abuse.

Formerly, when most entry-level jobs were found in factories the contradiction between an oppositional street culture and traditional working-class,
shop-floor culture was less pronounced—especially when the worksite was
protected by a union. Factories are inevitably rife with confrontational hierarchies; nevertheless, on the shop floor, surrounded by older union workers,
high school dropouts who are well versed in the latest and toughest street-
culture styles function effectively. In the factory, being tough and violently macho has high cultural value; a certain degree of opposition to the
foreman and the "bossman" is expected and is considered appropriately
masculine.

In contrast, this same oppositional street identity is nonfunctional in the
service sector that has burgeoned in New York's finance-driven economy
because it does not allow for the humble, obedient, social interaction—
often across gender lines—that professional office workers impose on their
subordinates. A qualitative change characterizes the tenor of social interaction in office-based service sector employment. Workers in a mailroom

or behind a photocopy machine cannot publicly maintain their cultural autonomy. Most concretely, they have no union; more subtly, there are few fellow workers surrounding them to insulate them and to provide them with a culturally based sense of class solidarity.[1] Instead they are besieged by supervisors and bosses from an alien, hostile, and obviously dominant culture. When these office managers are not intimidated by street culture, they ridicule it. Workers like Willie and Julio appear inarticulate to their professional supervisors when they try to imitate the language of power in the workplace and instead stumble pathetically over the enunciation of unfamiliar words. They cannot decipher the hastily scribbled instructions—rife with mysterious abbreviations—that are left for them by harried office managers. The "common sense" of white-collar work is foreign to them; they do not, for example, understand the logic for filing triplicate copies of memos or for postdating invoices. When they attempt to improvise or show initiative they fail miserably and instead appear inefficient—or even hostile—for failing to follow "clearly specified" instructions.

Their "social skills" are even more inadequate than their limited professional capacities. They do not know how to look at their fellow co-service workers—let alone their supervisors—without intimidating them. They cannot walk down the hallway to the water fountain without unconsciously swaying their shoulders aggressively as if patrolling their home turf. Gender barriers are an even more culturally charged realm. They are repeatedly reprimanded for harassing female co-workers.

The cultural clash between white "yuppie" power and inner-city "scrambling jive" in the service sector is much more than a difference of style. Service workers who are incapable of obeying the rules of interpersonal interaction dictated by professional office culture will never be upwardly mobile. In the high-rise office buildings of midtown Manhattan, newly employed inner-city high school dropouts suddenly realize that they look like idiotic buffoons to the men and women they work for. Once again, a gender dynamic exacerbates the confusion and sense of insult experienced by young, male inner-city employees because most supervisors in the lowest reaches of the service sector are women. Street culture does not allow males to be subordinate across gender lines.

"GETTIN' DISSED"

On the street, the trauma of experiencing a threat to one's personal dignity has been frozen linguistically in the commonly used phrase "to diss" which is short for "to disrespect." Significantly, back in the coffee-hacienda highlands of Puerto Rico in 1949, Wolf had noted the importance of the traditional Puerto Rican concept of *respeto*: "The good owner 'respects' [*respeta*] the laborer." Wolf pointed specifically to the role "respect" plays in controlling labor power: "It is probably to the interest of the landowner to make concessions to his best workers, to deal with them on a respect basis, and to enmesh them in a network of mutual obligations" (Wolf 1956*b*, 235; see also Lauria 1964).

Puerto Rican street dealers do not find "respect" in the entry-level service sector jobs that have increased twofold in New York's economy since the 1950s. On the contrary, they "get dissed" in their new jobs. Julio, for example, remembers the humiliation of his former work experiences as an "office boy," and he speaks of them in a race- and gender-charged idiom:

> I had a prejudiced boss. She was a fucking "ho'," Gloria. She was white. Her name was Christian. No, not Christian, Kirschman. I don't know if she was Jewish or not. When she was talking to people she would say, "He's illiterate."
>
> So what I did one day was, I just looked up the word, "illiterate," in the dictionary and I saw that she's saying to her associates that I'm stupid or something!
>
> Well, I am illiterate anyway.

The most profound dimension of Julio's humiliation was being obliged to look up in the dictionary the word used to insult him. In contrast, in the underground economy, he is sheltered from this kind of threat:

> Big Pete [the crack house franchise owner] he would never disrespect me that way. He wouldn't tell me that because he's illiterate too. Plus I've got more education than him. I got a GED.

To succeed at Gloria Kirschman's magazine publishing company, Julio would have had to submit wholeheartedly to her professional cultural style but he was unwilling to compromise his street identity. He refused to accept her insults and he was unable to imitate her culture; hence, he was doomed to a marginal position behind a photocopy machine or at the mail meter. The job requirements in the service sector are largely cultural—that is, having a "good attitude"—therefore they conjugate powerfully with racism:

> I wouldn't have mind that she said I was illiterate. What bothered me was that when she called on the telephone, she wouldn't want me to answer even if my supervisor who was the receptionist was not there. [Note how Julio is so low in the office hierarchy that his immediate supervisor is a receptionist.]
>
> When she hears my voice it sounds like she's going to get a heart attack. She'd go, "Why are you answering the phones?"
>
> That bitch just didn't like my Puerto Rican accent.

Julio's manner of resisting this insult to his cultural dignity exacerbated his marginal position in the labor hierarchy:

> And then, when I did pick up the phone, I used to just sound *Porta'rrrican* on purpose.

In contrast to the old factory sweatshop positions, these just-above-minimum-wage office jobs require intense interpersonal contact with the middle and upper-middle classes. Proximal contact across class lines and the absence of a working-class autonomous space for eight hours a day in the office can be a claustrophobic experience for an otherwise ambitious, energetic, young inner-city worker.

Willie interpreted this requirement to obey white, middle-class norms as an affront to his dignity that specifically challenged his definition of masculinity:

> I had a few jobs like that [referring to Julio's "telephone diss"] where you gotta take a lot of shit from bitches and be a wimp.
> I didn't like it but I kept on working, because "Fuck it!" you don't want to fuck up the relationship. So you just be a punk [shrugging his shoulders dejectedly].

One alternative for surviving at a workplace that does not tolerate a street-based cultural identity is to become bicultural: to play politely by "the white woman's" rules downtown only to come home and revert to street culture within the safety of one's tenement or housing project at night. Tens of thousands of East Harlem residents manage this tightrope, but it often engenders accusations of betrayal and internalized racism on the part of neighbors and childhood friends who do not have—or do not want—these bicultural skills.

This is the case, for example, of Ray, a rival crack dealer whose black skin and tough street demeanor disqualify him from legal office work. He quit a "nickel-and-dime messenger job downtown" to sell crack full-time in his project stairway shortly after a white woman fled from him shrieking down the hallway of a high-rise office building. Ray and the terrified woman had ridden the elevator together and coincidentally Ray had stepped off on the same floor as her to make a delivery. Worse yet, Ray had been trying to act like a "debonair male" and suspected the contradiction between his inadequate appearance and his "chivalric" intentions was responsible for the woman's terror:

> You know how you let a woman go off the elevator first? Well that's what I did to her but I may have looked a little shabby on the ends. Sometime my hair not combed. You know. So I could look a little sloppy to her maybe when I let her off first.

What Ray did not quite admit until I probed further is that he too had been intimidated by the lone white woman. He had been so disoriented by her tabooed, unsupervised proximity that he had forgotten to press the elevator button when he originally stepped on after her:

> She went in the elevator first but then she just waits there to see what floor I press. She's playing like she don't know what floor she wants to go to because

she wants to wait for me to press my floor. And I'm standing there and I forgot to press the button. I'm thinking about something else—I don't know what was the matter with me. And she's thinking like, "He's not pressing the button; I guess he's following me!"

As a crack dealer, Ray no longer has to confront this kind of confusing humiliation. Instead, he can righteously condemn his "successful" neighbors who work downtown for being ashamed of who they were born to be:

When you see someone go downtown and get a good job, if they be Puerto Rican, you see them fix up their hair and put some contact lens in their eyes. Then they fit in. And they do it! I seen it.

They turnovers. They people who want to be white. Man, if you call them in Spanish, it wind up a problem.

When they get nice jobs like that, all of a sudden, you know, they start talking proper.

SELF-DESTRUCTIVE RESISTANCE

Third- and second-generation Spanish Harlem residents born into working-class families do not tolerate high levels of "exploitation." In the new jobs available to them, however, there are no class-based institutions to channel their resistance. They are caught in a technological time warp. They have developed contemporary mainstream American definitions of survival needs and emotional notions of job satisfaction. In short, they are "made in New York"; therefore, they are not "exploitable" or "degradable." Both their objective economic needs as well as their personal cultural dignities have to be satisfied by their jobs. They resist inadequate working conditions. Finally, they are acutely aware of their relative depravation vis-à-vis the middle-level managers and wealthy executives whose intimate physical proximity they cannot escape at work.

At the same time that young men like Julio, Willie, and Ray recognize how little power they have in the legal labor market, they do not accept their domination passively. They are resisting exploitation from positions of subordination. They are living the unequal power struggle that a growing body of anthropological and ethnographic literature is beginning to address (Bourgois in press; Foley 1990; Fordham 1988; Willis 1977; Wolf 1990*b*, 590).

Unfortunately, for people like Julio and Willie, the traditional modes of powerless resistance—footdragging, disgruntlement, petty theft, and so forth—which might be appropriate in traditional peasant or even proletarian settings (see Scott 1985) contradict the fundamental "technological" requirement for enthusiastic "initiative" and "flexibility" that New York's finance-driven service sector demands. In manufacturing, resistance can be channeled through recognized institutions—unions—that often reinforce class consciousness. In fact, oppositionally defined cultural identities are so legitimate on the shop floor that they even serve to ritualize management/ worker confrontation.

In the service sector, however, there is no neutral way to express cultural nonconformity. Scowling on the way to brewing coffee for a supervisor results in an unsatisfactory end-of-year performance evaluation. Stealing on the job is just cause for instant job termination. Indeed, petty theft is the avenue for "powerless revenge" most favored by Willie and Julio. They both were skilled at manipulating the Pitney-Bowes postage meter machines and at falsifying stationery inventory to skim "chump change."

More subtle, however, was the damage to Julio's work performance due to his constant concern lest Gloria Kirschman once again catch him off guard and "disrespect" him without his being immediately aware of the gravity of the insult. Consequently, when he was ordered to perform mysteriously specific tasks such as direct mailings of promotional materials that required particular combinations of folding, stuffing, or clipping, he activated his defense mechanisms. Julio had rarely received direct mail advertisements in his project apartment mailbox; consequently, the urgency and the precision with which his supervisor oversaw the logistics of these mailings appeared overbearingly oppressive and insulting. Gloria appeared almost superstitious in the rigor and anxiety with which she supervised each detail and Julio refused to accept the "flexibility" that these delicate mailings required—that is, late-night binges of collating and recollating to make bulk-rate postage deadlines coincide with the magazine's printing and sales deadlines. Furthermore, to Julio, it was offensive to have to bring over the assembled promotional packets to Gloria's home for a last-minute late-night inspection:

> It would be late and I would be at the office to do these rush jobs: collate them, staple them, fold them in the correct way ... whatever way she said. It was always different. And it had to be just the way she wanted it. I'd stuff them just the right way [making frantic shuffling motions with his hands] and then seal the shit.
>
> I used to hate that. I would box it and take it to the 38th Street Post Office at 10:30 at night.
>
> But then sometimes she would call me from home and I would have to bring papers up to her house on 79th Street and 3rd Avenue [Manhattan's silk stocking district] to double check.
>
> And she would try to offer me something to eat and I would say, "No, thank you," because she would try to pay me with that shit. 'Cause she's a cheap bitch.
>
> She'd say, "You want pizza, tea, or cookies?" She had those Pepperidge Farm cookies [wrinkling his face with disgust].
>
> But I wouldn't accept anything from her. I wasn't going to donate my time man.

She thought I was illiterate. She thought I was stupid. Not me boy, charge *every penny*. From the moment I leave the office that's overtime all the way to her house. That's time and a half.

I used to exaggerate the hours. If I worked sixteen, I would put eighteen or twenty to see if I could get away with it. And I would get away with it. I'm not going to do that kind of shit for free.

And that bitch was crazy. She used to eat baby food. I know cause I saw her eating it with a spoon right out of the jar.

If Julio appeared to be a scowling, ungrateful, dishonest worker to Gloria, then Gloria herself looked almost perverted to Julio. What normal middle-aged woman would invite her twenty-year-old employee into her kitchen late at night and eat baby food in front of him?

Julio's victories over his employer, Gloria, were Pyrrhic. In the cross-cultural confrontation taking place in the corridors of high-rise office buildings there is no ambiguity over who wields power. This unequal hierarchy is constantly reasserted through the mechanisms of cultural capital so foreign to participants in street culture. For example, when someone like Willie, Julio, or Ray is "terminated" for suspicion of theft, the personnel report registers an insulting notation: "lack of initiative," "inarticulate," or "no understanding of the purpose of the company." Julio correctly translates this information into street-English: "She's saying to her associates that I'm stupid!"

Willie and Julio have no frame of reference to guide them through service employment because their social network only has experience with factory work. In their first factory jobs, both Willie and Julio were guided by older family members who were producing the very same products they were making. Still today, for example, Julio's mother is a sweatshop/homework seamstress and Willie's uncle is a factory foreman in the Midwestern town where his metal-chroming company relocated. In contrast, the only socialization available to Willie and Julio in the service sector comes from equally isolated and alienated fellow workers. Willie, for example, who has always been precocious in everything he has done in life—from dropping out of school, to engaging in street violence, to burglarizing, to selling drugs, to abusing women, to becoming a crack addict—immediately understood the impossibility of his supervisor's maintaining an objective quality control in the mailroom where he worked prior to being hired by Julio at the crack house:

I used to get there late, but the other workers wasn't never doing shit. They was *lazy* motherfuckers—even the supervisor.

They all be sitting, asking each other questions over the phone, and fooling with video games on the computer. And that's all you do at a place like that. My boss, Bill, be drinking on the sneak cue, and eating this bad-ass sausage.

Finally, the precarious tenure of entry-level jobs in the service sector is the immediate precipitating factor in Willie's and Julio's retreat from the legal labor market. When they were not fired for "bad attitude," they were laid off due to economic retrenchment. The companies employing them fluctuated with the unpredictable whims of rapidly changing "yuppie fashions." Julio, for example, lost two different positions in fragile companies that folded: (1) Gloria Kirschman's trendy magazine, and (2) a desktop publishing house.

Surprisingly, in his accounts of being laid off Julio publicly admitted defeat and vulnerability. On repeated occasions I had seen Julio brave violence on the streets and in the crack house. I knew him capable of deliberate cruelty, such as refusing to pay for his fifteen-year-old girlfriend's abortion or of slowly breaking the wrist of an adolescent who had played a prank on him. Downtown, however, behind the computer terminal where he had held his last job "in printing," he had been crushed psychologically by the personnel officers who fired him. Ironically, I registered on my tape recorder his tale of frustration, humiliation, and self-blame for losing his last legal job as a printer only a week after recording with him a bravado-laced account of how he mugged a drunken Mexican immigrant in a nearby housing project:

> I was with Rico and his girl, Daisy. We saw this Mexican.... He was just probably drunk. I grabbed him by the back of the neck, and put my 007 [knife] in his back [making the motion of holding someone in a choke hold from behind]. Right here [pointing to his own lower back]. And I was jigging him *HARD* [grinning for emphasis at me and his girlfriend, who was listening, rapt with attention]!
>
> I said: *"No te mueve cabron o te voy a picar como un pernil* [Don't move motherfucker or I'll stick you like a roast pork]." [More loud chuckles from Julio's girlfriend.] Yeah, yeah, like how you stab a pork shoulder when you want to put all the flavoring in the holes.
>
> I wasn't playing, either, I was serious. I would have jigged him. And I'd regret it later, but I was looking at that gold ring he had. [Chuckle.]
>
> The Mexican panicked. So I put him to the floor, poking him hard, and Rico's girl started searching him.
>
> I said, "Yo, take that asshole's fucking ring too!"
>
> After she took the ring we broke out. We sold the ring and then we cut-out on Daisy. We left her in the park, she didn't get even a cent. She helped for nothing. [More chuckling.]

As a knife-wielding mugger on the street, Julio could not contrast more dramatically with the panic-stricken employee begging for a second chance that legal employment had reduced him to:

> I was more or less expecting it. But still, when I found out, I wanted to cry, man. My throat got dry, I was like ... [waves his hands, and gasps as if struck by a panic attack].

They called me to the office, I was like, "Oh *shit!*"

I couldn't get through to them. I even told them, "I'll let you put me back to messenger; I will take less pay; just keep me employed. I need the money; I need to work. I got a family."

But they said, "Nope, nope, nope." I left.

I just stood right outside the building; I was fucked, man. All choked up. *Me jodieron* [They jerked me].

THE NEW IMMIGRANT ALTERNATIVE

The flooding of cocaine and then crack onto America's streets during the 1980s infused new energy into the underground economy, making drug dealing the most vibrant equal opportunity employer for Harlem youths. Normally, in order to fill jobs adequately in the expanding service sector, New York's legal economy should have to compete for the hearts and minds of the growing proportion of the inner city's "best and brightest" who are choosing to pursue more remunerative and culturally compatible careers in the underground economy. A wave of cheaper, more docile and disciplined new immigrant workers, however, is altering this labor power balance. These immigrants—largely undocumented—are key agents in New York's latest structural economic adjustment. Their presence allows low-wage employment to expand while social services retrench. This helps explain, for example, how the real value of the minimum wage could have declined by one-third in the 1980s while the federal government was able to decrease the proportion of its contribution to New York City's budget by over 50 percent (Berlin 1991, 10; Rosenbaum 1989, A1). The breakdown of the inner city's public sector is no longer an economic threat to the expansion of New York's economy because the labor force that these public subsidies maintain is increasingly irrelevant.

Like the parents and grandparents of Julio and Willie, many of New York's newest immigrants are from remote rural communities or squalid shantytowns where meat is eaten only once a week, and where there is no running water or electricity. In downtown Manhattan many of these new immigrants are Chinese, but in East Harlem the vast majority are Mexicans from the rural states of Puebla and Guerrero. To them, New York's streets are still "paved in gold" if one works hard enough.

Half a century ago Julio's mother fled precisely the same living conditions these new immigrants are only just struggling to escape. Her reminiscences about childhood in her natal village reveal the trajectory of improved material conditions, cultural dislocation, and crushed working-class dreams that is propelling her second-generation son into a destructive street culture:

I loved that life in Puerto Rico, because it was a healthy, healthy, healthy life. We always ate because my father always had work, and in those days the custom was to have a garden in your patio to grow food and everything that you ate.

We only ate meat on Sundays because everything was cultivated on the same little parcel of land. We didn't have a refrigerator, so we ate *bacalao* [salted codfish], which can stay outside, and a meat that they call old-meat, *carne de vieja*, and sardines from a can. But thanks to God, we never felt hunger. My mother made a lot of cornflour.

Some people have done better by coming here, but many people haven't. Even people from my barrio, who came trying to find a better life [*buen ambiente*] just found disaster. Married couples right from my neighborhood came only to have the husband run off with another woman.

In those days in Puerto Rico, when we were in poverty, life was better. Everyone will tell you life was healthier and you could trust people. Now you can't trust anybody.

What I like best was that we kept all our traditions ... our feasts. In my village, everyone was either an Uncle or an Aunt. And when you walked by someone older, you had to ask for their blessing. It was respect. There was a lot of respect in those days. [Original in Spanish]

Ironically, at sixty, Julio's monolingual Spanish-speaking mother is the only one of her family who can still compete effectively with the new immigrants who are increasingly filling Manhattan's entry-level labor market. She ekes out a living on welfare in her high-rise housing-project apartment by taking in sewing from undocumented garment industry subcontractors.

Rather than bemoaning the structural adjustment which is destroying their capacity to survive on legal wages, street-bound Puerto Rican youths celebrate their "decision" to bank on the underground economy and to cultivate their street identities. Willie and Julio repeatedly assert their pride in their street careers. For example, one Saturday night after they finished their midnight shift at the crack house, I accompanied them on their way to purchase "El Sapo Verde" (The Green Toad), a twenty-dollar bag of powder cocaine, sold by a reputable outfit three blocks away. While waiting for Julio and Willie to be "served" by the coke seller, I engaged three undocumented Mexican men drinking beer on a neighboring stoop in a conversation about finding work in New York. One of the new immigrants was already earning five hundred dollars a week fixing deep-fat-fry machines. He had a straightforward racist explanation for why Willie—who was standing next to me—was "unemployed":

OK, OK I'll explain it to you in one word: Because the Puerto Ricans are brutes! [pointing at Willie] Brutes! Do you understand?

Puerto Ricans like to make easy money. They like to leech off of other people. But not us Mexicans! No way! We like to work for our money. We don't steal. We came here to work and that's all. [Original in Spanish]

Instead of physically assaulting the employed immigrant for insulting him, Willie turned the racist tirade into the basis for a new, generational-based, "American-born," urban cultural pride. In fact, in his response, he ridiculed what he interpreted to be the hillbilly naivete of the Mexicans who still believe in the "American Dream." He spoke slowly in street-English as if to mark sarcastically the contrast between his "savvy" Nuyorican identity versus the limited English proficiency of his detractor:

> That's right, m'a man! We is real vermin lunatics that sell drugs. We don't want no part of society. "Fight the Power!"[2]
>
> What do we wanna be working for? We rather live off the system. Gain weight, lay women.
>
> When we was younger, we used to break our asses too. [Gesturing toward the Mexican men who were straining to understand his English] I had all kinds of stupid jobs too ... advertising agencies ... computers.
>
> But not no more! Now we're in a rebellious stage. We rather evade taxes, make quick money and just survive. But we're not satisfied with that either. Ha!

CONCLUSION: ETHNOGRAPHY AND OPPRESSION

America was built on racial hierarchy and on blame-the-victim justifications for the existence of poverty and class distinctions. This makes it difficult to present ethnographic data from inner-city streets without falling prey to a "pornography of violence" or a racist voyeurism. The public "common sense" is not persuaded by a structural economic understanding of Willie's and Julio's "self-destruction." Even the victims themselves psychologize their unsatisfactory lives. Most concretely, political will and public policy ignore the fundamental structural economic facts of marginalization in America (see Romo and Schwartz 1993). Instead the first priority of federal and local social "welfare" agencies is to change the psychological—or at best the "cultural"—orientations of misguided individuals (Katz 1989).

Unfortunately researchers in America have allowed the gap to grow between their hegemonically "liberal" intellectual community and an overwhelmingly conservative popular political culture. From the late 1970s through most of the 1980s, inner-city poverty was simply ignored by all but right-wing academics who filled a popular vacuum with scientifically flawed "best sellers" on the psychological and cultural causes of poverty in order to argue against the "poisonous" effect of public sector intervention (cf. Gilder 1982; Murray 1984). Their analyses coincide with the deep-seated individualistic, blame-the-victim values so cherished in American thought.

There is a theoretical and methodological basis for anthropology's reticence to confront devastating urban poverty in its front yard. Qualitative researchers prefer to avoid tackling taboo subjects such as personal violence, sexual abuse, addiction, alienation, self-destruction, and so forth, for fear of violating the tenets of cultural relativism and of contributing to popular racist stereotypes. Even the "new advocacy ethnography" which is confronting inner-city social crises—homelessness, AIDS, teen pregnancy—in an engaged manner tends to present its "subjects" in an exclusively sympathetic framework (Dehavenon n.d.). The pragmatic realities of a new advocacy anthropology require published data to be politically crafted. A complex critical perspective therefore is often stifled by the necessity of contributing effectively and responsibly to a "policy debate." Defining policy as the political arena for engagement can demobilize both theory and practice.

Regardless of the political, scholarly, or personal motivations, anthropology's cautious and often self-censored approaches to social misery have obfuscated an ethnographic understanding of the multifaceted dynamics of the experience of oppression and ironically sometimes even have served to minimize the depths of human suffering involved. At the same time, there is a growing body of ethnographic literature at the intersection of education and anthropology—sometimes referred to as cultural production theory—which provides insight into how contradictory and complicated forms of resistance often lead to personal self-destruction and community trauma (Foley 1990; Fordham 1988; MacLeod 1987; Willis 1977). Nevertheless, perhaps even these more self-consciously theoretical attempts to grapple with an unpleasant reality tend to glorify—or at least to overidentify with—the resistance theme in order to escape a "blame-the-victim" insinuation (see Bourgois 1989).

Much of the problem is rooted in the nature of the ethnographic endeavor itself. Engulfed in an overwhelming whirlpool of personal suffering it is often difficult for ethnographers to see the larger relationships structuring the jumble of human interaction around them. Structures of power and history cannot be touched or talked to. Empirically this makes it difficult to identify the urgent political economy relationships shaping everyday survival—whether they be public sector breakdown or economic restructuring. For my own part, in the heat of daily life on the street in El Barrio, I often experienced a confusing anger with the victims, the victimizers, and the wealthy industrialized society that generated such a record toll of unnecessary human suffering. For example, when confronted with a pregnant friend frantically smoking crack—and condemning her fetus to a postpartum life of shattered emotions and dulled brain cells—it was impossible for me to remember the history of her people's colonial terror and humiliation or to contextualize her position in New York's changing economy. Living the inferno of what America calls its "underclass," I—like my neighbors around me and like the pregnant crack addicts themselves—often blamed the victim. To overcome such a partial perspective when researching painful human contexts it is especially important to develop a sensitive political economy analysis that "articulates the hidden histories" of the peoples raking themselves over the coals of the latest forms of capitalism.

NOTES

The author would like to thank the following institutions for their support: the Russell Sage Foundation, the Harry Frank Guggenheim Foundation, the Social Science Research Council, the National Institute on Drug Abuse, the Wenner-Gren Foundation for Anthropological Research, the United States Bureau of the Census, and San Francisco State University. Helpful critical comments by Jane Schneider and Rayna Rapp changed the shape of the article. Finally, none of this could have been written without Harold Otto's moral support and typing, as well as final work on the keyboard by Henry Ostendorf and Charles Pearson.

1. Significantly, there are subsectors of the service industry that are relatively unionized—such as hospital work and even custodial work—where there is a limited autonomous space for street culture and working-class resistance.

2. "Fight the Power" is a song composed by the rap group Public Enemy.

NINE

The Great Bambi War:
Tocquevillians versus Keynesians in an
Upstate New York County

Edward C. Hansen

A comparison of the householding strategies of two distinctive populations in Putnam County, New York, illustrates why the poorer of the two has a better chance of surviving capitalist recessions than does the richer. Like many other anthropological enterprises, this undertaking was an unintended outcome of its author's life experiences. Insufficent income led to my residence in Putnam from 1970 to 1980. At first, I had no wish to meet local people, much less to study them. In most particulars, I was part of one of the two populations: people who reside in the county, but who derive their cash income from union-scale salaries earned in New York City. As was the case with the New York City firefighters, police officers, schoolteachers, and low- to middle-level functionaries who make up the heart of this stratum, residence in Putnam County allowed me a middle-class lifestyle that I could not have afforded in the city or in the suburbs. If ever there was a fringe middle class, defined in terms of standard of living, we were it. A major human cost for the very modest home and meager yard was the fifty-mile commute to the city, undertaken either by car over bad roads or in an antediluvian train from Brewster. My own circumstances were such that I could not afford a residence in one of the nucleated settlements straddling the highways or at the railhead. What I could afford was a rundown rental property deep in the woods. My new location brought me into immediate contact with the other population of Putnam residents. Early on the second morning of my tenancy, I was jolted by a shotgun blast followed by violent but shortlived thrashing about directly outside the front door. Upon opening the door I saw that a dead and very bloody deer lay athwart the adjacent yew bushes. The second observation was yet more jarring. Less than fifteen feet from me stood the agent of the deer's undoing. Here was a stocky short fellow with exaggerated Elvis sideburns clad in greasy coveralls, shitkicker boots, and a filthy plaid cap with earflaps. Even more unsettling was his malevolent glare at me, heightened by the fact that his shotgun was pointed at my person. His words to me were: "Your house, our woods." That stated, he slung the deer over his shoulder and departed thunderously in a battered pickup truck. Even though I was a veteran ethnographer and this was a fellow American, I felt that this peremptory encounter rendered the meaning of The Other more profound than had my research and travel in the Gran Chaco, Mato Grosso, or the Catalan litoral.

My initial unnerving experience of local alterity was compounded many times over during the next several weeks. Every move I made to settle in brought me into hostile contact with similar beings who popped out of nowhere each time I turned around, to suggest, in minimalist monologues, that whatever I was doing was actually or potentially offensive to "us woodchucks." It swiftly became clear to me that (1) "woodchucks"—the semiferal, rustic majority of the county's population—are the same people who are vulgarly and variously called peckerwoods, kickers, rednecks, or white trash elsewhere in the nation; (2) a standard model woodchuck male exhibits a style best described as Proto Masculine, that is, we are speaking of a legion of hard drinking, gun toting, violent, aggressive, male-bonded individuals for whom male sensitivity is not an issue; (3) I was now a resident of a heavily armed, very surly version of Dogpatch; and (4) if I were to enjoy economic easement and the tranquility to publish in pursuit of tenure and promotion, I should have to make some accommodation with these people, lest sheer physical survival become my major problem.

This essay is one by-product of that process of accommodaion. While undergoing the rigors of adaptation, I began to realize that the conflicts between woodchucks and exurbanites had a bearing on certain key issues concerning American social stratification. Principal among them was that of social mobility, the ideological touchstone of American polity. The exurbanites measured mobility primarily in terms of first-time home ownership, however encumbered by mortgages that might be. Woodchucks held small acreages through inheritance and were concerned with stability, not mobility. In terms of standard of living, woodchucks actually enjoyed an edge over the exurbanites as they owned more substantial estates, capital equipment, and stocks of food. This is remarkable insofar as woodchucks are officially classified by both federal and state authorities as a poverty population (New York State 1990*b*). Virtually all woodchuck families are officially unemployed for five months annually, that is, they are eligible to receive unemployment benefits during cold weather (November through March). The poverty image of the woodchuck could be bolstered by considering their salient sociometric characteristics apart from their low incomes. First, their official income derives from traditionally low-paying skills, essentially those related to the construction trades. Second, their educational levels are low for the decades 1970 to 1990; less than 50 percent held high school diplomas (Kent Board of Education 1991). Some 30 percent are functionally illiterate, and woodchuck children are notoriously poor students, truants, and the instigators of the fights that blight the reputations of local secondary schools. Yet to suggest that woodchucks, on the basis of such income data and sociometric parameters, are truly a poverty population or an emerging rural underclass (Auletta 1983) would be to embrace reification.

What begs to be explained is why woodchucks enjoy the standard of living that they do, why it is currently more secure than that of the exurbanites, and why there is such antagonism between the two strata. The strata discussed here did not emerge as a consequence of a hierarchical sorting out of local peoples via impersonal market forces operating in situ. What we have instead is the collision of two populations whose household economies were forged in different historical eras in different locales and are now enclaved together. As I shall argue below, the conflict between these two populations, which causes palpable discomfiture to each, is that between Jeffersonian/Tocquevillian yeomen and a middle class of the Keynesian compromise. Simply put, woodchucks hold productive private property, and the Keynesians reside on private property that is actually owned by banks, which entails staggering personal debts. Woodchucks assume that their property and traditional rights to forest resources are the basis of their livelihoods. They bitterly resist any intrusions of the state that might undermine these assumptions, especially when such intrusions involve raising property taxes. In a word, woodchucks are forest anarchists. By contrast, the Keynesians are creatures of government, the beneficiaries of labor struggles of the 1930s that resulted in wages having a political dimension, coupled with cheap credit.

These different historical points of economic origin and political position lie at the root of the confrontations between the two populations and express themselves in conflicts over the very definition of resources and who should have access to them. Nowhere is this clearer than in the case of deer hunting. To the woodchuck, deer is meat; to the Keynesian, it's Bambi, appealing and decorative. An effective comparison of these populations requires consideration of their respective "household resource packages," that is, the totality of activities that constitute production, consumption, and social reproduction within the home. This includes cash income, the disposition of family, kin, and network around subculturally defined resource bases, and household strategies to evade constraints and to exploit opportunities presented by the political order. To elaborate this concept, I first provide a brief history of Putnam County, and then consider the workings of woodchuck and exurbanite households.

PUTNAM COUNTY: TWO CENTURIES OF
OFFICIAL ECONOMIC FAILURE

One of the remarkable featues of the United States is that people continue to live in areas that are economic backwaters. It is easier to explain why so many people settle in New York City, Chicago, or Los Angeles than it is to explain why others still live in Kayenta, Arizona, or Climax, Michigan, or Putnam County. Conventional wisdom asserts that a lengthy depression in agriculture commencing around 1900 led inexorably to the flow of people away from agricultural proprietorship in the countryside to wage labor employment in big cities. Thus, in 1900, 50 percent of the American labor force was deployed in agriculture, but by 1957 the ratio had shrunk to 4 percent. By 1957, the average Iowa farmers' earnings were at roughly $2 per hour (Davidson 1990). Small wonder that so many rural people went urban. But others did not, and the question remains, Why? Were these folks simply those incapable of adapting to the new economic order, or people who rejected progress?

Putnam County offers a case in point that contradicts the conventional wisdom. The area is no stranger to economic depression. In fact it has known no other condition since the American Revolution. Here, literally, nothing has worked out well economically for two centuries. Putnam County derives its name from Colonel John Putnam, who, as head of the local militia during the revolution, was rewarded with a substantial acreage at the conclusion of hostilities, a gift that swiftly impoverished him. His reward came at the expense of the loyalist De Phillipses family, who had hoped to make money—apart from farming—by mining lead to make musket balls for the British army. The lead turned out to be of inferior quality, just as their farmland proved to be worthless (Puerrefoy 1956). There is at present not a single farm operating in Putnam County; the last one, a dairy enterprise, shut down in 1970.

Prior to 1940, most of the county's residents were classified as farmers; in the aftermath of the depression, most residents no longer farmed at all. Whenever possible, they subdivided their farms and sold tracts to local realtors, who in turn further divided and sold the properties to an increasing number of New York City dwellers seeking summer cottages. Local realtors who bought deep-woods property found little resale market; those who bought waterfront properties near the lake and reservoirs profited modestly. In fact, real estate only became a flourishing part of the county's economy after 1970 (Carmel Chamber of Commerce 1990). At present, real estate is the only viable part of the official current economy. Simply put, there is no farming, no industry; Putnam is too far from New York City for most commuters, and no large business has yet established a branch in the county. Even real estate has been a depressed economic sector for seven years of the decade 1980–1990. It is simply somewhat less depressed than other sectors.

Not surprisingly, Putnam County has been classified as an official poverty county since 1970, in spite of the fact that the area's villages are largely inhabited by refugee New York City civil servants and local businessmen whose earnings are middle income (New York State 1990*b*). Indeed, these urban refugees have disposed of sufficient income to stimulate the development of several malls along the county's highways. The malls are the local centers of social life and consumption for the Keynesians, the focal points of weekend activities. In fine, income in New York City, a home in or near one of the small towns, and access to a mall are the key ingredients of economic and social life for the Keynesians, who constitute roughly one-third of the county's population.

Clearly, the officially poor are the woodchucks, the other two-thirds of the county's population. Virtually all of them live along the serpentine dirt roads that crisscross the low mountain, secondary forest wilderness that physically defines the county. For generations, woodchucks have tried to wrest a livelihood from this unyielding terrain. Many collapsed farm buildings, crumbled stone walls, abandoned roads, and overgrown family cemeteries testify to the failure of previous economies. Yet the numerous substantial fieldstone and wood dwellings built by woodchuck hands on retained acreages, marked by all kinds of vehicles, ruined or operative, bear witness to the woodchuck capacity for survival. In general, their survival stems from retention of family acreages, albeit reduced in size, and aggressively pressed claims to forest resources, including those to which they have no de jure property rights. The energies they expend in defending and exploiting these resources are so extensive that for woodchucks New York City, so close at hand, is not to be visited, and, via television news, becomes a metaphor for all the world's evils. In Putnam County New Yorkers are at best woodchuck cash cows; at worst, they are potentially the end of the woodchuck natural order.

The county's official poverty rating is not simply a function of the inexorable workings of extralocal economic forces. Woodchucks themselves have been active agents in the political arena promoting the persistence of official poverty. They constitute an electoral majority, and they have consistently used their voting strength to prevent the establishment of industry in the county, to block muncipalities from applying for any revenue-sharing funds that might require contributions from locals, and above all, to ensure that only new properties (i.e., those that change hands) or new construction have their taxes reassessed. To woodchucks, who is elected to be mayor, or to serve on the school board, or to the post of tax assessor is more important than who is elected to be president of the United States. As long as they can control the local electoral process, woodchucks can stop both external capital investment and governmental expansion. That they have voted Republican by overwhelming margins for more than four decades underlines their perception that Republican government means less government, and therefore less local taxation, and less bureaucratic interference in their ability to protect their resource bases. Unemployment insurance is one form of government insurance that woodchucks accept, insofar as it is regarded as a cash bonus to household income; yet only 53 percent of those eligible do so. In other words, government in any form is not a benefactor but a clear and present danger.

Having established context, we turn to examine the comparative resource packages of Tocquevillians and Keynesians. It will be seen below that the conflict between the two has not only a material base, but also a related aesthetic struggle that arises over estate disposition and deer hunting. The struggle is not merely about who gets what, but also about the different cultural styles through which material goals are pursued. As simultaneously an intimate participant in the lives of both populations, an ethnologist with a profound political economy bias, and a cynic, I was struck by the fact that issues of style were more vital to all informants than those of substance on the level of discourse. I shall below offer some explanation of this seeming triumph of style over substance.

WOODCHUCK AND EXURBANITE HOUSEHOLD RESOURCE PACKAGES COMPARED

The fundamental bases of any exurbanite's household resource package are middle-income salaries and the credit that accrues to people who earn such salaries. The salary anchor of any exurbanite family of four is at least one salary earned at union rates in New York City. Police officers, firefighters, and teachers in the city have been unionized for a long time, and their pay and benefit packets reflect that fact. A universal perception among this population is that although union-scale wages are "decent," they are insufficient to meet household consumption needs. Credit is thus a necessary bridge between need and salary shortfall. All exurbanite homes were purchased with mortgages; since 1980 there has been a dramatic increase in doubly mortgaged homes. Informants cite overextension of credit and children's college costs as the primary reasons for second mortgages. Automobiles, an absolute necessity for commuters, are purchased with either bank or dealer credit. High-ticket consumer items—stereos, washing machines, and so forth—are purchased with credit cards in the local malls, to the point where mall vendors of high-ticket items joke about being unable to identify U.S. currency. Mall consumption on the credit card-wielding exurbanite's part is commonly described as "plastic fantastic." Material life here is not about owning anything free and clear, but about enjoying consumption now with the promise to pay for such enjoyment later.

Several assumptions underlie this behavior, assumptions that have well served many post-depression Americans by their own cultural compasses, but which now threaten to annihilate them economically. Principal among these assumptions is the conviction that their salaries will steadily rise, via union salary scales, thus allowing them to convert debt into equity at least in terms of home ownership. Once they pay off the mortgage(s), the home will be theirs, at (they believe) a higher value than they paid for it. Such equity could be used for either a more comfortable retirement than that afforded by union pension alone, or to provide a modest inheritance for their children, or for some combination of both. Second, they have labored so hard at their jobs, and are willing to labor yet more to increase salaries, that they believe they are deserving of this level of consumption. The ambitious schoolteacher, firefighter, or police officer can work overtime or study to take civil service exams to achieve higher salaries faster than by simply awaiting raises accruing from union seniority. The key assumption is that wages will steadily increase, thus providing an ever-higher standard of living, both for themselves and for their children.

At present, the exurbanite's faith in these assumptions is being sorely tested by a deepening recession. Features of the recession include loss of real earning power, union bashing by Republican national administrations (Newman 1987), the general shrinking of entitlements (e.g., health and unemployment benefits), and the reduction of the public sector workforce as debt-ridden states like New York are forced to make draconian budget cuts to balance their budgets (Blumberg 1980). The exurbanites of Putnam County are very vulnerable to these developments, especially since all their economic eggs are in the one decaying basket of unionized public sector employment. Nevertheless, exurbanites have annually outearned woodchucks by roughly 3:1 over the period 1970–1990 (New York State 1990*b*). Hence, it appears that if exurbanites are sweating it, then woodchucks must really be sunk. The official incomes of woodchucks seem to confirm this opinion. In 1990, a woodchuck family of four earned $16,700, while the exurbanite family of four collected $44,800. Yet cash income as recorded in governmental documents is only that which is logged in taxable transactions. Few social science analysts seem to take into account the fact that one of the most elaborate sporting contests in this society has long been that between ratepayers and governmental revenuers, even though resorting to outside coaching (accountants) is a widespread practice among such analysts. Although the exurbanite, unlike the analyst, may not be able to pay for a personal accountant, suffice it to say that H & R Block does very good business in Putnam County—but not among woodchucks, who operate in a host of cash and carry, off the books economies. Simply put, the tax hedge of the woodchuck is the U.S. dollar, the passage of which from one hand to the next is vastly harder to trace than the computerized payroll checks issued to the exurbanites, the latter's credit card transactions, or, for that matter, the electronic cash register recordings of mall merchants. When woodchucks sell their skills to exurbanites, they offer substantial discounts for off the books payments in cash. Few exurbanites refuse such discounts. Thus, the gap between woodchuck and exurbanite incomes is not as large as official records indicate: the exurbanites earn more money, but a substantial amount of woodchuck cash earnings is unofficial and therefore nontaxable.

Woodchucks cannot readily avail themselves of standard credit devices, as their official income is too low to qualify them for home mortgages or credit cards. But home mortgages mean little to the woodchucks, who have owned homes with sizable acreages for generations, and credit cards are not essential for their domestic consumption. Woodchucks occasionally need bank loans in order to buy capital equipment and must use their properties as collateral to secure such loans. The need to purchase a new back hoe or a bulldozer constitutes a serious household economic crisis. Yet the general lack of credit is currently a blessing in disguise for the woodchucks. Simply put, they cannot use credit to run up the staggering private debts that now threaten to sink the exurbanites.

Although woodchucks do participate to a limited extent in the official cash economy, their principal and basic economic orientation is toward household self-sufficiency. In a depression, this means simple subsistence, defined in terms of food and shelter. At the heart of the woodchuck subsistence economy is an intricate combination of family estate, forest resources, household organization, a range of specific and generalized economic skills, and extensive kin and friendship networks. Taken together, these mean that woodchuck families have a greater ability to resist economic downturns than do exurbanites. In a word, their strength is in economic diversification, a term that has meaning to the exurbanites only when they converse with the managers of their share portfolios. The dispersing of diverse eggs in diverse baskets is the key to woodchuck survival. Let us turn to consider what these elements are, their combinations, and how these contrast with the exurbanites' resources.

The starting point of woodchuck economy is the family estate. These estates were long ago amortized; that is, they carry no debt. The size of this property ranges from 5 to 40 acres, the remainder of the 60- to 180-acre grazing farms that failed two or more generations ago. In fine, woodchucks long ago sold most of their estates to realtors in order to raise cash. Yet the 5 to 40 acres that remain are more productive than the farms ever were. All are forest properties, which are unsuitable for any form of commercial agriculture. Yet somewhere within this acreage is a half acre (or larger) garden capable of providing virtually all vegetable needs of a woodchuck family. Woodchuck wives spend long hours cultivating these gardens in the summer and preserve a wide variety of vegetables for the winter months. Potatoes and turnips are stored in antiquated but functional root cellars.

The bulk of the woodchuck estate is not farmland, but secondary forest wilderness. This is the supreme province of Man the Hunter, a.k.a. the woodchuck male. These woods are teeming with deer, the woodchucks' principal source of lean red meat. Although the official hunting season is but six weeks long, woodchucks shoot deer anytime they see a void in their half-ton freezer chests. In the ten years I lived there, I cannot recall a day unpunctuated by rifle fire and the baying of mammoth woodchuck hunting dogs. Nor are deer the only game in the woods; rabbits, guinea fowl, and pheasants also abound. The latter are tame birds bred by the New York State Conservation Commission, which turns them loose on woodchuck properties. They are not shot, but rather strangled by woodchucks who easily stalk these unwary birds. The streams, ponds, and reservoirs of the county are brimful with fish, among them the desirable smallmouth bass and German trout. Finally, the forest is a source of fuel. All woodchuck homes are essentially woodburning with limited use of fossil fuel.

In short, woodchuck households are largely self-sufficient in terms of food and fuel. In a depression, they could survive without supermarkets and fuel deliveries, but the exurbanites could not. Currently, woodchucks take modest fuel deliveries—all own modern gas furnaces, water heaters, and stoves—and do some shopping at supermarkets. The exploitation of estates and forest resources thus currently translates into a significant savings over what exurbanites must pay for food and fuel. In 1990, the average woodchuck paid about $400 for fuel and $3,100 for groceries annually. Corresponding figures for an exurbanite family were $1,900 and $10,700, respectively. Such savings go a long way toward explaining why the woodchuck standard of living in fact differs little from that of the exurbanites. Nor is it difficult to understand why both woodchuck estates and the forest are stoutly defended from encroachments by exurbanites and authorities.

Woodchuck economy is not limited to the exploitation of family estates and the woods. As I noted earlier, woodchucks depend for cash income largely on exurbanites, who are literally woodchuck cash cows, there to be milked whenever possible. Woodchucks sell their skills and labor to the exurbanites, and these are the same skills necessary to implement the woodchuck subsistence economy. A major difference between these two populations is that woodchuck economy depends upon the possession of a number of specific personal skills, of a variety of additional generalizable skills, and of a prodigious capacity for labor of all kinds. In contrast, the exurbanites depend on salaries gleaned from one profession and sometimes two, when both spouses are employed. In fine, the exurbanites are highly specialized, whereas woodchucks are flexible.

Let us inventory the repertoire of woodchuck skills. All woodchuck males practice at least one of the following crafts: carpentry, electrical repair and installations, masonry (including the use of native fieldstone, a common ma-

terial used in the construction of houses, fireplaces, chimneys, and fences),
plumbing, heavy equipment operation, welding, metalwork, mechanics (repairs of any form of equipment, not merely of automobiles, which virtually
everyone does themselves), well drilling and maintenance (critical in a
county where most water is derived from private wells), landscaping, road
building (important in a county where half the roads are privately owned
and maintained), and all kinds of tree work (the county is essentially a big
forest). All these skills are simultaneously essential to woodchuck subsistence economy and salable to the exurbanites. At best the exurbanites are
weekend do-it-yourselfers. Many are capable of painting a room, fixing a
leaking faucet, planting flowers, and so forth. But when an exurbanite's
home has structural damage from age or storms, when the well freezes
over, or the septic tank oozes, the exurbanite contracts a woodchuck to effect repairs. What the woodchuck does for free at his own home becomes
cash income when carried out at the exurbanite's place.

Possession of such skills is obviously a critical part of woodchuck household economy. More subtle are the ways in which such skills are deployed.
One of the most important characteristics of woodchucks is the degree to
which they manage to control their own time as households. Simply put,
woodchucks try to avoid institutional arrangements of all kinds, especially
routinized full-time jobs. Critical to their mode of social reproduction is
the tapping of multiple resources, which are available variously in different
times of the year and different hours of the day. Frequently, the pursuit of
multiple resources causes conflicts in woodchuck households, which recali-
brate their labor deployment on a daily, sometimes hourly basis. If you
have to finish a paying construction job, but your freezer is low, do you
complete the job to collect the money or bag a deer? Common complaints
of the exurbanites who contract woodchuck labor are that no one can guarantee when the woodchuck craftsman will show up for work, and in what
condition. The woodchuck may well have spent the night cleaning fish obtained illegally from the Hudson River, dressing out a poached deer, or
brewing applejack in his garage still. If seen tapping a healing beer from
his Igloo cooler—a standard 4 × 4 pickup accessory—for his breakfast, he
probably had a rough night at one of the country and western boozers found
along the county's back roads.

The exurbanite's lament underlines a real source of tension in woodchuck households, which boils down to this: when do you commit to the pursuit of what resources, and who will be involved in this commitment? This
tension reaches a peak in warm weather months, when all resources are
available simultaneously. Paid work is at its peak; fish, game, and fuel are
abundant; and gardens must be tended. Woodchuck families are poorest
but calmest during winters; with the onset of spring, their households become frenetic, as their resource package has to be bundled in these seven

months of the year. Part of the tension stems from the fact that it is not merely a household struggling to make appropriate time commitments to gleaning diverse resources, but also that other woodchuck households with the same decision-making problems are critical to successful resolution of these problems. That is, successful woodchuck householding depends upon maintaining intricate labor exchange and barter arrangements with other woodchuck households, who are generally kin, as much as it depends upon effective exploitation of all household labor.

The complexity of labor allocation decisions regarding multiple resource exploitation injects a measure of anarchy into the daily activities of wood-chuck families. It is literally impossible to solve all problems smoothly in this context. Woodchuck men frequently have trouble deciding which task is most important on any given day; woodchuck wives may be interrupted while putting up food, gardening, or helping children with homework by unanticipated visits by clients or kin, or incessant phone calls from cash clients as to the whereabouts of their husbands. Woodchuck children, particularly boys, may be pulled out of school to help their fathers at work, to garden, to cut wood, or to go fishing or hunting with dad. Woodchucks consciously weigh the value of child labor against the benefits of formal education, and do not hesitate to emphasize the former. Exurbanite children, in contrast, are a drain on the family budget. In short, the woodchucks continue to be committed to multiple resource exploitation, in spite of its tensions. There is no way that they will commit themselves or their children to dependence upon nine to five jobs for their livelihoods. For them, it's forest anarchy forever.

The organization of time by exurbanites is radically different. Earning a paycheck as a police officer, firefighter, or teacher involves a fundamental commitment to the forty-hour week. Police officers and firefighters average four hours a week overtime, and this is their principal means of obtaining additional money. All three jobs have professional social requirements as well; an amorphously defined but very palpable part of these jobs is collegiality. Crudely put, this means that to survive at work, the employee must hang out with other employees while he or she is officially off duty. Failure to grease social skids outside work will lead to on-the-job problems. Police officers and firefighters are notorious for after-hours bar communing (Kaprow 1990); teachers give dinner parties and picnics. These particular exurbanites have an additional time-consuming problem: the primary wage earner spends fifteen hours a week commuting to New York City.

Exurbanite time commitments are scarcely defined by jobs alone; it takes plenty of off-the-job time to fulfill the status requirements of middle-class membership. Time must be expended maintaining the appearance of one's home and its provisioning: in a word, shopping. The better part of one day each weekend is spent at the mall, most of the other in trying to put the home in order. Additionally, there are marital and familial requirements for togetherness, best addressed on weekends, since there is little other "free time," that classic oxymoron of middle-class life. Children further complicate the picture: their school, physical, and "activities" needs must be kept up to speed, lest they wind up as mall shoplifters or dopetakers, or as such poor students that they cannot get into a decent state college, or even as teenage suicides. Overcommitment to pursuit of income and status frequently means undercommitment to kids, who sometimes turn out rotten. All told, the time and money commitments of middle-class status often threaten the survival of the household.

CONCLUSION

Clearly, it would be folly to explain the relationships between woodchucks and exurbanites in terms of income differentials, as a pineywoods version of the unceasing struggle between poor people and the middle class. Despite the fact that exurbanites earn much more money than do woodchucks, both populations enjoy a similar standard of living. What woodchucks lack in cash income is offset by what they gain from labor exchanges, barter, and above all, the exploitation of multiple resources. To paraphrase the Bible, man—or woman—does not live by income alone. The woodchucks are certainly proof of that. Moreover, the woodchucks are more likely to survive capitalist recessions than are the exurbanites, insofar as they are well suited to live in a self-generated subsistence economy, whereas the exurbanites are absolutely dependent on cash income, credit, and governmental services for their economic and social well-being. In the current recession, these mainstays of middleclasshood are rapidly contracting, leaving the exurbanites in a much more precarious situation than the woodchucks.

Although the conflicts between the woodchucks and the exurbanites have a clear material basis—contested forest rights and divergent definitions of resources—the spirit of these conflicts cannot be understood without reference to the American Dream and its historical transformations. In a word, the woodchucks seem to have stepped right out of the pages of Jefferson's and Tocqueville's vision of the Dream, whereas the exurbanites are creatures of Bloomsbury's John Maynard Keynes, midwifed by Franklin D. Roosevelt for American consumption. In each version, private property and individual initiative occupy ideological center stage, yet the definition of property and the context of initiative are radically different in the two.

Time and space considerations permit no more than a sketch of these two visions. The Jeffersonian/Tocquevillian version foresaw a nation of modestly prosperous yeomen, economically self-sufficient by virtue of ownership of property that could generate a livelihood through prodigious household self-exploitation. In the Jeffersonian vision, American society would thus be classless, as all men would become proprietors of familial businesses. In the Tocquevillian (1835, 1840) variant, although differences in wealth were bound to emerge, the spirit of the whole society would be profoundly democratic, to the point of vulgarity, coarseness, and rudeness. For both authors, the role of government was minimal and that of business everything. This vision was attuned to the reality that, as Dan Rose (1989) points out, the United States is the only country in the world to be founded as thirteen separate businesses. Not surprisingly, social personhood depended upon acquiring property that generated minimally a livelihood, and hopefully prosperity. Perhaps the sine qua non of property was land, as the United States remained a profoundly rural society until the end of the Civil War. From the end of the Civil War to the present, the likelihood of individual households sustaining themselves from land-based businesses has declined with each passing year, to the point where by 1980, there were roughly 11 million such businesses for 235 million Americans. Despite the conversion of Americans into a wage earning (rather than propertied) society, the political and social ideology of the country is still focused on ownership of land as an ultimate symbol of personal realization. Only the land now consists of a dwelling surrounded by grass, shrubs, and perhaps a picket fence (stockade in urban areas). Instead of generating income, it produces private indebtedness. Where once it was central to production, it is now the paramount object of national consumption. Then it offered the prospect of household independence; at present it requires dependence on government subsidies.

One of the supreme triumphs of the American political system has been the preservation of the symbol of ownership, while radically changing its content. Nowhere is this success more apparent than in the Depression-era policies of the Roosevelt administrations and their successors that created the modern middle class. In their totality, these policies vitiated the downside effects of business cycles on major segments of a very contentious American polity. What evolved was an elaborate system of subsidies for different strata of the polity, which we cannot discuss here. The subsidies of concern for this essay were those concessions made to organized labor. Salient among these were the establishment of FHA mortgages, the recognition of a political dimension of wages, and the extension of consumer credit through various banking and currency reforms. Viewed through the bleak lens of classical political economy, these acts made it possible for a whole new class—the contemporary middle class—to enjoy a standard of living that it clearly did not merit through market competition. In other words, the contemporary middle class is the supreme political creation of the Roosevelt era; it is not an economic class at all, but a political artifice.

The ideological underpinnings and cultural validation of the new middle class consisted of social mobility from the working class via home and automobile ownership, plus additional credit to purchase consumer durables. The trade-off for mass consumption was increasing private indebtedness for households, an indebtedness that was relatively painless as long as government maintained subsidies and the economy continued to expand. The property of the Tocquevillians now became the home of the new middle class. Production was now converted into consumption through Keynesian economic formulae, but cultural symbols were preserved in the transformation. The conflictual coexistence of the woodchucks and the exurbanites can be best understood as the collision of old and new versions of the American Dream.

If, as Wolf (1956a) proposed, the local arena is best understood as a cross-cutting manifold, a point of intersection or overlap among diverse relational fields, then Putnam County is a case in point. Here, webs of group relations, each the terminus of a distinctive set of articulations with the state and of a distinctive history, are, as Wolf suggested they could be, "wholly tangential to one another" (1956a, 1065). Such a model of the local level draws much-needed attention to the cultural and stylistic aspects of intergroup conflict; cultural style is shown to be an integral part of the wider articulations and of the respective histories of the groups involved. These differences of external linkage and history influence not only how people think but also how they organize time, run households, relate to neighbors, approach local government, and respond to a deer transfixed by headlights at the side of the road.

NOTE

I wish to acknowledge a PSC-CUNY grant and a Queens College Presidential Award, which provided time and money to begin systematizing information collected between 1970 and 1980. I would like to thank Geoff Bate, Warren De Boer, Geraldine Grant, Mimi Kaprow, Sharryn Kasmir, Gloria Levitas, Dan Rose, Steve Thompson, and Brackette Williams for constructive criticism of this version of the manuscript. I own thanks for both intellectual support for this project and a whole lot of reciprocal labor for the construction of Iron Ball Mountain to Fred and Ethel Adams, Jeremy Beckett, Howard and Peg Carpenter, Gilda and Joplin Hansen, Mo and Goo Littlejohn, Bill Dorson, Delmos Jones, Ellery McClatchy, Mervyn and Joan Meggitt, Peter and Jane Schneider, Sydel Silverman, and Eric Wolf. All are absolved from construction defects in this paper and that dwelling.

TEN

In the Shadow of the Smokestacks: Labor and Environmental Conflict in a Company-dominated Town

Josiah McC. Heyman

We know what company towns are, or at least we think we do. The company owns every corner of the community; it controls every civic function. Town managements are either benevolent and omniscient, or they are unremittingly exploitative. The company town is thus a domain of total power, or correspondingly heroic but doomed resistance. This stereotype of monolithic company towns is not merely exaggerated; it is fundamentally false.

The monolithic stereotype does not adequately explain conflict in corporately dominated settlements because it treats local power as a single entity. During quiet times the corporation exercises power hermetically. It is difficult to understand why conflict would ever break out.[1] If resistance to the corporation does emerge for some reason, totalizing assumptions about the nature of company town communities give no guidance for fine-grained study of the social composition of conflict; we are left with no other model than that the entire community rebels against the corporation that held them in thrall for so long.

The conflicts that I will describe took place in Douglas, Arizona, a small city on the United States-Mexico border.[2] Douglas was built around a large copper smelter owned by the Phelps Dodge corporation. Douglas was not a pure company town in the sense that Phelps Dodge owned all property and privately governed the municipality (as it did, in fact, in several other Arizona copper towns), but the corporation's domination of Douglas extended beyond being its largest employer. It launched the small city's elite, it owned the largest store and the hospital, and its hiring and pay policies profoundly affected the town's physical and social-racial (Anglo and Mexican American)[3] structure.

A protracted, and ultimately unsuccessful, national strike against Phelps Dodge began in 1983. A series of hearings in 1985 brought environmental conflict to the fore; townspeople and outsiders debated (on various sides) whether or not to close the Copper Queen smelter. Underlying both conflicts were several critical, but silent decisions made by Phelps Dodge which effectively deindustrialized Douglas. What was extraordinary about Douglas was the synthesis of several distinctive issues into a fundamental argument over the future of the city: should Douglas beg Phelps Dodge to continue to dominate, or should it break with the only history the town had ever known? The public debate engaged sentiments that were not explicitly part of either original conflict. Anger and loyalty toward Phelps Dodge were rooted in unequal experiences of growing up in Douglas's neighborhoods, schools, and city government, experiences based on a peculiar company town fusion of race, labor, and attitudes toward the corporation.

Corporately dominated communities vary enormously in physical layout and extent of company ownership (Knight 1975). They also vary because early in their planning and construction important patterns of residence and power were built into place. Corporate intervention in nonproductive municipal life—building houses, extending credit through stores, managing the intricacies of civic life—is a complicated and sometimes costly undertaking. Companies only step into these functions, I hypothesize, when the labor market is insufficient to pin down flows of laboring people or it acts too greatly in favor of workers in high demand. This may occur simply because of geographical isolation, or broader regional history may inform us that working people move about and seek jobs for their own purposes, often escaping or even battling corporate rationality. Stratified segments of the workforce have different motivations and roles in the enterprise and the regional labor market. Workers thus require of company planners differentiated means of attraction and control within a single corporately sponsored settlement. Complex patterns do not cease with construction, but continue to emerge from action and counteraction in the town's history.

No matter how empirically diverse, then, corporately dominated settlements do share a process in which enduring physical and social alignments emerge from pattern-setting confrontations between owners and diverse laboring peoples, especially those early in municipal history. Eric R. Wolf, in his articles on peasant community types (1955*b*, 1957), has recourse to encompassing comparisons about processes (colonialism in Mesoamerica and Java, say), while at the same time his framework requires that the historical trajectory within each setting be specified. A general type, such as the one I propose for corporately dominated communities, is useful insofar as it delimits the set of potential cases and indicates lines of substantive inquiry into individual cases that are specifically relevant to that delimited set. A typology that identifies central processes engaging multiple parties encourages discovery, reaching even the point of creating new knowledge to challenge its own assumptions, rather than (as in the worst of typologies) restricting vision to those traits that best conform.

The portrayal of corporately dominated communities emerging, in all their complexity, from key conflicts requires a compositional and relational theory of power. Power, in the convergent approaches of Wolf (1990*b*) and Steven Lukes (1974), is not limited to explicit shows of force. They conceptualize strength and vulnerability within a series of increasingly general levels of analysis. The broadest analysis, and ironically the one that most informs us about the minutiae of local society, is "structural power" which, in Wolf's words, "shapes the social field of action so as to render some kinds of behavior possible, while making others less possible or impossible" (1990*b*, 587). Wolf then notes that what may be composed may also be discomposed. Each level of power offers the potential for both parties to act on each other, though with unequal resources for the contest. Each engagement provides alternative possible results. Therefore my approach, which specifies certain types of power alignments in corporately dominated communities, remains open about the endpoints of conflicts in particular local histories.

The first level of power is overt. The corporation may legally direct elements of municipal life: it may act as landlord, creditor at banks and stores, doctor at the clinic, even police force. Each service provided by the company may then become a claim of rights by residents. Corporations in dominated settlements exercise considerable overt power even when they provide limited services (as in Douglas); they make public threats to remove jobs and tax payments if satisfactory responses from workers, populace, and city officials are not forthcoming. These forms of power are nearly overwhelming, but elected local governments in single-enterprise towns may also fall into the control of labor unions or other explicit critics of the outside corporation (see Gutman 1977, 321–343).

Far more insidious is a second, hidden level of power: the events that never happen; the alternatives that are cut short. Management's ability to control real estate, zoning, and bank loans enables them to block competing employers. Local dependency, systematically created and maintained, forces individual working people, unions, and elected governments to think in terms of the well-being of the dominant local enterprise, even when no overt pressure has been exerted. The strike and environmental hearings in Douglas brought into the open whether Douglas was better off with or without Phelps Dodge.

At the structural level of power, however, corporately dominated communities demonstrate their most distinctive characteristics. Such towns are an extreme, and otherwise rarely encountered, distillation of the wage earning situation in which foundational aspects of the labor market are repeated endlessly outside of work, leaving little or no way of constructing diversified sets of social involvement. One knows exactly how a person stands in corporate power from the size of the house, the placement of the neighborhood, and the circle of friends. Perceptive observers cite the overlap between workplace and residence as a critical feature of company towns (Bulmer 1975; Zapata 1977). Affiliation with the corporate hierarchy can hardly be avoided even by nonworking family members. Adjunct occupations such as doctors, lawyers, and merchants, on the one hand, and disabled and retired workers, peddlers, and small shopkeepers, on the other hand, are attached at appropriate places.

Under these circumstances the social field of action—everyday give and take among people—is strongly coherent. The nature of social interaction in one domain, let us say segmented pay in the job market, is likely to be reproduced in another, say among children in school. Grievances accumulated at the company store by women overlap with grievances accumulated in the mine shafts by men. One's self-understanding, such as "race," is synonymous with other self-understandings, such as "union," as A. L. Epstein (1958) pointed out with the term "unitary structure." Residents take stances of loyalty or opposition to the ever-present company which persist for years, transmitted through family, union, and city politics. The redundancy of social relationships may make difficult the initiation of conflict with the company, but it also provides a range of recruitment and cohesion-making strategies outside the worksite which is unusual in other settings.

HISTORICAL BACKGROUND

Smelters reduce ore concentrates to nearly pure metal (the final stages are performed in often distant refineries); smelters are often located at central points inside large ore fields, surrounded by mines (which employ many more workers) and their adjunct concentrating mills. Two smelters were built in Douglas beginning in 1901, the Copper Queen and the Calumet and Arizona, and merged in 1931 under the auspices of Phelps Dodge. Douglas was placed on the United States-Mexico border, in the middle of a great copper field that spanned both nations. Douglas served the mines of Nacozari, Sonora, and Bisbee, Arizona. In its early years, it drew on a flux of copper workers who readily moved across the international boundary.

From the 1890s to the 1940s racial discrimination was the order of the day on both sides of the Arizona-Sonora copper region, the result of a tripartite struggle between American copper companies, Anglo American skilled (and often unionized) miners, and unorganized, but hardly passive, Mexican and Chicano miners (in these circumstances, the two groups were treated much the same). Corporations and Anglo American workers saw eye to eye over the "need" to pay discriminatory salaries to Mexican working men, but Anglo miners feared their cheapness and thus wanted to restrict their numbers; conversely, corporations wanted to increase their numbers and use them to undercut Anglo unions. Mexican miners, the weakest in terms of formal power, staged independent strikes and, even more important, sought less abusive conditions by moving from worksite to worksite on both sides of the border. The result was that each mine, mill, and smelter developed its own peculiar balance of ethnic composition. Douglas was one of several locations known for its heavily Mexican workforce. All of the copper region, however, adhered to the uncompromising principle of racial discrimination called the "Mexican wage": a level of pay worth at least a dollar a day less than comparable Anglo wages, as well as job segregation and blocked entry into skilled careers (Park 1961).

The company town mechanism was unusually effective in this regard, projecting the insecure segmentations of work onto the absolute racial boundaries of daily life. Anglo skilled miners, because of their market monopoly, had to be attracted to remain with the company; they and the Anglo managerial elite benefited from such privileges as company housing and segregated schools. The Mexicans, who often formed the bulk of unskilled labor, moved easily among mines in two countries. They were in a sense more replaceable, and thus few provisions were made for their housing; often they were left to build their own houses on unplanned, undesired margins of town. Companies tried, however, to calibrate Mexican turnover through use of company stores that sold consumer goods from food to furniture on a payroll deduction system. This system encouraged men to continue to earn and pay, while carefully not risking too much credit to potentially mobile households (see Heyman 1991).

Douglas manifested these patterns even though it was not built as a pure company town. Phelps Dodge gave over construction of Douglas, "a great financial melon" (Jeffrey 1951, 6), to key executives and their friends, who formed the International Land and Improvement Company. This group allocated among themselves public functions such as the utilities, hotel, and bank, and subdivided real estate to be sold for stores and houses. Douglas was incorporated as a self-governing municipality, but its formative political and social elite was intertwined with Phelps Dodge.

To Phelps Dodge, Douglas was not just another production site. It was honored with the name of Dr. James Douglas, the metallurgist who purchased many of the copper prospects that made Phelps Dodge great. Phelps Dodge, an old East Coast (New York) firm, had virtually all of its major operations in the Southwest. Douglas came to host the western regional offices, so that this city was the home away from home for Phelps Dodge's managerial and technical staff.

Phelps Dodge Mercantile, the company store, was the largest store in Douglas, though other commercial outlets were tolerated. Phelps Dodge provided a company clinic and a staff of doctors. Town boundaries were cleverly drawn so that the smelter was exempt from municipal taxes, but the corporation did pay county property taxes which supported the school system.

Douglas schools were segregated by race, reinforcing the divisions of labor between Anglo and Mexican Americans. Houses made yet more visible the interlocking of local stratification and the segmented labor market, even though there was never any systematic residential segregation in Douglas. Just uptown of the commercial district lay a well-designed park. It was ringed by handsome houses; some were owned by Phelps Dodge for its managers, whereas others were built privately for the Anglo American professionals in real estate, law, and medicine. The corporate and other elites saw one another each day as neighbors. Douglas's core was surrounded by smaller bungalows privately built and sold to Anglo American foremen and workers. Several marginal patches, inside the city and out, were left for Mexican families, who either built their own homes or lived in shabby rows of apartments.

Beginning in 1942 the Copper Queen smelter was unionized by the United Mine, Mill, and Smelter Workers (the "Mine-Mill" union). This union differed from prior hard-rock mining unions in its philosophy of non-racialism. The union broke the "Mexican wage" by insisting on equal pay and promotion into craft jobs. The union's success at the smelter indirectly affected racial segregation within the town. Pay raises won in a bitter strike in 1946 and afterward permitted Mexican American workers to buy or build better houses. The de facto housing segregation of Douglas crumbled. The union local was the springboard for the first local Mexican American political officeholder, a city councilman elected in 1948. Schools were desegregated in 1952. The synchronicity of these changes, within and outside the workplace, add to the case for Douglas as a company-dominated town.

The Mine-Mill union was destroyed in 1963 when former Communists in its national leadership were prosecuted by Attorney General Robert Kennedy. The United Steelworkers of America replaced it in the copper industry. The attack on Mine-Mill leaders confused the Mexican American smelter workforce, many of them patriotic World War II veterans, who nevertheless were fiercely loyal to the Mine-Mill. The change in unions dovetailed with a bitter local rivalry among two smelterworkers for leadership of the union and the Mexican American community. This period of disorientation and recrimination began the decline of the "G.I." political generation of the 1940s.

As the 1960s and 1970s progressed, a new political generation emerged. Educated activists associated with the 1960s and 1970s Chicano movement concentrated their energies on the still-entrenched Anglo American town establishment. Younger smelterworkers, however, faced the problem that the United Steelworkers, unlike the Mine-Mill union, was initially weak on workplace grievances. In the 1970s and early 1980s they gradually rebuilt the local's shop-floor strength.

Beneath the visible changes in Douglas politics, its social structure as a company-dominated town matured and gradually dissipated. The Arizona-Sonora copper region changed in the 1940s; copper producing centers in Mexico mostly closed whereas the ones on the Arizona side stabilized. Production systems were made more capital intensive. Smelter manpower in Douglas, for example, fell from 1,700 in 1913 (Jeffrey 1951, 25) to 350 in 1982 (in a roughly constant population of 12,000), much of the reduction coming in 1931 when the two smelters in Douglas merged, and in the late 1960s to early 1970s, when the smelter was automated. Copper work in Arizona, made more attractive and permanent by better pay, open career ladders, and the decline of Sonoran mines, drew less and less on the fluid immigrant labor market surging up from Mexico. In the specific case of the Douglas smelter, the closing of mines in Nacozari in 1949 and most of Bisbee in 1965 eliminated its geographical rationale, though it continued to serve more distant Phelps Dodge mines very productively.

Promotion of Mexican Americans into crafts eliminated the preserve of the Anglo American worker and caused the gradual Mexicanization of the workforce. Anglo American workers never completely disappeared from Douglas, but they became a small, loyal segment of a union led by, and generally identified with, Mexican Americans. Other Anglo Americans remaining in Douglas formed a thin upper-middle class and elite. Mexican Americans sustained a new group of professionals on top of a large working class.

This local working class was, however, increasingly divided between the smaller group of prosperous smelterworkers whose jobs opened up rarely and were often passed among kin, and a larger working class engaged in the low-pay, high-turnover service and commercial sectors of Douglas which cater to shoppers from Sonora. Douglas, as a border port, receives a small but constant stream of new immigrants from Mexico. This group, which might have entered the mines in the earlier epoch, was less likely to find jobs there (though the possibility was never completely absent in Douglas).

Meanwhile, the union, through repeated strikes, brought its members prosperity notable by the standards of Mexican Americans in the Southwest; in 1983, for example, a laborer in the smelter started at $10 an hour, $20,000 a year before overtime, with generous health benefits for the entire family. Smelterworkers became avid consumers, able to buy cars, finance their children's education (often with impressive results), and furnish their houses on loans, in part gladly supplied them by Phelps Dodge Mercantile.

As the economy of Douglas changed, strikes in the smelter appeared more and more to be segmented labor conflicts typical of urban America.

The pronounced racial and class structures of Douglas faded on the surface. However, Douglas remained a company-dominated town as much in its social alignments as in Phelps Dodge's economic presence; it would take bitter events and struggles in the 1980s to fulfill Douglas's gradual historical trajectory from smelter town to border city.

THE DEINDUSTRIALIZATION OF DOUGLAS

Phelps Dodge deindustrialized Douglas in a blunt exercise of first-level power. The aging Copper Queen smelter, which essentially dated to 1913, had no pollution controls, except to capture gold-bearing heavy metals from the smokestacks. It was the largest point-source of sulfur dioxide in the western half of North America. In 1977, when the Environmental Protection Agency issued a Non-Ferrous Smelter Order (NSO) giving Phelps Dodge ten years to clean up or close the plant, the company thus had to choose to invest several hundreds of millions of dollars either in updating the Douglas smelter or in building a new facility; it had further to decide whether to invest this money in Douglas or elsewhere.

Phelps Dodge chose to build a new smelter some seventy miles to the east, in Playas, New Mexico. Playas is closer to Phelps Dodge's largest mine in Tyrone, New Mexico, and it is located on an extensive supply of groundwater (a necessity for smelters). In addition, the Playas smelter was nonunion from the start. A new plant in Douglas would have faced a town full of workers experienced at shop-floor conflicts and imbued with union loyalties; in molding its new workforce, the company transferred only chosen employees to the Playas smelter, which lay within driving distance. In spite of the new smelter's opening in 1981, Phelps Dodge continued to utilize the Douglas smelter, which was extremely efficient, and thus put off its closing for environmental reasons as long as possible.

Phelps Dodge delivered a second blow to Douglas in 1981 when it removed its western regional headquarters from Douglas to Phoenix. This signaled a fundamental loss of commitment to Douglas. Phelps Dodge executives had tired of this quiet desert town, with its two-story offices and handsome old mansions. They chose instead the fifteenth floor of a shining glass building in Phoenix, an overgrown tangle of stores, boulevards, and suburbs.

The corporate relocation meant in practical terms that about thirty-five houses were put up for sale, a number (which I have not been able to determine) of well-paid staff jobs were transferred out, and the Phelps Dodge clinic was closed (the county hospital was available to replace it). In social structural terms, the withdrawal removed the functional basis for an Anglo American company town elite; they did not disappear, but their persistent social identification with the corporation became vestigial.

The deindustrialization of Douglas was worsened by the long-term exercise of second-order power, the ability to prevent things from happening. The opponents of Phelps Dodge and of the entrenched town leadership accused the company of blocking competing major employers. In 1985 Douglas possessed only a marginal electronics firm, a low-wage garment manufacturer, several seasonal chili packeries, and branch offices and warehouses of several large American factories in Agua Prieta, located directly across the international boundary. Within my direct observation, the passive role of the city government before Phelps Dodge departed in 1987 (and their fervor for an industrial and commercial park on land developed by Phelps Dodge since then) certainly fits the definition of "non-decision making" (Lukes 1974, 42; citing Crenson 1971).

THE PHELPS DODGE STRIKE IN DOUGLAS

The six corporations that make up the U.S. copper industry sat down in 1983 to negotiate a new national contract with the bargaining council of twenty unions (the Steelworkers and diverse craft trades). Strikes at contract time, averaging six to eight weeks, were normal in the copper business; there had been one every three years since 1968. Workers grew accustomed to strike time; they saved for it or found temporary work, such as agricultural labor. Pattern bargaining, in which one corporation sets the standard for the industry, eventually settled each strike. In 1983, however, Phelps Dodge refused to follow the pattern set by Kennecott (no pay raises other than a cost-of-living allowance, or COLA). It demanded elimination of the COLA as well as additional cuts in wages and benefits. (For the issues and general events of the strike I draw on the fine work of Kingsolver 1989.)

Why did Phelps Dodge act in this manner? It is unusual among copper companies in that it has no other source of capital, and completely depends on the metal. Kennecott, the pattern leader, is owned by Exxon. Phelps Dodge, though it has foreign investments, is largely a domestic producer. Since it depends on U.S. copper, Phelps Dodge felt particularly threatened during the early 1980s, when copper prices were quite low, by high domestic costs (labor, older mines, and environmental regulation). Furthermore, Phelps Dodge is an extremely conservative organization, with a bitter labor history, and for years it barely tolerated the existence of unions. Though unions sensed the toughness of Phelps Dodge, they did not foresee that this strike would be different from other tough negotiations, that Phelps Dodge's objective was not concessions, but the complete removal of unions.

The contract with Phelps Dodge expired on 30 June 1983 and on 1 July the workers struck across Arizona and New Mexico. The stoppage affected large mines in the pure company towns of Tyrone, Ajo, and Morenci (the focal point of the strike, along with its twin settlement, Clifton, which is mine-dominated but privately owned), and smelters at Morenci and Douglas. The nonunion smelter at Playas continued to operate. In Douglas, unionists picketed the junction of the smelter road with the highway. Officeworkers and foremen entered in convoy to operate the plant. The first court injunction against mass obstructive picketing in the strike was issued at Douglas, citing five names and two hundred "John Does" (Kingsolver 1989, 26). The Arizona Department of Public Safety arrived in Douglas to enforce restriction to ten pickets who could not obstruct traffic. On 7 July, a letter was sent to strikers telling them to return, or else.

Six weeks into the strike, replacement workers ("scabs") entered various Phelps Dodge operations. (Arizona is a so-called right to work state, meaning that one does not have to belong to a union to work in a union plant.) The bitterest period of the strike began largely at Clifton-Morenci, with sympathetic echoes to the south in Douglas.[4] Arizona governor Bruce Babbitt declared a ten-day "cooling-off period" with no picketing or plant operations allowed; this effectively prevented the masses of strikers and their families from blocking convoys of strikebreakers. When strikers refused the terms of the cooling-off period (they wanted no operations until the contract was settled in order to pressure Phelps Dodge), Governor Babbitt called the National Guard down on Clifton-Morenci. When the cooling-off period expired on 19 August, the National Guard, tanks and all, forcibly protected the scabs and broke the strike.

In Douglas, events were not quite as dramatic; there, a mere two hundred armed Department of Public Safety Officers guided scabs past the strikers' shouting lines. Once Phelps Dodge had its replacement workforce, it moved to terminate the strikers, selecting the activists for first dismissal, while trying to induce other strikers to return. Luis Acedo, a striker, showed me a letter from Walter L. Gage, superintendent of the Douglas works, dated 3 August 1983. It listed ten points designed to frighten strikers, such as item three (paraphrased very closely from the original): the company has 1,500 permanent jobs to fill, but 2,250 strikers and layoffs—several hundred ("possibly including *you*") won't have a job with the smelter; it's like a game of musical chairs—what if your family doesn't have a job when the music stops!

Negotiations resumed on 23 January 1984; they broke off as Phelps Dodge raised its demands. On 8 June 1984 the unions offered concessions greater than Phelps Dodge's original demands: a COLA freeze, a $2 an hour pay cut for six months, and a payroll deduction for medical coverage. But Phelps Dodge simply asked for more. They demanded that strikers return below scabs in seniority. Phelps Dodge clearly had no intentions of settling a strike under any terms with a union. Decertification elections, removing the unions as bargaining agents, were held in October 1984. Only union members can vote to decertify their own union; the question for the

National Labor Relations Board was whether terminated strikers or only the union members who returned to work could vote. The union had lost all decisions and appeals by 1987.

Phelps Dodge's ability to recruit strikebreakers was critical to breaking the strike at the local level. Although I could not compile a list of scabs (as I did through the Steelworkers for their strikers), my interviews with five strikers and several scabs indicate some sources of those who broke the strike and those who did not. Some strikebreakers were smelterworkers who broke ranks and crossed the picket line. This group was important early in the strike; Phelps Dodge's ability to restart the smelter, I was told by strikers, rested on six repairmen who kept the plant operating. Another source was local men, without skills but attracted by smelter jobs, who were hired to break the strike. I conversed with one such scab, a legal immigrant from Mexico.[5] He saw the smelter as an opportunity to remove himself from poorly paying agricultural and construction jobs. The presence of these replacements reflects the segmented working class in this border port. However, foremen and experienced scabs were required to teach such workers. Finally, outside strikebreakers may have been imported.

Why did some smelterworkers respect the strike and others cross the picket line? The evidence points to consumer pressures, perhaps deliberately manipulated by Phelps Dodge.[6] Smelterworkers, through their own effort, had achieved high earnings and consumer expectations; they were entangled in debt and time-payment. Douglas smelterworkers had been laid off because of low copper prices for twelve of the eighteen months before the strike. After six months off and three on, they were laid off for Christmas of 1982. This lasted from October 1982 to March 1983. Then, before the contract negotiations in June 1983, employees were given three months of work: "a little taste of the paycheck," as one striker expressed it.

Throughout this time, as in previous years, workers were able to survive on credit from the company store, Phelps Dodge Mercantile. Phelps Dodge offered goods on special terms, called "PD specials," essentially sale incentives through credit. Many families took advantage of PD specials for Christmas 1982. They did not have to pay off the credit while they were laid off, but the bills undercut their paycheck as soon as they returned to work. For a year into the strike, Phelps Dodge Mercantile did not collect money from the strikers, and then it hired a collection agency to pursue the bills. Better-off Douglas families also frequently shopped in Tucson, where prices were lower, and in this manner accumulated other time-payment debts. Strike benefits (as of 1985) were $60 a week, and the union was helping with doctor, utility, and some credit bills.

A scab told me that he had entered the smelter after two and a half years in the military; he had $6,000 in debts plus the mortgage on a five-bedroom house. None of the five strikers reported large debts; several stated that they avoided PD specials and also owned their own houses.

Why are strikes within the confines of corporately dominated towns so often confrontational? First, we must realize that picketing and mass harassment of scabs are not simply emotional crowd behavior, nor are they an unfocused form of intimidation. Harassment is often aimed at specific individuals well known to the strikers. Strikers know that key tasks and skills are carried by fellow workers who cross the line. They understand the choices such persons face, and by picketing and pressure tactics they attempt to force the issue. It is therefore very much in the interest of strikers to use all of their local friendship networks, family ties, veteran's clubs, bars, baptisms, and weddings to put pressure on individuals. One incident, described to my wife Merlyn by a woman who had just witnessed it, involved the wives of strikers stabbing the wives of scabs with their high heels on the dance floor during a wedding in the Bushmaster's club. This may not succeed, in the face of the power of the state and the corporation, but it is, as James Scott (1985) has pointed out, a weapon the weak do possess.

Such weapons inevitably ramify in the unitary social structure of a corporately dominated community. Here we are concerned with the redundant social alignments of Douglas in terms of the features internal to the smelter working class: the overlap of anticompany, pro-union identity with ethnicity and historical identity, family alliances, and a form of gender roles particular to male wage-earner towns. In each case the strike by necessity fractured other social ties; it could not be segmented from the rest of community life. Senior to junior relations had transmitted knowledge of discrimination in the smelter long after it disappeared and thereby renewed the unification of Mexican American identity and unionism. Thus it was that a leader of the strike spoke with estrangement as well as grudging admiration of his former supervisor who had taught him about the history of segregation in the smelter and the years of struggle to bring in the union; this man, as a manager, had remained working, indeed helped the smelter operate at the beginning of the strike.

Families divided into angry segments when men[7] were on opposite sides of the strike. Northern Mexican men are likely to seek alliances of trust and equality among brothers, brothers-in-law, and first cousins (that is, nonfictive same-sex kin of the same generation). When the strike split apart these horizontal allies, the ties of bilateral kinship (which are maintained only through interpersonal relationships) easily frayed into smaller family factions. I refrain from using the examples I collected in order to avoid causing embarrassment since unity of family continues to be a strongly held ideal.

Conflicts were equally expressed among women. The topic of women's roles in the Phelps Dodge strike is covered by Barbara Kingsolver (1989) and Judy Aulette and Trudy Mills (1988). There is little I can add to these excellent accounts, other than to note an understanding given to me by Adela Gonzalez, a wife of a striker and an active office manager for the

Steelworkers. She described how each wife faced a fundamental choice: to assert her role as a consumer by pressing her husband to return to work, or to affirm her commitment to the strike with a resolve born of the depth of this decision. This choice occurs in a particular type of company town where the male is a head-of-household wage earner, house owner, and debt-worthy consumer. The wife and children are socially related to the community and company through the husband and rarely construct interests and networks independent of him.[8] As June Nash (1979, 113 116) and Louise Tilly (1981) indicate, this social structure may ironically strengthen the role of women in defense of male pay, consumption, and rights to jobs against strikebreakers.

ENVIRONMENTAL HEARINGS IN A
COMPANY-DOMINATED TOWN

The Douglas smelter, without additional pollution controls, was slated for closure at the end of 1987. The enforcement of this deadline was in the hands of the Environmental Protection Agency. In addition, the plant required a yearly operating permit issued by the Arizona Department of Public Health. Phelps Dodge was eager to keep it operating indefinitely, since it was still quite efficient. A tightly organized group of environmentalists who lived outside Douglas were pressing the state governor to guarantee that the smelter would close. Would they find a community unified in defending its major employer, or would they find allies in a largely Mexican American and poor Douglas?

The extended case method (Van Velsen 1967) highlights such conflict sequences. Public situations are recorded and analyzed for the carefully crafted presentations of different actors. Behind each speaker lies a complex web of alliances and disputes indirectly represented in public. I observed two public hearings in 1985. Wolf's emphasis on historical composition within fields of power renews this valuable tool of anthropologists; the case of Douglas is best understood in terms of the redundant social cleavages of class, race, and community politics inherited from the epoch of Phelps Dodge domination.

The first event, held in January, was a town meeting called by a nervous congressman trying to sound out public opinion. It was a disastrous ambush of Phelps Dodge. Thirteen persons from the audience spoke; all but one of them criticized the smelter. Five individual strikers and an official AFL-CIO representative spoke against the smelter. Four of the strikers appeared by last name to be Mexican American, and one was Anglo American. Another Mexican American spoke on behalf of the strikers. Four speakers came from the environmental movement, all of them Anglo American. Several volunteers from the audience could not be identified; one said that pollution had not caused him health problems (*Arizona Daily Star*, 18 January 1985, 2G, provides a corroborating account).

A former city councilman and retired smelterworker gave the most dramatic speech. To considerable enthusiasm, he compared giving Phelps Dodge a permit to giving "a crazy man a gun for three years: are you going to let him keep the gun, or take it away from him?" I later found out that the Steelworkers local had invited the speaker to the meeting. He represented an older, but still influential, generation of leadership in the Mexican American community.

An important element of the argument against Phelps Dodge emerged at the meeting in a series of statements by two strikers sandwiching a reply by the local Jobs Training Partnership Act (JTPA) director, a member of the environmental network. (The head of the Steelworkers had a job at the JTPA office.) They established not only the technical point that strikers were eligible for retraining *if* they fit the low-income guidelines, but also the general point that no alternative employers would come to Douglas as long as Phelps Dodge was there. This sequence was very important because it kept the "jobs versus environment" dynamic from forming. The congressman was on the defensive the entire evening. He was never able successfully to develop his own angle, blaming cheap foreign copper for lost jobs and new Mexican smelters for pollution, thus exculpating Phelps Dodge while appearing sympathetic to displaced workers.

Having this experience in mind, officials of the state of Arizona in consultation with local politicians prepared much more carefully a hearing in April for issuance of a state health permit. Not that it was one-sided; it was simply rigid and formal, with most speakers representing named organizations and recognized in a balanced turn-taking of supporters and critics. It was, furthermore, designated an "informal" (nonbinding) hearing, with the "official" hearing to be held at state health offices in Tucson (*Arizona Daily Star*, 9 April 1985, C11).

The meeting, held in the high school gymnasium, had an audience divided into fairly clear and vocal factions that I could readily identify. On the left-hand side, facing the panel, were a cluster of male strikers in the upper benches, and families of strikers and other Mexican American sympathizers in the lower benches. On the right-hand side, toward the panel, sat the Anglo American environmentalists, whereas back from the panel sat the pro-Phelps Dodge townspeople and officials. In the upper rafters, opposite the strikers, sat the scabs, indicated by shouted insults and whistles as they entered under police escort.

Twenty-eight persons spoke. Seventeen of them opposed the permit; ten supported it; one politician waffled. A vice-president of Phelps Dodge spoke, and a supervisor at the smelter presented a petition with "4,800 signatures" asking to keep it open. The then-current mayor of Douglas spoke in favor of the smelter. The mayor was a lawyer on retainer for Phelps Dodge; his father had been a mine manager and a rancher, as well as one of the members of the International Land and Improvement Company that founded Douglas. Another key Anglo speaker was a former mayor, county supervisor, and political boss.

Most of the critics of the smelter this time came from the environmental movement, which could supply endless organizational affiliations, unlike the individual strikers who dominated the earlier meeting. Representatives of the state of New Mexico, the Sierra Club, the Environmental Defense Fund, Threshold, and the Group Against Smelter Pollution (GASP) all opposed the permit. The local environmental organizer brought out three of the same local citizens (two farmers and a high school biology teacher) who had spoken at the earlier meeting.

The union was represented by only one officer, and they also brought a representative from AFSCME (the public service workers union) in nearby Sierra Vista, a military base town. Ben Wilson of the Committee for Justice, a local border human rights group, spoke of possible carcinogens and other environmental and economic damage left by Phelps Dodge to Douglas.

The net result of the meeting was that it was impossible for the mayor to claim that a unified Douglas opposed the closing of the smelter imposed on them by outsiders and environmentalists. As a public meeting, it failed to produce the consensus Phelps Dodge needed. The permit was issued, however, for that year.

Support for the smelter in the two meetings was relatively simple. It consisted of scabs, with no public voice, and a vocal Anglo American minority in both audience and speakers. They were older persons from the small town elite who identified completely and unquestioningly with Phelps Dodge. One older Anglo American woman remarked at the first town hall meeting that she just couldn't understand why people criticized Phelps Dodge after all the good things they had done for Douglas, such as provide scholarships; a Mexican American woman asked me, "But how much have they taken out of Douglas?" Anglo American supporters of Phelps Dodge could not leave behind the fusion of corporate with local social hierarchy, even after the corporation withdrew its headquarters from their beloved town. The racial dimensions of loyalty to Phelps Dodge were the last echoes of the third order of power, the old way of recruiting and dividing labor in the Arizona copper fields.

Opposition to the smelter was more diverse: it included environmentalists; strikers; and a small but influential band of opponents of the old order in Douglas as a whole. A post-1960s activist-entrepreneur who lived in the mountains outside Douglas skillfully orchestrated national and state political contacts and a base of local environmentalists. They were younger Anglo

Americans (either from Bisbee, a former mine town and the county seat which now subsists on governmental jobs, or farmers angry with smelter pollution).

The environmentalists' alliance with the strikers was purely instrumental. Both groups wanted to punish Phelps Dodge, and they coordinated action between their leaders, but they remained distinct constituencies. The strikers were working class, largely Mexican American, in a way still proud of the smelter, and (in interviews) very much ill-at-ease with the post-1960s back-to-the-country environmentalists. In addition, the strikers were in a difficult position because in 1977 their local president was on record as supporting the smelter during a trip to Phoenix sponsored by the company.

The reason labor and environmental issues fused was not because articulate links were developed but because advocates drew on the appeal within a former company town to any and all resentments of Phelps Dodge. Struggle in Douglas inevitably awakened racial divisions, which had cut deeply in the laboring past. Corporately dominated communities are unusual in that their social alignments are palpably redundant rather than loosely overlapping within a wider arena of unequal institutional powers. In this context it is not helpful to categorize particular conflicts as old-fashioned labor struggles versus new social movements; even conjoining reified labels, "race" and "class," is less rewarding than analyzing the historical making of additive social alignments.

In the end, the keystone of the alliance was the group that was critical of the political order in Douglas. Hector Salinas, a young city councilman and member (with Ben Wilson) of the Committee for Justice, had voted against a city resolution putting Douglas in favor of extending the smelter's lease on life. Salinas, a draftsman, is the son of a smelterworker, and the brother of a striker, as well as cousin of a strikebreaker. His loyal following is in city Ward 1, the old barrio of Douglas. The old barrio is a poor, largely Mexican American neighborhood. Few smelterworkers remain there, but it was a launching place of both the union and of Mexican identity in opposition to Anglo American domination. Since 1972 Ward 1 elected a series of active councilmen from the Chicano generation of political leadership, up to and including Salinas. Salinas's popularity came from his efforts to get city services (such as sidewalks and curbs) from a city government seen as distant and prejudiced, from his impressive series of defensive maneuvers in local politics (using the Department of Justice to prevent the city from dropping nine hundred names from the voting rolls, for example), and especially from two major cases of torture and death in Agua Prieta (in Mexico across from Douglas) which he and his two colleagues Ben Wilson and Leo Sierra doggedly exposed. Salinas and Wilson brought environmentalism to a Mexican American and poor constituency.

Councilman Salinas and the mayor were opposites. One was the son of a smelterworker, the other a company lawyer and son of a town founder. They fought over visions of Douglas, one of a Douglas freed from dependence on Phelps Dodge, and the other a Douglas loyal to the company and the old town hierarchy. The debating points included the environmental effects of the smelter, the question whether Phelps Dodge discouraged other employers from coming to Douglas, and the rise or fall in the town's 2 percent sales tax once Phelps Dodge quit spending money there. The argument was conducted in a setting of complete uncertainty, since no one knew what effect losing the Phelps Dodge payroll would have on the range of service and commercial jobs in the city. Indeed, the two opponents were not so much projecting a future as they were taking positions on the past. Company domination offers but two choices, faith or principled opposition. This stark dichotomy is learned early, and at an emotional level: social race is learned among one's schoolmates; class is seen in one's parents' house (the mayor's house was, of course, the most notable of the great houses of Douglas); and allegiance to either company or union is transmitted in one's upbringing. Thus the political battle was, in a sense, a struggle to force Douglas's social structure to change, well after Phelps Dodge had removed its economic rationale.

The Douglas smelter closed at the end of 1987. It is hard to know how much local struggles affected the decision to let the EPA go ahead and shut it down. It is possible that the lack of effective local consensus in favor of the smelter made it difficult to mobilize politicians at a higher level.[9] Three hundred and fifty jobs were lost. Some well-paid blue-collar jobs were replaced with the opening of a state jail, a leading product of America in the 1980s. A branch of AFSCME opened in the Steelworker's hall, and they now represent the prison guards (eight of whom were hired among the strikers as of 1985). Douglas itself has had a commercial boom, with shoppers streaming over from northern Sonora, as they long have. Even a Wal-Mart has arrived, located partly on Phelps Dodge land. Douglas, which was once exceptional, now has become a typical American-side border town, resting on Mexican shopping, smuggling, and new immigrants. In 1991, the twin stacks of the smelter were tumbled, forming a cross as they descended, and the scrap of the Copper Queen was sold to Japan. Douglas no longer lives under the smoke of the company.

CONCLUSION

Eric Wolf taught anthropologists to think within a framework of relational power and to use that framework to understand social classes within historically composed regions. Though anthropologists now often delineate locally studied people as members of such classes rather than members of a community or a culture, the older tools for examining social structure remain valuable. These are particularly helpful for illuminating complexity within classes and the enactment of relationships between classes. Working people, as among all social classes, live out life within local systems of stratification; this motivates powerful emotions toward highly particular understandings of oneself and others. Sequences of conflict uncover strongly motivated social alignments, and offer insights about the less penetrable—but equally important—times of stasis. In this manner the study of heavily structured power can also become the study of how people make their history.

NOTES

I would like to thank numerous informants in Douglas on both sides of the issues. Whatever the final results, I wish the town the best. All responsibility for interpretations and errors of fact are mine alone. This paper is dedicated to my teacher, Eric Wolf, for his gentle wisdom. I thank James B. Greenberg for introducing me to Douglas in 1982 and for many enlightening conversations since then. I also thank Teresa Hanley for sharing her company town fieldwork on the persistence of social structure after the initial rationale in labor control has passed. This material is based on research supported by the National Science Foundation under grant BNS-8403884, a fellowship from the Doherty Foundation, and a grant-in-aid from the Wenner-Gren Foundation for Anthropological Research.

1. A historian who addresses the difficulty of explaining a sudden outburst of labor conflict from a setting of enveloping paternalism is Larry Lankton (1991). John Gaventa (1980, 37) also notices the curious contradiction between his portrayal of quiescence in south central Appalachia and the usual generalizations about mining communities as militant isolates. In an otherwise very fine book, *Workers' City, Company Town*, Daniel Walkowitz (1978) is unable to explain convincingly why the textile mill community of Cohoes, New York, sustained a prolonged strike after having argued that their prior passivity reflected corporate domination.

2. I observed Douglas during two periods. The summer of 1982 came shortly after the decisions to build a new smelter away from Douglas and to withdraw corporate headquarters. From September 1984 to May 1986 I witnessed the later stages of the Phelps Dodge strike (begun in 1983), interviewed scabs and strikers, and observed an important but incomplete segment of the environmental debate which ended in 1987. In 1991 and 1992 I returned to Douglas and conducted some retrospective interviews.

3. Anglo American, or Anglo for short, is the regional cultural term in the western United States for non-Hispanics, non-Indians, and nonblacks. It does not refer in usage to putative Anglo-Saxon ancestry. Rather, it is a contrastive term (Anglo versus non-Anglo) whose roots in regional history, schools, and labor markets are evident from the text. Terms for persons of Mexican ancestry in Douglas are more complex. People refer to themselves variously as Mexican American, Chicano, Hispanic, Latin (or Latino), or Spanish. In fact, most often people spoke of themselves and others as Mexican or Mexicano, although they may have been U.S. citizens with lengthy family roots inside the territorial United States. To avoid confusing the

reader, I have adopted Mexican American (a term today passing somewhat out of usage) as most clearly conveying the operative ethnic distinction.

4. Kingsolver (1989) and several strikers in Douglas attributed the fact that the Douglas strike did not as completely envelop the community as in Clifton-Morenci to the less complete overlap with the enterprise in the border city.

5. So-called green-carders already have legal permanent residence in the United States; people cannot immigrate as strikebreakers per se.

6. James Greenberg by chance conversed with a Phelps Dodge psychologist who indicated that the prestrike layoffs were a deliberate strategy to prepare the ground for the strike.

7. I had a list of strikers belonging to the United Steelworkers; all but one were men.

8. This situation in mine company towns and its opposite, with important female managerial roles in heterogenous border cities, is described in Heyman 1991, chap. 5.

9. Another possible explanation is that the Arizona or U.S. government pressed Phelps Dodge to give in, so as to have a bargaining chip in negotiations with Mexico over pollution controls for two smelters opened in the late 1980s in northern Sonora. This was the strategy proposed by a border environmentalist who had a good working relationship with then Arizona Governor Bruce Babbitt.

ELEVEN

Risky Business: Genetic Counseling in a Shifting World

Rayna Rapp

One of the central problems described throughout the scholarship of Eric R. Wolf concerns the risks working people must confront in their efforts to wrest security and make meaning in an inherently unstable world. "Closed corporate" peasants and "new working classes," caudillos and commissars all confront risks to their livelihood; some succeed better than others in diminishing or transforming this problem (Wolf 1966*b*, 1982*a*; Wolf and Hansen 1972). Yet throughout Wolf's corpus, there is no direct examination of the concept of risk itself. In this chapter, I offer an analysis of one area of contemporary American life in which the idea of risk has become increasingly central. One goal of this essay is to examine the multiple and conflicting meanings this idea may hold.

"Risk" appears to be a dominant, empirically based category of later twentieth-century American culture, closely linked to medical definitions of social and biological factors affecting individual health. Yet this was not always the definition of "risk"; recent scholarship on the history of mathematics and statistical thinking suggests that the European invention of statistical generalizations about the human condition owes much to theories of gambling and insurance from the early eighteenth century forward. These ideas were first applied to generalizations about births, deaths, and marriages, and only became focused on patterns of disease during the nineteenth century (Daston 1987; Hacking 1990).

Here, I examine one arena where such medical definitions of risk proliferate, the genetic counseling interview that precedes a pregnant woman's decision to use or forgo amniocentesis. Amniocentesis is one of the most routinized of the new reproductive technologies; it is used to detect chromosomal problems and neural tube defects in fetuses during the second trimester of a pregnancy. At that time, if a "positive diagnosis" is made (i.e., that the fetus carries a trait that will lead to a serious disability), a woman and her supporters must decide to continue or end the pregnancy.

In studying amniocentesis as a cultural anthropologist, I am especially interested in how medical analyses of risk are constructed as biological, individual, and containable through the discourse of genetic counseling. The language and assumptions of this discourse are very powerful, often muffling other strategies by which pregnant women from diverse cultural backgrounds understand risks to themselves and their children. In New York City during the last decade, when much of my fieldwork has been conducted, "risk" also adheres in broader social conditions as distant as the fluctuating value of the dollar and the price of oil; as near as the rise of drug trading in the neighborhood playground; as abstract as real estate investment strategies that transformed the City from a renters' to a buyers' market for housing; as concrete as the cutbacks in sanitation, transit, and police services which have made it more difficult to define and defend a viable neighborhood. Powerful medical definitions of risk intervene in and demean these more commonsense meanings that inhere in the practical consciousness of daily life. Different understandings of risk then affect the reproductive decisions that clients sent for genetic counseling must negotiate. The political economy of risk is thus a culturally contestable domain.

THE RISE OF RISK

"Risk" is on the rise as a cultural category, at least in advanced capitalist societies. Its conceptual power is surely intertwined with the rise of statistical and probabilistic thinking from the eighteenth century forward in the West. These descriptive and predictive technologies are themselves closely linked to patterns of governmentality (Foucault 1979), increasingly used to claim control over resources as diverse as fitness and availability of recruits to national armies, morbidity and mortality rates, and economic trends and taxation. As many scholars have pointed out, the deployment of such "knowledge/power" complexes has enormous effects at every level of social interaction, from the most bureaucratic-abstract to the most subjective-individualistic (e.g., Miller and Rose 1990).

The impact of discourses of probability and risk is nowhere more apparent than in the field of modern medicine, where from at least the mid-nineteenth century forward, powerful professional movements and policy trends reflected a growing awareness of the measurable interaction of social factors and public health. Initially labeled "social medicine," this sensibility was at once scientific and political, prone to a belief in technocratic resolution of health problems and implicitly critical of individual solutions to collectively generated social ills. Social hygiene, health education, and eugenic thinking were commonly linked in this perspective (Kevles 1985; Porter and Porter 1988; Starr 1982).

Powerful advances in clinical medicine—the diagnosis and treatment of

illness focused on and within the individual—both challenged and transformed this more social focus. The newly emergent germ theory of disease
both used and advanced a series of overlapping metaphors: first, the body as
machine with all its attendant connections and breakdowns; then, military
metaphors of disease and disfunction as sites of warfare; and, since World
War II, cybernetic and computer-based languages to describe the body
as an information-processing system (Haraway 1988; Martin 1990; Montgomery 1991). Some sociologists and historians have recently argued that
biomedicine has entered a "post-germ theory" paradigm state that has consequences for the discursive focus of medical interests. The relative decline
of contagious diseases and the subsequent visibility of chronic conditions in
the developed world has been accompanied, they argue, by a new attention
to immunology and genetics, two fields that attempt to describe the "information systems" out of which bodies develop, function, and misfunction
(Baird 1990; Lippman 1991; Todd 1990). An "informatics" approach to
biomedicine then feeds back into older preoccupations with health and illness, for it has implications for both professional and popular understandings of prevention and cure (e.g., "lifestyle" considerations in promoting or
stressing immune responses; promoting "preconceptual" health before conceiving babies) (Lyon 1993; Raab 1987).

Many of these preoccupations are deeply consonant with powerful and
long-standing themes in American culture: individual health and illness
have often been pictured as the product of a person's own actions, although
for some subcultures, they are also predestinational signs. The power of the
individual to condemn or save him/herself on the basis of righteous living
holds sway in many strata of American culture. There is a strong belief in
the "self-made man" whose core resources are internal. This celebration of
the self-contained individual stands in tension with the idea that genealogi-
cally transmitted resources also strongly influence an individual's achievement, as well as her or his group identity. Genetics provides ample resources for metaphorical productions of what an individual is and what an
individual's resources and limits might be.

This melding of core cultural beliefs and modern biomedical foci is particularly evident in the development, takeoff, and routinization of prenatal
diagnosis. The technologies designed to detect chromosomal and neural
tube problems in fetuses are built into an emergent worldview that Lippman labels "geneticization": "an ongoing process by which differences
between individuals are reduced to their DNA codes, with most disorders,
behaviors, and physiological variations defined, at least in part, as genetic
in origin" (1991, 19). Geneticization promotes the view of risk as individual, and located in the body. It encodes variations in life-chances into the
life-force itself, foregrounding a biomedical worldview, backgrounding
more obviously social differences in the risks and possibilities that individ-

uals necessarily confront. I will return to the question of foreground and background in the cultural articulation of risk below. But first, I will describe the empirical research context in which my understandings of "risk" have developed.

RESEARCHING RISK

For the last nine years, I have been studying the social impact and cultural meaning of amniocentesis and related reproductive technologies. A technology is not a village, an ethnic group, or a ritual; in short, it is not the sort of object usually studied by anthropologists. But it is a cultural product of human labor, it has a political-economic and social history, and its distribution and impact reflect power differences. All of these can be studied. In order to understand an emergent technology, I have had to develop a methodology that does not rely on a concept of a coherent community or continuous social interactions as its main framework. I have come to think of my method as the construction of a Venn diagram: overlapping domains of interaction characterize multiple sites of investigation. Whereas some of these domains are dense with daily interaction (laboratories as workplaces, for example), others are only ephemerally constructed by my own efforts to interview patients, doctors, and parents of disabled children who may very well never have met one another. Yet all have lives that are touched by the technology I seek to understand.

The layers into which I have delved begin with the Prenatal Diagnosis Laboratory (PDL), founded by the Health Department of New York City in 1978 explicitly to provide outreach to the urban poor. The PDL is the largest cytogenetics lab attached to a public health facility in the United States. Its three to five genetic counselors are circuit riders, servicing both private (that is, middle-class) and clinic (that is, working-poor) patients in five to seven hospitals, and its laboratory analyzes amniotic fluids for twenty-four municipal hospitals. The population served by the lab is one-third African-American, one-third Hispanic, and one-third white. But we should be cautious about such census categories. Recent Haitian immigrants coming from the society with the poorest medical services in the Western Hemisphere are lumped together with native New Yorkers whose families have been in this country many generations longer than my own. The "old migrants" from Puerto Rico and the Dominican Republic end up in the same census box as recently arrived, war-torn Salvadorans and Nicaraguans and middle-class Argentinians and Colombians. And the exotic "white" race includes Ashkenazi and Sephardic Jews; Polish, Italian, and Irish Catholics; Greek and Russian Orthodox; and Pentecostalists and Anglican Protestants, as if they were a unified racial and cultural group by dint of not belonging to the minorities under surveillance. The historical and contemporary complexity of New York's fluid racial-ethnic map is thus erased by the very categories of "difference" we are given. The same caveats apply to my more recent observations at Beth Israel Medical Center, where I am particularly interested in observing and talking with working-class and lower middle-class patients sent for genetic services by the Hospital Insurance Plan (HIP), New York's oldest HMO. Beth Israel, too, serves a richly multilingual, multicultural patient population, approximately 7 percent of whom are drawn from New York's Chinatown.

Using the standard anthropological methods of participant-observation, I have watched more than three hundred intake interviews with pregnant women who are potential candidates for the test, trying to understand their questions, silences, and responses to the information genetic counselors give them. I have also interviewed more than sixty women (and fifteen men) at home after they have had the test to see what they thought about it, and scores who refused to have the test, to find out why a "routinizing technology" doesn't always stay on route. Thirty-five genetic counselors and ten geneticists spoke with me about the cultural diversity of their patients' backgrounds and their own attitudes about prenatal testing, disabilities, and diversity in responses to it. And an internship at the city lab revealed something of how technicians think about their work. Families in a support group for parents whose children have Down's syndrome, the most common diagnosable cause of mental retardation, and the most common reason most pregnant women are recommended for, or seek out, the test, helped me to understand the difference between a medical and a social definition of a chromosomal disability. In the overlapping of these layers, I hope to locate the social impact and cultural meaning of a new technology.

In sum, my field-based study reaches out to many people affected, or potentially affected, by amniocentesis. It assumes that the experts I want to hear from are pregnant women and their supporters, and mothers (and when possible, fathers and other relatives) of disabled children, as well as the medical service providers involved in the routinization of this new reproductive technology. The professionals articulating a scientific discourse of risk; women and their families "at risk"; and a range of social institutions and contexts, such as early intervention services for developmentally delayed children and media representations of genetics, genetic testing, abortion, and disabled children and adults, all provide powerful clues toward understanding the intersection of multiple risk-laden discourses.

REDUCING RISK

In the State of New York (and in many other states), no pregnant woman is offered amniocentesis unless she has been counseled about the risks and benefits of the test. This presentation is usually made by a genetic counselor, a new category of health professional trained to interpret the cutting edges of genetic technologies and tests to a lay audience. The discourse of genetic counseling is both fluid and negotiated in relation to the questions and seeming comprehension of the client, as I have tried to indicate elsewhere (Marfatia, Punales-Morejon, and Rapp 1990; Rapp 1988). Genetic counselors must quickly assess the spoken and unspoken bases of knowledge and concern of their diverse patients, allowing for chasms in education, sophistication in handling statistics, and interest in "preventing birth defects" versus "accepting God's will," to name the most obvious poles of patient positions. In a forty-five-minute genetic intake interview, the counselor must: take an individual and familial reproductive health history; ascertain "background factors" (e.g., age, parity, ethnicity, familial causes of morbidity and mortality) which might affect appropriate screening and diagnostic tests to be offered; and make sure that the client understands the benefits and risks of testing. She must also open up spaces in an otherwise medically dense dialogue to respond to any specific questions the client may have. This is a daunting agenda, and, in urban hospitals, one that is often pursued in the client's second (or third) language, with or without the aid of an appropriate interpreter. The opportunities for miscommunication as well as communication are thus many.

"Risk" is central to the information genetic counselors seek to convey. The technology of prenatal diagnosis was explicitly developed in order to allow the selective abortion of fetuses facing serious disabilities because of atypical chromosomes and genes (Cowan 1991, 1992; McDonough 1990). The language of genetic counseling is intended to enhance awareness of the age-related risk of chromosomal problems, but counselors rarely speak directly about "disability" or "abortion decisions," unless a problem is detected. Counselors describe their goals quite differently: to give "reassurance." "Reassurance" consists of being returned to the "general population," which has a "background risk" of 2 to 3 percent of giving birth to a child with a disability, rather than undertaking the larger risk entailed by forgoing amniocentesis, which adds one's age-related risk to that generic background risk. This language of "added risk," "background risk," and "reassurance" is consistently deployed by all the genetic counselors I have observed at work. It thus foregrounds a statistical, medical, age-related, universal, and wholly individual model of risk. In the process, what Lippman (1991, 31) labels "iatrogenic anxiety" is also constructed: whereas "older" women have long known they were more likely to give birth to babies with Down's syndrome than younger ones, it is only the present generation of statistically graded pregnant women who have been given specific risk figures, and thus been led to identify generic pregnancy anxieties with their specific age and statistic. The same worldview that measures this risk and constructs its iatrogenic anxiety also offers relief by providing a new piece of medical technology to assess and assuage the problem. Using such powerful and totalizing models of risk silences many "background factors" whose risks are empirically much higher, as I hope to show below. Dominant medical frameworks lay claim to the conceptual space in which many alternative ideas of risk can and do flourish.

The overwhelming majority of clients for amniocentesis are sent to see a genetic counselor because of a.m.a. (advanced maternal age), which adds to the risk of giving birth to a baby with abnormal chromosomes. Although all pregnancies carry a small risk of "birth defects,"[1] chromosomal problems are the only screenable prenatal conditions that systematically increase with age. For example, a twenty-year-old woman has a 1 in 1500 chance of giving birth to a baby with Down's syndrome; a thirty-five-year-old's risk is 1 in 360. At forty, women have babies with Down's once in every 106 births. Here, the relationship is numerical and straightforward: using age charts, graphs, or birth ratios (that is, numerical graphics), counselors explain a general risk pattern, then derive a specific risk ratio, based on the particular mother's age at estimated date of delivery. Increasing age is considered a "risk factor"; having amniocentesis and receiving negative results (i.e., that the fetal chromosomes are normal) removes the "added risk" that accompanies age, and returns the pregnant woman to the "general patient population." These numbers (and thus the "risk" and "reassurance" discourse that accompanies the technology) appear as universal, uninfluenced by the general health or nutritional status of the parents, or their country of origin. Because chromosome problems are the only test routinely performed on genetic material in an amniocentesis, and Down's syndrome accounts for about 50 percent of the chromosome problems detected, Down's looms large in the discourse of genetic counseling. There are, however, about four hundred much rarer, much more arcane genetic disabilities that can now be diagnosed prenatally. A pregnant woman's amniotic fluid would only be tested for one of these (at great expense) should her family history provide a medical indication. Most childhood disabilities are not, of course, either chromosomal or genetic, for they are caused by the scourge of low birthweight which accompanies poverty and insufficient prenatal care, or by accidents and infant illnesses. But the routinization of amniocentesis and its limits describes the universe in which Down's syndrome has become iconic.

Advanced maternal age is not the only "risk" that genetic discourse can describe and whose consequences can be diagnosed. Increasingly, autosomal recessive conditions, many of which run at heightened frequencies in specific ethnic groups, can also be picked up. Thus, sickle cell anemia (among people of African descent); Tay-Sacks disease (most prevalent among those of Ashkenazi Jewish background); the thalessemias (which are most common among Mediterranean and Asian populations) can now all be diagnosed.

Prenatal screening for cystic fibrosis, the most common autosomal reces-
sively transmitted "ethnic" disease encountered among white North Europeans, is now being piloted. Although some of the available screens are
close to 100 percent accurate (e.g., sickle cell anemia; Tay-Sacks disease),
others are probing for conditions caused by a series of functionally related
genetic mutations that vary between families and among ethnic groups
(e.g., presently available cystic fibrosis screens are most effective for Scandi-
navians, less effective for Italians, and least effective for Ashkenazi Jews).
Carrier and/or fetal testing may therefore net more statistical probabili-
ties, rather than absolute yes/no diagnoses. And although some conditions
(e.g., Tay-Sacks disease) are dramatically and tragically consistent in their
trajectories, a much more common occurrence is that "degree of pene-
trance" and "degree of expressivity" (described in the language of probability) are quite variable. Even a 100 percent accurate diagnosis of sickle cell
anemia does not indicate how mildly or severely affected a particular fetus
will be, nor can a diagnosis of CF or the late-blooming Huntington's disease
predict age at onset of symptoms, itself a powerful indicator of life span and
"quality of life" (Bluebond-Langner 1991). I do not mean to underestimate
either the seriousness or the consequences of carrying and transmitting a
genetic condition, for which increasingly sophisticated clinical interventions
as well as genetic screens are rapidly being developed. I do, however, want
to underline that the powerful language of risk attached to age, ethnic background, or family genetic history muffles other possible subject positions and
social interpretations from which people actually respond to disease. There
is little room for cultural variation in this individually grounded, causative
model of genetic risk.

THE LARGER REALM OF RISK

Of course, the world in which risk is empirically constituted is much broader
and more stratified than what its geneticized referents would seem to indicate. The rise of prenatal screening has accompanied other dramatic and
less individually based transformations in the lives of pregnant women.
Most obviously, throughout the United States and in New York City, where
my data have been collected, the dramatic increase in women's participation in a highly stratified labor force has become lifelong, with implications
for themselves, and their children. Divorce rates are up; so is multinational,
multicultural migration to conditions of urban poverty. Cyclical welfare
dependency for mothers and children is both heightened and threatened
by dramatic cutbacks in entitlements and means-tested benefits since the
1980s.

Concomitant changes in medical economics accompanied these large-
scale political-economic and demographic trends. It is only since the 1950s

and 1960s that most Americans have paid for their medical services via third-party insurance; prior to that time, fee-for-service arrangements predominated. And by the 1970s, a body of case law driven by malpractice suits and emergent "standards of care" responded to parents and children suing respectively for "wrongful birth" and "wrongful life," claiming that available tests should have been offered in order to avert the birth of children with prenatally diagnosable disabilities (Clayton 1993). The world of genetics, obstetrics, and the newly developing field of reproductive medicine were strongly influenced by these limiting conditions and increasingly made the offer of prenatal testing an aspect of prenatal care. In the same period, birthrates dropped, abortion was legalized, and the professional reputations of medical service providers involved with any aspect of pregnancy, birth, and the neonatal period came to rely increasingly on producing "high quality" results that were technologically dependent. By the late 1980s, prenatal testing, especially genetic testing, had shifted into the realm of commercial, for-profit laboratories, away from the academic medical centers where it had initially developed. The process of routinization has moved rapidly from "experimental" to "outreach-service" to "health care industry." Genetic risk assessment increasingly conforms to the laws of business, a trend that health care providers expect will only grow more significant. These macro-indicators only begin to hint at the shifting and often-unsupported base on which pregnant women stand when they are offered the "reassurance" of a "risk-reducing" prenatal technology.

Although American politicians are once again debating some minimal form of national health insurance, "the hollow state"[2] in which most Americans live no longer provides many benefits for mothers and their supporters raising children; public school budgets have been gutted, libraries and park programs are rapidly closing, and media representations of urban violence heighten an already fearful sense of being unable to protect children from the vagaries of daily life. Under these circumstances, raising children with disabilities seems a daunting proposition. Long-standing fears and biases expressed against disabled people make it hard to separate the fantasy of the burdens of raising a child with special needs from a sound knowledge base of both the exigencies and accessible resources.

In reality, there are many excellent programs designed for developmentally delayed children, but their spread and availability are uneven. Although a history of the social construction of disability and disability services in the United States has yet to be written (see Biklen 1987; Finger 1984; Hahn 1988; Miringoff 1991; Murphy 1987), variations in what is obtainable are enormous. Although some states (e.g., Michigan and Minnesota) have pioneered innovative services for both disabled children and their families, New York's services are more spotty: there are some excellent programs funded through the Family Court, but placement varies dramatically by borough. Some churches, private foundations, and philanthropies also provide very fine services. Learning one's way around this network can become a full-time job.

Mothers of children with Down's syndrome I interviewed estimated that they spent 25 percent of their time locating appropriate services and arranging for their use when their children were small. Of course, the need for parental intervention is cyclical; the diagnosis of a baby with special needs puts a family into high-gear activity; so does graduation from an early intervention program (in which children often stay until the age of five), and preparation for the bureaucratic hoops involved in placing a child in an appropriate, state-funded special education setting. Families with more economic and educational resources sometimes locate and use private schools and even residential programs; occasionally, they may successfully buck the bureaucracy, getting such services subsidized, but this has become increasingly rare. If an educational setting is satisfactory, a family may remain relatively unstressed until their disabled member reaches young adulthood, when the cutoff of educational services stimulates the search for a day-program, sheltered workshop, or other adequate work position, depending on the individual and her/his family. In the intervening years, routines of care may be less intensive.

Women and their families experience the costs (and benefits) of nurturing a child with a serious disability quite differently, depending in part on their sociocultural background. Two African-American women with whom I spoke, for example, wanted amniocentesis despite the fact that both were adamantly opposed to abortion. Each expected to rely on a kinship network for sustained support, should the child be born with a health problem. One said she wanted the test in order to know whether she should move back to Georgia where her mother would help her to raise a disabled child. Not everyone experiences a label like Down's syndrome as all-encompassing. As one African-American mother said, "My kid's got a heart problem. Let me deal with that first, then I'll figure out what this Down's business means." Although a group of committed activists in the Manhattan-Bronx Parent Support Group (for families who have children with Down's syndrome) succeeded, after many years of research and agitation, in getting a Catholic parochial school to fund and organize an excellent enclosed classroom for twelve primary-level children, these activists were overwhelmingly white and upper-middle class. Their strategy contrasts dramatically with that of a Colombian hospital orderly, who described her experiences:

> What does it mean to have this child? That I will be a mother forever, that this one will never leave home. That's OK, I'm glad I'll have him with me forever. Only I worry if I die before he does. I don't want anything else from the schools, there's no point in that. He's happiest right here at home, where I can

take care of him. (Anna Morante, mother of an eight-year-old with Down's syndrome)

An African-American welfare-dependent mother of three children told me this story about the birth of her son with Down's syndrome: she had been planning to put the newborn up for adoption, a decision she had reached shortly before his birth due to the domestic stress and violence with which she was living. When the baby was born and diagnosed, a white social worker came to see her about placing the child. The mother asked what would become of her baby and was told, "We'll probably find a rural farm family to take him." "Then what?" she queried. "He'll grow up outside, knowing about crops and animals," was the reply. "Then what?" the mother repeated. "Maybe he'll even grow up to work on that farm," the social worker replied. "Sounds like slavery to me," answered the mother, who decided to take her baby home. This imagery, and its legacy, contrast with the stories of many white mothers, who often fantasize peaceful, outdoor, small-scale life as the perfect placement for their children with Down's syndrome.

> I read somewhere that there's a community for retarded people in the mountains, somewhere in Europe. They play music, and they run a farm. Kids like this are very loving, they're good with animals, it's like the music of the universe is inside of them. If only the rest of us could listen, maybe they could teach us to hear it better. (Judy Kaufman, white Jewish nurse, mother of a seven-year-old with Down's syndrome)

Indeed, the very reasons for accepting or rejecting prenatal testing are deeply embedded in different collective histories of social risk. When I interviewed a thirty-six-year-old Puerto Rican UPS package inspector in a rundown neighborhood in Queens, for example, she seemed to have accepted an amniocentesis without great introspection. As the mother of two teenaged boys from a former marriage, she "just wanted everything to be all right." During the course of an hour's home interview, my tape was filled with her disinterested answers, interrupted by the flamboyant and sonorous testimony of her fervently Pentecostalist husband. He described his vivid visions of the infant Jesus protecting his own infant-to-be, swore that the prayers of his co-congregants had already healed all manner of potential problems the child might have faced, and used the occasion of my visit to witness the benefits of faith. It was a stunning performance. Later, Mari-Carmen walked me back to the subway, and without the pressures of husband or tape recorder told me the following story: Pentecostalism was saving her husband, who had twice been jailed on drug charges and from whom she had separated because of his infidelities. Her chief worries centered on her older sons, both having problems in school, one involved with a neighborhood gang. If "having a baby for him" would stabilize the family, she would accept the pregnancy, and the amniocentesis, and any other advice the doctor gave her, just as she had accepted the Pentecostalist congregation. Without the benefit of this shadow interview, I might well have coded Mari-Carmen's answers as "medically compliant" with the discourse of older women's increased risks. But the real risks in her life—a dangerous neighborhood and substandard schools for her children; a husband involved in drugs and other threats to family stability—were far more pressing, and external to medical definitions of her situation.

The reasons for rejecting prenatal genetic testing are quite varied. When a well-known white Anglo-Saxon Protestant economist heard about this research, she told me her own amniocentesis story: pregnant with a third child at thirty-eight, she read extensively in the medical literature and discovered that the birthrate of liveborn children with Down's Syndrome was 25 percent lower than the figures quoted for the prenatal detection of this condition. She reasoned that the test was less accurate (that is, that it produced 25 percent false positives) than what the geneticists were claiming and rejected it on that basis. The difference between the two rates (at mid-trimester, via amniocentesis; at birth, among liveborns) is actually based on another "fact" that she failed to turn up in her reading: chromosomally atypical fetuses remain vulnerable to miscarriage and stillbirth throughout the pregnancy; late spontaneous abortions of Down's fetuses account for the difference in rates. Her "informed consent" to reject the test was based on a strategy I have often observed among white, upper-middle-class professionals: they "fight with numbers," testing whether the discourse of genetics actually includes their own particular case and can respond to their sophisticated statistical interpretations. They feel comfortable deploying the discourse of statistics, even if only to argue to the point of conviction, accepting or rejecting the counselor's expertise. The economist's rejection was thus based on her own cultural values and skills.

When I interviewed an African-American Wall Street secretary about her decision not to have an amniocentesis at thirty-seven, she spoke about her husband's reaction to the consent form they were asked to sign. The form only covered lab procedures for analyzing the chromosomes extracted through the test; it was not a permission to perform the test, which is inscribed in different documents. But the lab form, which is written in quite technical language (and often skimmed or skipped by those committed to undergoing testing) included a proviso granting the geneticists rights to use discarded amniotic fluid anonymously for experimentation. Reading intensively, the husband was disturbed by this clause, citing the Tuskegee experiments and other examples of abusive research conducted on black people as his reason for rejecting the test. A sentence written in scientific bureaucratese here touched a culturally and historically sensitive memory of racially abusive medical domination.

These culturally specific, historical legacies deeply influence how the offer of an amniocentesis or an abortion for an affected fetus is placed in the foreground or background of consciousness. Some risks are more experience-near or experience-far, to use conventional anthropological wisdom. As one savvy genetic counselor queried, "How do we convey a 25 percent risk of sickle cell anemia when a low-income pregnant Afro-Puerto Rican woman experiences a 100 percent chance of running out of food stamps this month, a 25 percent risk of having one son or brother die in street violence, and an 80 percent chance of getting evicted by the end of the year? A 1 in 180 chance of having a child with a chromosome abnormality at age thirty-five is probably the best odds she is facing." What looms large for the counselor may seem quite small to the pregnant patient. The extreme vulnerability of undocumented immigrants or children with severe school problems are problems of *now*. The same cannot be said of potential risks to the unborn fetus. Even with the best of intentions, priorities between counselors and patients may vary dramatically. Numbers are relative: despite the universalizing language of genetics, the odds of life are not evenly distributed. Of course, most of the "odds of life" are inscribed in social relations not amenable to genetic definitions and medical control. Whether a child's life will be damaged through accidents or drugs, or its potential distorted by an education system in crisis which cannot prepare low-income youth for an economy in which they are basically redundant—these are problems that cannot be described medically. The risks of living in a world where invisible and geopolitically unbounded economic and social forces influence the life chances of pregnant women, their supporters, and their fetuses, are not so easily contained by medical discourse. The ongoing risks inherent in the social construction and consequences of class, racial, ethnic, religious, and gender differences, and the deeply stigmatizing but specific attitudes held about disabilities all enter into the way prenatal testing is received. It is only when we screen out these "background risks" that amniocentesis appears to "cut risks" and "offer control."

Ideas about risk are culturally and historically embedded, as I have tried to show in this chapter. What constitutes an "acceptable risk" will vary among individuals and communities. And some social groups are more self-conscious about socializing risks and their costs than others. Anthropologists have long studied how peasant communities and ethnic enclaves level out their resources through ritual and enforced relations of sharing. Thus the risks of poverty and an uncertain political world can sometimes be collectivized (see Wolf 1966*b*; Wolf and Hansen 1972, 200). Although some groups in New York City are able to hold on to stable and dense relations of sociality through which risks are shared, many more are subject to the rapid velocity of social change which accompanies multiple migrations and the unpredictable problems and possibilities of urban life. How might risks be shared under such shifting circumstances?

The emergent disability rights movement offers one set of answers to this question, insisting that problems of prejudice and stigma, not absolute biological incapacities, set the limits on the quality of life their constituencies may achieve. Using the rhetoric and strategies of the civil rights movement, disability activists have successfully agitated for national and local legislation to make jobs, transportation, housing, and public spaces more accessible (Scotch 1984; Miringoff 1991). They have made a powerful claim that the costs of disabling risks can and should be socialized. In place of amniocentesis, they self-consciously counsel agitation. Other groups define persistent risks to pregnancy and children and their alleviation quite differently. Minority participation in movements against hospital and clinic cutbacks and for electoral and school board reforms, may be interpreted, too, as statements about what constitute "experience-near" risks to family life. Perceptions of the political economy of risk are culture- and community-specific. However much powerful chromosomes may loom in the matrix of medicine, they offer only one possible explanation of risk and its potential reduction in a shifting and multicultural world.

NOTES

Portions of this study have been funded by the National Science Foundation, the National Endowment for the Humanities, a Rockefeller Foundation "Changing Gender Roles" fellowship, the Institute for Advanced Study (Princeton, N.J.), the Spencer Foundation, and a sabbatical semester from the New School for Social Research. I am grateful to them all and absolve them of any responsibility for the uses I have made of their support. I want to thank the many health professionals who have aided this work because they believed in the necessity of better understanding their patients' experiences. Above all, I am grateful to the many pregnant women and mothers of children with disabilities and their supporters who shared their amniocentesis stories with me. All their names have been changed to protect their confidentiality. Comments from Faye Ginsburg, Shirley Lindenbaum, and Jane Schneider helped to transform an earlier draft of this essay, and I am deeply grateful for their ongoing support.

1. The medical language of "birth defects" is highly contested by the disability rights movement. "Potential disabilities" would provide a more socially accurate and neutral description.

2. The concept of "the hollow state" flows from discussions between Jane Schneider and myself about how to characterize the political forms now emerging in the rubble of regulatory social democracies throughout many Western countries. Although the United States never had many of the social democratic programs that

became the norm in much of Western Europe, especially Scandinavia, after World War II, it did have a more dense set of connections between federal, state, and municipal social services than currently exist. The "Reaganization" of such programs (which actually began under the Carter administration and continued in the Bush years) was premised on the rhetoric of "turning power back to the states" by drastically cutting and redistributing funding. In that process, large urban municipalities like New York City were particularly hard hit.

TWELVE

From Trash to Treasure: Housewife Activists and the Environmental Justice Movement

Harriet G. Rosenberg

STUDYING MOBILIZATION: DEEP BACKGROUND

It is not communism that is radical, it is capitalism.

BERTOLT BRECHT
(CITED IN WOLF, *PEASANT WARS OF THE TWENTIETH CENTURY*)

In the last decade, hundreds of popular protests have been led by North American housewives, who have mobilized politically in response to community exposures to toxic wastes.[1] The most famous of these protests has been the case of Love Canal; but whether well known or locally contained, the majority of the protests have been organized, staffed, and led by working-class women and women of color.

Disempowered housewives, like peasant insurgents studied by Eric R. Wolf (1969a), often find that their mobilization may begin with a conservative stance: a defense of children, family, and home. But for many this initial position has led to radical critiques of state and society and an undertaking of political actions of which they never dreamed themselves capable. To understand this pathway to mobilization, one needs a conception of politics that is not confined to or defined by the electoral process. Coming of age with the literature on patron-client relationships, friendships, coalition formation, and alliance patterns, I have looked for systems of human activity that are socially and culturally more intricate and historically deeper than can be disclosed by analyses of voting patterns or political parties.

In writing *Peasant Wars of the Twentieth Century* (1969a), Wolf combined historical and political economy analyses to make the case that peasants calculated and executed strategic decisions, formed alliances, and ultimately picked up arms based on logical assessments of opportunities and constraints. This insight was an important intellectual liberation at a time when many theorists, hampered by racist and antipeasant stereotypes, were struggling to explain how peasants in Vietnam could be besting the United States militarily and ideologically.

Wolf's typology of mobilization in *Peasant Wars* argued that strategic/ structural positioning and historically contingent opportunities opened to middle peasants arenas of maneuverability closed to under-resourced poor peasants and ideologically constrained rich peasants. Thus, he not only disagreed with the concept that peasants were incapable of authentic action and must be led by outsiders, he also disputed the notion that it is the most oppressed who mobilize. This was both a subtle and respectful position to take: it was neither dismissive nor triumphalist. This analytic framework applies to housewife activists as well.

The concept of "housewife activist" is popularly viewed today with the same sense of contradiction and implausibility with which peasant insurgency was viewed twenty-five years ago. Thus I am arguing here that housewife mobilization, based on the powerful ideology of maternalist child-protection, has situated housewives in a structurally analogous position to middle peasant insurgents. Women act not only because they feel themselves to be grievously wronged, but also because they have a strategic base that validates support, credibility, and the potential to form important alliances across race, class, ethnic, and gender boundaries.

To pursue this kind of analysis, I draw inspiration from Eric Wolf's methods which lead us to trace relationships from the local to the global level and to expose connections between seemingly unrelated events (1982*a*). On the informal level, we have learned from him respect for the data, respect for the people, and respect for the struggle.

HISTORY

Ill fares the land, to hastening ills a prey,
Where wealth accumulates, and men decay.
OLIVER GOLDSMITH, *THE DESERTED VILLAGE*

The history of the rise and expansion of industrial capitalism is also the history of the spread of industrial pollution of the environment of the worker and working-class families. The evils of environmental destruction became a theme for early anticapitalist sentiments enshrined in pastoralist literature and also gave rise to an elitist natural science-based social movement incorporating themes of nature as moral guide, romanticized ruralism, anti-urbanism, and managerial conservation of soil and forest as economic and spiritual resources. Concern for the health impacts of industrial pollution on humans was largely absent from early ecological theory (Bramwell 1989).

However, environmental health was of concern both to states and to working-class radicals. Elites feared the spread of epidemic disease from working-class neighborhoods, and activists struggled against the poor quality of life and lowered life expectancy of workers and their families. The British state sponsored numerous statistical expeditions concerned with disease and mortality rates in the poor districts of industrial towns, the most famous of which was Sir Edwin Chadwick's surveys in the early 1840s. Chadwick's public health solutions were the now familiar technological response of managing pollution as a postproduction phenomenon through the development of sewerage and water purification (Finer 1955; Ridgeway 1970).

Later in the century when imperial dreams were construed as being threatened by high infant mortality rates, public health expanded into public hygiene campaigns that targeted working-class mothers. These activities were usually framed in the discourse of economic rationality rather than a moral appeal to child-rescue. For example, a London medical officer of health presented his profession's mission in these decidedly unsentimental terms:

> Over-production lessens, under-production enhances the value of commodities. Considering the life of an infant as a commodity, its money value must be greater than 35 years ago. It is of concern to the nation that a sufficient number of children should be produced to more than make good the losses by death; hence the importance of preserving infant life is even greater now than it was before the decline of the birth rate. (Alexander Blyth 1907, cited in Davin 1978, 11)

Like previous state interventions these campaigns did not link capitalist production practices to health outcomes (Davin 1978). The most famous radical critique of the health impacts of capitalist practices was Friedrich Engels's survey of English industrial towns in 1844. Engels held the industrial bourgeoisie and the state directly responsible for the noxious practices of capitalism. He used the terminology of the workingmens' associations, "social murder," to signify the intensity of the crisis he was observing (Engels 1975 [1845], 394).

However, this signification did not become a basis for oppositional mobilization, in part because public health bureaucratic interventions were able to defuse crisis construction (Davin 1978; Enzensberger 1982; Ridgeway 1970).[2] Recent dramatic environmental health disasters, like Love Canal, have once again raised the possibilities of a social movement based on a radical analysis, which links industrial capitalist practices and state regulatory complicity to health crises. Crisis construction has been facilitated by the credibility of apocalyptic language within mainstream environmentalism, a social movement constituted, for the most part, by white, urban, well-educated supporters. Hans Magnus Enzensberger has argued that when the middle class fears for its future, then imagery and ideology are universalized—for the end of class privilege is truly the end of the world (1982, 191–194).

Although middle-class mobilization has enhanced the respectability of environmental concerns, it has, in the main, not been truly universal, since it has not dealt successfully with cross-class issues. Robert Bullard (1990) notes that this elitism has estranged the movement from poor and minority peoples in the United States who are concerned about environmental issues, but who are uncomfortable with and feel unwelcomed by mainstream organizations. He describes three categories of elitism: (1) compositional elitism (environmentalists come from privileged backgrounds); (2) ideological elitism (environmental reforms appear to be self-interested); and (3) impact elitism (environmental reforms frequently operate in a jobs versus the environment mode that discounts the issues of poverty and social justice for workers and poor people). Unlike mainstream organizations, grassroots groups dealing with specific community-based health and environmental problems have successfully organized cross-class and interethnic alliances.

TOXIC TREASURE

Thinking of making money? Hazardous toxic waste is a billion-dollar-a-year business. No experience necessary. No equipment necessary. No educational requirements. Think of your financial future and call now for exciting details.

ADVERTISEMENT IN THE *INTERNATIONAL HERALD TRIBUNE* (CITED IN CENTER FOR INVESTIGATIVE REPORTING AND MOYERS, *GLOBAL DUMPING GROUND*)

In the last thirty years, waste disposal has developed into one of the most profitable industries in the world. It is dominated by two U.S. transnationals (Waste Management Inc. [WMI], and Browning-Ferris Industries [BFI]) and Laidlaw Environmental, a Canadian corporation. The largest is WMI. Today these private companies and smaller independents have turned waste disposal into a virtual private utility in many parts of North America. The history of this industry is a compressed version of the history of capitalist development. It begins with small independent haulers and ends with vertically and horizontally integrated North American monopolies and "garbage imperialism" overseas (Center for Investigative Reporting [CIR] and Moyers 1990; Russell 1989).

Privatized waste disposal began with horse and buggy operations at the turn of the century. In the 1950s and 1960s in the northeastern United States and Florida, much of private garbage collection was in the hands of various organized crime families who set prices, allocated territories, and handled "grievances" when haulers attempted to steal customers or customers attempted to switch to other companies. These "property rights" arrangements were enforced by bribes, threats, beatings, arson, and murder (Block and Scarpitti 1985).

Private firms also handled industrial toxic waste disposal. Since they had no pretensions at technological skills, and since landfills were virtually unregulated, disposal was a haphazard affair. They dumped in municipal landfills, down sewers, along roadsides, in abandoned gravel pits, in farmers' fields, abandoned warehouses, or abandoned coal mines. They mixed toxic liquid wastes with oil and sold it to rural municipalities to spread on dusty roads or they mixed it with fuel oil and sold it in cities (Brown 1981; Block and Scarpitti 1985; CIR and Moyers 1990; Freudenberg 1984; Jackson et al. 1982).

One technique revealed to an Associated Press reporter involved the filling of a tanker truck with hazardous liquid waste, waiting for rain or snowy weather, and then driving along a highway with the tanker valve open. It takes about sixty miles to get rid of 6,800 gallons of cargo, a driver reported. "The only way I can get caught is if the windshield wipers or the tires of the car behind me start melting" (Block and Scarpitti 1985, 61–62).[3]

Manufacturers, who generated toxic wastes, tended to dispose of the wastes themselves. Hooker Chemical in Niagara Falls, New York, for example, dumped toxic wastes for over a decade into the Love Canal and then sold the site to the Niagara Falls school board for $1. Working-class housing and an elementary school were built over an estimated 43 million pounds of chemicals, many of which were known to be hazardous to human health. The deed of sale included a disclaimer that Hooker could not be held legally responsible for any adverse health outcomes (Levine 1982, 11).

Between the mid-1960s and mid-1970s the garbage industry changed rapidly. Environmental consciousness raised regulatory questions and governments in Canada and the United States responded with a variety of laws and the creation of agencies and ministries at various levels of government. The efficacy of these state actions has raised political controversies, but the legislation had a galvanizing effect on the garbage industry.

As an environmentally configured discourse emerged, names like Ace Scavenger Service disappeared and companies like Waste Management Inc. were born. Garbage was no longer dumped—waste was managed. Men with serious expressions, hard hats, or space-age protective gear appeared in company literature, trade journals, and popular media signifying that science had taken charge of garbage. Waste disposal became an engineering problem of risk assessment best left to the professionals. Profits skyrocketed.[4]

This alchemist's dream was accompanied by a rapid consolidation of the garbage business from about 12,000 private haulers, dump operators, and recyclers in North America in the 1960s to a few giant agglomerations today (Crooks 1982, 7). From the very beginning the industry has been riddled with antitrust suits, environmental violations, and criminal prosecutions.[5]

RACE, CLASS, AND NOXIOUS SITES

The results of these disposal practices has been the creation of a North American landscape covered with hundreds of thousands of contaminated

sites. Approximately 275 million metric tons of hazardous wastes are produced annually in the United States, of which 90 percent is estimated to be
improperly disposed (Edelstein 1988, 3). It is also estimated that there are
600,000 contaminated sites in the United States, of which 888 fall under
the Superfund cleanup program.[6] Another 19,000 sites are under review
(Edelstein 1988).[7]

Given past disposal practices and current industry and government siting
strategies, working-class people or poor rural dwellers, and especially black,
Hispanic, and Native peoples, are most likely to be exposed to noxious sites
or have new waste disposal facilities located in their neighborhoods.

One report commissioned by the State of California to assess potential
political opposition to incinerator sitings speaks to issues of class by concluding that

> middle and upper socioeconomic strata possess better resources to effectuate
> their opposition. Middle and higher socioeconomic strata neighborhoods
> should not fall within one-mile and five-mile radii of the proposed site. (Cer-
> rell Associates 1984, 42–43)

Activists have mobilized with their own investigation of waste and siting
patterns. The United Church of Christ commissioned a study on race and
toxics which reported that three out of every five black and Hispanic Americans live in a community with uncontrolled toxic sites and that race, not
hydrogeology, is the best predictor of waste siting (Commission for Racial
Justice 1987; Bullard 1990).

For people in exposed communities, environmental politics has become
an additional dimension of struggles against racism and poverty. Poor communities often find themselves torn between economic and health concerns.
In Emelle, Alabama, for example, where WMI runs the world's largest
dumpsite in a poor, predominantly black community, the county receives
$2 million a year from the company, which it uses for basic social services
including road, fire, ambulance, library, law enforcement, and school equipment (Bullard 1990, 69–73; Collette 1988, 13). The local mayor has expressed his frustration with this seemingly insoluble contradiction in saying
"[We are] like dope addicts. We can't live with the poisons they're putting
into the ground, but we can't live without the money" (Collette 1988, 13).

Mobilization against toxic waste disposal has led to wide-ranging political
analyses and coalitions that cut across class, race, and gender lines. In
Emelle, Alabama, where race politics and economics have been described
as typical of "Old South" apartheid-like relationships, a small but growing
segment of the local community has forged alliances across race and class
lines and developed analyses that encompass social justice and environmental goals (Bullard 1990, 73). The multiplicity of issues and the intersection of
interests that toxics mobilization addresses is described by one activist this
way:

People don't get all the connections. They say the environment is over here, the civil rights group is over there, the women's group is over there, and the other groups are here. Actually all of them are one group and the issues we fight become null and void if we have no clean water to drink, no clean air to breathe and nothing to eat. They say, "Now Miss Tucker, what you really need to do is go back to food stamps and welfare. Environmental issues are not your problem." And I say to him, "Toxic wastes, they don't know that I'm black." (Cora Tucker, keynote speaker at the 1987 conference, "Women in Toxic Organizing," cited in Zeff, Love, and Stults 1989, 5)

MATERNALIST MOBILIZATION AND CORPORATE COUNTERMOBILIZATION

Although concerns about social justice, nature conservation, and fairness in risk distribution are all part of the language of toxics mobilization, it is the discourse of motherhood and child-protection that has become central in attracting women to the movement and legitimating their sustained involvement. For many women activists it seems inconceivable that their vision of child-protection would not be greeted with an immediate suppression of potential dangers. The language of risk-benefit analysis is not meaningful to them, not because they do not understand statistics (as their opponents often contend) but because for them maternalism is a much more powerful ideology than science.

Maternalist discourse has had a complex history in Western capitalist ideology. For the last one hundred and fifty years varieties of state maternalism and familism have emerged to justify state intervention into the family (e.g., compulsory education, residential schools for Native children, public health campaigns, criminalization of birth control and abortion, etc.) or to justify withdrawal of social services that are supposedly better performed in the family (daycare). These policies have been associated with the endless production of maternal devotion imagery (Bridenthal, Grossman, and Kaplan 1984; Davin 1978).

The child-saving movement and its ideology of child-protection at the turn of the nineteenth century has been the underpinning for the development of innumerable middle-class professions including psychology, teaching, pediatrics, nursing, children's literature, public health, home economics, and social work (Nasaw 1985; Sutherland 1976; Zelizer 1985). Although the movement itself had many contradictory impulses, which at times seemed more inclined to punish than protect, it has become a dominant force in the sacrilization of the child which has virtually replaced the utilitarian child as essentialist ideology (Zelizer 1985). Children are no longer construed as workers or future soldiers (Davin 1978), nor in polite society should children be viewed in economic terms. In the course of the twentieth century, the construction of the priceless, sentimentalized, vulnerable child (Zelizer 1985) has produced a focus for the multibillion-dollar cartoon, toy, movie, and television industry. Indeed, it is difficult to think of a stronger cultural icon.

Child-protection is completely naturalized for parent activists. As a mother with Concerned Citizens of South Central Los Angeles, a poor community with 78 percent unemployment, said in explaining her opposition to the siting of a solid waste incinerator:

> People's jobs were threatened, ministers were threatened ... but I said, "I'm not going to be intimidated." My child's health comes first, ... that's more important than a job. In the 1950s the city banned small incinerators in the yard and yet they want to build a big incinerator ... the Council is going to build something in my community which might kill my child ... I don't need a scientist to tell me that's wrong. (Charlotte Bullock, cited in Hamilton 1990, 217)

Maternalist ideology is an enormous source of mobilizing energy and has been met with a variety of corporate counterstrategies. The oldest counterstrategy to maternalist mobilization by state and corporate officials has been to label women "hysterical housewives" and dismiss their epidemiological data as "housewife statistics" (Brown and Mikkelson 1990; Gibbs 1982; Levine 1982; Rosenberg 1990*b*). A more recent and much more subtle corporate engagement of maternalist discourse has been to express direct concern for children. In doing so the companies avoid addressing emotionally charged health issues directly and concentrate on educational campaigns urging children and housewives to reduce litter, create less solid waste, and encourage recycling (Rosenberg 1990*b*, 131).

This strategy bears a striking similarity to nineteenth-century sanitary education campaigns (Davin 1978). In both cases the individual mother is exhorted to accept personal responsibility for a crisis that she is said to be able to ameliorate through private practices within her household. And in both cases, a radical critique of the structural determinates of crisis are vitiated by an appeal to maternalist duty.

These environmental education campaigns also serve to transform corporate images: polluters become environmentalists. The techno-eco modernist ("ecocratic") gesture within environmentalism (Sachs 1990) permits waste generators and disposers to speak with credibility as experienced eco-managers, sharing their know-how with the public in such matters as solid waste management or recycling. Such companies also reinforce their self-representation as environmentalists by donating to mainstream nature conservationist organizations and by sitting on their boards of directors.[8]

An example of reputation metamorphosis is encapsulated in a contest sponsored by WMI, through its Recycle America program. The "From

Trash to Treasure" contest aimed at getting "our kids involved in cleaning up the mess around us." Contestants were invited to submit works of art using paper, aluminum, plastic, and "lots of imagination" in their efforts to demonstrate the possibilities of recycling. First prize was an all-expense paid trip to Disney World (*Ladies Home Journal* 1989, 188).

A quick deconstruction of this tactic reveals mystification of corporate responsibility in "mess" production; the desirability of the amelioration of "messes" by individual solutions (which require lots of privatized "imagi nation"); and the quick reward of escape into fantasy, which is not identi- fied as yet another corporate mess.

Corporations dislike housewife activists because women do not see child health as a negotiable category. "We must not compromise our children's futures by cutting deals with polluters and regulators," urges Lois Gibbs, Love Canal housewife activist and founder of the Citizen's Clearinghouse for Hazardous Waste (CCHW). She insists that grassroots activists name names and hold government and corporations directly responsible for their actions.

In public, industry assessments of grassroots mobilization express dismay at their wrongheaded naivete:

> Grassroots local groups, many of them misinformed, wield increasingly disrup- tive power. "... [They] are concerned about the value of their homes and the health of their children. That means they are relentless. In general, unlike mainstream environmental groups, they are not interested in compromise or mediation." (Stephenson, environmental public relations consultant, cited in Kilpatrick 1990, 54–55)

In private, companies express much stronger fears about grassroots radicalism:

> CCHW is one of the most radical coalitions operating under the environmen- talist banner. They have ties into labor, the communist party and all manner of folk.... In October, at their grassroots convention, they developed the at- tached agenda which if accomplished, in total, would restructure U.S. society into something unrecognizable and probably unworkable. It's a tour de force of public policy issues to be affecting business in years to come. (Internal memo from Clyde Greenert, 14 Nov. 1989, to other Union Carbide execu- tives reviewing CCHW Grassroots Convention; cited in Mueller 1990, 18)

This private analysis has led to corporate strategies of intimidation. One significant technique has been "SLAPP" (Strategic Lawsuits Against Popu- lar Participation). This tactic targeted local groups and researchers with multimillion-dollar suits based on industry claims that they have been libeled by local activists. When successful, such suits have caused fear among grassroots groups as they assess their meager funds in comparison to large corporations, have dispersed energies away from environmental health issues, and ultimately may have caused some local groups to fall apart. The effectiveness of this tactic has subsided as it became identified as malicious prosecution and local communities began launching counter-suits against corporations.

Given the links that some corporations may still have or have had to organized crime, some activists also fear physical attack. One informant told me that she always paused anxiously before putting her key into her ignition after a meeting because she feared that her car was wired to a bomb.

The newest corporate countermobilization has been to sponsor local groups that mimic grassroots groups in organizational style and public self-presentation. These industry-financed groups have targeted job development and job security. They appeal to local citizenry on the issue that has been called "the weakest link" of the environmental justice movement (*Everyone's Backyard* 1991, 1). The collision between child-protection discourse and the imperatives of employment is one of many contradictions that housewife activists face.

CONTRADICTIONS OF MATERNALIST IDEOLOGY

Although maternalism is manipulated by corporate/state strategies, it also has its own internal contradictions that constrain mobilization. Complex processes of stigmatization occur in communities exposed to toxic wastes, where parents blame themselves for their children's present or potential health problems and are paralyzed into inaction (Brown and Mikkelson 1990; Edelstein 1988; Levine 1982; Madisso 1985). Sometimes their activism is delegitimated by the view that they are manipulators who are attempting to construct and then exploit a crisis situation to their own material advantage. Thus activists in Legler, New Jersey, reported being told, "There's nothing wrong with your water, you're only out for the money" (Edelstein 1988, 114). And mothers at Love Canal were accused of "trying to make a bundle" from the government (Levine 1982, 185).

Visible disasters like floods or hurricanes produce community consensus and mutual support with relative ease; however, toxic crises are invisible and require agreement on an analytic framework that relates events in the distant past to health outcomes in the present and the future (Vyner 1988, 1–26). Parent activists, who might also be caring for sick children, are often also required to address forces of dissensus within the community.

Nonbelievers in the crisis (often nonparents or older residents, or those more geographically distant from the exposed area) may attack activists because of declining real estate values as a result of negative publicity. Thus activists who represent themselves as protecting the family are frequently attacked for undermining financial, social, and emotional investments in the home and turning the home from sanctuary into trap (Rosenberg 1990*b*).

The struggle to mobilize and to sustain mobilization is also played out within the family. Children and husbands may resent the time and energies that women put into antitoxics activism. Preserving familist ideology, in theory, often results, in practice, in long absences from the home, unprepared meals, undone laundry, and kitchens turned into offices. When women become active publicly, their husbands may resent their new confidence and skills. A United States support group for toxics activists (CCHW) has found these tensions so widespread that it has prepared educational material on managing household stresses as a result of activism which suggests that women involve their children and husbands as much as possible.

A Mothers of East Los Angeles (MELA) activist analyzed the transformation in her marital relations (and her husband's political education) this way:

> My husband doesn't like getting involved, but he takes me because he knows I like it. Sometimes we would have two or three meetings a week. And my husband would say, "Why are you doing so much? It is really getting out of hand." But he is very supportive. Once he gets there, he enjoys it and starts arguing too. See, it is just that he is not used to it. He couldn't believe things happen the way they do. He was in the Navy for twenty years and they brainwashed him to believe that none of the politicians could do wrong. So he has come a long way. Now he comes home and parks out front and asks me, "Well, where are we going tonight?"(Erlinda Robles, cited in Pardo 1990, 4)

In other households, tensions are not resolved this easily and the outcome has been separation and divorce (Gibbs 1982; Madisso 1985).

Maternalist essentialsm is also the underpinning of a very different social movement: New Right antifeminism. Based on similar initial constructions of defense of home and child-protection, New Right women have mobilized around a different view of crisis, seeing feminism and abortion as the biggest threats to the family. For many women the maternalist child-protection mission seems at complete odds to the pro-abortion position. When these positions intersect, the contradictions embedded in maternalist ideology emerge and environmental health mobilization may fall apart.

In 1981, for example, a United States group attempted to bring together women, workers, and environmentalists in the "Coalition for the Reproductive Rights of Workers." The coalition ultimately disintegrated, in large part because the right to reproductive protection position could not be reconciled with the abortion rights position (Freudenberg 1984, 222).

The discourses of toxics mobilization and abortion can in fact intersect but configure in yet another way. In Italy, the Seveso disaster in 1976[9] coincided with a national debate on the decriminalization of abortion. The town of Seveso had been exposed to dioxins and when pregnant women were offered the option of legal abortion, those holding anti-abortion positions argued that the health hazards of exposure were being exaggerated in order to grant legitimacy to the abortion cause (Reich 1981, 105–112).

Although state health officials tried to prove that dioxins were dangerous, a majority of community members mobilized around the position that "it's all an invention of the politicians" (Reich 1981, 105), supported their priests in the reoccupation of their homes, and narrowly avoided armed clashes with the police who were trying to keep them out.

Children's health was seen to be adversely affected by the exposure to toxic chemicals, but this observation did not become a central mobilizing focus. On the contrary, unlike residents of Love Canal, residents of Seveso fought overwhelmingly for repatriation and against environmental health crisis construction.

Finally, there is another possible interpretation of exposure to toxics. If the connection between exposure and negative fetal and child health is taken as a given, it may not always be industry and government who are deemed responsible for negative health outcomes. Women may find themselves being held responsible for mutagenesis and teratogenesis. Mothers may be labeled abusers and their fetuses may be seen as appropriate recipients of biogenetic and legal interventions. As Lin Nelson (1990) points out, women's bodies have already been defined as hazardous environments in some workplace "fetal rights" legislation. Thus the logic of prenatal rights discourse could produce litigation, based on the following argument:

> Once a pregnant woman has abandoned her right to abort and has decided to carry her fetus to term, she incurs a "conditional prospective liability" for negligent acts toward her fetus.... These acts could be considered negligent fetal abuse resulting in an injured child.... Withholding of necessary prenatal care, improper nutrition, *exposure to mutagens and teratogens, or even exposure to the mother's defective intrauterine environment* ... could all result in an injured infant who might claim that his right to be born physically and mentally sound had been invaded. (Attorney Margery Shaw, cited in Nelson 1990, 187. Emphasis added.)

These clashing discourses mediate the possibilities of alliances with pro- and anti-abortion groups, fetal rights groups, and disabled rights groups. The collision of competing "rights" under capitalism offers no easy predictor of alliances and can fracture coalitions based on maternalist essentialism.

THE ENVIRONMENTAL JUSTICE MOVEMENT

For many women the experience of toxics activism is transformative. Said one Mother of East L.A.:

> You should have seen how timid we were the first time we went to a public hearing. Now, forget it, I walk right up and make myself heard and that's what you have to do. (Aurora Castillo, cited in Pardo 1990, 6)

At present these transcendent experiences operate on the local level to educate and mobilize other potential activists and to establish information sharing and support links with other similar groups. This decentralized pattern is in the process of transforming itself into a broad-based social movement. A CCHW grassroots organizing conference has urged women to commit their housewife skills to a professional career as community organizers (Zeff, Love, and Stults 1989).

In the United States activists situate this movement in the tradition of the civil rights movement, the labor movement, and the women's movement (Zeff, Love, and Stults 1989) and distance themselves from mainstream environmentalism. The humanist social justice-based radicalism of the environmental justice movement often puts it in opposition to biocentered tendencies in mainstream environmentalism.

The following summary of a story, told by Lois Gibbs, illustrates these differences (Edelstein 1988, 167).

The scene is a hazardous waste site hearing in Louisiana several years ago. The group opposed to the siting has set up an aquarium filled with contaminated drinking water from their wells. They loudly announce their plan to place fish into the tank, claiming that these fish will be dead by the time the hearing is over. Environment officials and traditional environmentalists instantly protest, but the audience begins to chant "Kill the fish."[10]

Gibbs interpreted the chanting to mean that animal protection should be secondary to child protection and human protection: "If we have to kill the fish to make the point, we'll do it. We're sacrificing our children" (Edelstein 1988). Her view is congruent with critiques of mainstream environmentalism and Deep Ecology, which argue that they mask race, class, and gendered interests by claiming a spurious universalism (Bradford 1989a, 1989b; Enzensberger 1982).

For toxics activists and victims, the environment is not a "teacher" or "moral guide" (Devall and Sessions 1985) that can reveal new lifeways through contemplation and meditation. Rather it is a ticking time bomb, carelessly and ruthlessly set in place by the practices of state and capital. For them the lesson of nature is social and political and already inscribed in the bodies of their children.

NOTES

Versions of this paper were given at the Women and Development Seminar and the Department of Anthropology Seminar in the Fall of 1990 (University of British Columbia), the American Anthropological Association Meetings (Chicago) 28 November 1990, the Health and Society Speakers Series (York University) April 1991, and the Department of Anthropology Seminar (University of Connecticut, Storrs) May 1991. Thanks to all the organizers and participants for allowing me a forum to test the ideas presented here. And a special thanks to the following for their sustaining interest and support: Alan Block, Julie Cruikshank, Richard Lee, Richard

Rosenberg, Irene Silverblatt, Mary Vise, and members of the Frankel-Lambert Action Committee (FLAC).

1. A note on terminology: In the United States many activists organizing against residential toxic waste exposure have designated their mobilization as a struggle for "environmental justice" (CCHW) or "environmental equity" (Bullard 1990), or the toxics movement, or toxics environmentalism to distinguish it from mainstream environmentalism. These terms are not current in Canada.

2. Later in the nineteenth century, Ibsen's play *Enemy of the People* (1882) used the device of an environmental health disaster (poisoning of town baths by factory effluent) as a vehicle with which to critique middle-class corruption. The play resonated with strong antistate and anticapitalist sentiments when performed during the late nineteenth and early twentieth centuries (Ibsen 1966, 12–14).

3. In August 1978, waste oil contaminated with PCBs was disposed of this way along a rural highway in central North Carolina (Freudenberg 1984, 182–183). When a landfill site was selected for the contaminated soil, in 1982, in a predominantly African-American community, local grassroots groups and national civil rights leaders began organizing protests. Ultimately 414 activists were arrested, marking the first time in the United States that anyone had been jailed for trying to halt a toxic waste landfill (Bullard 1990, 35–38).

4. Big profits were being made in all forms of garbage disposal but the biggest profits were being made in the high-tech specialty of hazardous waste disposal. As of August 1990, Chemical Waste Management, a subsidiary of WMI, was charging its customers in Emelle, Alabama, $112 a ton; the site normally handles 800,000 tons a year (Kemesis 1990, 40). The United States "hazwaste" market is currently valued at about $32 billion (Rotman 1990). WMI as of 1986 reported gross revenues of over $2 billion (Moody's *Handbook of Common Stocks* 1987). Its executives are among the highest paid in the United States: its president earned over $14 million in 1987 (Citizen's Clearing House 1988, 4).

5. For example, WMI has faced countless charges of fraud, bribery, price-fixing, illegal dumping, and unsafe practices. Between 1982 and 1987 WMI paid over $30 million in fines for violations of environmental regulations but it has been estimated that it took the company only six days to earn the revenues to pay these fines (Vallette 1987, 7). WMI regularly makes political donations to officeholders in the United States (Vallette 1987) and Canada (Rosenberg 1990*a*).

6. Inventories of the number of contaminated sites have not been undertaken on a national level in Canada, but in southern Ontario alone, it is estimated that there may be between 2,000 and 3,000 unrecorded sites (interview with Environment Canada official, October 1990, Jackson et al. 1982, 18).

7. In addition there are 400,000 municipal landfills in the United States, which may have received unregulated toxic wastes, hundreds of thousands of deep well injection sites, and 300,000 leaking underground storage tanks threatening groundwater (Edelstein 1988).

8. In 1987–1988, WMI disclosed donations to environmental groups, which included the National Wildlife Federation, the National Audubon Society, the Natural Resources Defense Council, and the Sierra Club of California (*Action Bulletin* 1989, 9). In 1987, WMI's Chief Executive Officer joined the Board of Directors of

the National Wildlife Federation. Over the years, WMI has hired people from various mainstream environmental groups, including the former director of the Environmental Defense Fund, who currently runs WMI's Public Relations Department (Collette 1988).

9. In July of 1976, a toxic plume of contaminated gas escaped the Swiss-owned ICMESA factory that produced industrial perfumes and pharmaceutical chemicals and settled over the northern Italian community of Seveso. Pregnant women came under close observation by public health authorities. Women, on an individual choice basis, were offered the opportunity to have abortions. This was the first time legal abortions were permitted in Italy (Reich 1981, 73–139).

10. Pardo (1990, 4) describes a similar narrative told to her by a Mother of East L.A. about the placement of an oil pipeline through the center of their community.

PART FOUR

National Integration and Disintegration

THIRTEEN

Structuring the Consciousness of Resistance: State Power, Regional Conflict, and Political Culture in Contemporary Peru

David Nugent

All through the afternoon of 17 November 1975, "neighborhood committees of struggle and faith" (*lucha y fè*) in the sierra town of Chachapoyas, capital of the department of Amazonas in northern Peru, met to decide what action should be taken with regard to the recently appointed Prefect —local representative of the military regime in Lima. Since 1968 the townspeople, and Peru as a whole, had suffered through a dictatorship in which all elected political positions had been eliminated, political parties had been outlawed, and the military government in Lima had appointed individuals of its own choosing to govern in the provinces without consulting local interests. The new Prefect was but the most recent in a series of "politicos" imposed upon the townspeople by the central state.

During the previous seven years the military regime's lack of familiarity with and insensitivity to local needs had resulted in long-standing regional problems reaching crisis proportions. The period of military rule had witnessed the virtual total breakdown of the infrastructure of communication and transportation which linked the department to the rest of the nation. By 1975 the region's major trunk highways were impassable, important bridges were washed out, air transport to Chachapoyas (precariously maintained under the best of circumstances) had been discontinued, the city's public lighting system was inoperative in 90 percent of the urban area, and telephone and telegraph links to the outside had broken down. So serious were these developments that even the city's ability to provision itself with basic foodstuffs was in question.

Although the developments of the previous seven years severely tested the patience of the townspeople, those of 1975 pushed them past the breaking point. A crisis in the national economy resulted in a coup in August of that year, and the military leader who came to power (Morales Bermudez) appointed the controversial new Prefect for Amazonas. This man, it was said, was guilty of the worst kind of professional and personal abuses. He squandered the little money available for infrastructural development by awarding work contracts to "friends," who then did little or nothing with the funds granted them. He also appointed unqualified individuals to administrative posts throughout the department solely on the basis of who offered him the largest bribes. They in turn were said to be using their posts as a means of personal enrichment, by exploiting their ties with the Guardia Civil (the National Police) in order to coerce wealth out of those under their jurisdiction. Finally, he seriously offended the dignity of local society by bringing a woman of "highly questionable moral background" into the town as his wife (or companion, no one was quite sure which) and presenting her at proper social and political functions as the "first lady of Amazonas."

Responding to the deteriorating conditions of the national economy, and anticipating the coup of August of that year, "neighborhood committees of struggle and faith" emerged in each of Chachapoyas's four neighborhoods early in 1975. It was these same committees that met on 17 November to decide what to do about the Prefect. Everyone agreed that the time had come to do something about the "immoralities" they had been forced to endure over the previous seven years of military rule. After debating a number of alternatives they finally reached a consensus and by early evening committed themselves to a serious course of action. All decided that it was necessary to "take the Prefecture," arrest the Prefect, and to install a Prefect of their own choice who would rule until the central government was willing to name an acceptable replacement. Only in this way could the immoralities of the previous seven years be brought to an end.

Each of the committees spread the word through their respective neighborhoods that people were to converge on the Prefecture at 9:00 P.M., stopping first at the Bishop's Palace to ask for his support. By the appointed hour a massive show of support for the action was evident. More than 5,000 people (out of a population of 11,250), led by the Bishop, had marched from all corners of the dark town, carrying torches and lanterns, to the doors of the Prefecture. The Prefect was promptly "arrested" by the citizenry and delivered for safekeeping to the local head of the Guardia Civil. Using the radio transmitter housed in the Prefecture, the Bishop then called the Ministry of Government in the capital to inform Lima of what had transpired and to request that a new, satisfactory Prefect be appointed to Amazonas. The regime in Lima complied, and within a month the department had a new Prefect.

The neighborhood committees of struggle and faith had actually developed a working relationship with the Bishop prior to the taking of the Prefecture. Jointly, the committees and the Bishop had organized the Communal Representative Commission of Amazonas in early 1975. The purpose of the Commission was to protest the neglect of the region by the government and to develop more effective strategies for advancing the cause of the department in the nation's capital, but to do so in as seemingly apolitical a manner as possible. To this end, the Commission avoided all connections with partisan political organizations (which were illegal at the time), drew up no charter, collected no dues, and had no formal membership apart from a few Commission representatives—despite the fact that a significant proportion of the town's population, representing all economic and social sectors, regularly attended the monthly meetings of the committees of struggle and faith. Rather than being a partisan political organization, the Commission was constituted as a group of patriotic citizens concerned only with the welfare of the region.

On the basis of discussions carried out within the committees of struggle and faith, the Commission drew up a list of projects that were considered integral to the department's future. They focused on improvements in roads, bridges, and footpaths; in health services; in the availability and distribution of food staples; and in air transport. After costly visits to Lima by Commission representatives and lengthy delays in the capital, the efforts of the Commission finally bore fruit: the central government was successfully petitioned for funds and machinery. For a relatively brief period following, virtually the entire local population was mobilized, largely through the efforts of the committees of struggle and faith. Led by "vecinos" with long-standing reputations for service to and sacrifice for their community, the committees induced their fellows to labor voluntarily without recompense on projects deemed beneficial for the region as a whole.

REGIONAL PROTEST AND STATE EXPANSION

This movement of regional protest in Chachapoyas is far from unique within Peru as a nation. In the last two decades regional movements have broken out in virtually every major and many minor urban centers and have been an important factor in the central government's decision to institute a plan of decentralization and regionalization.[1]

These movements have a number of characteristics in common. First, protest is couched and demands are made in terms of the interests and needs of specific regional arenas. Second, protest is predominantly urban in nature; it is generally organized and led by urban elites, and its main participants are likewise urban dwellers. Third, the various classes and class segments involved in the movements are not consistent from one region to the next. Rather, each represents a somewhat different coalition of class segments. Fourth, local, usually municipal, government plays a central role in the movements, and provides the institutional basis for protests to the central state.

These movements, in other words, are urban-based alliances whose class content varies significantly according to region which use the local governmental apparatus to express regionally specific grievances with the central state. As such, they differ considerably from the form of protest one would expect in industrial capitalist contexts. Rather than representing a broad movement whose interests and demands are generalized by social class, and which unites and divides on this basis, protest in Peru is more cellular in nature. It defines common interest on the basis of control of space, of region, and brings together variegated groups in the process.

This difference in the basis of mobilization—one in which domination has as its referent an undifferentiated social class regardless of social space, the other in which its referent implies control of a differentiated social space regardless of social class—points to a key feature of the political economy of contemporary Peru. To understand the causes of this "regional problem" we must inquire into the way that the state has come to control the national space during this century. Following Eric R. Wolf (1956a, 1969a; Wolf and Hansen 1967), I will argue that the massive expansion of North Atlantic capital into Peru toward the end of the nineteenth century initiated a process of social transformation and state centralization that brought to an end the caudillo politics that had dominated the nineteenth century. The centralizing state, however, was unable to challenge anything but those aspects of local class power that posed a blatant threat to central control—specifically, the unrestricted use of armed force by local elites for their own private interests, as opposed to those of the state. As a result of this partial integration of the countryside by the state, most existing property and production relations were left intact. The majority of these were what Wolf (1982a) has called "tributary"—production was controlled directly by primary producers, and extraction depended on "extraeconomic" mechanisms and relationships. Thus, although the state imposed an increasingly unified and centralized political/administrative apparatus on the territory of the nation toward the end of the nineteenth century, distinct political-economic regions with interests opposed to the state continued to operate.

In this context of incomplete integration of the countryside, and unresolved tensions between region and state, the latter subsequently came to rely on two interdependent mechanisms in order to "nationalize" (Fox 1990b) its population and control its territory. First, in order to weaken the hold that regional elites exercised over local resources, territory, and people, the state expanded its apparatus in the countryside so as to absorb many powers and privileges enjoyed by regional elites. In the process, the state increasingly undermined the position of these elites as mediators, controlling the flow of local resources from region to state and dominating subaltern classes within their spheres of influence.

The second mechanism employed by the state to integrate its population and control its territory involved what can be called the "annihilation of regional space." Until the early twentieth century there was a very limited basis upon which to conceive of the nation as a single community. Virtually all important interdependencies—material, social, political, and religious— were regional in nature. The state was greatly hindered in any attempt to overcome these boundaries and to replace regional with national inter- dependencies by the physical difficulties of moving people, material goods, and cultural messages through the tortuous topography of coast, sierra, and jungle. Governments of the twentieth century have consistently attempted to overcome these limitations through massive investments in the infrastruc- ture of communication, transportation, and education. These changes have contributed to the nationalization of the population and the control of space in several interrelated ways. First, by vastly expanding the circulation of commodities, produced either in one of Peru's few urban industrial centers or outside the country, the state has created new material dependencies among its populace and has linked individuals to a growing national (as opposed to regional) economy via the market. Second, by expanding and integrating its control over communication and education the state has extended the ideological and cultural bases upon which individuals may imagine the nation as a single community and themselves as its citizens. Finally, the progressive annihilation of regional boundaries has made it pos- sible for the state to apply armed force with greater ease throughout more of its territory.

Despite the integrating effects of these changes, the state was only par- tially successful in its attempt to undermine the power of regional elites and to gain control over the national space. Its success varied enormously, and its efforts proceeded at very distinct rates, in different regions. More important, however, in most regions the state did not transform the tribu- tary nature of extraction, but rather attempted to absorb into the central governmental apparatus the most important of the tributary powers exer- cised by regional elites—to shift tributary responsibilities from region to center. The effect was to impose a strengthened, national tributary struc- ture on a series of weakened, but still functioning regional arenas, and thus to leave conflicts between the state and local elites for control of tributary revenue unresolved.[2]

Chachapoyas was one such outlying, relatively autonomous region. The following sections of the paper return us there to trace the historical devel- opment of region-state relations and in the process reveal the way that the regional problem has been transformed but not done away with during the twentieth century. We begin with the organization of regional society and the relation between region and state in the decades prior to state expan- sion (circa 1930), when a local, landed elite assumed responsibility for most tributary functions and the state for relatively few. We then turn to the emergence of an alliance between the state and members of a regional protest movement—who referred to themselves as the "moral community"—that had begun to challenge the landed class prior to state expansion. This alliance made it possible for the state to seize control over tributary functions formerly monopolized by the landed class, and to redefine region-state relations. Finally, we consider the most recent manifestation of the regional problem—the way the moral community, like other regional populations throughout Peru, organized so as to protect regional interests and oppose the state during a subsequent phase of state expansion in the 1970s. These developments return us to the Communal Representative Commission of Amazonas discussed earlier.

STATE-REGION RELATIONS, 1883–1930: NOBLE CASTAS AND REGIONAL HEGEMONY

As a legacy of the caudillo politics of the post-Independence decades (as of the 1820s; see Bonilla 1972; Wolf and Hansen 1967) and the devastation caused by the War of the Pacific (1879–1883), at the turn of the twentieth century Peru was an internally fragmented polity (Burga and Flores Galindo 1979, 88–94; Caravedo 1979; Cotler 1978, chap. 3; Gorman 1979; Wilson 1982, 192; Yepes del Castillo 1980, 305–310). The state apparatus was controlled by the Civilista Party, which, during its period of dominance (1895–1919), represented the interests of select, regional elites: north coast plantation owners involved in sugar production for the international market (Gonzales 1985; Klaren 1973); mine owners (and those who provided services to the mines) in the central sierra, also involved in export production (Caravedo 1979; Mallon 1983*b*); and Lima industrialists and merchants (Mallon 1983*b*, chap. 4; Pike 1967, 168–186). Not only was the mass of the population excluded from participation in the political process, but so too were the other regional elites scattered about the national space: mine and hacienda owners from the northern sierra (Taylor 1986); large estate owners in the central sierra (Mallon 1983*b*, chap. 4); and wool merchants and hacendados from the southern highlands (Basadre 1968–1969, 10:102–143; Cotler 1978; Flores Galindo 1977; Klaren 1988).

The state maintained connections with these marginalized elites and nominal control over the outlying regions in which they lived through clientelistic ties with particular elite groups in each region (see Jacobsen 1988; Miller 1982). The strength and character of these ties, and thus the degree of autonomy from state control, varied considerably from region to region. In virtually all cases, however, much of the regional elite was denied access to political power; at any given point in time, the state favored only a few at the expense of the remaining elite families. In many regions, this resulted in endemic conflict, as elites struggled among themselves to control the local apparatus of the state (Favre 1965; Mallon 1983*a*; Taylor 1986).

Chachapoyas was one such region. Prior to the consolidation of state control circa 1930, five noncorporate political coalitions (Schneider, Schneider, and Hansen 1974), each made up of a core of kin-related, landed families and their extensive network of clients, dominated the social landscape of Chachapoyas. These coalitions, which were referred to by the local populace as *castas*, competed with one another to occupy four key political positions that would insure their hegemony within the region: Senator and Deputy (elected positions), and Prefect and sub-Prefect (appointed, respectively, by the President of Peru and the Ministry of Government). Control of the elected offices carried with it the right to dictate the appointed posts, and thus all four were normally occupied by a single casta.[3]

Political hegemony granted the ruling casta the powers and prerogatives necessary to carry out key administrative functions for the state: collecting tributary revenue and keeping the peace. In return, the state allowed the casta to manage regional affairs as it chose and supported it in case of threats from other castas. Fulfilling the obligations upon which privileged, client status was based, however, was a far from simple task, for most revenue had to be extracted from primary producers coercively, in the form of taxes. At the same time other coalitions, each of which could quickly assemble an armed force of fighting men, constantly challenged the hegemonic position of the ruling casta. The department-wide, multiclass coalitions that characterized casta rule, and the selective use of intimidation and favoritism upon which they were based, reflected the exigencies of maintaining control under these trying conditions of forced extraction and resistance.

In order to extract wealth and keep the peace, the ruling casta had to maintain effective control over the regional space in the face of constant threats from other castas. Its ability to do so was a function of the wide powers it exercised by virtue of its monopoly on the aforementioned four political positions. These powers included the ability to control coveted appointments to virtually all administrative, extractive, and judicial posts for the entire department, and thus to recruit clients by elevating fortunate individuals to positions of governance in every province, district, and subdistrict. In addition to acting as the official representatives of the central state (and thus the ruling casta) within their zones of jurisdiction, appointees were responsible (directly or indirectly) for collecting the taxes that were the ruling casta's main source of revenue—which provided it with another key resource in recruiting and maintaining its network of clients (see below).[4]

By virtue of its powers of appointment and extraction, then, the ruling casta was able to construct a single, department-wide political machine whose members were united behind the common cause of extracting tributary revenue and reproducing casta power. Because it controlled appointments to administrative positions throughout the department, the ruling casta was assured an official presence in all sections of the regional space, even where landed property ownership made opposing coalitions strong, and thus could more effectively carry out its duties for the state.

The ability of the ruling casta to maintain control over this tributary structure was in large part a function of yet another power it exercised as the central state's privileged client—its control over the local police, the gendarmes. The casta controlled all appointments to the gendarmery, and it was specifically the Prefect (in consultation with the other key politicians) who appointed its personnel. He generally named as head of the police a member of one of the kin-related, landed families that led the ruling casta. The rank and file, by contrast, was made up of local men with limited economic opportunities, little education, and no training, who would feel deeply indebted to casta leaders for the opportunity afforded them.

Even so, the loyalty of the gendarmes could not be taken for granted. Because of the key role they played in maintaining the status quo, in order to insure their allegiance the ruling casta added funds of its own to the rather meager salaries provided by the central state, drawing upon the local tax revenues over which it exercised monopoly control.

The gendarmes were concentrated in the town of Chachapoyas but were also distributed in smaller numbers in select provincial and district capitals throughout the department. Working in concert with the casta's local political appointees, they maintained "order" according to the dictates of their patrons, patrolling their zones of jurisdiction with rifles, constantly on guard against challenges from other castas. Whenever this local constabulary proved unable to contain threats from other coalitions, the state sent in the army to restore order.

The ruling casta combined favoritism with intimidation to insure the loyalty of its clients. To those who were strategic in maintaining order and extracting wealth, casta leaders dispensed special favors, ignoring their "diversion" of (some) funds for private use, and shielding them from paying taxes, from serving in the military, and from fulfilling labor obligations for public works (the last two were particularly important to peasant households). Should they "overstep their bounds," however, they might be demoted to a lesser position within the casta hierarchy, "reprimanded" (by temporarily withdrawing some of their privileges), or simply abandoned by the casta.

The ruling casta also used its powers to weaken other coalitions, removing their leading members from positions of influence and extraction, denying their clients employment, seizing their property, and persecuting them as much as possible, at times to the point of torture and assassination. Only the threat of retaliation by other castas placed an upper limit on the rapaciousness of the dominant coalition.[5] Membership in one of the castas was therefore crucial in helping to insure the safety of one's person and property against predations by members of other coalitions.

Each of the important castas had exercised political hegemony at some time, during which they had established clientele both in the town of Chachapoyas and throughout the region's smaller towns and peasant communities. The fact that such hegemony was unstable and shifting, however, meant that each coalition had only temporary control over the means of force, with which it could augment its tributary control over space, people, and goods for relatively brief periods. The rise of a new casta signified a complete changeover of the personnel controlling the tributary/redistributive structure.

The relation of region to state during this period is perhaps best expressed by a direct descendant of one of the region's ruling castas:

> In 1913 the President [of Peru] appointed a new Prefect for Amazonas, who traveled from Lima to Chachapoyas, where he expected to begin his duties. My great uncle—who was Senator at the time [and thus was living in Lima] —was opposed to the appointment, and when the new Prefect attempted to take up his post he was informed that Senator Pizarro would not allow it; he [the new Prefect] was denied entrance to the Prefecture. After waiting for several weeks at El Molino [a hacienda of an opposing casta, located just outside Chachapoyas], he returned to Lima. Shortly thereafter the President called my great uncle into his office for an explanation. Challengingly, he asked my great uncle, "Who rules in Amazonas, you or me?" My uncle replied, "It looks like I do, doesn't it!"

The notion of regional community prevalent at the time is best expressed by another informant:

> Before 1930 we didn't have national political parties with ideologies in Chachapoyas. We had only Pizarristas, Burgistas, Rubistas, etc.

"LA DEMOCRATIZACIÓN" OF REGIONAL SOCIETY: CHACHAPOYAS CIRCA 1930

It was in an effort to undermine such regional autonomy, and the fragmentation that accompanied it, that the state began to employ the two mechanisms of centralization referred to earlier: (1) the expansion and reorganization of the state apparatus in the countryside; and (2) the annihilation of regional space. The magnitude of its task was truly monumental. In the 1920s and 1930s, both before and after the world economic crisis of 1929, large-scale movements of secession or revolt broke out all across the nation. And for a brief period in 1931 there were two, according to some sources three, different men in different parts of Peru simultaneously claiming to be the President. In short, the national space was anything but securely under central control.

The state took major steps to end the autonomy of regional centers throughout the 1920s and 1930s. Concerted efforts began in Chachapoyas in the early 1930s, as the state attacked the powers and privileges upon which casta rule was based—the ability of coalition leaders to appoint clients to key positions of extraction and administration throughout the department, to use the gendarmes to protect these clients and their extractive activities, and to maintain the loyalty of these clients through the selective use of patronage, favoritism, and intimidation.

The ruling casta lost the ability to appoint its members to extractive and administrative posts throughout the department, and thus to maintain hegemonic control over the regional space, in 1931. The National Election Law of that year, which promulgated the secret ballot, extended the franchise, and made voting obligatory, caused it to be impossible to continue to manipulate elections through intimidation and fraud, as castas had in years prior.[6] As a result, no one casta could control the four key political positions upon which regional hegemony had been based. Rather, these positions, and the administrative posts throughout the department to which they gave access, came to be divided among different classes and class segments, with no one casta or class able to exercise exclusive hegemony within the region. This was a key factor in breaking casta control over the regional space, for from this time forward political appointees no longer functioned as the local cogs of a single, overarching political machine, acting in concert to extract wealth so as to reproduce casta power.

Not only did ruling castas lose the ability to monopolize administrative posts throughout the department, but the posts themselves changed in character. With the growing state integration of the region, political appointees who, in concert with the gendarmes, had once organized extractive activities for their casta, were relieved of these responsibilities. In place of this local structure of control the state imposed central control in the form of state institutions directly responsible for the collection, monitoring, and use of tributary revenues.[7]

By assuming tributary duties directly the state denied casta leaders control over much of the revenue and many of the positions of employment that they had formerly used to construct and maintain coalitions. No longer could ruling castas redistribute revenue to key clients (such as the gendarmes), so as to insure their loyalty, and thus help maintain the hegemonic position of the casta. Nor could castas continue to name their clients to positions within these institutions. Rather, as of the early 1930s the state replaced a regional with a national tributary structure, as most local tributary revenues came under the direct control of the central government.

Finally, casta leaders lost their control over the gendarmes, who had played such an important role in supporting the extractive activities of the ruling coalition, and in intimidating and persecuting the opposition. In 1933 the national government replaced the gendarmes with a new "peace-keeping force," one that would not act in the short-term interests of local powerholders, but instead would be directly responsive to the will of the state. The new force, the Guardia Civil, was a well-trained and disciplined order, made up of men from outside the region, who were rotated in and out of Chachapoyas after several years duty.[8] One of its first major activities was to sweep the countryside, disarming each of the region's major castas.

Casta leaders were able to construct broad-ranging coalitions prior to 1930 because the privileges, powers, and protections that only they could grant were indispensable to the rest of the population. Coalitions emerged as people traded casta loyalty for these necessary privileges and protections. As a result of the centralizing changes of the early 1930s, however, the vast majority of these powers were absorbed by the state. Denied the ability to reward or to threaten, castas found themselves with little to offer those formerly so beholden to them.

From this time onward the state imposed a more impartial regime of law and order on one and all. By guaranteeing the safety of individuals and the security of their possessions, it broke the interdependent ties that had formerly linked patron, police, and general populace. This in turn made extra-individual, group loyalties unnecessary and made it possible for a new relationship to be established between wealth and power, the individual and the state.

THE BIRTH OF THE MORAL COMMUNITY CIRCA 1930

The increased state integration of the Chachapoyas region, however, was not simply a question of the application of state power. Prior to state integration local, subaltern social movements had begun to project a form of regional community in radical opposition to the powerful castas—one of equality rather than inherited privilege, individual rights and protections rather than group-based coercion. Leading these movements was a politicized generation of young Chachapoyanos—privileged youth who, like provincial elites from around the country, had gone to Lima in the first decades of the century to take advantage of the expanded, postsecondary educational opportunities being offered by the state (part of the state's attempt to annihilate regional space by molding a stronger, national consciousness among its citizenry). At precisely this time, however, radical and populist ideologies increasingly dominated intellectual life in the national capital (Cornejo Koster 1968; Ingenieros and Haya de la Torre 1928; Paz Soldan 1919; Stein 1980). A new brand of organic intellectual (Gramsci 1971) emerged out of this encounter as "provincianos" seized upon notions of equality and progress and applied them to the particulars of their home regions. In the process, they expressed the dissatisfactions of social groups that had long been marginalized by casta power. The result was a serious challenge to the existing state of affairs.

In the latter half of 1929 fifteen to twenty adolescents began to meet in secret on Sundays, at midnight, in the cemetery of Chachapoyas. The vanguard of a new, outlawed political party (the APRA),[9] they were deeply committed to remolding regional society in a new form—one of equality and justice, in which the individual would be freed from relations of servitude with the more powerful. They met, in reverence, at the grave of one Victor Pizarro—ironically, the favorite son of one of the town's ruling castas. Victor Pizarro had gone to Lima in his teens so that he could pursue university training in one of the professions and return to Chachapoyas to occupy a position of responsibility for his casta. While a student in Lima, however, he became caught up in the radical currents that dominated university life at the time and subsequently spent a number of years in the Soviet Union. In the late 1920s he returned to Chachapoyas and for several years gave lectures on Marxism three times a week to a group of wide-eyed youth in a broken-down shack on the edge of the town, where he lived as a pariah from his casta family. He died of kidney failure in 1929, the result of injuries sustained during an anti-Communist police raid in Lima.

The APRA remained an outlawed party, its members forced to organize in secret due to the vicious persecution they suffered at the hands of the central government. At approximately the same time that the APRA was first emerging, however, a related social movement began to unfold which embodied many of the same ideals. It was less radical than the APRA, however, was a local rather than a national movement, and was not outlawed by the government. A number of closet Apristas therefore gave visible support to this alternative movement while continuing their clandestine party activities. The origins and ideology of this second movement were the following.

In 1926 the son of an impoverished branch of a landed family, Ricardo Feijoo Reina, who like Victor Pizarro had traveled to Lima in his teens to pursue a professional career, began publishing a newspaper that was distributed in Chachapoyas. The new image of regional society presented in this paper had much in common with the transformed society envisioned by the town youth involved in the APRA who met in secret in the local cemetery. Both images were in stark contrast with the existing state of affairs. The newspaper depicted the rule of the powerful castas as fundamentally immoral, based on inherited privilege, brutal coercion, greed, and outright theft.

Coexisting with the powerful casta families was a hidden form of community, said the paper, a moral community. Local society, it argued, was made up predominantly of defenseless and powerless people who, in the absence of adequate protections by the state, had been left to be abused and mistreated by the casta families. Rid of such coercive influences, guaranteed their constitutionally granted, individual rights by the state, and led by responsible politicians, these people would be free to act according to their true natures, with a sense of moral responsibility to society at large, to "the people" (*el pueblo*). Honesty and responsibility were thus seen to be the key features of the "unencumbered" Chachapoyano. Working together, such liberated persons would form a new kind of collectivity, one based on consensus and organic interconnection rather than coercion and conflict. In the new community those who did not work for the common good would be working against it; the good of one would be the good of all. Service to and self-sacrifice for the wider collectivity were seen as the requisites of proper social participation in this new moral community. Finally, such a collectivity of freed individuals would create a new future for the region, one in which the squandered opportunities of the casta-controlled past would be replaced by material progress and advancement that would benefit all. This imagined community based on moral obligation to one's neighbor and personal responsibility for one's actions as an individual first appeared in a newspaper called *Amazonas*, whose name was later changed to *La Voz del Pueblo* (The Voice of the People). By 1930 still another newspaper, *Redención* (Redemption), appeared, enunciating many of the same principles.

The influence of this new image of regional society and its morally based appeal may be gauged by the following: Ricardo Feijoo Reina, publisher of *La Voz del Pueblo*, decided to run for political office as Deputy of Amazonas in 1931 and became the first politician in the history of the department to oppose and defeat the ruling castas.

Who were the members of this moral community, and what was the social process that led to a redefinition of regional society and its relation with the state? Briefly, the "egalitarian impulse" that emerged in the late 1920s appealed predominantly to the "middle sectors" of Chachapoyas—the town's artisans, muleteers, petty shopkeepers and merchants, cantina owners, and public employees. This impulse was given ideological expression, however, by the aforementioned politicized generation of upper-class youth who participated in the "educational revolution" in Lima in the first decades of this century. The middle-class artisans, muleteers, and so forth were individuals who, although partially involved in what Wolf (1969*b*) has called the "power domain" of the casta families, nonetheless retained considerable autonomy due to the independent manner in which they gained a livelihood (Wolf and Hansen 1967). They had been sufficiently integrated into national culture to have internalized and valorized the rhetoric of constitutional rights and individual protections that had been present in state discourse since Independence from Spain (1824) but were painfully aware of how few of these privileges they actually enjoyed. They experienced the abusive, arbitrary aspects of casta rule, knew few of its benefits, and had aspirations and self-conceptions in opposition to it. Social movements that promised the end of such abuses and called upon individuals to act as members of a moral community of equals were therefore very appealing.

The privileged youth who helped give ideological expression to the movements of democratization constituted a true stratum of elite, organic intellectuals, however. Many returned to Chachapoyas after finishing their education in Lima to become primary and secondary school teachers, lawyers, judges, and politicians—all positions that gave them ample opportunity to disseminate and/or act upon the new set of egalitarian values that helped define the moral community.

Without some structural shift in the organization and distribution of power, however, such as took place in the early 1930s, it is unlikely that the democratization of local society could have been achieved. The previously discussed process of state integration, which undermined the power of the castas and strengthened the autonomy of the individual, was therefore crucial in opening a new political space in which the moral community could become a political reality. For just as the moral community was calling for equality before the law, freedom from oppression by the powerful, security of person and property, and for an end to inherited social privilege, the centralizing state was taking actions that advanced these very causes. It was therefore the articulation of these subaltern social movements with the goals of the expanding state, the partial complementarity of what were for the most part opposed political processes, that combined to precipitate a rupture in the structure of regional society.

REGION-STATE RELATIONS TRANSFORMED:
CHACHAPOYAS, 1930–PRESENT

Free of casta domination, the new "moral community" found itself in a stronger position with every passing decade, assuming greater control over local government, managing the department's remaining tributary revenues, and negotiating regional affairs with the state.[10] Simultaneously, the state made its presence felt increasingly in the region as it faithfully pursued its strategy of centralization. The government bureaucracy expanded in importance, absorbing growing numbers of the local populace, whereas the infrastructure of communication, transportation, and education developed steadily under its sponsorship. In this way the state replaced the castas as the source of patronage and protection for the local community and in the process established direct dependencies with an emergent, national citizenry that it helped to create and whose rights it protected.

As part of the same process of expansion that "liberated" the "moral community," the state also established the conditions in which national commodity circuits could penetrate the region more fully than ever before.

For with the dismantling of the casta structure, in which the personnel and the property of opposing coalitions had not been safe from the predations of the ruling casta, the state underwrote the safety of individuals, the security of their possessions, and their ability to move through the regional space unmolested. A small group of merchants from outside the region responded to this change immediately and began to import a wide range of manufactured goods into Chachapoyas on a scale never before possible. As the region became progressively integrated into national commodity circuits in the decades thereafter, local people (and products) were increasingly drawn into a national, exchange-based economy that provided them with most of the material necessities of life.

The expansion of commodity circulation thus helped reinforce in the economic sphere the key point of connection between the state and the "moral community" in the political sphere—the autonomy of the individual. Only because the centralizing state pursued policies that strengthened individual autonomy was it able to make common cause with the "moral community" and thus to give the local populace an alternative to casta rule. As long as these relationships remained viable the "moral community" was able to thrive, and relations between region and center remained calm. Within several decades, however, the state found it increasingly problematic to maintain these ties. Cyclical problems stemming from Peru's position in a global political economy began to reassert themselves (see Thorp and Bertram 1978), and the state responded to the national economic crisis that ensued (Thorp and Bertram 1978, chap. 14) by launching another phase of centralization—in the late 1960s and early 1970s.[11]

The structure of power that the state attempted to impose in the Chachapoyas region at this time resembled pre-1930 casta rule, but in a more centralized form. Under the new regime the Prefect, a state appointee, was given virtual monopoly control over the state political apparatus for the entire department. Along with those he appointed to administer the department's provinces, districts, and subdistricts, he was free to govern largely according to his own prerogatives, without "interference" from elected politicians, political parties, and the host of other formal and informal mechanisms and organizations by which the local populace had formerly made its influence felt in local affairs.

In this way the state did away with the institutional framework within which its reciprocal pact with the "moral community" had been played out in prior decades. Rather than arbitrate, mediate, and redistribute according to the seemingly impartial, universalistic principles of the "moral community," there was little to prevent state representatives from using their recently expanded powers in more personalistic terms—as a source of patronage, to construct coalitions of support that would reinforce state control.

Assisting them in this regard was the Guardia Civil. The Guardia continued in the role established for it in the 1930s—that of enforcing the will of the state, as articulated by its local representatives, the Prefect and his appointees. In the context of the centralized coalition-building that began to characterize regional politics, however, the Guardia's role became that of protecting the ruling coalition and helping to carry out members' dictates.

In the process, the state established the conditions in which the basic constitutional guarantees and individual protections of much of the population were progressively undermined. With the Guardia to support them, political appointees began to use their positions as a means of personal enrichment, by coercing wealth and services from those within their jurisdictions. As a result, the bulk of the local population found itself subject to increasingly arbitrary and insecure conditions of life.

Unlike the earlier phase of state expansion (that of the 1930s), then, this second phase found no marginalized group in the countryside with which it could make common cause; nor did it produce organic intellectuals that could give voice to the dissatisfactions of such a group.[12] Rather, this second phase of centralization threatened the very configurations of power and property that had emerged since the state's first efforts at expansion in the 1930s—not only in Chachapoyas, but in the majority of the regional arenas found within the territorial boundaries of the state. As a result, protest movements such as the one discussed at the beginning of the paper broke out across the country as regional communities rose up to protect themselves from the centralizing state.[13]

The mobilizations carried out in the 1970s in Chachapoyas by the neighborhood committees of struggle and faith and the Communal Representative Commission of Amazonas exemplify the defensive posture of regional communities around the country. For rather than greet the state and its integrating efforts with open arms, hailing it as natural ally and potential savior (as it had in the 1930s), the "moral community" attempted to thwart state efforts to expand. Furthermore, it did so in the name of the same notions of equality, community, and individual autonomy that earlier had caused it to embrace the state as friend and liberator.

The activities surrounding the taking of the Prefecture in 1975, and those of the committees of struggle and faith and the Communal Representative Commission of Amazonas, were decisive in halting further state incorporation of the region. By taking the Prefecture, the local populace signaled to the state that they would no longer tolerate its efforts to undermine all that they had achieved in the political sphere during the preceding four decades. The state's efforts to impose an autocratic form of centralized rule, in which the individual had no voice in regional matters, little personal autonomy, and few protections from the arbitrary decisions of indifferent power-holders, therefore reached an upper limit as the local community seized the seat of local government. Their success in forcing the military to appoint a Prefect who would respect established, local patterns of governance represented a triumph of regional over central forces.

The committees of struggle and faith and the Communal Representative Commission of Amazonas likewise played an important role in returning control over local affairs to the moral community—by demonstrating that the regional populace was far more capable of identifying and solving regional problems than was the state. The Commission was able to bring to the attention of the state a series of key, regional problems, which the state was either unaware of or indifferent to, and to propose solutions that relied primarily on the energies of the local populace (and required only minor state involvement). By acquiescing to the proposals of the Commission the state conceded its inability to identify and resolve regional problems, relinquished to the moral community the right to do so, and thus tacitly admitted the failure of its own policy of centralized rule. The fact that, subsequently, virtually the entire local populace labored voluntarily in order to carry out these projects, whose importance they had themselves decided upon, further emphasized the efficacy and legitimacy of local rule and thus the failure of state policies.

Although the political mobilizations of the 1970s mark an important turning point in the shifting balance of power between region and state, they represent more than simply a struggle for regional dominance. The moral community was not truly defiant of the state in the 1970s. At the basis of its resistance to state expansion was its belief that the state had violated basic principles of civil society upon which legitimate political rule is based—principles of democracy, consensus, and cooperation. The centrality of these principles is revealed not only in the public discourse it generated as it confronted the expanding state, but also in the consensual, egalitarian forms of organization and action that it spontaneously chose in doing so.

As the local populace mobilized to oppose the controversial Prefect of 1975 they generated a public discourse concerning the legitimacy of political rule based on a contrast between consensus and coercion. They branded the military regime as "immoral" because it was based on the use of raw power and coercion, and thus violated the consensual relations among autonomous individuals that had been the basis of legitimate political rule since the 1930s.

So strongly did those of the moral community believe in consensus as the only legitimate basis of political rule that, in order to restore it, they asserted their right to use force to oppose the state; they forcibly took the Prefecture, removed the Prefect from office, and insisted on an "acceptable" replacement. By their actions, they suggested that the state had temporarily forfeited its right to govern because it had violated the consensual basis upon which legitimate rule is based—but further, that it was the obligation of the "moral community" to reestablish the proper balance. As one informant explained, "only in this way could the immoralities of the regime be eliminated."

The only way that the local populace, as a moral community, could justify using force to oppose the state, however, was to transform force from "coercion" into "public will"—to organize its resistance according to the very egalitarian, consensual principles that it insisted the state had violated. All aspects of the mobilizations of the 1970s were implicitly democratic and noncoercive in nature, from the meetings of the committees of struggle and faith to the work projects in which virtually all townspeople participated, to the actual taking of the Prefecture. Throughout, the local populace met as a community and through a drawn-out, consensual process settled on measures that all agreed were necessary in light of the difficulties, and the immoralities, they were being forced to endure. The fact that the general public participated in these developments en masse helped legitimize them as reflecting the true "will of the people."

The mobilizations of the 1970s were essentially conservative in nature. They were intent upon preserving the integrity of person, property, and community that the state had helped establish as of the 1930s—and that it was intent upon violating in the 1970s. The local populace did nothing more, then, than insist that the state honor its pact with the moral community—obligations upon which legitimate political rule must be based.

CONCLUSION

The regional movements of resistance that broke out across Peru in the 1970s express unresolved contradictions in Peruvian state formation, contradictions that stem from the state's relation to global and national arenas. As Peru became more fully integrated into the global arena in the late nineteenth century, the state marshaled the resources necessary to embark upon a process of national integration and state expansion. Although it was able to achieve greater control over its national territory in the process, it was not able to do away with the tensions between region and center that prefigured state expansion.

Thereafter, because of Peru's dependent position in this global political economy, the state has been forced to confront cyclical, national economic crises, which have brought to the surface otherwise dormant conflicts between the central state and the many regional arenas still found within its territorial boundaries. In attempting to resolve these crises, the state has drawn upon mechanisms that would impose unity (in the form of greater central control) over the multitude of conflicting, regional interests with which it has been confronted.

Its success in doing so has decreased steadily through time. Early in this century the state was able to effect a more complete integration of territory and nationalization of populace by weakening the coercive powers of regional elites and establishing direct interdependencies with those formerly under elite control. It succeeded in this endeavor, however, in part because (and to the extent that) regionally specific, subaltern class coalitions had already begun to challenge the privileged position of local elites. In the Chachapoyas region, the coalitions in question generated a public discourse on the legitimacy of political rule based on a contrast between consensus and coercion. Seizing upon notions of individual rights and constitutional guarantees that had been present in state discourse since Independence from Spain (but which had existed in name only), a coalition of marginalized "middle sectors" and organic intellectuals sought to delegitimize local, elite rule by characterizing it as coercive. Simultaneously, these groups sought to free themselves from coercive, elite rule by appealing to the state to enforce the individual protections that would make possible rule by consensus. Coincidentally, the policies of the expanding state promised to provide these very individual protections and constitutional guarantes, and thus a reciprocal bond emerged between formerly marginalized groups and the centralizing state.

By the 1970s, however, the state was frustrated in further attempts to resolve the national crisis by imposing greater central control over economy and polity. For in carrying out its second phase of centralization, the state attempted to implement policies that threatened to subsume the very individual rights, democratic processes, and constitutional guarantees that the success of its first phase of centralization was based upon. As a result, regional communities around the country rose up to resist what were seen as "encroachments" into their own legitimate terrain. Furthermore, they did so by invoking the same public discourse concerning the legitimacy of political rule that they had used to justify state intervention during the 1920s and 1930s—one based on a contrast between consensus and coercion.

Such ideological continuity, and the transformation of ideology into action, has important implications for understanding the bases and the limits of state centralization in twentieth-century Peru. For it suggests that regional configurations of power and property act as effective barriers beyond which centralization can proceed only with great difficulty or violence.

NOTES

I would like to thank Joan Vincent, Ashraf Ghani, Gerald Sider, Tom Biolsi, Jane L. Collins, Adam Weisberger, Sonya Rose, Christine Bowditch, Jane Schneider, and Rayna Rapp, all of whom have made important contributions to the ideas in this paper. My greatest debt is to Eric R. Wolf, whose scholarship has long been a source of inspiration. The research upon which this article is based was generously funded by the Henry L. and Grace Doherty Charitable Foundation, Sigma Xi, the Scientific Research Society, the MacArthur Foundation Pre-Doctoral Fellowship Program, the Fulbright-Hays Pre-Doctoral Program Abroad, the Colby College Social Science Grants Committee, and the Colby College Interdisciplinary Studies Grant Program. I gratefully acknowledge their generous support.

1. This policy of regionalization, which actually preserves considerable power in the hands of the state, is an outgrowth of provisions of the 1979 Constitution and was instituted during the government of Alan Garcia Perez (1985–1990). For a useful review of regional protest, see Slater 1989.

2. Local government became a primary locus of conflict and protest because local government exercised tributary control over designated territorial arenas. Symptomatic of the unresolved tensions between region and center is the fact that regional autonomy versus central power has been an important issue in National Constitutions (those of 1823, 1828, 1856, 1867, 1920, 1933, and 1979), and in a series of key "Organic Laws" (during the nineteenth century, those of 1873 and 1886, and their many revisions in subsequent years) ever since Independence from Spain.

3. Landed families struggled among themselves for control of the political apparatus because it was virtually the only means by which they could prosper. Unlike many other regions of Peru, in Chachapoyas the landed class controlled little in the way of arable land, peasant labor, or the product of peasant labor (see Nugent 1988, chap. 4). Being removed from the sphere of production, secondary extraction via political office (and taxation) represented the key alternative.

4. Taxes were assessed primarily on local businesses (merchants, artisans, breadmakers, bar owners, and market vendors), on the transport and sale of select, local products (food staples, livestock, hides, and coffee), on rural and urban property, and on property sales (this list includes the tax collection responsibilities of Municipal Government as well, whose members were likewise appointed by the ruling casta). The ruling casta also controlled appointments to the offices responsible for taxing "specialty" products—salt, tobacco, opium, liquors of various kinds, and chancaca (brown sugar).

5. At this time local judges were appointees of (or were easily "influenced" by) the dominant coalition, and their legal decisions generally reflected this fact. The nearest high court—which was free of influence from the ruling casta—was located eight days ride to the west in the city of Cajamarca and had only formal jurisdiction over Chachapoyas.

6. Before 1931, a system of public voting—in which voters signed their names along with their votes (Basadre 1980)—had allowed the dominant casta to control the electoral process.

7. The same central state institutions made responsible for collecting departmental tax revenues (first the Caja de Depositos y Consignaciones, and later the Banco de la Nación) were also charged with distributing the funds provided by the state to pay its employees and maintain/build infrastructure within the region. This further undermined the material base of casta coalitions and significantly increased the tax revenue of the central state (see Bardella 1964, 182).

8. This new Guardia was a recent phenomenon nationally and the first of its kind

in the history of independent Peru. In 1923 the government commissioned a team of Spanish experts to open a new training school for its police—one that professionalized and disciplined them during a year of rigorous physical, technical, and ideological training (Basadre 1968–1969, 8:284–286; Zapata Cesti 1949). See Nugent 1991 for a more in-depth discussion of the process by which the Guardia replaced the gendarmes in the region.

9. Alianza Popular Revolucionaria Americana, or Popular American Revolutionary Alliance. The "cells" of the APRA that met in secret in Chachapoyas at this time were segregated by gender—there were separate groups of young men and women. The following account is based on interviews with the few surviving members of these original Apristas, all of whom are male.

10. For the sake of convenience, the new political bloc that the state helped to empower through its centralizing activities of the 1930s—which consisted largely of formerly marginalized "middle sectors," but included merchants, public employees, and professionals—will be referred to hereafter as the "moral community."

11. A military regime initiated this second phase of state expansion. For an overview of the specific policies of the military regime, see Lowenthal 1975 and Booth and Sorj 1983.

12. DeGregori (1990) describes a similar set of developments, at the regional level, in the department of Ayacucho, in tracing the emergence of Sendero Luminoso (the Shining Path).

13. In many other regions in Peru, regional movements similar to those of Chachapoyas broke out in the early 1970s in the aftermath of the military government's sweeping Agrarian Reform program. Many analysts argue that the destruction of regional, landed elite power via the expropriation of estates by the military resulted in a power vacuum at the local level, which made it possible for formerly marginalized groups to make their voices heard—in the form of regional protest movements. This scenario does not fit the sequence of events in Chachapoyas. Agrarian Reform came late to Chachapoyas—the first expropriations began in 1976, *after* the mobilizations discussed at the beginning of the paper. Thus, the landed class still controlled their properties at the time of the mobilizations, they had not been forced from regional dominance, and there was no power vacuum for anyone to fill. Furthermore, expropriations began in Chachapoyas the following year *despite* the changed relation between region and state signified by the mobilizations of 1975 described in the text. These facts indicate just how far the landed class had fallen in influence since the 1930s and how removed they were from the center of regional politics in the 1970s.

FOURTEEN

Notes toward an Ethnography of a Transforming State: Romania, 1991

Katherine Verdery

Over the past several decades, the work of anthropologists in complex societies has moved from focusing primarily on single communities (Foster 1967; Gillin 1947) to seeing communities as "part societies and part cultures" (Redfield 1956) and relating them ever more explicitly to the larger organizations of power and economy in which they are embedded (Steward 1955; Wolf 1956a, 1957, 1966a). This movement has required, in turn, more sophisticated conceptions of the nature of both "power" and "the state," considered as power's most concentrated expression. Just as some anthropologists now raise doubts about the reification of "society," increasing numbers have begun calling into question what "the state" means as they grow uneasy about writing of the state as "it"—a unified subject (rather like a person) that "intends" and "acts."

In consequence, the state itself, seen less as a thing than as a set of social relations or processes, is becoming the object of ethnographic inquiry. Varied approaches to an ethnography of the state can be found in the work of people such as Ann Anagnost (1988) on the "socialist imaginary" and the Chinese state, Ashraf Ghani (n.d.) on state-making in Afghanistan, and John Borneman (1992) on nationness in the two Germanies. Additionally enhancing the possibilities for an ethnography of the state are the writings of Eric R. Wolf. As Ghani's paper in this volume clearly shows, Wolf has built his corpus around an inquiry into the nature of public power, viewed not in terms of essentialized "societies" or organizations but in terms of processes that occur in "fields of forces acting within fields of forces" (Wolf 1977b, 33; see also Wolf 1990b, 591). Such emphasis on process positively invites ethnography.

The present essay accepts that invitation (if tentatively), contributing data on the early phases of state transformation in postsocialist Eastern Europe. Rarely has such an objective had so propitious a moment: the speed with which "actually existing socialist" states are decomposing and being transformed into something more (or differently) receptive to capitalism makes it possible to research this process literally as it happens. Even brief visits or periodic reading provides much material for an ethnography of the post-socialist state.[1] Two things make these notes toward an ethnography—using an "ethnographic present" that is more ephemeral than ever—very provisional, however. One is the pace of the changes in Eastern Europe, together with the remarkable openness of the world-system conjuncture in which they are occurring; the other is the conceptualization I employ. If the state is indeed a process, a project always to some degree in the making, then it is ongoing locally based political action within a fast-changing world that will determine what may eventually be viewed as "the outcome" of this process. No one, at the moment, can predict how these changes will unfold.

The one certainty is that as different groups in Eastern Europe work to create their versions of democracy, markets, and private property, the role "the state" should play will itself be under contention. Some members of the former elite will resist the dismantling of the bureaucracy that was their power base, whereas others, hungry for gain as new economic managers, will strive to wrest property rights from state control; opponents of the old regime will press for a reduced state presence, if only to show that socialism is dead; some workers, threatened with unemployment, may demand more state welfare functions and protection from the market, whereas others may resist this as diminishing their possible earnings with higher taxes. The emergent social interests may coalesce into social movements precisely around the issue of how much and what kind of state is best. All across the region political activists will influence state forms by the kinds of institutions and relations they establish—for "the state" is itself a set of political, economic, social, and cultural relations, bound up in institutions.

An ethnography of the transforming postsocialist state ought to do at least three things. First, it should specify the international and internal "fields of forces" within which the socialist state is being broken down and a new one constructed in its place. That a new one is being constructed is unmistakable; an ethnography of the postsocialist state may help to clarify why and how some sort of state is reconstituted. As a process, this is part of the present global reconfiguration of capitalism, and its agents are both international actors and shifting coalitions of groups inside each formerly socialist country; an ethnography of the transforming state ought to characterize both. Second, this ethnography should illustrate the mechanisms, the arenas, and the specific social processes within and through which the changes are occurring. How, and where, and by whom, in what contexts, is the state of socialism being challenged and undermined and a new one arising? Third, an ethnography of state transformation in Eastern Europe should show both what is common to all these cases and also how their historical and sociological peculiarities make their paths diverge. How will the new form of state and the processes making it in Romania, whose bloody "revolution" left the structures and personnel of Communist party rule more intact than elsewhere, differ from the same forms and processes in the Czech lands, with their "velvet" revolution, or in Poland, where ten years of underground Solidarity honed people's political capacities to an unusual degree? As differing patterns in the region begin to crystallize, we may begin to perceive a singular process with variants. This will enable a comparative analysis of state re-formation.

The present essay does not attempt to do all three of the above tasks. It concentrates on the second: to illustrate some of the mechanisms and arenas of state transformation. This is the task to which ethnography can most readily contribute, given how chaotic and ill-understood are both the international world-system reconfiguration and the localized political fields that mediate it. Most of my examples come from Romania, where owing to the extreme fluidity of political forces and coalitions, the emergent social movements are unstable and hard to define. I offer provisional accounts of what is happening more broadly in the region as of 1991, but I do not attempt here either a comparative or a macro-systemic analysis.

For my provisional ethnography of the postsocialist state as "process," I rely on earlier work concerning the nature of socialism as a system (Verdery 1991*a*, 1991*b*). In particular, because the state's corporate ownership of property fundamentally determined political processes in socialism, the divestiture of this property will cause major changes in both the power of the state and its nature. The changes will be especially visible in certain privileged arenas. I believe that a central arena is so-called privatization, seen as the reconstitution of private property rights in the hands of jural individuals by redistributing the corporate rights that the state bureaucracy once held—and that formed the basis of its power. Even as some aspects of privatization undermine the power base of the socialist state, however, other processes tend to reconstitute a political center. Let me call these contradictory processes of undermining and reconstituting the political center "destatizing" and "restatizing" tendencies.

"Privatization," like "democracy," "markets," and other elements of the transition from socialism, is both a symbol and a set of processes through which that symbol is acquiring new and multiple content. As a symbol, and again like democracy and markets, one of its functions is to generate external and internal support by signifying the end of socialism—thus qualifying its users for Western aid, credits, and investments, as well as for the allegiances of voters wanting the decisive end of the old order. This ideological significance of "privatization" probably explains why discussion of alternatives to it has been largely squelched—such as (1) *reorganizing production,* instead of redistributing property rights, (2) distributing not *ownership* rights but *use* rights, perhaps collective and overlapping rather than individual and exclusive, and (3) wider advocacy of ownership by workers as opposed to managers.[2] Each of these alternatives would favor different groups and would produce different state-economy relations from those now emerging.

Aside from its symbolism, privatization is a set of processes that range from altered laws to changes in pricing policy to a complete resocialization of economic actors. I treat it here as the locus of contradictory destatizing and restatizing tendencies. State property enters into private hands in very different ways in each East European country; in each, it encounters tremendous obstacles and is the subject of extended, often bitter, political debate.[3] The debate hit the ground running in 1989, for covert privatization had been appearing even before that unusual year. Jadwiga Staniszkis (1991a, 128) places its beginnings in about 1987 for Poland, David Stark (1991, 364) as early as 1984 for Hungary. Romanian friends, too, suggested to me that the "transition" was merely furthering processes already apparent two to three years before. Indeed, a number of scholars believe the very impetus for perestroika was growing pressure from socialist bureaucrats (known as the *nomenklatura*) to become owners rather than mere managers of state property.

Among the main forms these pre-privatizations took were incursions by managers of firms into the ownership prerogatives of the state and expansions of the so-called second economy—those informal activities operating in integral relationship to the formal state-run production system but in its interstices. (Both were especially far advanced in Hungary, where legalization of the second economy through "subcontracting" became so prevalent in the late 1980s that it produced the joke, "What is the quickest way to build socialism? Contract it out.") I will discuss these two areas—privatizations of state property, and expanded second economy—in turn, even though a strict separation of them is as impossible analytically as it was in practice. Their overlap is especially great in the system of distribution and provisioning, which I describe in passing. For each sphere, I will show how "privatization" itself is being produced—and a new state along with it—through a struggle between forces promoting divestiture of state property and other forces promoting the accrual of paternalist and oversight functions in the state.

For several reasons, such as difficulties in establishing a suitable purchase price for firms and abuses that give the former elite an edge in acquiring property, privatization has so far been a nightmare. Because the socialist economy was not run according to market-based principles of valuation and profitability, it is almost impossible to assess the book value of state firms so as to sell them. Thus, any estimate of their value is shot through with politics. Evidence points to a systematic devaluation of state assets, in part through controlled bankruptcies; this means that the cash paid by managers or foreign buyers is much less than the potential value of the holding acquired.[4] Throughout the region, newspapers frequently report scandals in which a piece of valuable property has been sold at a derisory price, leading to accusations that public assets are being squandered and to calls for state regulation of the process. Properties are sold in auctions at which only one bidder presents himself; or companies are allowed to go bankrupt, conveniently reducing their purchase price. Since most firms have not yet learned how to do without state subsidies, and since the supply of raw materials is more uncertain than ever because economic ministries no longer seek to assure them, it takes no effort at all to bankrupt a firm.

Beyond this, many former apparatchiks and managers of firms took advantage of uncertainties in the status of property law, thereby gaining possession of properties before their acquisition could be legally regulated. All over Eastern Europe, major factories and department stores quickly went from being state property to being joint-stock companies, "owned" collectively by groups of former apparatchiks and managerial or engineering personnel. Likewise, ownership of state farms and parts of some collectives is passing into the hands of those who managed them before. In one village I know, many of the cows in the collective's seven hundred-cow dairy farm had been sold at auction (with a single bidder) to the engineer who ran the agricultural machinery station for the area's collectives; he had also acquired other lands and equipment and was busily setting himself up as a capitalist farmer. I will call such people "entrepratchiks," to indicate their dual status as owner-entrepreneurs and as former or present managers, including members of the state bureaucracy.

Not only legal uncertainties but also the extraordinary complexity of the arrangements for privatizing serve to restrict access to property. David Stark's (1990, 374) account of how firms develop institutional cross-ownership, with managers of several firms acquiring interests in one another's companies, makes it clear that only people with extensive inside information and contacts will be able to participate in such schemes. Published descriptions of Romania's proposed "stock give-away plan," in which the public receives certificates amounting to 30 percent of the value of newly created joint-stock companies while the other 70 percent is held in state management firms, were so complicated that I, for one, found them impenetrable, and I seemed not to be alone. From correspondence columns in the press, it was clear in the summer of 1991 that average citizens suspected they were being hoodwinked by these schemes and that what was presented as a windfall for them will prove to be yet another swindle, in the time-honored tradition of Romanian political life. Similar plans exist for other countries of the region as well.

In each country the groups acquiring former state enterprises have slightly different compositions and different intermixtures of foreign capital, but in all, those who are benefiting the most are the former privileged groups. These include former high Party personnel and also the "technocratic elite" that was challenging their power before. They have acted fast: in Poland, for example, already by mid-1990, 10 to 20 percent of all fixed capital was in nomenklatura hands (Staniszkis 1991*a*, x). Stark (1990) vividly labels what is happening a transformation not from plan to market but from "plan to clan." Staniszkis carries the analysis even further, suggesting that just as socialist industrialization was built at the expense of agriculture, what she calls "political capitalism" will occur at the expense of the state sector. Nomenklatura companies attached to that sector will throw their costs onto the state, using their dual assets as owners/managers and political cronies to increase their own profits and accelerate the formation of capital. Given that prior capital accumulation *outside* the state was almost nonexistent under socialism (except in Hungary), this decapitalization of the state sector is almost the only source of "new" capital, aside from foreign investment. Thus, says Staniszkis, political capitalism is the Trojan horse in the state sector, the instrument of accelerated accumulation that must precede true privatization (see Staniszkis 1991*a*, 206–208). As is obvious, this drain on the assets that structure the state inevitably debilitates it, perforce changing its nature.

That many old elites are settling into new favorable situations is not surprising, nor has it escaped notice. One of several forces favoring some sort of *re*statization is political pressure. It originates partly in popular outrage at the speed with which old managers have become the new elites and partly in machinations by those among the old elites who did not move fast enough and found themselves left out. Michael Burawoy and János Lukács, as well as Stark, describe how privatization in Hungary led to "bringing the state back in" so as to regulate illegalities in the process of property transfers. Owing to public outcry against the amazing profits that Hungary's former elites had amassed so quickly, in January 1990 Hungary's Parliament passed a Law for the Defense of State Property, hoping to prevent further abuses by retarding privatization.[5] A major topic of debate in Eastern Europe thus became whether dismantling socialism's centralized political economy is possible only by strengthening the state further, so it can better manage the process of its own dissolution. This, say some, may even require expressly *re*nationalizing property from its precocious owners, so as to *de*nationalize it. The problem is worst in Hungary, where "pre-privatization" so diffused property rights that they cannot now be easily distributed without being first renationalized (Sajó 1990).

Not only the public but sometimes also the heads of newly privatizing firms help to re-create a central authority. A high government official in Bucharest observed to me in June 1991 that his economic program had eliminated central planning, but firms kept coming to him to ask for plans and regulation. Discussing with doctors irate at the government's failure to provide adequate supplies for health, a government minister asked why they didn't consider private practice. One replied to him bluntly, "Why should I pay to rent space and to get insurance, material stocks, and all that expensive equipment when the state can do it for me? And besides, where would I get the money?"

Comparable demands for state intervention or support come from all quarters but are especially vociferous in the domain of culture. Romania's Minister of Culture described to me how editors of publishing houses had resisted his plan to privatize the publishing business and begged him instead for subsidies. As he put it, "Everyone shouts 'Down with Communism!' and with their next breath 'Up with the State!'" Following a visit to New York's Metropolitan Museum, where he learned how the museum raises funds by such gambits as selling earrings like the ones in a famous Rubens painting, this minister proposed that the directors of his own cash-strapped museums do the same. The reaction: "That is a debasement of art! Museums should not have to become commercial operations, the state should subsidize them!" Archaeologists seek state protection against privatization of land, because now peasants do not want them digging up old Roman ruins any more on soil that could produce marketable crops. Literary magazines run stories with dire predictions that Romanian culture will expire unless the state controls the price of paper, thus subsidizing the publication of books and journals. In the most dramatic such case, numerous literary magazines appeared in mid-December with their front page blackened; one headline blared, "Romanian culture at an impasse! Journals of the Writers' Union suspend publication ... until the government assumes its necessary responsibility to support the national culture."[6]

Yet another example reveals not *requests* for intervention but people actually re-creating it themselves. The example comes from the sphere of teaching, rather than from economic privatization. An acquaintance told me of a discussion she overheard late on New Year's Eve, at a party of high-level university personnel. They were talking about the need to restore surveillance of the students, to re-create dossiers with notes as to what political parties each student favored, what political attitudes they held, and especially what views they had of the ruling National Salvation Front (which those present obviously supported). From the way they talked, it was quite clear to my friend that this was *their own* idea, not an order sent down from some higher authority. Thus, the professors who had replaced discredited Marxist-Leninist hacks in university chairs were now reconstituting for themselves a position of omnipotence based in a hopeful alliance with a new, intrusive political center.

These examples show us how Romanians accustomed to the presence, subsidies, and interventions of socialism's paternalistic state respond to its seeming disintegration by reconstituting a center to which they can continue to appeal. Although the state's power has been deeply compromised, they continue to anticipate it in their plans. Any ethnography of the post-socialist state must take account of the ways in which such appeals will help to produce a new state more paternalistic and centralized than the one that advisers from the United States and the international lending agencies are seeking to impose.

Results similar to these consequences of privatization and reform in the official, state sector of the economy can also be seen in the growth of "private enterprise" through an expanded second economy. By second economy, I mean all those income-generating activities that workers in socialism carried on outside their formal job—often using equipment or time or even the physical premises of their formal job, but often doing so unofficially, and sometimes illegally. Workers who drove black-market taxis in their off-hours, construction crews that borrowed tools and supplies from their work-site so as to build houses for themselves and their friends, clerks in stores who held goods under the counter to sell to someone who had given them a gift or bribe or was a friend or relative, and peasants cultivating the plot of land allotted them by the collective farm—all were engaged in socialism's second economy. It is important to note that these activities were not a suppressed form of entrepreneurship struggling valiantly to survive: their success *depended* upon their integration with the state sector. Hence, for such entrepreneurs the state's demise would be far from good news. Here are some examples of how people were expanding these sorts of activities in Romania, as of the summer of 1991, and how they continued to implicate a political center in their plans.

The most visible form of this kind of enterprise, to my traveler's eye at least, was that the former black-market taxi business had now been transformed into private taxis competing with the state taxi company. For the first time in eighteen years of going to Romania, I was able to get a taxi almost whenever I wanted one. Since I took at least a hundred taxis during one six-week stay and interviewed in all, I can speak about private taxis with some authority. I will not expatiate upon what I learned, other than to mention three noteworthy aspects of privatized taxi trade. First, it entered an open niche because the socialist government had invested so little in the transport infrastructure during the 1980s—especially in the infrastructure for "consumers," many of whom could not buy their own cars owing to exorbitant cost and lengthy waiting periods. This left a void into which private taxis could easily move, in typical second-economy fashion. Second, privatization via taxis requires no capital investment on the part of the petty entrepreneur: all who go into this business have already made the one capital investment necessary—they bought themselves a car—some time ago. Thus, the fact that average citizens (as opposed to the wealthy political-economic elite of socialism) have very little access to capital is not an impediment to becoming a private taxi driver. In effect, the main change from before is that people who used to hang around outside hotels and pick up the odd foreigner, nervously watching out for the police, can now do this legally.

Third, and most interesting, although every last cabbie said he made more money with his cab than with his regular job (and for many of them, the cab supplemented either temporary unemployment or wages inadequate in the present inflation), only one had left or would leave his state-sector job to become a fully "private entrepreneur." Thus, every last one of these drivers who had not been forced out of his official job was driving the cab outside regular working hours. They preferred to see the state sector retained so as to siphon off resources from it, even though the result was a tremendous lengthening of their working day (one recalls Marx's analysis of the extraction of surplus value). In some cases, the official job was directly tied to taxi work: an employee of an auto service firm would borrow tools and supplies, in the best tradition of the socialist "second economy," in order to keep his taxi in good repair. More often, the state sector's importance for them is in anticipated job security, benefits, and pensions these drivers do not want to or know how to provide on their own.

An additional area in which second-economy practices are flourishing in Romania is the well-stocked secondhand stores called *consignatii*, of which each major city has a large number. Some of the goods in these stores are in fact secondhand; the owners obtain other goods through their networks or extensive travel; still other goods are doubtless bribed from state warehouses. Consignatii sell things like coffee, cigarettes, stockings, Western liquor, shampoo, cosmetics, shirts, shoes, and so forth. Many of the goods are foreign, and they sell for Romanian currency at prices cheaper than those of the state-run hard-currency shops, which used to monopolize this trade and which the consignatii are now evidently displacing. Both the displacement and unanimous popular opinion suggest that the owners of consignatii are former apparatchiks, Secret Police operatives, and others who have connections and money adequate to procuring both centrally located spaces and large stocks of goods—in a word, entrepratchiks. The one employee I was able to interview in such a place said that his boss was always traveling around getting goods from as far away as the United States and that he had both money and "highly placed connections." It is appropriate to see them, therefore, as petty commerce of the sort that *de*statizes, displacing stores that generated hard-currency profits for the state budget with a company that generates wealth for a private owner. Yet these stores also gain from access to the state—thus they are eager to see a political center maintained—for some of them turn profits by selling the packages of clothing and food that Romania's state representatives have continued to receive as foreign aid for the hungry and the orphans.

These consignatii (along with other forms of petty commerce I have not discussed) flourish in the intersection between socialism's shortage economy and the effort to introduce markets. This intersection creates many openings for people who aim to mediate shortages (especially of the consumer goods that the socialist state always neglected) and can now do so more legally than before. Any activity that supplies consumer markets and eases pressure on the official distribution system is therefore at a premium; the disintegration of that unreliable system reinforces opportunities further. In Romania shadow networks had already begun to displace it before 1989, through bribery or by setting up auxiliary channels. In some sectors, such as food provisioning, those in power are anxious to see distribution occur by whatever means. In other sectors, one suspects that distribution is purposely lax, such as with the dissemination of the independent press and oppositional party electoral material—which, in the 1990 elections, somehow never made it out to the provinces. Whatever the reason, opportunities for privatized distribution arise, and they have consequences for the developing form of the state.

A final area in which privatization via expansion of the second economy occurs at the expense of (and therefore undermines) the formerly state-run sector is through decollectivization: the redistribution of agricultural land. Procedures for decollectivizing vary from one East European country to another, and there is much disagreement as to what form it should take: in a 1991 survey conducted in Hungary, for example, 24 percent of the respondents supported the return of lands to former owners, 41 percent thought the members of each collective farm should decide the question, 23 percent wanted the collective farms to remain as they were, and 5 percent backed selling the land to the highest bidder (Szelényi and Szelényi 1991, 15). Despite these disagreements, however, some form of decollectivization is in progress in every country, regulated by complicated and varying redistribution laws.

How the laws will work out in practice is doubtless very complex. In Romania, despite a presumably uniform Law on Landed Property, there is variation from one village to another as to whether one receives one's old parcel, an equivalent amount elsewhere in one's village, or nothing at all. Because the redistribution begun in 1991 was not going to be completed by spring planting time, in many localities farm members simply occupied lands by plowing and planting them. Some people occupied what they had owned before; some who had had no land or had moved into the village and worked in the collective now occupied lands to which their claim is uncertain. In other villages, the farm leaders encouraged people to farm in common for that season and to divide the produce in proportion to people's former landholdings. In still others, leaders broke up the farm preemptively, redistributing land to those who wished and pooling the rest in "Associations." These comprised all with rights to land who preferred not to work it themselves (in most cases, because they were elderly or lacked adequate implements); proceeds would be divided in proportion to the land each person committed to the pool. These Associations are being touted as possible models for Romania's future.

By no means were all villagers in Romania (and elsewhere) initially enthusiastic about return of their lands. I heard many expressions of reluctance during a visit in the summer of 1990, although a year later, many people had changed their minds.[7] In 1991 I happened to arrive precisely on the day when the mayor posted the allotments each household was to receive as owners. Villagers who felt they had been shortchanged had five days to register complaints, or contestations (*contestatii*). Talk of contestations filled the four days of my visit, because for a variety of reasons, virtually no one had received the exact amount they had held in 1959, when the collective was formed. Many people who had owned land got nothing back at all, since the law returns only the land held in *collective* farms. This leaves former owners of about 30 percent of Romania's arable surface—the amount held in *state* rather than collective farms[8]—ineligible for property restitution, while substantial resources remain in the hands of the persons who (mis)managed them under socialism. Not surprisingly, many of the disenfranchised are upset.

The specifics of decollectivization, then (like privatization more broadly), are crucial to the way class relations are being reconfigured in Romania, and all over Eastern Europe. Everywhere, the potential ownership and autonomy of cultivators is being resisted by the group this would dispossess: the former presidents, directors, agronomists, veterinarians, and accountants of collective and state farms. In Romania, these people are mounting a determined effort to see to it that newly propertied cultivators view the new Associations as their chief option (no one was talking about credit for acquiring agricultural implements; no one was accepting offers from England and Italy to send in cheap tractors). In advance of the 1990 elections, villagers informed me, farm leaders had urged them not to vote for opposition parties who would supposedly disband the collectives and take away everyone's pensions. I suspect that such disinformation was not ordered by politicians in Bucharest but was a local initiative, reflecting a defense of privilege. Even where these local elites do not see their salvation in a new form of collective farm but are willing to become capitalist farmers themselves, they must struggle to gain control of property that villagers see as rightfully their own.

Many villagers angrily resist such efforts. I discussed at length with one old friend her resentment at having received no land at all in the proposed redistribution. She was convinced that the mayor and others were in cahoots to make sure *they themselves* ended up with land even if by cheating the villagers: only if there is some pool of land besides the two- and three-hectare parcels of the new peasant owners, she said, will those officials have any livelihood. When I asked what she would do with the land if her contestation succeeded, she replied, "Give it to the Association, of course! I haven't got a horse or tractor to work five hectares with, and I'm too old to buy them! My children have all moved to the city; *they* have no interest in farming the land." When I expressed surprise that she was going to such lengths to get land that she was going to turn over to yet another form of collective, she disagreed vigorously. "The important thing is not to let those people *rip me off again!*"

In this new version of class struggle in the countryside, all parties are in various ways both allying themselves with the state (and thus shoring it up) and undermining its power. That is, decollectivization, like other forms of privatization, is serving as an arena in which some form of central control is being both destroyed and recomposed. Officials of collective and state farms swing their weight behind those forces at the political center who want to brake the decomposition of the resources on which state power has rested. They use the state prosecutor to pursue peasants who walked off with farm property, such as cows or horses or carts. At the same time, by abusing decrees about land redistribution and by other acts in which they demonstrate that they are no longer under central control, they arrogate power from the center as they struggle locally to stabilize their life-situations.

Those cultivators pressing for decollectivization also diminish the center, in the most obvious of ways. Collective farms constituted one of the forms of collective property whose management buttressed the bureaucracy's power; any reduction in centrally controlled assets, through the redistribution of lands to villagers, *eo ipso* diminishes the state, and many villagers are insisting on precisely this. But the legal nightmare that has resulted from occupations of land and from the thousands of contestations shows us a contrary *re*composition of central power, in another sphere. The job of resolving the contestations and sorting out the tangled property claims that have emerged falls to the state judicial system. It is to this system that villagers will look for the justice they believe local officials are denying them. Through thousands of court cases, a reconstituted central apparatus will reshape plaintiffs into new legal subjects, who look not to themselves or their local boss but to the center for redress of wrongs.

By claiming their lands and contesting the questionable decisions of local officials, then, villagers are both subverting and also reconstructing state power. Better said, they participate in reshaping it. They are also, potentially, reshaping themselves as subjects. Among the goals of an ethnography of the state should be an inquiry into how meaningful subjects are constituted, either by the actions of the center or in resistance to it. In contestations and forcible occupations of land we see the resistant self-constitution of subjects who perceive their personal efficacy as wrapped up in becoming possessors once again. Many villagers, I believe, now see their sense of personhood as depending on a diminished sphere for the state, with its decades of ever-greater intrusions into their household activities, the organization of their time, the crops they could plant on their so-called private plots,[9] and even their sex lives (for like all Romania's women, peasant women had had to undergo regular gynecological exams, monitoring for illegal abortions). As one villager said to me about her land, "Even if I just turn it over to the Association, it's still *my land*, as it wasn't before. If I don't like how they're running the thing, or if I think I'm not getting a big enough share, I can withdraw my land from the Association and sell it or give it out in sharecropping." Others made similarly clear that their sense of themselves *as owners* and as *respectable persons*, persons who would not be ripped off, was at stake in decollectivization. For these cultivators, a meaningful life means being able to make their own decisions about the disposition of their labor and its products.

One can imagine the concerns of the various groups I have mentioned congealing into social movements that back different political parties and promote variant conceptions of the state. In thousands of local contexts across Eastern Europe, the 1990s will witness a struggle of these conflicting preferences among villagers and between them and local authorities; the struggle will surely reverberate into national politics. The results will have consequences for the kind of state people will live under and the kinds of persons they will become. Although the persistence of collective property forms may press toward a state resembling the earlier paternalist one, contestations may help create a center of a new kind: the "law-governed state" so often invoked in postsocialist rhetoric, rather than one governed by fiat, arbitrariness, and terror.[10] Depending on whether political action in domains other than those treated here manage to separate judicial from executive functions, the state and the subjectivities it implies may differ markedly from before in their form.

That will be the case, however, only if entrepratchiks are reined in, if they do not succeed in penetrating the judicial process and turning it to their own ends. One could bring forth many examples of entrepratchik resistance to the rise of a "law-governed state." In one example, charges of calumny were brought against archnationalist entrepratchik Corneliu Vadim Tudor for untruths published in his newspaper, *Greater Romania*. As the date for the trial drew near, *Greater Romania* issued an appeal to its supporters to overwhelm the courtroom in defense of the "unjustly accused" victim. On the appointed day,[11] mobs of people did indeed overwhelm the courtroom and successfully prevent the trial from taking place. Police were barely able to control the crowd, many of whom called for the head of the prosecutor bringing the charges. Telephoned death threats to others who have sought to bring legal charges against local potentates (of whom Vadim Tudor is one) show similar attempts to dismantle inconvenient forms of state power.

An ethnography of the postsocialist state would follow cases like this one, as well as the progress of decollectivization and its attendant contestations. It would look for points at which one or another actor appeals to the once-paternalist state to intervene, would inspect the terms of those appeals and their acceptance or rejection, and would examine the process of law-making that sets out new tasks for institutions, the state, and individuals. It would speculate upon the implications of these different state tasks—regulating property acquisition, enforcing contracts, subsidizing culture and medical care, and so forth—for the emergent political and cultural relationships and the institutions that would "become" a new state form. It would focus on events in which forms of violence the state is supposed to monopolize are wielded (as was frequently happening in Romania during 1990 and 1991) not by branches of the state but by disaffected groups—miners, Secret Police, and the like—whose very action makes manifest and simultaneously reproduces the state's incapacity. Examining these and many other arenas, of which privatization is a fundamental one, will enable us to see how the fields of forces around Eastern Europeans are changing, bringing new forms of domination to replace that of socialism.

NOTES

I am grateful to Ashraf Ghani, Emily Martin, Jane Guyer, Jane Schneider, and Michel-Rolph Trouillot for comments on earlier drafts of this essay.

1. This essay is based on two visits to Romania in the summers of 1990 and 1991, as well as on reading Romanian newspapers and the work of scholars for other countries of the region, as cited in the bibliography. Although my data are not extensive, they are sufficient to show how an ethnography of the postsocialist state might begin.

2. For the first, see e.g., Burawoy and Lukács 1992, 10, 26; for the second, Burawoy and Lukács 1992, 154, and Hann n.d., 2–3, 9, 19–20; for the third, Burawoy and Lukács 1992, 159–167, and Stark 1991, 24.

3. An excellent summary of these debates for Hungary is found in Stark 1990.

4. Burawoy and Lukács 1992, 154. See also Stark 1990, 360.

5. Burawoy and Lukács 1992, 155; Stark 1990, 366–369, 376.

6. From *România literara* for 19 December 1991, p. 1.

7. Kideckel likewise found, in the summer of 1990, considerable variation in people's interests in decollectivizing. He shows this variation to be directly related to people's household economic strategies and the availability of labor. See Kideckel 1990; see also Hann n.d., 6–7, for Hungary.

8. The percentage of the land that was held in state as opposed to collective farms varies significantly by country across the region. Romania and the Soviet

Union, for example, had unusually high percentages of land in state farms, Poland and Hungary much lower percentages.

9. In Romania starting in 1984, villagers were given a list of amounts and crops they were required to contract to the state from their private plots. This meant that their own plan for their household consumption had to be subordinated to this new drain from outside. See Verdery 1992 for further elaboration.

10. Talk of the "law-governed state" has become yet another symbol of the transition from socialism. In each country of the region there is a specific expression that has this meaning, best rendered with the German *Rechtsstaat* (*statul de drept*, in Romanian; *jogállam*, in Hungarian; *pravo gosudarstveno*, in Russian, etc.). The term shows up constantly in the press, as people complain that a law-governed state clearly does not yet exist, or else argue that a given behavior would help to construct the law-governed state.

11. This is according to newspaper reports I had no opportunity to confirm.

FIFTEEN

The Timely Significance of Supernatural Mothers or Exemplary Daughters: The Metonymy of Identity in History

Pamela Wright

> *Guadalupe is important to Mexicans not only because she is a supernatural mother, but also because she embodies their major political and religious aspirations.*
> ERIC R. WOLF, "THE VIRGIN OF GUADALUPE"

The last ritual I expected to observe in my fieldwork with the Garifuna of Belize was a beauty contest. Yet, after many months of working in Belize, I began to understand this beauty contest was one of the major expressions of ethnic identity for Belizean Garifuna. It revealed how important national-ism had become in the signification of ethnicity. It also indicated how edu-cated leaders were consolidating their leadership, redefining "Garifuna-ness" through the figure of "Miss Garifuna," regarded as an exemplary daughter of the ethnic group. As with the Virgin of Guadalupe, which rep-resented not only a "holy mother" for seventeenth-century mestizos in Mexico but also their political and ideological rights in a state, the ethnic daughter of the "Miss Garifuna Contest" constitutes symbolically the political and ideological aspirations of certain Garifuna in a postcolonial nation-state. Here I examine how the beauty contest comes to stand for a particular asso-ciation of identities in historical context.

IDENTITIES IN HISTORICAL CONTEXT

Anthropologists increasingly study how ethnicity is constituted in context. Ethnicity itself is now understood as a historically bound phenomenon that, like other processes of identity and conceptions of a group's history, differs through time (see, for example, Hill 1988). With recent examina-tions of the history of nationalism we begin to look specifically at the con-tent of both nationalism and ethnicity and how they are produced by spe-cific agents. In the case of nationalist ideologies, much symbolic production takes place at the local or middle levels of societies, where educated or inter-stitial groups mediate processes of more global levels (Schneider and Schneider 1976; C. Smith 1984; Vincent 1990). The study of such symbolic production tells us much about the formation of nationalism, contentions over ethnicities and nationalism, and the role of intellectuals in establishing legitimacy for different states (see Fox 1990*c*; Verdery 1991*b*, 429).

Some anthropological accounts of ethnicity privilege its political or instrumental uses, often stressing also its changing dimensions through time (Bentley 1987; Keyes 1981). Abner Cohen's (1985) work on ethnicity, by declaring it political, utilizes a maximization model to focus on utility in struggles over resources. Other accounts emphasize primordial aspects pointing to the continuity of central symbols and their links through time (see Geertz 1973). A third approach speaks of "invented traditions" whose links to the past create an illusion of invariance in the present (Hobsbawm 1983). To transcend these limited choices that treat ethnicity as either "primordial," "instrumental," or "invented," I propose to analyze the symbolic content of cultural production from the perspective of political language and the political uses of symbolism. Such a perspective includes consideration of indirection or other specialized speech genres for political language, the combination of the sacred or traditional symbolizations with contingent political agendas, and the indexical centering of symbolizations in person, place, and time (see Brenneis and Myers 1984 on political language; Hanks 1987 on discourse genres; Gal 1991 for a recent example of a symbolic analysis of cultural production). Through a careful consideration of economic and political interests as they are couched in symbolic productions and take meaning in historical contexts, we can illuminate symbolic meaning and agency in constructions of identity (Fox 1990*c*). In this chapter, I will examine complex symbolizations of ethnicity, nationalism, and gender among the Garifuna of Belize within the first ten years following Belizean independence. I shall first elaborate on Roman Jakobson's symbolic concept of metonymy as it applies to a consideration of identity in history.

THE METONYMY OF IDENTITY IN HISTORY

Jakobson's concept of metonymy can prove fruitful for this quest as it has for others. Jakobson[1] (1960, 1971) defines metonymy as the symbolizing practice of contiguity and contextualization of symbols in which meaning is produced and transformed (in other words, he asks us to consider how symbols are linked to one another in particular contexts). He contrasts this with the more singular concept of metaphorical symbolization, in which meaning adheres to the symbol itself. Applying Jakobson's concepts to group symbolizations in history we might say that each ethnic group is its own metaphor of identity, whereas the relations of groups in social context provide significations of "groupness" and make for the metonymy of identity. Seeking to understand nation-states as "imagined communities," we might examine how psychologists have interpreted metaphor and metonymy as they are played out in dream and other symbolizing of human minds. The psychologist Jacques Lacan refers to metonymic symbolization as displacement, contrasting this to metaphorical symbolization, which, he suggests, coincides with Freud's concept of condensation. Such observations should serve to remind us that identities disseminate onto other things and peoples and that power and emotion are bound in identity symbols. Central metaphors persist through time, connoting a powerful complex of meanings, often considered sacred and irreducible. Metonymic formulations, by contrast, allow for shifts and new links in meanings at higher levels of complexity as group relations are transformed through history.

Examining metonymy becomes particularly important in looking at combinations of ethnicity with nationalism in particular social formations or types of nationalisms (Fox 1990c; Verdery 1991b; Williams 1989, 1990). If we understand that power inhabits signification (Wolf 1990b), this negates a facile dichotomy of primordial sentiment versus instrumentality in categorizing these combinations. Such symbolizations convey knowledge about identity, sentiment, and power, drawing upon local and supralocal meanings to bind groups together. The engendered symbol of the Mexican nation, the Virgin of Guadalupe, serves as a classic example (Wolf 1958). The Virgin (superimposed on the site of the female earth and fertility goddess Tonantzin) came to symbolize the Mexican nation-state, assuming special significance in the seventeenth century as an expression of the political aspirations of colonial mestizos vis-à-vis metropolitan Spain. As Wolf considers the psychological import of the symbol of the Virgin by looking at family forms and gender relations for both Indians and mestizos, he also tells us that the political function of the symbol for mestizos was to secure their place in the social order.

If seventeenth-century mestizos wielded an indigenous Virgin to legitimate their Mexican state and lay claim to their place in it, then Garifuna have utilized an educated ethnic beauty queen to promulgate nationalized ethnicity within their ethnic group and secure where they stand in the Belizean nation-state. As we will see below, beauty queen symbolization is embedded in presentations of central ethnic symbols such as the sacred food, cassava, and its production by women; dances to propitiate the ancestors; and homecomings to the island Irumei of the groups' Caribbean past—all in an annual national holiday celebration called "Garifuna Settlement Day," observed on 17 November in Belize.[2] This potent complex of new and old ritual culminates in one event, the Miss Garifuna contest, during some seven days of celebration surrounding this holiday. Together old and new symbols are enlisted in the constitution of a new ethnic identity that reinforces that of the nation-state, giving meaning to its new authority, new relationships, and new leadership. The combination does not exhaust old symbols of identity but, rather, harnesses their meaning and history to the new identity of nationalism in a metonymy of ethnicity.

As an ethnic group the Garifuna afford illustrations of both stasis and change in culture and identity (see Wright 1991): anthropologists have studied the effects of warfare and displacement under colonialism on the Garifuna identity (see Whitehead 1988), and the changing racial composition of the group resulting from the sixteenth-century incorporation of African slaves into an Amerindian cognatic clan, followed by intermarriage with other African groups into the present (see Crawford 1984). Their shifting place in the ecology and economy of Central America has also been of interest. Nancie L. Gonzalez (1970, 1988) cites the ability of the group to change and produce new culture rapidly (she calls it a "neoteric" culture), whereas other ethnohistorical work such as that of Mary Helms (1981) indicates continuities between Garifuna and pre-Columbian Caribbean culture. According to the linguist Douglas Taylor (1977), the ethnic group's language, Garifuna, has changed little from the Arawakan dialect reported in the mid-seventeenth century by Raymond Breton. I have studied both the early connections between the Garifuna and other lowland Amazonian groups, occurring in the pre-Columbian period through colonialism (in the fifteenth to eighteenth centuries), as well as the more recent profound change of an intergenerational language shift. Currently in Belize, the younger Garifuna speak only Belizean English (versions of Creole and Standard West Indian English), even though they understand the Garifuna spoken to them by their parents and elders (see the detailed study of the dynamics of this language shift in Wright 1986). This chapter, with its focus on the cultural production of ethnicity, suggests ways in which the intergenerational language shift[3] is related to the new nationalized form of ethnicity.

Garifuna-speaking peoples have inhabited the countries of Belize, Guatemala, Honduras, and Nicaragua since the end of the eighteenth century (see Gonzalez 1988, 10). Many kin ties and links existed among the Central American Garinagu (the term for the collective body of Garifuna) until Garifuna became involved in the nationalisms of those countries after 1840 (see Wright 1991, 26–29). How nationalist they have since become is difficult to judge from the anthropological literature, which has focused on the maintenance of "traditional rituals" of the various groups (see Gonzalez 1988; Kerns 1983; but see Adams 1991, who notes nationalism among Garifuna in Honduras). Although I have discussed the involvement with nationalism of Garifuna of the various nation-states (see Wright 1991, 26–30), I have most closely studied the situation in Belize. Among the Belizean Garifuna, older women have successfully maintained many older elements of religion and ritual, yet simultaneously others, especially the young, are involved in new ways of being Garifuna.

The Belizean nation-state officially gained independence on 21 September 1981. At the time, the nation-state was searching to produce its identity through local symbolization replacing the older colonial symbols of British authority vested in the white-gloved Queen, British flag, and mother England (still held dear by some aged Belizeans). In this historical context, the symbolization of the Miss Garifuna contest gained much of its value, through a defining of "Garifunaness" as Belizean. The contest marks educated Garifuna as both ethnic and national leaders, being a ritual construction not just for one ethnic group but for the entire state's public culture.

BELIZE AS A POSTCOLONIAL NATION-STATE

The public culture of states involves a constant production and formulation of symbols of peoplehood and at the same time, the changing forms of the state enable new forms of culture and new identities. The state has powers to enfranchise new ethnic groups and classes and sometimes appropriates symbols of local groups as a state identity; this process creates new divisions and new contentions in nationalist ideologies. For example, Brackette Williams (1990) has described how Guyanese appropriated the Shi'ite Islamic festival of Moharram for nationalized celebration, adding elements of drinking and gambling. Muslims reclaimed the festival from its despoilment in national celebration. They were able to do so because the tradition of British compartmentalization of ethnic groups gave Muslims rights over this tradition. The process of appropriation of local symbols into national ones is only beginning for Belize. Thus most of the battles over national culture seem to be attempts to establish hegemony or at least parity among Belizean ethnic groups. For example, heated political disputes on immigration into the country have centered on fears that this immigration would upset the country's ethnic and racial balance. Thus far, immigration to Belize has been primarily responsive to Central American conditions and hence "refugee" communities of Spanish-speaking peoples have served as the primary addition to the Belizean population (see Bolland 1986, 41; Palacio 1990).

The current national ideology is that Belize is a composite of all of its cultures (see Bolland 1986, 41). Table 15.1 summarizes the ethnic composition of the Belizean nation-state. As I describe below, the British relinquished the government to a group of expatriate and Creole landowners and businessmen with the national participation of the lower-class Creoles in the state coming as a later political victory. Creoles are the descendants of former Scots-English landowners and African slaves, who spoke Standard West Indian English and Creole English. The British sought to maintain the Anglo-European cultural and linguistic hegemony in the state and the Central American region more generally (see Olien 1987 on the Spanish and British battles over the region) by containing the Spanish and Mayan power

TABLE 15.1   Ethnic Composition of the Belizean Nation-State, 1980

Ethnic Group	Primary Region	Percent of Population (N = 145,353)
Creoles	Belize District	40
Mestizos	Corozal & Orange Walk	33
Garifuna	Stann Creek District	8
Maya (Mopan)	Corozal	7
Kekchi	Toledo	3
East Indian	Toledo	2
Other		7

in the state. Thus despite the proportional representation of ethnic groups (see table 15.1), the national culture of the Belizean nation-state must be understood in terms of its national legacy, derived primarily from its British colonial heritage. At the same time that rituals and public performances create a new plural "Belizean" identity, education as well as political and economic forces serve to reinforce the colonial legacy of English identity in the Central American region.

The local cultures (officially recognized as Spanish, Mayan [Kekchi and Mopan], Garifuna, and Creole) are promoted as "Belizean cultures" in performance by selected groups in public national festivals or celebrations. Some aspects of these ethnically identified cultures have been appropriated for national culture. For example, the dance of *punta*, derived from the Spanish dance of *culio* (dancing in which the buttocks are wiggled suggestively), has consistently been performed in national festivals by Garifuna dance troupes and presented as Garifuna culture, along with other Garifuna dances. More recently, the dance has become a symbol of Belizean identity. In 1987, Trinidadian Calypso Rose, who often performs at Belizean national celebrations along with Lord Lara and other calypso stars from the Caribbean, wrote and performed a calypso song about dancing punta. She performed the song at the national independence day celebration, unaccompanied by any Garifuna dancers or singers, and danced the dance to calypso music rather than the traditional Garifuna singing and drumming.

The elevation of Garifuna culture to national status I describe above seems to have met no protest. Other cultural appropriations have not been received so sanguinely. For example, at a 1983 national meeting of Belizean Rotary clubs (the association of businessmen based on and affiliated with those in the United States), each club was asked to perform a skit representing its local identity. Although the Corozal district club performed a series of Spanish dances, the Stann Creek district club performed a skit about the history of the Garifuna (emphasizing, among other things, the "fact" that the Garifuna were once a nonblack race). Dangriga Garifuna, knowing of the meeting, which was held in their district, pointed out that the local high school principal was the only member of the Rotary Club who was Garifuna and protested the performance as an appropriation of Garifuna culture by other Belizeans.

One reason why Belizean national culture is still identified with the British has to do with the relationship of the nation to its border state, Guatemala. A fear of invasion by the Guatemalan military has shaped Belizean national politics (see Stone 1989, 98 and n. 20), and a British military presence remains today as one of the conditions under which the country would agree to become independent, accounting for the seventeen-year delay after Belize was granted early self-rule in 1964. In Guatemala, the dominance of a white elite has prevented the development of a national culture (see Adams 1991; Smith 1990), maintaining mestizo and Indian peoples as separate. Many Belizeans are fearful of the loss of patrimonial rights in a postcolonial British state, should the military power that supports this Guatemalan elite take action on political claims to Belizean territory (Guatemala's 1945 constitution officially defines Belize as Guatemala's twenty-third department; see Bolland 1986, 110).

THE BELIZEAN ECONOMY, ETHNIC GROUPS, AND CLASSES: TEACHERS AND NATIONAL CULTURE

After independence in 1981, the colonial administration of the British was only slightly modified by excluding non-nationals. The colonial educational apparatus was left intact with the financing, administration, and staffing of education shared between missionary societies from the United Kingdom, the United States, and the Belizean nation-state. Although government and educational employment may not be significant in the economies of many industrialized nations, the Belizean economy is another matter. The chief production for foreign exchange is sugar in the northern districts and citrus in the south, although with the fall of sugar prices in the world market, the sugar industry of Belize has declined. Most agricultural work is seasonal and fluctuates with global trends. Tourism operates on a small scale, with no large international companies participating. Like many Caribbean countries, remittances are a significant source of income for many people although there are no reliable figures.

In such an economy, employment in education and education-related positions (teaching and community work in the civil service, work with religious or missionary endeavors) constitutes the most stable available source of full-time work. Labor in the informal sector is comprised of petty trading, subsistence agriculture, and small market and craft production, whereas

TABLE 15.2   Employment by Sector in Belize

Sector	Total	Male	Female
Agriculture	30.0%	38.0%	10.1%
Forestry	0.8	1.0	0.1
Fishing	1.3	1.7	0.5
Quarrying	0.2	0.4	0.0
Manufacturing	10.3	10.8	8.9
Electric, Water	1.5	1.9	0.3
Construction	4.9	6.6	0.8
Commerce	11.2	8.5	17.9
Transportation	5.0	5.9	2.7
Banking, Insurance	1.4	0.8	2.9
Government	15.4	9.9	28.9
Community Service	16.0	12.1	25.8
Other Services	2.0	2.4	1.1
Total	100%	100%	100%
Number Employed	40,700	29,045	11,655

many people are unemployed and rely on remittances from other family members to provide support (see Wright 1986, 161–173). In terms of income, church and civil service workers make up a larger "middle class" (Wright 1986, 174, 395) than small merchants or other professionals, both in number and income level.[4] If we examine the labor statistics from the period shortly after independence (1982–1983) given in table 15.2, we see that workers who are employees of the government and other church agencies comprised 30 percent of the labor force in Belize, matching that of agriculture (also 30 percent). When these statistics are broken down by gender they prove even more dramatic: 22 percent of available labor for men is in this education-related work, whereas approximately 55 percent of all work for women is in this domain (Belize Labor Force Survey 1983–1984).

The history of Garifuna access to educational opportunities is complex. Under British rule the Belizean teaching profession and civil service were dominated by the Creole ethnic group. Like the majority of Creoles, the Garifuna are a phenotypically black ethnic group. Some Garifuna have even "passed" as Creole when in Belize City. Despite this common racial distinction, the groups have always used other criteria to distinguish themselves (see Taylor 1951, 39–40; Wright 1991). One criterion for not hiring Garifuna was that the British sought to perpetuate the English language in the schools and many Garifuna were Spanish-speaking in the early nineteenth century. Indeed, the British trained the Creoles, who had already been socialized in much of the culture and language of England by church and state. According to many Garifuna, they were ill-served by the Creoles, who rarely considered the interests of the Garifuna ethnic group. As the British relinquished control of the Belizean state during the period of internal self-rule in Belize (1964–1981), large numbers of Garifuna men, who spoke English by this time, entered the civil service as teachers. Other non-Creole groups were also allowed into civil service positions as they sought to gain control over their own schools and local government. Although the majority of Garifuna entered into teaching at this time, a small number had begun training as teachers a century earlier. Some men worked with missionaries from the Methodist Church of the United Kingdom as early as 1838 (Ashcraft and Grant 1968). Catholics were also training Garifuna teachers during the late nineteenth and early twentieth century. (Unlike the British, the Catholics also trained the Spanish-speaking ethnic groups for work in teaching.)

By 1947 the Jesuits were sending young Garifuna men to secondary school in Belize (see Lundberg 1978 on recruitment; Wright 1986, 272–280, on training and advancement). These young men were to repay their scholarships by working in schools during the period of their studies and teaching for several years after graduation. The Jesuits were based in the United States and many Garifuna were sent to that country for higher education.[5] The advanced education the Jesuits provided allowed Garifuna men to become teachers and principals as soon as secondary schools were opened by the Belizean government in the 1960s. Garifuna male teachers had already been teaching in elementary schools in all regions.

These men were socialized in their educational training in a way that differed from Garifuna pursuing other ends: in addition to mastering an English education and the English language, their employment required that they maintain Western-style dress and habits as well as stable legal/religious marriages. Church authorities also required the wives of male teachers to accompany their husbands to the teaching sites, located far from Garifuna towns or villages. This practice deprived women of their traditional agricultural production for subsistence and marketing and made these families increasingly reliant on purchased foodstuffs, as women were seldom able to secure land in the villages of other ethnic groups. Most important, "teacher's wives" were increasingly expected to conform to Western gender roles by Catholic and Methodist church authorities who supervised the male teachers.

The system of church education included one elementary school in most villages. Catholics sent Garifuna teachers to teach in the Kekchi and Mopan Mayan villages, located in remote areas of Belize where Creoles refused assignment. Secondary schools were located in larger towns. As more Garifuna became involved in teaching, their lifestyles reflected their steady wage income as well as their new socialization to Western dress and a patriarchal family form. In the town of Dangriga, a substantial portion of the

Garifuna population became involved in this work. Dangriga Garifuna maintained Western-style houses with electricity and plumbing, wore different forms of dress, and developed cultural practices that continue to distinguish them from Garifuna who live in villages.

Garifuna socialization and employment in the educational system of their nation-state had a profound effect on subjectivity and the promulgation of ethnic identity. In the words of Nicos Poulantzas (1978, 29) "state apparatuses enter into the process of determining classes as the embodiment and materialization of ideological and political relations"—an apt characterization of how civil servants and teachers come to fulfill the role of a "medial" or middle class both economically, socially, and symbolically.[6] I use the word "medial" to convey the importance of such classes in perpetuating social orders, a role that Marx observed for the petit bourgeoisie in capitalist formations. Benedict Anderson (1983, 74, 115) also emphasizes the medial role of teachers and other public sector workers both in Europe and in postcolonial nation-states where their propagation of nationalism has been decisive. David J. Banks (1990) similarly points to the importance of novels written by teachers and other political figures in the creation of national culture in Malaysia. For Anthony Smith (1983, xxii), civil servants are a "professional intelligentsia," whereas for Alvin Gouldner (1979) such intellectuals assert the authority of their "professional language" over that of traditional social forms. Ethnographic studies of medial classes by anthropologists now include not only postcolonial nation-states but also Europe and the United States (see Ortner 1991). As Sherry Ortner (1991, 186) tells us, we must recognize "both the ways in which various pieces of the society may be mutually constituting . . . and the ways in which all the pieces are at the same time constituted by the larger histories and structure that encompass them."

According to Cedric Grant (1976, 285), civil servants play an especially important role in Belizean society because of the absence of a large established local elite. Public sector workers are particularly important in casting meanings of the individual, society, knowledge, and authority through which national and ethnic identity are negotiated and in legitimating education in the new social order of the postcolonial nation-state. Of course, the ideological influence of civil servants and educational workers, as well as the evaluation of education within different nation-states, varies according to the relationship of the formal sectors of the labor market to the state. The multiple studies of such medial groups are only beginning to provide data to allow their comparison both in relation to the historic character of specific states and in relation to world and local economic formations. In postcolonial nation-states, often education and other public sector institutions are maintained through the support of the missionary societies of various churches, worldwide agencies such as the United Nations, financial and administrative aid from former colonial powers, and contributions of the state itself. This means that the cultural forms, knowledge, and authority that public sector workers utilize are also drawn from these realms. Just as Mexican nationals drew on the Christian religious symbol of the Virgin, which legitimated pan-state power and authority in Europe, to assert their authority as a nation-state, so education also becomes such a pan-national basis for the legitimation of an ethnic group within the postcolonial nation-state of Belize.

AN ETHNIC BEAUTY CONTEST: MISS GARIFUNA OF BELIZE

In discussing the Miss Garifuna contest I want to focus on the cultural production of the educated group and the metonymy of ethnicity—that is, the combination or concatenation of important ethnic symbols and the way in which these legitimate new social relations and subjectivities. In this process of combination and concatenation, social meaning is directed by individuals who serve as agents of change, linking the state to local groups. This beauty contest takes its meaning only within a more general consideration of the role of "ethnic" leadership of teachers, other civil servants, and local leaders during national holidays.

Carlos G. Vélez-Ibañez (1983) has demonstrated how the medial role played by local-level leaders in national integration is particularly evident in the rituals of national holidays. His description of a political movement (Congreso Restaurador de Colonos) based in an informal sector population in Mexico City shows how leaders of local movements are co-opted by elites. Vélez-Ibañez calls these holidays "intermediate rituals" expressing "proper relations" of political dominance and subservience between national and local level politicians and leaders of local movements. In these "intermediate rituals," local leaders serve not only in the role of "disciples" [my term] seated at the governor's right hand, but actually provide buses full of "the people" [my term], especially those who specialize in forms of cultural production: musicians, folk dancers, and others carrying decorations, banners, and flags (Vélez-Ibañez 1983, 207–208).[7]

Several similar rituals comprise the series of celebrations of the Belizean national holiday known as Garifuna Settlement Day, consolidating ethnic control for the educated leaders while promulgating national integration. In these rituals ethnicity is formulated symbolically to indicate a new combination of identities consistent with the medial position of the educated leaders. Established as a national holiday through the efforts of several public sector workers in Dangriga in the 1960s, this holiday has become a central celebration of "Garifunaness" for Garifuna throughout Belize and in migrant communities in the United States as well. A week of activities in Dangriga culminates on 19 November with a reenactment of the Garifuna making the voyage from Irumei, their island homeland, to the Central American shores: hence the name of the holiday, Garifuna Settlement

Day. The holiday celebrations are run by a committee composed almost entirely of schoolteachers. The committee organizes parades, speeches by local and national politicians, food fairs, and a contest for the selection of an ethnic "queen" known as "Miss Garifuna."

Past celebrations of the holiday have been preserved in multiple media: speeches of one year were published in a book entitled *Luwani Garifuna*[8] (1975), translated as *The Soul of the Garifuna*. This publication with another book of poetry, *Chulua Dan* (1977), translated as *It's About Time*, became the first "Garifuna" literature. The authors are notable male teachers and educators, young male Garifuna leaders, a teacher's wife, and an old Garifuna village woman renowned for her poetry. All of the writings in *Luwani Garifuna* are in English, with some of the poems in *Chulua Dan* appearing in both English and Garifuna. Although the expository forms of the speeches and the free verse of the poetry are English genres learned through formal education, most contain potent symbols or metaphors for the Garifuna, usually expressed in Garifuna words. This combination of Garifuna metaphors, drawn from the Garifuna language, combined with English literary genres and discourse are significant examples of the "metonymy" of ethnicity as it exists in textual form (see Wright 1986, 256–265, and 1990 for other examples and a detailed analysis).

The Miss Garifuna contest also makes such metonymic combinations in the many ethnic enactments that comprise the event. The format is that of a beauty contest: individual contestants display various costumes and perform individual dancing and speaking skills, while judges evaluate the performances and rank the contestants. Beauty is not the main criterion for evaluation of the contestants; instead, "ethnic knowledge" is the measure of the candidates. In the Belizean Miss Garifuna contest, however, the emphasis on "young girls," the individuated competition culminating in a question-answer format conducted by an "emcee," and the evaluation by "judges" quite clearly follow the Western form of a "beauty contest" (despite the stress on ethnicity or "Garifunaness," coined in the native language as *Garifunaduó* for the contest). The practice of publicly displaying young girls is in marked contrast to the older Garifuna practice of confining young girls to the private domain of the home and family, with older middle-aged women dominating the more public spheres (see, for example, Kerns 1983; Khan 1982, 1987). The presentation of ethnicity in this "beauty contest" format also alters the ethnic forms displayed: various Garifuna dance steps performed at rituals or for celebrations are demonstrated in sequence by each of the contestants, accompanied by Garifuna drummers who play the appropriate drum beats. Traditionally the most sacred of these Garifuna dances, *hungú-hungú*, is performed in the ten-day to two-week ritual curing ceremony known as *adugurahani* by a group of kin and fictive kin who dance, linked in a

circle, around a local temple or *dabuyaba*. This dance is not performed individually but always with a group of kin, who all must act to propitiate an
offended dead ancestor to restore order. Other traditional dances are
punta, *chumba*, and *sàmbéi*, performed at local level rituals such as a *beluria*
or wake celebration. These dances also stress group participation, although
individuals or couples may perform for the group in turn.[9] Although all the
traditional Garifuna dances are named and performed correctly in the
beauty contest, each has been truncated and individuated into a performance to be evaluated by the judges; they are now "dance steps" to be mas-
tered and performed devoid of their earlier social contexts and functions.

Like the speeches and poetry in the new Garifuna literature, the contest
speeches and question-answer format of the "beauty contest" are clearly a
non-Garifuna genre of speech. Like the dances, too, these are forms of "individual ethnic display" which the contestants perform for the judges and
for strangers (the local audience and the radio audience). This anonymous
individuation and performance by adolescents is familiar to young Belizeans and their teachers through education, where students perform individually while teachers judge.[10]

For the beauty contest, teachers and other public sector workers sit on
the panel of judges, usually those who have attained the highest positions
or have nationwide prestige. In 1983, the beauty contest was hosted by a
young male student teacher and featured a Garifuna dance group, *Igemeri*,
"The Light," composed primarily of young male and female teachers. The
judges of the contest were higher-level civil servants whose ages ranged from
thirty to forty; the majority were male. A chorus of singers, comprised of
older Garifuna women, sang the excerpts of traditional songs required for
the contest dance performances. Neither the old women who sang nor the
older men who provided the drumming necessary for the contest spoke
publicly. Both groups sat offstage where they could not be viewed by the
audience. Thus, although their music was essential to the contest and they
received an acknowledgment from the "emcee," the older men and women
formed an unseen and silenced backdrop.

The winner of the contest is the contestant who is judged best in speech-
making (in the Garifuna language), "traditional" dancing, and in answering
impromptu questions about Garifuna history or culture in both Garifuna
and English. The several Garifuna villages and two Garifuna towns, Dangriga and Punta Gorda, produce candidates for the contest; a victory is considered a win for the entire locality as the candidate becomes Miss Garifuna,
the exemplary daughter of the Garifuna.

To participate in the regional Miss Garifuna contest, towns and villages
of the southern Belizean regions of Toledo and Stann Creek hold local contests to determine their candidate among Garifuna girls in high school. The

regional contest is broadcast over Radio Belize, the national radio station, in conjunction with the celebration of Garifuna Settlement Day. International, national, and local dignitaries are invited to the contest. The announcer on Radio Belize provides a commentary on the contest and often gives explanations and historical references for the Garifuna role in Belizean history. The contest has existed since the early 1960s when it was much more like a standard beauty contest and the winner's title referred to the region, "Queen of the South," rather than the ethnic group.

Beauty contests are common in Belize and their presence is important in many political events. For example the celebration of Belizean independence in 1987 involved the presentation of some seven beauty queens, including not only the Queen of the Bay[11] and Miss Belize World but also three queens from Belizean emigrant communities in the United States (Miami, Los Angeles, and New York City).[12] In the past the grand prize for the Miss Garifuna contest was a free trip to the United States donated by a local airline. By 1982 some Garifuna objected to this prize, claiming that the reward for "ethnic excellence" should not be a trip to the United States. However, a new destination was not easily agreed upon.

Through the Miss Garifuna contest and its array of symbols, local intellectuals direct new social meanings and propagate these new symbolic formulations for society. The contest itself represents the direction of ethnic meaning by the teachers and civil servants who conduct, perform in, and judge the contest in a national forum. The contest creates nationally recognized leadership positions and styles of public display which differ from those of shamans, traditional specialists, union leaders, farmers, and respected elders among the Garifuna. Many Garifuna ethnic practices employed within this "beauty pageant" form are truncated fragments of older Garifuna ethnic practices reformulated in Western genres stressing individual performance.

Dance steps are taken from dances drawn from sacred and profane contexts and equated as "ethnic forms of dance" in the young girls' performances. The individual performances of young women become synecdochical references to the chorus of older women who sing excerpts from the traditional songs and the men who drum the appropriate sequences for the different dances. The contestants themselves do not sing or drum. The background function of the elders is underscored by their presence offstage. The old and young Garifuna combine to produce this ethnic presentation; yet it is the new "young" ethnic formulation that is center stage; the elderly and old forms are only referenced. In this symbolization, the contest at once creates new leadership positions for the public sector workers and recasts traditional ethnic practices in forms that align, rather than oppose, the authority of traditional specialists with that of the public sector workers.

Of course, the Miss Garifuna contest is not only a new symbolization of ethnicity but emblematization in a gendered form. As with the Virgin of

Guadalupe, a female symbol is employed to represent the group, rearticulating categories of person and group with a sexual symbol. Instead of a Virgin, this engendered symbol of the group is an ethnic queen, with the English title of Miss Garifuna. Just as Wolf's analysis of the Virgin indicates how this figure legitimated mestizos and their attempt at control of the Mexican nation-state in the seventeenth century, the Miss Garifuna contest legitimates the educated leaders and their ethnic nationalism. Writing thirty years after the publication of Wolf's "Virgin of Guadalupe" (1958), Joan Scott (1988, 88) explains how gender is critical symbolically and politically "as a story of the creation of political identity through representations of sexual differences." The Miss Garifuna contest proffers an exemplary daughter who provides fecund power to a new political identity, nationalized ethnicity. Gender[13] as a central social symbol becomes a vehicle to establish the political.

At the same time, the contest provides changed role models for young women. The former productive activities of women are truncated and folklorized. The young women may be asked to describe the growing and making of the cassava bread, or the implements involved in cassava production, but do not produce cassava. Gender is constituted through an individuated model and one that selects as an "ideal woman" a "young, educated woman."[14]

Like the speeches published in *Luwani Garifuna*, the Miss Garifuna contest is part of a national legitimation of the ethnic group. This is more obvious in the literate cultural production of the intellectuals, where nationalism is often fervently espoused and the rhetoric is clearly aimed at a national instead of a local audience. Forms of authority and individuation drawn from Western education are expressed in this ritual, as individuated performances of young women are evaluated by the judges, who are teachers or other public sector workers. However, the role of the educated ethnic leaders as organizers and judges of the beauty contest belies their role in the nation as the representatives of the ethnic group and the articulators of ethnicity with nationalism. As the hierarchy of the civil service is dominated by men, these men have claimed a stake in the state, transforming it to include their interest and that of their ethnic group. In these holiday speeches, performances, and the beauty contest, they establish a nationalized ethnicity and underscore their own role as ethnic and national leaders. For Miss Garifuna not only represents her ethnic group but her nation as well—she is Miss Garifuna of Belize.

The relationship of the metonymic formulations of ethnicity by the Garifuna intellectuals to an intergenerational language shift in the group as a whole can be more clearly seen in the Mini Miss Garifuna contests held in the elementary schools in the town. Although the Miss Garifuna contest is conducted entirely in Garifuna, the contests for elementary school girls are conducted entirely in English, consisting only in the question and answer format and the dance performances. And even though the requirement for speaking Garifuna in the Miss Garifuna contest for adolescents would imply that all contestants speak fluent Garifuna, in fact many have had to memorize their speeches with the help of older speakers. Some even falter in speaking during the contest. Several Garifuna remarked to me that in future contests, speeches in Garifuna would be eliminated, a certainty if the language shift proceeds on course.

The analysis of the metonymy of identity allows us to portray identities as they are combined and concatenated in symbolic formulation. Such combination makes for new social formations and concepts of people over time as well as the advancement of the political and economic interests of particular groups. In this chapter, I have indicated a triarchy of identities formulated in the Miss Garifuna contest. Nation, ethnic group, and gender are all symbolized in her, just as nation, ethnic group (mestizo-indio), and gender are symbolized in the Mexican Virgin. This metonymy of ethnicity makes for a new concatenation of identities in which Garifuna claim a past as well as a new present. Much about the symbolic forms comes from global as well as Garifuna society, making for new subjectivities (see Wolf 1990*b*, 593; Wright 1993). Here I depict how Garifuna at the local level recast themselves through combination and reproduction of these symbols. The symbol of Miss Garifuna can legitimize not only tradition but also change for a culture that accorded power and respect to male and female elders (Kerns 1983, 1985; Palacio 1987). For symbolized in the contest along with ethnicity, nation, and gender is also youth. Significantly, Mini Miss Garifuna, judged the "most Garifuna" of all the girls while speaking English to her Belizean audience, indicates that the power of both mother and mother tongue are now in the Garifuna past, rather than their future.

NOTES

I would like to thank Jane Schneider and Rayna Rapp (supernatural mother herself) for their patient editing and insightful comments on this paper, B. F. Williams for her discussions and writing on ethnicity, and Lorna Martin and Roy Cayetano for *wadumuruhanya*.

1. I have departed here from the more commonly used concept of metonymy to indicate part-whole references, equating metonymy with synecdoche. As Jakobson (1960, 370) reminds us, anything sequent is a simile, an observation particularly important in the polysemy of identity constitution. Thus we should note in ethnic formulations the combinations and concatenations of symbols which include nationalist, religious, and other identities to produce and legitimize meaning in context. White (1973, 31–35) rejects Jakobson's use for a related idea of the "container for the con-

tents" and identifies metonymy as apprehensions of phenomena existing in the modality of part-part relationships (not, as in metaphor, object-object relationships). Other scholars, especially folklorists (see Stoeltje 1981, 251–252, who also derives her analysis from Kenneth Burke), have utilized Jakobson's terminology, though not often emphasizing historical change as I do here. Although Jakobson does not explicitly discuss historical change, his formulation does stress context as well as the content of symbolic production.

2. This is the symbolic representation of the Garifuna landing in Central America; their exact arrival in Belize is uncertain. Many Garifuna arrived in Belize following wars in Honduras after the 1830s, and by 1841 they appear to have made a substantial settlement in Dangriga and Punta Gorda; they are cited in Belize City historical documents in 1911 (see Bolland 1986, 25–26). The British fought the Garifuna in their Caribbean home and deported them from the islands of St. Vincent in the Lesser Antilles (known to the Garifuna as Irumei) to Roatan, an island off the coast of Honduras, in 1797. However, Irumei is also represented in ritual and has a cosmological reference as well as a literal geographical reference to the island of St. Vincent.

3. Sociolinguists are now connecting the social processes of language shift with other processes of social change, particularly cultural production (see, for example, Gal 1991).

4. Most merchants in the southern region of Belize where the Garifuna reside are Chinese, who maintain international links to overseas Chinese suppliers and investors, primarily in Hong Kong. They dominate mercantile activity, effectively preventing any growth in this sector. A Salvadoran elite family has also opened small businesses in addition to their other financial endeavors.

5. Many Garifuna intellectuals pursued postsecondary education in the United States or Britain (see Wright 1986, 249–253, 401, for relevant statistics on education levels among Garifuna). Methodist church officials were often instrumental in securing scholarships for various Garifuna to continue their education in the United Kingdom, whereas Catholics sent their followers to the United States. This initial migration for education led to later migration for work. Educated Belizeans secured visas to emigrate more readily than their uneducated compatriots.

6. Fox (1990*b*, 7) points out that class analyses provide information on "material interests and structural conditions that enter into intellectual confrontations." Following Poulantzas, I have identified this group in Belize as a medial class rather than a bureaucratic elite as have other authors.

7. Although Vélez-Ibáñez does not use the term "cultural production" he clearly presages this concept by his application of ritual to political performances of the state. He characterizes these as "rituals of inequality," following Edmund Leach.

8. In the titles of these books and in other Garifuna words I have used an orthography for the Garifuna language developed by Roy Cayetano (1982). I prefer this orthography to that of Douglas Taylor, who transcribed all Garifuna words according to a strict phonemic analysis (see Taylor 1951, 1977). Cayetano is Garifuna and has based his orthography on the IPA symbols that are available on a standard typewriter and on English orthography. He differs from standard American IPA by representing the affricate |č| as |ch|. I have strayed from Cayetano's orthographic representation of the mid-central unrounded vowel in Garifuna as |u| by representing this as ʉ, sepa-

rating this vowel from the high back rounded vowel which I represent as |u|, since both of these phones have phonemic status. I have chosen to represent nasalization with the diacritic | ~ | while writing |n| where it is pronounced, differing from Cayetano's representation of nasalization as |n| whether it is a surface segment or not. I indicate stress only where it does not conform to the rule of stress in Garifuna: primary stress is predictable in Garifuna with a pattern of stress on the second syllable of words of three or more syllables and on the first syllable in two-syllable words.

9. During Beluria, wake, or holiday gatherings, solo performances of individual dancers are commented upon by members of the audience and some onlookers take the role of challengers as they take over the dance floor. These challenges discourage lengthy solo performances, however, and should a dancer fail to give up the floor, the audience may soon depart (see Gonzalez 1988, 78–79, 95n.; Wright 1986, 290–292).

10. The question and answer format of the beauty contest is particularly homologous with the emphasis on individualized task accomplishment and "teacher talk" (Cazdan 1979) in Westernized classrooms in Belize. Speaking of teachers in Samoa, Elinor Ochs (1988, 204) has described "teacher talk" as extensions of practices of speaking from Westernized care-giving to Westernized classrooms. In such talk, rhetorical questions simplify a proposition by breaking it down into two separate utterances and draw a child's attention to certain information (topic) in one utterance, then a predication (comment) in a separate utterance.

11. The Queen of the Bay, like other symbols of the Baymen, represents the British/Creole heritage (see Grant 1976, 52, 109, 273). This heritage was long celebrated on St. George's Cay Day, a holiday honoring the victory of the British against Spanish invaders in 1798. As the efforts of African slaves proved decisive in the fight against the invaders, this contribution has been put forth as a rationale for the rights of the black Creole population. The People's United Party regarded the celebration of St. George's Cay Day as National Day. Some factions wanted Belizean independence to occur on this day as well. The Queen of the Bay is an ethnic national symbol like that of Miss Garifuna but is a symbol in which the state has been displaced onto an ethnic group rather than the opposite, which is the case for Miss Garifuna.

12. Each of these beauty queens holds political significance, with Miss Belize World signifying the new national recognition in a world venue and the three queens from the United States signifying those transnational links and the emigrant communities' regard for their national origins. The Queen of the Bay described above may be representative of Creoles or the Belize City locale of the independence day celebration. Variations of the Miss Garifuna contest also occur in the Garifuna emigrant communities in New York and Los Angeles. The contests in New York that I have attended from 1981 to the present, however, are nostalgic reminders of Central America, with little of Garifuna "traditional culture" being celebrated.

13. See Jane Schneider's (1971) work on the symbolism of Virgins in Mediterranean cultures for a historical perspective on virginity and its significance. Also see Bynum 1986 and Scott 1988 on the complexity of gender as a social symbol. Ortner (1991, 185) asks us to see that there is a social power underside to sexual difference.

14. Or at the least, a woman certified by an educational elite. However, despite the emphasis on youth and individual performance in this context, the Miss Garifuna contest has also been invested with meanings from Garifuna culture in the rejection of beauty or ambiguous "talent" as criteria for evaluation. Would that all contests were so transformed. The young woman who won the contest in 1983 when I observed it was a stout village woman with few of the Western attributes of "beauty." Her determined speech won over both the judges and the crowd.

SIXTEEN

Being a Good Swede: National Identity as a Cultural Battleground

Orvar Löfgren

BEING NATIONAL

One night I was following a couple of detectives through the seediest streets of New York. Behind the bar in a dance hall I found a girl from Dalecarlia in folk costume. I went up and talked to her. The dialect revealed that she was of the true kind.

"You shouldn't wear this dress here," I told her.

"Why not?" said Brita. "There isn't a finer dress in the whole world."

"That's why," I said. "It's a national costume, which tells the world that Dalecarlia is the home of manly courage and female virtue. That's precisely why it is too good for a place like this."

And when I left, Dalecarlia-Brita sat crying with the apron over her head.

This confrontation with a Swedish immigrant in New York is described by Cecilia Milow (1904; my translation), member of the Swedish Society for Temperance and Popular Education, in a report from visits to Swedish immigrants in the United States at the beginning of this century. Her pamphlet was titled *Do You Love Your Country?* and was part of a drive for moral rearmament which swept over Sweden as people in the thousands voted with their feet and left for North America.

Mass migration from Sweden resulted in an intensive public debate. Pamphlets, social surveys, and government papers were produced, in order to come to terms with this drain on Swedish human resources. To a great extent the debate came to center around the lack of national loyalty as a major cause of the migration. A new patriotic consciousness among the masses was needed. It was during this period that epithets like "traitor to your country" were frequently heard, and it was also this period that produced the long-lived myth about Swedes being bad patriots.

It is this role of "the national" as a contested terrain, where solidarity with the state is affirmed or rejected and where competing versions of national identity are put forward by different social movements, classes, and interest groups, which is the focus of this paper. My examples are mainly taken from nineteenth- and twentieth-century Sweden, with a few American parallels, but my approach is rooted in the kind of historical and comparative anthropology that Eric R. Wolf has advocated over the years. The very nature of a chameleonic phenomenon like nationalism makes such an approach vital.

The interesting paradox in the emergence of modern nationalism is that it is an international ideology that is imported for national ends. This was the case at the end of the eighteenth century, when the revolutionary national experiments in Northern and Southern America inspired European intellectuals on the other side of the Atlantic, and this is still the case at the end of the twentieth century, when new national movements appear in the Third World or old national projects are called to life in the disintegrating Second World.

In this perspective we may view the ideology of nationalism as a gigantic do-it-yourself kit. Gradually a more and more detailed list of ideas is developed as to what elements make up a proper nation. Fixed conceptions emerged in the nineteenth century about how a cultural heritage should be shaped, how a national anthem should sound, and what a flag should look like. National galleries were founded; national literature was published. In this parallel work of nation-building, cultural matrices were freely borrowed across national frontiers. For example, national museums of folk culture were built in Europe, following the model in Berlin, and areas of native beauty were selected for transformation—after an American idea—into national parks (see the discussion in Löfgren 1989).

The interesting point is the ways in which national projects are made transnational, are imported and transformed into new, unique national settings. There is a problem of timing here which is crucial. Some nations manage to appear as self-evident, God-given creations rather than historical accidents, whereas others make their claims at the wrong time and in the wrong form. That is why many of today's nations include a number of failed or frustrated national projects, whose advocates either bide their time or have given up completely. It is this national latency that constantly causes political surprises—sudden revivals and new confrontations.

The problem is simply that the nations that see themselves as "old" products of natural growth can easily adopt an ironizing, big-brother attitude to more recent nation-building. This aloof stance often contains a more or less conscious evolutionary idea: that nationalists in the remains of Eastern Europe or in the Third World are representatives of an old-fashioned national rhetoric. They parade in folk costume and wave their flags in a way that the first nations abandoned long ago.

We thus reach the other great paradox of nationalism, that it can survive by ostensibly withering away. Nationalism has an ability to be mobilized—

as both idea and practice—by widely diverse political groupings. In this adaptability it changes form in a way that often means that it appears to be dead or fading.

A historical anthropology of nation-building thus needs to explore the complex relations between culture and power. We must look at the ways in which the cultural ideology of nationalism has been linked with the institution of statehood in the evolution of the modern nation-state, one of the most successful political structures developed over the last centuries. The analysis of the making of this institutional framework calls for the kind of approach Eric Wolf has advocated in his 1991 essay "Facing Power: Old Insights, New Questions." He argues that we need to pay much more attention to the ways in which power structures are formed, reproduced, and challenged over time, in a way that combines a study of the social and political organization of power with a cultural analysis of its symbolism. The making and constant remaking of the modern nation-state seem to me a most fruitful arena for the kind of study he advocates.

To understand why the nation-state has often been such a successful machine for political mobilization and cultural homogenization, displacing or overruling other traditional loyalties and allegiances, we have to develop a broad approach that includes studies not only of how the national framework is generated and used in political struggles and administrative procedures but also of how the nation-state is materialized in the everyday life of the ordinary citizen. As Wolf has underlined in an earlier work (1982*a*, 388ff.), we need to study ideology as a social process, examining the ways in which (in this case) nationalism is articulated and put to work in different cultural domains and social situations.

My general aim is thus to explore some of the cultural processes behind the nationalization of citizens on several levels: how is the nation-state made visible and tangible in everyday life, what kind of ties are created between the state and its citizens, and what kinds of cultural sharing exist between fellow countrymen?

THE DISINTEGRATING NATION

In 1911 five hundred Swedish schoolchildren were asked "What person whom you have seen, heard, or read about would you like to emulate if you could?" In this listing of culture heroes the three most popular suggestions turned out to be martial kings of Sweden's heroic past: Gustavus Adolphus who fought the Papists during the Thirty Years' War in Germany, Gustavus Vasa who saved the country from the Danes, and Charles XII who tried to conquer Russia (Andolf 1985). The list suggests that the traditional national rhetoric emphasizing the glorious past and the role of monarchy as a national rallying point was still working—or was it?

A couple of years earlier another public survey gave a different picture. As part of a major government inquiry into the causes of Swedish emigration a collection of letters from abroad was published. A number of Swedish immigrants in the United States had been asked to give their view of the old motherland and state their reasons for leaving it.

The frustration and anger aired in these letters mainly focus on the outmoded political structure of Sweden. There are bitter memories of being bawled out by the haughty lieutenant during national service, being ridiculed by the local schoolmaster or admonished by the pompous village vicar, or just the knowledge that one was subject to the whims of those in power: in short, people remember being treated as second-class citizens without political rights. (The most common reason given for emigration is to escape the dreaded military service, which was not seen as a national duty but as a compulsory ordeal.) In comparison with the United States, Sweden is depicted in these letters as a decaying, ossified monarchy, hopelessly out of touch with modern realities.

Similar memories of humiliations surface in working-class life histories from those who stayed behind in early twentieth-century Sweden, and the interesting thing is that it is precisely those institutions that had once been seen as tools of national integration that are most severely criticized: the Lutheran state church, national military service, school, the royal family. The representatives of these institutions are not seen as symbols of unity. They stand for a system where workers and peasants cannot get a fair hearing or just treatment. Both the letters and the life histories thus describe a system of integration or a machine for producing loyalty which is crumbling: old ties of allegiance are no longer working.

For many contemporary observers it seemed as if the nation was falling apart. Some of their worried rhetoric belongs to a classic genre—the disintegrating nation—a type of discourse that has been with us for most of the history of modern nationalism. It would be more exact to say that what we are witnessing here is a power struggle between the old conservatives and the new radical and liberal forces that are on the attack. Conservative thinkers saw the lack of both national pride and loyalty to the state among the masses as the roots of the problem. Their remedy was an intensified national rhetoric, emphasizing the glorious past and the role of the monarch as the national rallying point, but these patriotic appeals no longer worked. On the whole, the very fact that these were years of intense national rhetoric tells us that old allegiances were being questioned.

In these turbulent times liberal intellectuals accused the conservatives of propagating an outdated chauvinist message of national loyalty. A new less bombastic rhetoric was needed which could unite the nation and stand above class strife. In this relocation of the national discourse the focus was shifted to a different arena.

NATIONALIZING NATURE

In the same year as the proposal for a national monument, a more successful public appeal was made, with a proposal in parliament for the creation of national parks in Sweden. This idea had a strong patriotic flavor. In Sweden at the turn of the century there was a strong belief in nature and its appreciation as an educational tool. In the proposed law on nature conservation of 1909 it was pointed out how important it was that the new national parks should be "visual material for teaching patriotism" (Sörlin 1988, 82).

Elsewhere I have discussed the ways in which nature was nationalized step by step during the nineteenth century and charged with new symbolic meanings (Löfgren 1990), but it was in the decades around 1900 that this process really accelerated. The nationalization of the landscape became an important part of the construction of a national heritage. Certain landscapes and scenes were selected as "typical" and charged with powerful symbolic meanings, through a process of cultural condensation.

The national landscape was discovered through collaboration between painters, authors, travelers, and political debaters. It was a process that transformed everyday natural scenes into "homelands," permeated with history and national symbolism. This sacralization is seen in the new national anthem, which also mirrors the Swedish focus on nature:

> Thou ancient, thou free-born, thou mountainous North!
> Thou silent, thou beauteous and joyful!
> I hail thee, o fairest of lands upon earth,
> Thy sun, thy heavens, and thy verdant climes.

The praise of the mountains which introduces the Swedish national anthem is due more to the emotional than to the topographic map. Most of Sweden is rather flat with few mountains, yet here we find the same alpine focus as in the 1909 proposal for national parks, which applied primarily to the mountain regions. It could be said that the idea of national parks gained currency at the same time that the cult of the mountain as a landscape type culminated around the turn of the century. The eighteenth-century observer scarcely saw any patriotic or aesthetic value in the mountains.

The mountain wilderness represented a majestic and heroic nature, but in general the new symbolic landscapes turned out to be more intimate sceneries, reflecting the new and more low-key nationalism. This is the period when *the* most popular representation of Sweden developed: a scene with a humble, red cottage in a meadow of wildflowers at the edge of the forest, facing a silent lake. Today, a mere reference to "the little red cottage" conjures up a whole universe of images and associations in Swedish life and thought.

Such examples show how the nationalization of the landscape can be seen as a process of crystallization: typically Swedish sceneries have gradually been demarcated and concentrated in symbolic spaces. This selection and stereotyping has taken place through a number of media that have become instruments in an educational process. This is achieved in part through the consumption of music, pictures, and texts in every conceivable form, ranging from geography teaching in school to oil paintings in museums or the prints found in the home—from oleographs to picture postcards. It is also achieved through the growth of mass tourism and pilgrimages to particularly Swedish landscapes. In this way images of the landscape have been blended with landscape experiences in a very powerful way.

National identification in a way became more private and personal: love of nature opened up a new emotional territory in which different experiences could be had. But the nationalization of nature also created a new cultural battleground. As the Swedish landscape became a more sacred territory a new middle-class discourse on the correct ways of experiencing and handling nature emerged. On the one hand, the love of nature was naturalized—it was argued that it was a traditional and inbred trait in the Swedish national mentality. On the other hand, peasants and workers could be accused of lack of reverence or sophistication in their ways of using or experiencing nature. They showed the wrong love or not enough love for this national heritage, which meant that the masses had to be educated through everything from school excursions to the use of urban parks.

Politically, the nationalization of nature thus signaled a shift from a more vociferous conservative rhetoric to a more subdued liberal one in Sweden, but the new nature-loving liberals often failed to see how they came to introduce a new normative element about the proper ways of being a good Swede.

MODERNITY AS A NATIONAL PROJECT

With the emergence of a new political force, the Swedish Social Democrats, the politics of nation-building came to be redefined in an even more radical way.

At the turn of the century the growing labor movement was often accused of a lack of national loyalty. As the Social Democrats slowly established themselves as a political force, the accusations of putting class before national interests increased. The Social Democrats riposted by accusing the conservatives of using patriotic appeals to mask the interests of the old, ruling elite. The early twentieth century can be seen as a battle about who was acting in the best interests of the nation; compared to most other European left wing movements, the Swedish party was much more successful in wresting the national argument from conservative hands.

When the Social Democrats finally came to power in 1932 they created a new political rhetoric and practice, which has often been mistakenly labeled as internationalist. Their aim was to develop a welfare state based upon new ties between Swedes and the state, new forms of collective action and cultural sharing. In this phase of nation-building three concepts became central: democracy, citizenship, and modernity.

There is a large, interdisciplinary debate on the interesting relationships between nationalism and democracy in the nineteenth and twentieth centuries. The sociologist Zygmunt Bauman, among others, has discussed how the nationalization of the state blended the issue of political loyalty and trustworthiness with that of assimilation and cultural homogenization. In this process citizenship and cultural conformity tended to merge—"the second was perceived as the condition, but also as a means to attain the first" (Bauman 1990, 161).

The concept of citizenship was a child of the French Revolution and carried the idea of a new form of relationship between state and individual. The old allegiance to the king was to give way to a more abstract loyalty to the nation and the state. The traditional loyal *subject* to the king should be transformed into a modern citizen—a mature democratic individual with certain civic rights and obligations. The rhetoric of citizenship and the actual production of citizens took different forms in different national settings during the nineteenth century (see Bendix 1964; Hammar 1990), but a crucial feature of the process was the idea of reciprocity between the state and the individual. Only the state could offer (or withdraw) the rights of citizenship, but this gift had a counterclaim built into it, a claim to certain duties and loyalties.

In Sweden, where voting rights were extended to all men in 1909 and to women in 1921, the concept of the democratic citizen became especially powerful during the 1920s and 1930s. Here we also find the linking of the idea of the democratic citizen with that of the modern individual. Louis Dumont has pointed out that the democratic nation-state is usually defined both as a *collection of individuals* (a bounded group of equals sharing "national" traits) and as a *collective individual* (the nation as a single subject with a will, a destiny; see the discussion in Handler and Linnekin 1984, 277ff.). This paradoxical link between individualism and a new collectivism, as subjects are transformed into citizens, is very evident in Swedish interwar politics. The Social Democrats had visions of a new nation—a people's home as it was called—populated by modern individuals, who first had to be freed from traditional collective loyalties and identities in order to be nationalized into the new collective of modern citizens: a process of decollectivization and recollectivization.

In this project being modern was crucial. The making of the new welfare state carried the idea of collective progress: a nation moving united into the future. Old habits and traditions had to be discarded, old rhetoric about the glorious past had to be exchanged for visions of a common future. The good

Swede was a modern Swede, looking forward rather than backward. To be a traditionalist was to lag behind, to slow down the pace of modernization and to let the nation down. Such accusations could be directed toward the old elite clinging to traditional privileges, but also to peasants who were suspicious of modern times.

It has often been said that the Social Democrats replaced old national values and heritage with an ideology of internationalism and modernity, but I would argue that they developed new and even more powerful tools of homogenization and nationalization. Modernity became a very Swedish project, taking on national forms, which were very effective because they were based more upon everyday practice than ideological statements or national rhetoric. In the making of the new Sweden, there emerged new ties of dependence, loyalty, and sharing, as well as a new national pride.

It is important to see this integration process as occurring on several, very different levels. Through schools and mass media a new civic spirit was fostered. Novel kinds of symbolic or mental images of the nation were produced (creating a new kind of imagery and a new kind of "imagined community," to use Benedict Anderson's [1983] term). Even more important than this "mentalizing of the nation" were the ways in which the welfare state was materialized in administrative routines and bureaucratic procedures. The new modern citizens found messages, claims, and gifts from the state in their mail more and more frequently, learned to fill in tax forms and to apply for home building loans or pensions, had their health tested, answered questionnaires from the school about their children, and so forth.

Another often overlooked dimension of integration was the construction of new physical structures, linking households and communities to wider systems. The welfare state became most visible in new sewage projects, in national radio broadcasts, in road construction, and in the installation of electricity and telephone lines. This modernization process was often both described and experienced in the symbolic terms of binding the nation together.

In the 1930s the collective individual was also created through new habits and routines. Swedes learned to do things together: singing, exercising, hiking. This was, for example, the great period of community singing and gymnastics through which new feelings of collectivity and national sharing became part of the body as well as the mind (see Frykman 1992.) In the new craze for biking and camping during the summer holidays, Swedes from different classes met on the roads, united in a common quest for Swedish sights and experiences. People *made* themselves Swedish and experienced the nation in new ways.

There are of course many parallels to this modernizing process, sometimes labeled "the nationalization of the masses," but on the whole the debate has tended to focus too much on processes of assimilation and social control, or on the more noticeable totalitarian aspects of this phase of nation-building, drawing, for example, on the German and Italian Fascist experience. But the control aspect must not overshadow the fact that the making of the modern citizen had a very important emancipatory side as well. In becoming integrated through new and much denser relations with the state, citizens not only became more dependent but also acquired a new cultural competence in handling bureaucratic structures. People learned not only about their duties but also how to stand up for their rights.

LOCATING "THE NATIONAL"

In 1985 an international survey asked persons aged eighteen to twenty-four what they were most proud of in their countries. Young people in Sweden put nature at the top of the list, followed by "the welfare system." If we compare Swedish responses with United States responses we find both a different emphasis and a different symbolic language. The young Americans questioned were most proud of their history and national heritage. Such surveys would produce various answers during varying periods of national life, but they may also illustrate the ways in which "the national" is located in different arenas or cultural registers—not only between nations but also between social groups and classes.

The Swedish and American answers tell us something about the similarities and differences in the ways in which culture has been nationalized and how different styles and dialects of national discourse have developed. In Sweden love of the native land has to a greater extent than in many other countries been expressed in the metaphorical language of the love of nature, whereas the national history has been a less prominent part of the national symbolic estate. In contrast, the making and remaking of an American heritage has been discussed from many aspects (see Lamme 1989; Lowenthal 1983). One reason why this aspect of nation-building is more visible in the United States has to do with the very conscious efforts to develop a sense of historical belonging in the young immigrant nation.

Today, history is in many ways much more present and much more institutionalized in the United States than in Sweden. Compared with many European nations, America has built up a much more obligatory set of national sites, made for pilgrimage and remembrance: the past has become highly visible in many ways. Another kind of national visibility is found in the national toponymy, which, as the American geographer Wilbur Zelinsky (1983, 1986) has pointed out, seems more marked in the United States than elsewhere. Nationalistic names were bestowed upon all kinds of objects: people, firms, organizations, consumer goods, schools and other buildings, highways, streets, communities, and so on—names taken mainly from the American pantheon of culture heroes.

Turning to the ways in which the landscape has been nationalized in the

United States, there are also striking differences. In a paper on symbolic landscapes the geographer D. W. Meinig has discussed the idealization of American communities, stressing the central role two settings have acquired in American iconography. He points out that a steepled church set in a frame of white houses, elms, and maples around a common has become the most typical representation of traditional America. This New England scenery is found on Christmas cards, in children's books, in films and cartoons, often symbolizing the national hearth and heart. The other setting is Main Street in Middle America, also mass-mediated in many versions. Both settings have over time become charged with specific moral meanings: the village often standing as a model for "an intimate, family-centered, God-fearing, morally conscious, industrious, thrifty, democratic community" (Meinig 1979, 165), and Main Street for the backbone of America, the landscape of small-town and also small-business virtues.

The same moral and emotional dimension is found in definitions of national landscapes. In both Sweden and the United States the cult of the wilderness came to acquire strong national overtones during the nineteenth century, but the moral message in the symbolic uses of the wild was not the same. (See the discussions in Batteau 1990; Löfgren 1990.)

If we turn to the ways in which modernity was nationalized in the two countries, especially during the interwar years, we again find differences and similarities. In both countries a new kind of imaginary community was developed through the idea of an individual collective of modern citizens with similar aspirations, habits, and standards of normality (see Löfgren 1992). Let me just give one example of this parallel development. In 1930 the big commercial fair in Stockholm carried the message of modern functionalism to its visitors, but more important, this fair also emphasized new standards of normality, through an exhibition of "the typical Swede," jokingly termed "Mr. Medelsvensson" (Average-Swanson). This message was similar to that of the New York World Fair of 1939–1940, which, as Warren Susman (1984, 214) has pointed out, was marketed as everyman's fair, exploring the life of "the plain American citizen."

As in Sweden, an increased self-consciousness and self-exploration emerged in the public debate of the twenties and thirties. The new cultural language of national unity was mirrored in an interest in two personalities: *the average American*, living in "typical America," and *the common American*, residing in "real America." Susman (1984, 213) notes how concepts like "the American way of life," "the American Dream," and "the man on the street" were invented or became more popular during these years. This was also the period when Mr. Gallup started to survey how the nation thought, acted, and lived, and also a time when the media and market focused on the idea of the standardization and homogenization of American life.

If opinion polls and market research signaled one contribution of the social sciences to national self-understanding, anthropology provided the other. There was a general shift away from High Culture to American cultures, a new ethnographic interest emphasized in the frequent use of concepts like "plain Americans," "ordinary life," and "common folks" (see the discussion in Perry 1984, 319ff.). Parallel to the search for "the typical America" there developed an ethnographic quest for "real America," a different kind of mainstream, symbolized by projects like Staughton Lynd's *Middletown* and W. Lloyd Warner's *Yankee City*. This was a search for a different kind of "folk" than that of the folklorist's expeditions to the Appalachians at the turn of the century. At that time the quest was for the authentic English heritage, a folk culture that had to be salvaged and reproduced in order to stem the disintegrating forces both from Tin Pan Alley and from the new waves of proletarian immigrants (see Whisnant 1983).

That this process of cultural nation-building was particular to America is suggested by Swedish responses to it. When Swedes look at the national rhetoric of the United States it is often described as much louder and more patriotic (or even chauvinist) than back home. American politicians are seen as using a language that would be utterly out of place in the Swedish public debate, and in comparison with the very tame celebrations of the Swedish national holiday, the Fourth of July stands out as a massive outburst of rhetoric, festivity, and fireworks.

Such comparisons may get trapped in measurements of patriotic fervor or chauvinist tendencies. As I have tried to show they rather illustrate national variations and traditions in the discourse of "the national." Swedishness and Americanness are expressed in different cultural registers and through different symbolic languages. When Swedes describe Americans as a nation of flag-wavers and marvel at the morning flag ritual in American classrooms, they tend to forget that in Sweden, although the use of the national flag may be rather limited in public life, it is extremely common in the private rituals of family life. There are far more flags found in gardens, on birthday cakes, and in Christmas trees in Sweden than in the United States. Such seemingly trivial details may tell us quite a lot about the ways in which "the national" is both ritualized and made part of everyday life.

Sweden, which was one of the most heavily militarized nations of Europe during the seventeenth and eighteenth centuries, waging one war after the other on the Continent, has not been to war since 1814. This historical transformation has of course radically changed the national self-representation in the same way that it would be impossible to understand the American national discourse without reference to the wartime experiences from Gettysburg to Kuwait.

The transformation of Sweden into a nation redefining itself as a neutral outsider has been a gradual process, but not without its paradoxes. Military parades have disappeared from the national arena, but twentieth-century neutrality has been combined with a brisk and profitable arms trade, and it is hardly a coincidence that competitive international sport has become an extremely important arena for expressions of national pride. Sports commentators are allowed to use a language that in any other setting would be described as chauvinistic, bombastic, or even racist (see the discussion in Ehn 1989).

My examples have been chosen in order to illustrate how the siting (and constant relocation) of "the national" may vary between nations like Sweden and the United States. By using a historical perspective I have underlined the changing phases of nation-building. In Sweden the glorious military past was replaced with the emotional landscape, the old national heroes gave way to the celebrations of the common man, the modern citizen, and the national future took the place of the historical heritage. In the same way the processes of integration changed, as old loyalties were replaced by new ones.

Comparing two so different national formations as Sweden and the United States may be rather like comparing apples and pears, but my point is that such comparisons are necessary if we want to develop a more systematic analysis of the cultural politics of nation-building in the nineteenth and twentieth centuries. The comparative perspective may help us to understand the actual siting of the national experience, the arenas and situations in which national loyalty is materialized, expressed, or contested. The historical perspective makes it possible to see how each new generation creates its own definition not only of the national heritage but also of national loyalty. Such a perspective may enable us to escape a narrative structure in which nations are born, age, or disintegrate, and instead focus on the constantly changing patterns of national culture-building.

IDEOLOGY AND EXPERIENCE

I began by emphasizing the dialectics of culture and power, with reference to Eric Wolf's discussion. The very successful marriage between the idea of a national culture and the formation of the modern state illustrates both how culture is empowered by its connection to a state structure and how it is elevated to represent "national interests" or becomes part of "a national way" or "national values." At the same time, state claims of loyalty and support from its citizens are legitimized by cultural arguments in a way that makes state politics without the framework of a nation-state rather difficult. The history of nation-building illustrates how a territorial dimension is interwoven with the political institution of the state and the cultural dimension of identification. National identity is not only a question of a social label or shared knowledge, but also of an emotional commitment, a moral investment, a sense of belonging which makes this identification so powerful.

By linking the study of culture and power, we are also forced to focus on the ways in which "the national" has always been a cultural battleground, a contested terrain where different actors and interest groups are confronted. Furthermore, we must avoid a type of cultural analysis which limits itself to the study of symbolism and rhetoric. As Eric Wolf points out, we need to look at the ways in which cultural arguments become powerful through practice, how ideology is anchored in social life: "Symbolic work is never done, achieves no final solution. The cultural assertion that the world is shaped in this way and not in some other has to be repeated and enacted, lest it be questioned and denied" (Wolf 1990b, 18).

In my examples I have illustrated the ways in which symbols are used and appropriated for very different ends and also how ideology is constantly confronted by experience. Let me give one final example of this.

During the last decades Sweden has become an immigrant nation. Today, roughly 10 percent of the population stems from recent waves of migration. The official policy in handling this new situation has been one of cultural pluralism, shying away from too strong an emphasis on the need to conform to Swedish values. Against this idea of the new ethnic mix enriching the Swedish national experience stands a more and more often voiced popular fear of the threat to Swedish culture. Both arguments may underrate the ways in which the Swedish experience is assimilating immigrants.

Immigrant groups may apply for state funds to create local associations for celebrating their own cultural heritage, but as a recent study (Lundberg and Svanberg in press) has shown, once an association is formed with this kind of assistance it has to comply with all the rules and routines that traditionally structure the life of popular associations in Sweden (the ways in which the club should be organized, committees elected, how its activities must cater to children and women as well as men, and so on). This illustrates the ways in which a (well-meaning) rhetoric of cultural pluralism is effectively counteracted by a very Swedish practice.

One thing we can learn from a comparative study of national integration is the specific Swedishness of this national experience. Compared to the social and cultural organization of national expressions in the United States, "the national" is less visible in Swedish public life. National identity and emotions are articulated more in private, embedded in the routines of everyday life. Swedish values are also hidden in a language of modernity and rationality. The indirectness of this national language makes it in many ways a very powerful instrument of Swedification: there are many written but more unwritten rules about how to be a good Swede.

SEVENTEEN

Cultural Dis-Integration and the Invention of New Peace-Fares

Richard G. Fox

In an article summarizing the anthropological literature on war making, Eric R. Wolf (1987*a*) reviews the history of innovations in human destruction and destructiveness. Wolf links these innovations in war to major transformations in the modes of production, as cultures evolve from kin-based to tributary and then to capitalist production modes. At the same time, he suggests that innovative possibilities of "peace-fare" may arise along with these new forms of warfare (Wolf 1987*a*, 141).

Current research in the anthropology of war and peace does not entertain Wolf's question about the emergence of new forms of peace-fare. The reason, I believe, is that we have, under the rubric of the anthropology of peace and war, in fact mostly studied war. Some studies emphasize the cross-cultural variability of warfare and the technological or social structural evolution of collective violence (see Fried, Harris, and Murphy 1968; Otterbein 1970; see also the literature reviews in Greenhouse 1987; Wolf 1987*a*). Other studies do "thick descriptions" of the cultural meanings sustaining warfare, as, for example, the "frames of mind" (Pitt 1989, xv), the symbolic forms (Foster 1988, 189), the valuation of social order (Greenhouse 1986), and even the "institutionalized insanity" (Nader 1989, 80) that legitimate violence and war in American society or any other.

This nearly exclusive emphasis on collective violence comes about because "peace" is too often treated as a residual category in our culture and in our scholarship. That is, peace means nothing more than the absence of collective violence, and peace as a cultural construction remains underexplored and untheorized. The definition of peace is therefore problematic or artifactual (Young 1990, 6), and the major model sustaining scholarship, both within and outside anthropology, is the pursuit of ever-better forms of conflict resolution (see Foster and Rubinstein 1986, xii; Turner 1989, 175).

Alice Kehoe (1986) criticizes this conflict-resolution literature as culture-bound. The universal method of resolving conflict it hopes to establish or discover has a Western bias at its base, which Kehoe contrasts with alternative assumptions from the Third and Fourth worlds.

This literature is also time-bound, as Peter J. Taylor (1991) suggests. Most such studies, Taylor argues, operate with implicit definitions of peace either as "cease-fire" or "armistice"—that is, peace means the immediate cessation of war; or peace is taken as equivalent to "pacification"—that is, peace means a political process by which war may be prevented for a longer term, beyond an immediate armistice. These definitions make little allowance for the possibility that new forms of peace-fare can appear and that they can change the definition both of conflict and of resolution.

Taylor advances a third definition of peace, which is appropriate for understanding the *longue durée* over which humanity has attempted to refashion social life for the better. This "perpetual peace" (a term Taylor adopts from Johannnes Galtung) depends on revolutionary changes "whereby the fundamental structures of the social system negate violence. ... The logic of the system no longer rewards violence as a means of social change" (Taylor 1991, 80). Taylor, again following Galtung, emphasizes the "infrastructural" revolution that must undergird perpetual peace: material plenty, ecological conservation, population constraints, and the like.

An anthropology of peace-fares suggests that other necessary radical changes besides these infrastructural ones must be recognized, particularly if we wish to avoid a simpleminded "base-superstructure" distinction. For perpetual peace-fares to develop, infrastructural change is obviously necessary, but so also is the emergence of novel cultural understandings, for they too are material conditions that can redefine human capacities, in this case, the cultural capacity to live at peace in the longue durée. My premise is that peace is a cultural construction and can be (has been) inventively redefined from time to time. This premise generates the following question: what is the process of cultural invention by which new definitions of peace and violence, new forms of peace-fare, develop? I hope to answer this question here by chronicling a past instance: Gandhi's invention of nonviolent resistance within the context of, and in response to, his lived experience with the cultural definitions of violence (and nonviolence) in his day.

THE DIS-INTEGRATION OF CULTURE

My approach to Gandhi's invention of *satyagraha* here is quite different from that in my earlier work. Previously, I argued that individual innovations can truly transform mass social movements—that Gandhi and Gandhism did, in fact, make Indian nationalism different (Fox 1989). I also outlined the contingencies by which individual innovations, once invented, take off at the collective level—this through a class analysis of Gandhism, both before and after independence, including how it came to be hijacked by a violent Hindu nationalism in India today (Fox 1989, 1990*a*). In addition, I dissected the innovator we label "Gandhi" into the many predecessors and contemporaries who contributed to what we "know" as his discovery (see Fox 1989, chap. 7).

There remains an important—and antecedent—question, the one that informs this paper, namely, how Gandhi's individual invention was produced as he encountered and struggled with worldly experience, including existing forms of violence, social movements, and cultural (mis)understandings. Before new cultural understandings have (public) authority they have (private) authors; that is, new cultural understandings have to start out as individual projects, although these individual projects always emerge from the existing material and experiential conditions. As Wolf notes, "A culture is ... better seen as a series of processes that construct, reconstruct, and dismantle cultural materials, in response to identifiable determinants" (1982*a*, 387).

Anthropologists have recently begun to reconceive culture in line with Wolf's admonition. The "anthropology of practice," the "construction of culture," and the "invention of tradition" are labels for this significant revision of the culture concept. Culture now appears as a set of habitual practices or a consciousness under active construction by which individuals interpret the world around them. Or, in a more behavioral view, it is a tool kit or a set of scenarios that individuals use to implement or to stage their daily life (see Bourdieu 1977; Ortner 1984; Sahlins 1981). Culture in this view does not have the hard, fully formed, or configured quality attributed to it by anthropology two generations ago. Rather, culture is rubbery and mobile; it is the outcome of a constant process of cultural production.

Elsewhere, I have suggested the phrase "culture in the making." By it, I mean to conceive of culture as more rubbery and mobile than is usually accepted even in the revised conception of culture adopted by many anthropologists today (Fox 1985; also see Fox 1989, 1990*b*, for further discussion). If we want to say more about the human capacity for developing new forms of peace-fare today (as well as in the past), I believe we have to "dis-integrate" the culture concept even more, that is, we have to move much further away from any unexamined notion of society as integrated or culture as constitutive.

In this essay, I wish to show that culture is constantly being dis-integrated and reintegrated as individuals and groups confront their social worlds and try to (re)form them. To adequately dis-integrate the culture concept, not only is it useful to recognize that culture is constructed and practiced, as is now fairly widely accepted in anthropology, it is also helpful to see it as authored—and in this process, even broken into pieces and creatively reintegrated.[1] Recognizing culture as authored leads to research that locates the agents by which culture gets dis-integrated and (re)constructed (and, necessarily, assumes that [some] humans are effective cultural innovators; see Fox 1989). It works against a "leveling" tendency in anthropology, by which we studied the culture of an undifferentiated People rather than the diverse people literally "making up" a culture (for some precedents in anthropology, see Lesser 1978 [1933]; Wallace 1978, 478–485).[2]

Accepting the possibility that culture can be broken into pieces means that new combinations of cultural forms can be invented as institutions, customs, beliefs, and artifacts undergo a process of authorship. Through the actions of an innovator, odd bits of cultural belief and/or practice may get separated from an existing cultural complex, and they may combine with other cultural complexes to form new institutions, beliefs, and artifacts. Accepting culture as breakable speaks even more strongly against an erector-set rigidity to culture and against an assumption of functional integration that disallows the historical process of innovation and the social role of innovator.

The following pages show the way in which an innovative cultural form, Gandhian nonviolence, came to be authored out of Gandhi's everyday experiences, that is, as he dis-integrated existing cultural beliefs and practices and put them into new combination.

NONVIOLENT RESISTANCE AS CULTURAL INVENTION

The invention of nonviolent resistance is a most significant cultural innovation in the twentieth century, certainly the most promising fulfillment of Wolf's hope that new possibilities for warfare give rise to new ways toward peace. Today, we see that this cultural invention has attained a marvelous facticity, not only in belief but also in practice (much like Marx's invention of the proletariat, Freud's of the Unconscious, and Pasteur's of the microbe, as Bruno Latour [1988, 53] tells us). Few people in the late twentieth century need to be convinced that this human capacity exists. We see it validated, reinterpreted, even hijacked by groups like Earth First!, Mitch Snyder's Society for Creative Nonviolence, the radical animal rights advocates, the Pro-Life movement, and many others. Some organizations assert a Gandhian authority no matter what they do; others recognize no human origin and take the technique for granted or from God. What better measure of how deeply it has transformed our world than that nonviolent resistance is naturalized or "celestialized" and that its eponymous inventor is often mythologized or even forgotten.

The cultural invention of nonviolent resistance altered forever our global understanding of aggression, violence, passivity, peace, war, and civil resistance. It did so by inventing—that is, by asserting that there really was—a third human capacity, intermediate between physical aggression and passive nonresistance. I say "invented" to emphasize the innovative cultural construction, but Gandhi would have said he discovered this hitherto poorly known human trait from a series of experiments (his term again) he made between about 1896 and 1919. After its invention, it is all too easy to find anticipations or earlier exemplars of nonviolent resistance, for Whiggish history is not only a distinctive (and misleading) form of scholarship but also a fairly common way that people misrepresent the past.

Gandhi isolated the capacity for nonviolent resistance in himself first and gave it a distinctive name, satyagraha, or soul force. He disaggregated it from other capacities such as passive resistance or Christian nonresistance. This capacity exists in all humans, Gandhi believed, but, like any other part of the body, it has to be built up by exercise; it requires "long training in self-denial and appreciation of the hidden forces within ourselves" (*Collected Works of Mahatma Gandhi*, hereafter *CWG*, XXXI 1926, 439).

Satyagraha depends on a regimen of spiritual weight training. At its most muscular, nonviolent resistance offers a new alternative to humanity, in-between aggression and passivity: it is warlike but not warfaring, peaceful but not puny. Gandhian nonviolence provided an alternative construction of human capacity in two other important ways: satyagraha occupied a new, middle ground between mass warfare and individual martyrdom and between divinely inspired nonresistance and secular revolutionary acts.

GANDHIAN DIS-INTEGRATION AND RECOMBINATION

Gandhi's invention of nonviolent resistance depended on a novel arrangement of several "pieces" of culture, including: *civil disobedience*, motivated by individual acts of conscience like Thoreau's refusal to be taxed; and *passive resistance*, based on mass protest through boycotts and antitax and antirent campaigns. These had a strong secular and expedient character; they were weapons of the weak, usually employed because other, more violent weapons were not available or were not sustainable. As Gandhi came to recognize this fact, he tried to piece together civil disobedience and passive resistance in a new, noncoercive way, which was nonviolent in substance as well as in practice. I describe this dis-integration and reintegration in the later section on "the invention of noncoercive nonviolence."

Another piece Gandhi worked with was the *nonresistance* or noncompliance—that is, the martyrdom—of early Christianity and the Anabaptist sects, which had a strong sacred character. When Gandhi eschewed coercion from his nonviolence, he came to recognize that he would have to struggle against understandings of satyagraha as inactive. That is, the choices pre-Gandhi were between an active, secular, coercive civil disobedience (or alternatively, passive resistance) and a quietist, sacred, and noncoercive nonresistance. Although Gandhi struggled to invent a noncoercive nonviolent resistance, at the same time he had to make it understood that his noncoercive nonviolence was still active resistance not just nonresistance, as I show in the following section on "the invention of active passive resistance."

Still another piece Gandhi dis-integrated and then reworked was *ahimsa* or nonkilling, which testified in Jainism and some Hindu sects to an otherworldly devotion to God and an attempt to minimize karma in this world. I show (in the section on "the invention of a humanitarian ahimsa") how Gandhi completely altered the meaning of ahimsa so that it came to sanctify and "celestialize" worldly (secular) action, such as the practice of civil disobedience and even mercy killing.

To state it so baldly minimizes the very transformative event or events that I want to emphasize: the fact that the capacity for nonviolent resistance is constructed within conditions of time, place, and culture, and, furthermore, that Gandhi has to struggle hard—with himself, at first, and, thereafter, with the everyday world—to define the uniqueness of his invention. Throughout the first decades of the twentieth century, there was a strong tendency to assimilate nonviolent resistance to forms of resistance either the Indian world or the Western world already knew about, or, even more complexly, there was a tendency to assimilate it to forms of protest the Western world thought it knew about Gandhi's India or to what Gandhi thought he knew about the West.

For example, the Reverend Joseph Doke, one of Gandhi's earliest admirers in South Africa, thought he knew India well enough to assimilate Gandhi's nonviolence to traditional Hindu methods of passive protest like "sitting *dharna*,"[3] no matter that he also notes, "Mr. Gandhi attributes [it] ... to quite other influences," chiefly the Sermon on the Mount (Doke 1967 [1909], 100). Perhaps Gandhi was equally chagrined when his understanding of the West proved to be wrong, as when Europeans understood his original term for the South African protest—"passive resistance"—to represent a weapon of weakness rather than the forcefulness of the soul, as Gandhi intended.

Only over time and through (sometimes self, sometimes group) struggle did Gandhi realize his unique cultural invention and get others to realize it. To document this struggle and the inventive "twist" Gandhi gave to existing Western and Indian forms of protest, I now turn to three significant acts of cultural dis-integration and reintegration by which Gandhi authored nonviolent resistance.

The Invention of Noncoercive Nonviolence

The first of Gandhi's innovations I discuss was to make his passive resistance noncoercive as well as nonviolent. Militant British suffragettes early in the twentieth century seem to have provoked Gandhi into this initial dissociation of his program from even this nonphysical "violence."

Gandhi's initial response to the movement for women's suffrage was quite positive. When news reached South Africa in 1906 that suffragettes had forced their way into Parliament (to make known their views), that they had refused to pay the fines levied on them for this "trespass," and that they had therefore gone to jail, Gandhi was mightily impressed. He recommended their "suffering" and the "hardships" endured by these "British women satyagrahis" as models for the South African resistance he led, and he admonished his fellow Indians that "deeds speak louder than words" and "when women are manly, will men be effeminate?" (see *CWG* VI 1906, 29–30, 335–336; VII 1907, 65–66; VIII 1908, 188–189). When jailed suffragettes hunger-struck against being declared common criminals, rather than political prisoners, Gandhi, who was then in England, approved; often, this tactic gained suffragettes early release, which the women regretted—so Gandhi originally thought, for as late as July 1909, Gandhi recommended that "we have much to learn from Suffragettes" (*CWG* IX 1908–1909, 324–326).

Gandhi's attitude swiftly changed in the fall of 1909, as suffragettes threw stones (to damage property, not people) and mobbed the prime minister. He now condemned the hunger strikers in jail as thereby coercing the prison authorities to release them before their sentence was up. (Gandhi seems to have been right about their intentions; see Fulford 1948, 282; Pankhurst 1936, 92). For Gandhi, the jailed suffragettes were no longer "prepared to submit to suffering" and their hunger strikes only aimed to "force" the government's hand. Rather than condemn the prison authorities, who increasingly force-fed hunger strikers, Gandhi saw it as a just "desert": "If the women resort to physical force, they will necessarily invite similar force against them," he wrote (*CWG* IX 1909, 447–448, also 402, 433). "A satyagrahi's object," Gandhi later wrote (*CWG* XII 1913, 37), "is to get into a prison and stay there."

Coercion, thereafter, had no acknowledged place in Gandhi's nonviolent resistance, even though it was widely accepted in contemporary secular passive resistance campaigns, such as boycotts, strikes, hunger strikes, and the like, and even though it resonated with some traditional Hindu forms of protest, such as the aforementioned "sitting dharna," and even though many discerning persons, among them Jawaharlal Nehru (1930), questioned just how far Gandhi's later fasts (hunger strikes?), swadeshi campaigns (boycotts?),[4] and noncooperation movement (disruption of society) truly escaped coercion. Symbolic innovations perhaps need only operate symbolically.

The Invention of Active Passive Resistance
In the second innovation I discuss, Gandhi struggled to make understood the particular twist he gave to "passive resistance," whereby it became "active" without being "violent" or "coercive." His efforts, detailed in the

previous section, to dissociate his program from secular, coercive protest probably helped others to assimilate it to existing ideas about passive resistance, which Gandhi resisted with increasing fervor. Gandhi was running up against then common Western notions that the only truly nonviolent "passive resistance" was, in effect, a sacred "nonresistance," that is a "noncompliance" but also a "nonconfrontation" (as practiced, for example, by Christian martyrs or Quakers, who refused to obey certain laws, but who also refused to confront those laws actively and directly until and unless they were forced to). Similarly, by this understanding, the only truly "civil" civil disobedience did not threaten such a mass confrontation with the government that it might lead to anarchy. Gandhi came to understand some of the meaning Europeans gave to "passive resistance" while he was still in South Africa, but he continued to use this phrase for his protest because few people knew of, or understood, the neologism "satyagraha" he had coined in 1908 (see Doke 1967 [1909], 101). Later in India, he had to directly confront the fact that Europeans understood active confrontation as either violent or as a harbinger of violence, and, as I shall show below, he was hard-pressed to explain his program of confrontational nonviolence, which to them was a contradiction in terms.

In 1919, Gandhi testified before the Hunter Commission, which was investigating the violent aftermath (including General Dyer's infamous massacre at Jallianwala Bagh) to Gandhi's call for an all-India strike against repressive British colonial legislation.

> *Hunter Commission*: I see in your speeches that your movement is referred to sometimes by the phrase "civil disobedience," which comes apparently from Thoreau, and sometimes by the phrase, which is more familiar to an Englishman, "passive resistance." Now if an order comes to a man from Government or from anybody else, and if his conscience says that it is not right, it may be up to him simply to do nothing if not to obey, but civil disobedience goes further than that. Does it not?
>
> *Gandhi*: Certainly....
>
> *Hunter Commission*: ... the disobedience may be active as well as passive, but still be civil according to your satyagraha doctrine?
>
> *Gandhi*: Certainly.... That is why I have not called it a passive doctrine, because there is nothing passive about this thing. It is active, but not in the physical sense.
>
> *Hunter Commission*: For instance, if there is a law which says that you must not publish a newspaper unless you register it, and you publish it, is it not passive resistance?
>
> *Gandhi*: It is active and intensely active.
>
> *Hunter Commission*: In the same way you go and get yourself arrested when you are told not to go to Delhi and that would be active resistance?
>
> *Gandhi*: Certainly.
>
> *Hunter Commission*: What I want to know is whether you appreciate the fact, as it appears to me is the case, that civil disobedience as understood by you

and what is called passive resistance are really two very different things?
Gandhi: I accept that. There is a fundamental distinction. (*CWG* XVI, 406–407)

Gandhi did not persuade many British officials. In his testimony before the Hunter Commission (which was kept secret throughout the colonial era), J. P. Thompson, Chief Secretary to the Government of Punjab, likened Gandhi's disavowal of violence to an Irish republican's denouncing government and then telling his audience to go home quietly "and if you meet the village constable remember *not* to dip him in the pond" (India 1975 [1920], 63). When a commission member remonstrated against accusing Gandhi of intentionally inciting violence, Thompson answered: "His preachings would have that effect on a great many people." Even an Indian member of the commission, Sir Chimanlal Setalvad, pressed Gandhi to admit that satyagraha assumed a "high moral and intellectual equipment" that ordinary people lacked (*CWG* XVI, 407–413), in which case violence might accompany it because it seems to require extraordinary control over "ordinary human passions" (*CWG* XVI, 412). Sir Chimanlal then pressed Gandhi to consider that a satyagraha campaign is tantamount to a call for anarchy and to admit that the masses could understand disobedience to laws but could not understand that it should be nonviolent (*CWG* XVI, 416–420).[5]

Even before the event, Annie Besant, who had only recently finished her term as President of the Indian National Congress, predicted Gandhi's campaign would lead to "riot and bloodshed" (Besant, quoted in India 1975 [1920], annexure xxi). Another Indian nationalist, Rabindranath Tagore, also mistrusted an active passive resistance: in 1921 he wrote Gandhi that his program "in its passive moral form is asceticism and in its active moral form is violence" (*CWG* XX, 538). The Indian National Congress set up its own commission to investigate the 1919 violence, and, even with Gandhi as a member, it advocated "utmost caution" because "the preaching of the civil disobedience form of *Satyagraha* can easily lend itself to misinterpretation" (Indian National Congress 1976 [1920], 42).

Gandhi, we now know, eventually prevailed over these contemporary understandings of passive resistance. The 1930 Salt March, for example, gained wide legitimacy as nonviolent and noncoercive, but confrontational and civilly disobedient. His inventive twist, however, required many admonitions over a long term, and, today, in other places, when, for example, trees are spiked and abortion clinics blockaded in the name of "nonviolence," it occasions renewed scrutiny.

The Invention of a Humanitarian Ahimsa

Another Gandhi innovation, the last I detail, was to "rediscover" the Jain and Vaishnavite Hindu concept of ahimsa (sanctity of life, or nonkilling)—

to the dismay of the orthodox in India. In this case, too, an originally sacred or sanctified ethic gets used to gloss—and legitimate—a principle of secular living and, by extension, a program of nonviolent political protest. Today, animal rights advocates and vegetarian societies invoke Gandhi's ahimsa and presume, thereby, to enlist Indian civilization's "age-old" commitment to nonkilling. Little do they know the struggle by which Gandhi took non-killing, an act of piety, and reinvented it as an act of mercy that sometimes required killing.

Gandhi's experiments in ahimsa began with poisonous snakes and ended up with rabid dogs. He encountered the snakes in South Africa around 1912; they infested Tolstoy Farm, the utopian community Gandhi developed to house satyagrahis and their families during the South African campaign. With regret, Gandhi allowed poisonous snakes to be killed when they threatened the inhabitants, but he regarded his action as *himsa*, that is, an act of violence, and as the result of cowardice:

> To have a conviction that there is violence or sin in a certain course of conduct is one thing; to have the power of acting up to that conviction is quite another. A person who fears snakes and who is not ready to resign his own life cannot avoid killing snakes in case of emergency. . . . I saw that it was my duty to permit the . . . [killing of] the snake. I had not the courage to seize the serpent with the hand or otherwise to remove the danger . . . and I have not cultivated such courage to this day. (Gandhi 1972 [1928], 230–231)[6]

Gandhi's snake handling was in tune with some strains of Jain and Hindu orthodoxy, which held that human life regrettably gave no alternative but violence against living things; people had to consume vegetable foods and they inadvertently destroyed many unseen and unseeable creatures. No one, least of all Gandhi, claimed that such unavoidable destruction was ahimsa, however, and no one claimed that setting about to kill living things might be required by ahimsa.

In 1926 stray dogs made Gandhi stray from orthodoxy, or so it seemed to many. They wrote in large numbers to chastise Gandhi and shame him for approving the "mercy killing" (as Gandhi, not they, saw it) of stray, rabid dogs in Ahmedabad. Gandhi found himself having to condone—and then justify—violence, and worse, killing, at the same time as he presented himself as a votary of nonviolence. To his greater discomfort, he had had to come to the defense of his major benefactor, Ambalal Sarabai, a wealthy millowner, who had ordered the dogs exterminated to protect his workers. In the last months of 1926, Gandhi wrote eight installments on "Is This Humanity?" in which he not only defended his position but also increasingly criticized orthodox notions of ahimsa and departed from them, while retaining a claim on the term.

In the first article, Gandhi admitted that Hinduism (like most religions, he erroneously thought) regarded taking life as sinful, but he argued that killing a rabid dog was a lesser sin than failing to protect the population from a dread disease (*CWG* XXXI 1926, 486–489). "We have to drink in daily life," Gandhi confessed, "many a bitter draught of violence" (*CWG* XXXI 1926, 488). Gandhi therefore relinquished the high ground to orthodoxy, with its view of nonkilling as a pious act—an act, therefore, not to be confounded with notions of "mercy."

After many more angry letters and some bitter face-to-face interviews, Gandhi hardened, and he began to disavow an uncompromising nonkilling as the definition of ahimsa. He invoked a "religion of humanity," which would require dogs to be properly maintained, and, should they become strays, might make their killing unavoidable, because waiting until "they get rabid is not merciful to them" (*CWG* XXXI [28 Oct.] 1926, 506). Then Gandhi struck back with even greater conviction:

> The dogs in India are today in as bad a plight as ... men. It is my firm conviction that this sorry plight is due to our misconception of ahimsa, is due to our want of ahimsa. Practice of ahimsa cannot have as its result impotence, impoverishment and famine. ... [I]t is possible that the man who kills the dogs that he cannot bear to see tortured thus may be doing a meritorious act. Merely taking life is not always *himsa*, one may even say that there is something more *himsa* in not taking life. (*CWG* XXXI [4 Nov.] 1926, 524–525)

In his next installment, Gandhi twisted ahimsa into a merciful duty rather than a pious commandment:

> Taking life may be a duty.... [A]himsa does not simply mean non-killing....
> The destruction of dogs ... can ... be resorted to only when it is unavoidable.
> ... But I have not the slightest doubt that refraining from that destruction when it is unavoidable is worse than the destruction. (*CWG* XXXI, 544–546)

Thereafter, he cited the actual or potential suffering of the dogs to justify killing them as, in fact, ahimsa. That many of his Hindu correspondents devoutly believed this "mercy" toward dogs brought "dis-grace" to themselves—on this issue, Gandhi kept silent. Ahimsa had for him become a principle of secular living rather than of the otherworldly.

Correspondents, representing orthodoxy, continued to admonish him, however. One suggested that killing stray dogs even before they threatened anyone seemed preemptive and asked: "Where is the humanity of shooting innocent dogs whenever they are found roving? How can one wishing well to all living beings do this?" (*CWG* XXXII 1926–1927, 14). Another argued that ahimsa could be preserved by confining rabid dogs and allowing them to die unmolested. Still another accused Gandhi of having succumbed to the Western practice of killing "lower beings for the sake of man." Gandhi responded by consigning these criticisms to "an *instinctive* horror of killing living beings under any circumstances whatsoever" (*CWG* XXXII 1926–1927, 42; my emphasis). The arguments against him now could be said to come from nature, not religion; ahimsa was his.

Now, it is also ours, much the way the other segments of Gandhi's invention compel and enable belief and practice globally (although not universally).

CONCLUSION

Perhaps anthropologists should rediscover the wheel. Once upon a time, we gave serious attention to cultural innovations like the wheel. Obviously, there is no reason to return to material-culture trait-listing or evolutionary taxonomies of technology. There is, however, a pedigree for a different approach to cultural innovation, akin to Sidney Mintz's history of the cultural invention of sweetness and Wolf's survey of the European invention of People without History. Surely, no scrutiny of the "invention of tradition" and the "construction of culture" can proceed very far without recognizing specific inventions and constructions as well as inventors and construction workers—that is, unless we conserve the Culturological cop-out that innovation and inventors occur whenever Culture is ready for them. This rabid cultural determinism deserves a merciful death. We must, of course, set the innovators and their innovations within a cultural context—that is, we must document the historical relationship between individual creativity and cultural constitution (see Fox 1991)—"the intersections of biography and history," as C. Wright Mills (1961, 7) put it.

As anthropology turns increasingly to the study of "lived culture," we must also attend to "cultured lives." By rediscovering the wheel *and* the wheelwrights, we may stop hiding under our anthropology the human ability to work with "hand and mind" that Eric Wolf reminds us of, and we may thereby have more to say about the human capacity to innovate cultural meanings that might transform the terms of our existence, including or especially, let us hope, the possibilities for peace-fare.

NOTES

This paper is a revision of one delivered at the 1990 annual meeting of the American Anthropological Association in New Orleans. I thank Rayna Rapp, Jane Schneider, Katherine Ewing, John Richards, Bruce Lawrence, David Gilmartin, and members of the Triangle South Asia Consortium for many helpful comments.

1. The technique for cultural production I am referring to is clearly much like the *bricolage* that Claude Lévi-Strauss (1966) posits. The creative process I posit as being carried or furthered by this technique bears little resemblance, however, to

the reassemblage of given or a priori dualisms (nature-culture, life-death, etc.) to which Lévi-Strauss applies the concept of *bricolage.*

2. In his attempts to expand and revise Thomas Kuhn's concept of paradigmatic change, Anthony Wallace (1978, 478–480) posited a "paradigm development process." After its initial innovation, according to Wallace, paradigm expansion depended on the development of a "technical core" by experts or specialists who might work out the implications of a paradigm innovation over years or even generations, with the outcome not predetermined. Wallace thus allowed for the act of innovation, multiple authorship, and contingent development over time.

3. "Sitting dharna" was a practice usually reserved to Brahmins, who would starve themselves at someone's door in order to extract compliance with their wishes. Gandhi regarded this practice as coercive because it depended on fear of divine retribution should the Brahmin be allowed to die.

4. Gandhi countered accusations of coercion in the following fashion: "I have advocated a boycott only of *foreign cloth* and there is no violence done to the British workers who may be thrown out of employment because of the boycott of cloth manufactured by them, for the simple reason that purchase of foreign cloth is not an obligation undertaken by India.... A drunkard does no violence to the owner of a drink-shop when he becomes a teetotaller" (*CWG* XXXI 1926, 103).

5. The image of proper or true passive resistance that many British Indian officials and even many Indians had was probably akin to the protest methods used by English Nonconformists in 1902–1906 against legislation on education that they felt favored the Church of England. Protesters, organized by a National Passive Resistance Committee, refused to pay the education tax and allowed their property to be distrained or, in some cases, relinquished ownership of their property so that they could be committed to jail. Except perhaps in the latter cases, passive resistance meant noncompliance and acceptance of suffering, but it did not mean direct confrontation. For instance, protesters continued to send their children to the schools (compared with Gandhi's call in 1920 for noncooperation, including leaving British Indian schools). See Hunt 1986, 51–91.

6. Gandhi wrote this passage some fifteen years later, but there is no reason to think it does not accurately reflect his thinking around 1912. About this same time, Gandhi had asked his close friend and mentor, Raichandbhai, who was a Jain, what the proper reaction was when threatened by a poisonous snake. Raichandbhai advised him he should allow himself to be killed (*CWG* XXXII 1926–1927, 72). In any case, his position in 1912, as he remembered it later, is considerably different from the stance he struggled over in the mid-1920s.

PART FIVE

Political Economy and Cultural Identity

EIGHTEEN

The Reconstruction of "Tradition" and the Defense of the Colonial Order: British West Africa in the Early Twentieth Century

Michael Adas

Over two decades ago in his seminal study *Peasant Wars of the Twentieth Century*, Eric R. Wolf observed that a major contributor to peasant protest, particularly in colonized areas, was the ignorance and insensitivity displayed by alien European administrators to the underlying cultural repercussions of the systems of rule and the capitalist, market-oriented economies they imposed on conquered societies. The Europeans' obliviousness to the "cultural shock waves [that] propagate themselves through the traditional strata of society" and their woeful inability to "respond to social cues from the affected population" (1969a, 283–287), Wolf argued, had rendered them incapable of dealing effectively with the deeply felt grievances that frequently exploded into local rebellions and at times full-scale social revolutions.

There have indeed been many clashes between colonizers and colonized that the cultural myopia or outright arrogance of European administrators, missionaries, and traders have done much to precipitate. But as a considerable body of research carried out in the decades since Wolf wrote his study of peasant wars has demonstrated, if the Europeans missed or garbled cultural cues and misjudged the impact of their policies on colonized peoples, they did not always do so willfully or for want of effort. In fact, from at least the latter half of the eighteenth century, European company officials in Asia of the stature of Warren Hastings and William Jones did much to promote the systematic study of the languages, beliefs, social structure, and customs of the rapidly increasing numbers of overseas peoples who were being brought under European colonial rule. Voicing a view that would become axiomatic for able colonial administrators in succeeding decades, Hastings noted that "the quickest way to the heart of a people is through the language of the country," and he viewed "every accumulation of knowledge" between colonized and colonizer as "useful to the state" and a "gain for humanity" (Kopf 1969, 15, 18). In the following century and a half as European hegemony was established over much of Africa, Asia, and Oceania, the enterprise of collecting, codifying, and applying information gathered about colonized peoples and their cultures came to be regarded as an essential dimension of successful colonial administration.

How seriously colonial officials or missionaries undertook these tasks and the degree to which they evinced sensitivity to the cultures of the colonized varied widely by time period and the colonizers and colonized in question. But as was clearly demonstrated by disasters, such as those that marked virtually the whole of the early phase of Belgian rule in the Congo or the rebellions stirred up by British and German flaunting of the symbols and prerogatives of indigenous leaders in the Gold Coast and German East Africa, the cost of ignorance on the part of the colonizers and their failure to heed cultural cues could be very high.

The information on colonized cultures which was gathered and codified for official use tended to fall into one of two rather different categories. The first was exemplified by the writings of eminent Orientalists like Jones in India, Snouck Hurgronje in the Dutch Indies, and Silvestre de Sacy in the Middle East who focused their investigations on textual evidence relating to the "Great Traditions" or "high civilizations" of Africa and Asia. A second major source of information was the ethnographic data compiled by travelers and later colonial officials assigned to rural districts. This information proved critical to the efforts of European administrators to map the social contours and to decipher the cultural codes of the broader peasant base of colonized societies.

Like turn-of-the-century administrator-anthropologists in colonized areas and modernization theorists in the 1950s and 1960s, the practitioners of both approaches assumed that the colonized peoples of Africa and Asia (and later Oceania) had possessed age-old and clearly bounded cultural configurations of "traditions" that had been basically static—despite often far-reaching political and social changes—in the era before the rise of European domination. The lesson that influential colonial observers drew from violent rebellions by the colonized, such as the Great Indian "Mutiny," the Maji Maji movement, and the Ashanti rising of 1900, which they concluded were mainly in defense of these cultural traditions, was that these "revered" and essentially fixed cultural configurations needed to be shielded from the corrosive effects of European colonial rule and the spread of the market economy. In the first phase of European colonial advance into different areas, European officials commonly stressed the need for the *preservation* of indigenous cultural traditions, as they understood them, as vital to the maintenance of the still fragile colonial order and internal peace. In early nineteenth-century India, for example, East India Company officials like Mountstuart Elphinstone and James Tod urged that, wherever possible, the British ought to rule India through "traditional" elite groups and indigenous institutions. Though it was often unstated, their defense of the princely and landlord hierarchy, which they often misleadingly compared to the aristocracy and improving gentry at home, was premised on the assumption that the indigenous cultural "traditions," from which these invaluable allies drew their symbols and rituals of legitimacy, must also be preserved.

If the initial alliances between European colonizers and indigenous elites resulted in a stress on the preservation of tradition, the widespread transformations that accompanied colonial rule prompted European administrators to adopt a number of different strategies in the defense of colonial orders that in most instances rested on accommodating indigenous elite groups. As the works of Wolf (1969a; 1982a, esp. pt. 3) have shown, the forces of the market, "rationalizing" tendencies within colonial bureaucracies, and the growing cultural hegemony of the West invariably undermined the accommodations that the colonizers had originally worked out with princely allies and local notables. These transformations spawned new classes, ranging from market-oriented peasants (both those who were fairly prosperous and others mired in debt) to Western-educated professionals and politicians, which posed direct challenges to both the indigenous *collaborateur* elites and their European overlords. In order to buttress crumbling colonial edifices, astute European administrators turned to *invented* cultural traditions or worked for the *restoration* of what they believed to be (or at least tried to pass off as) the authentic cultural "traditions" of the colonized peoples.

Much of the cultural fabrication that Terence Ranger (1983) describes falls into the former category. Transferred to alien African contexts, the monarchical and public school rituals and "traditions"—often themselves recent contrivances—that the British exported to east-central Africa in the nineteenth century were *inventions*—that is, "production[s] of ... new method[s], ... art[s], kind[s] of instruments, etc. previously unknown"—in the *Oxford English Dictionary*'s most meaningful sense of the term. Though they relied a good deal more on the disembodied appropriation of fragments of the colonizeds' culture, the martial "traditions" that the British cultivated among the Sikhs of the Punjab and other Asian and African ethnic groups in the late nineteenth century (Fox 1985, esp. chap. 8) also represented invented traditions designed to bolster the increasingly unsteady colonial order in various areas.

Invented traditions, however, were just one side of the colonizers' attempt to repair or—in recently colonized areas—forge new accommodations with "traditional" African and Asian elites and cultures. Even more important in many colonial situations were conscious and systematic efforts to reconstruct what the Europeans believed to be the traditional political and social systems and the underlying culture of colonized peoples. Invention, in the guise of the imposition of British interpretations and monarchical rites on long-standing ceremonies like the durbar, was clearly at work in late nineteenth-century British strategies aimed at establishing symbols and ritual occasions to represent and legitimize their authority among the Indian populace (Cohn 1983). But much of what the British *thought they were doing* was recovering and restoring indigenous traditions that had been allowed to fall into disuse in the colonial period or had been diluted and degraded by the rationalizing campaigns of reform-minded administrators or missionaries and the impact of commercializing capitalism. In contrast to Europe itself in this period, where, Eric Hobsbawm argues, invented traditions were aimed at establishing or strengthening the cohesion of existing social groups (Hobsbawm 1983, 9), over much of Africa and Asia colonial administrators placed emphasis on the reconstruction of what they believed to be authentic, indigenous traditions that had been displaced or eroded by the advance of European imperialist hegemony.

This project of reconstruction depended upon an essentializing approach to the society and culture of colonized peoples that was premised on the assumption that the "tradition" to be restored consisted of innate and timeless ways of thinking and modes of social and political organization. Therefore, restoration began with the identification of the essential attributes of a given colonized people, a process that often involved the distillation of these attributes from composite cultural blends that had resulted from interactions between the "base" culture and foreign influences, particularly those emanating from Europe. Thus, colonial officials and ethnographers routinely justified policy decisions with references to the sort of essentialist assumptions that Eric Wolf has sought—usually implicitly, sometimes explicitly—to counter with decades of research and scholarship anchored in the specifics of social and economic organization, political mobilization, and cultural transformation in each of the wide range of societies examined in his works.

Of the many examples of efforts to reconstruct African and Asian cultural traditions to bolster European colonial control in the early twentieth century, I will concentrate in this essay on those associated with the establishment of indirect rule in British West Africa between the final years of colonial conquest in the late 1890s and the years after World War I. Not only was the project of the reconstruction of tradition associated in these and subsequent years with the imposition of indirect rule over much of West Africa among the largest—in terms of the numbers of the colonized affected—ever undertaken, it was also among the most ambitious, given the daunting diversity of cultures and societies into which the system was introduced. From the colonizers' point of view, indirect rule also represented the most conscious, systematic, and successful campaign to reconstruct what were believed to be traditional cultures, with the explicit intent of reducing social dislocations and staving off emerging threats to the European colonial order.

For the advocates of indirect rule, projects aimed at the preservation or restoration of indigenous cultures in the African context centered upon essentialized notions of tribal identity, organization, and institutions. As Terence Ranger (1983) has argued, the extensive employment of the lexicon of terms associated with the tribe by European ethnologists and colonial administrators served to codify and rigidify ethnic divisions that were much more fluid and permeable in the precolonial era. It also meant the misapplication of the tribal concept and associated terminology to African societies or ethnic groups that did not constitute tribes in any meaningful sense of the term. Nonetheless, in the early decades of the twentieth century, colonial officials came to see tribal identities and institutions as the core elements of the "traditions" they sought to restore. Ironically, these same identities and institutions were also appropriated by those—including often nationalist leaders—who sought to challenge European dominance and put an end to colonial rule.

In this essay, I will explore a number of key aspects of the project of reconstructing tradition that was embodied in the British imposition of indirect rule in West Africa. Following a survey of the conflicting and basically monocausal assessments of the motivations behind the early twentieth-century advocacy of indirect rule in Africa, I argue that the growing reliance on the reconstruction of what were believed to be authentic African traditions arose from a convergence of factors. Some of these were generated by conditions and challenges emanating from the colonized areas, such as the breakdown of "tribal" social organization and related perceptions of increasing social disruption as well as mounting challenges to the colonial overlords from urban, Western-educated African elite groups. Other motivations for the imposition of indirect rule were linked to social and intellectual currents in Britain itself, including the ascendancy of social evolutionist thinking and efforts to return to an imagined chivalric and gemeinschaft ethos of the preindustrial past. The essay concludes with some thoughts about the ways in which the reconstruction of African "tradition" through the imposition of indirect rule has shaped subsequent thinking about African cultures and the African historical experience.

I

There has been considerable disagreement regarding the motivations behind the turn-of-the-century reincarnation of indirect rule by British colonizers. Some scholars have stressed the lack of available manpower and financial resources that forced British administrators to devise ways of imposing "colonialism on the cheap" (Lackner 1973, 127–128; as quoted in Fox 1985). Other observers have stressed the pivotal role of F. D. Lugard. Variations of this interpretation range from Margery Perham's (1960, 138–144) near-hagiographic depiction of the great white leader in the

tropics singlehandedly forging a viable government through ingenious innovations on early precedents, to F. Nicholson's (1969) view that Lugard
favored indirect rule because it best served his personal need to exercise
paternalistic and autocratic authority. In sharp contrast to these Lugard-
centric interpretations, Michael Crowder argues that indirect rule was just
one of a number of ad hoc solutions to the problem of establishing colonial
authority over the bewildering diversity of states and societies the British
claimed in the last decades of the nineteenth century. Crowder traces the
West African precedents that Lugard drew upon in establishing indirect
rule in northern Nigeria, and he emphasizes the important roles the existing, indigenous political institutions and patterns of rule played in British
decisions to impose the indirect rule option (Crowder 1968, 130–137,
165–166, pt. 3, chaps. 3 and 4).

Focusing on the British side of the motivational forces behind indirect
rule, Mark Girouard (1981, 226) sees the late nineteenth-century aristocratic and upper-middle-class retreat to colonial refuges in the face of de-
mocratizing forces at home as the key to the turn-of-the-century determination on the part of Lugard and other prominent administrators to bolster
princely allies in India and rule through indigenous elite groups in Africa.
Yet another view of indirect rule was voiced by Western-educated leaders
in the areas the British colonized in this period and those who later
struggled for independence. They charged that Lugard and his successors
had quite consciously pushed the system of indirect rule because they
wished to bolster the position of traditional elites at the expense of the
newly emerging commercial and professional classes in the towns (Crowder
1968, 212, 220, 223). Gérard Leclerc concurs with the view that the system
was intended to shore up "traditional" African cultures. But he sees the
growing influence of the first generation of British anthropologists and
the more favorable views of African society and culture that their research
and that of their French counterparts had engendered as the key factors
behind the shift in British official preferences from direct to indirect rule in
this era (Leclerc 1972, 44–52, 83–84). Writing on this shift in preferences
in the context of the French debates over assimilation and association,
Raymond Betts has stressed the impact in this era of social evolutionist
thinking on colonial policy formation more generally (Betts 1961, esp.
106–132).

Each of these explanations for the advocacy of indirect rule by British
administrators at the turn of the century highlights individual facets of a
larger configuration of causal factors that was responsible for the colonizers' increasing preference for governance of the colonized through indigenous elites. But none takes fully into account the past precedents or begins
to comprehend the complex convergence of ideological assumptions, pragmatic political calculations, and resource constraints in various colonial

locales that prompted British officials to push for indirect rule and the preservation or reconstruction of the cultural traditions of the colonized in this era. Nor do any of these explanations deal with the underlying disintegration that was endemic to the British colonial order in ironically the very decades when the empire peaked in size and apparent power—a process of dissolution that was to take on crisis proportions in the years after World War I.

The origins of the broader British project of reconstructing what were seen to be the authentic cultures of the colonized, which was the wellspring for official advocacy of specific systems of indirect rule, cannot be understood unless they are analyzed in a framework that is both diachronic and comparative. Lugard's thinking on the policy of indirect rule, for example, very likely originated in and was certainly shaped by long-standing British practices regarding rule through the princely states in India as well as in Malaya. It was also influenced by both his earlier contacts with the administrative hierarchy of the Ganda kingdom in Uganda and his familiarity with the stratagems pursued by George Goldie and the Royal Niger Company in Yorubaland in the 1890s (Lugard 1968 [1893], 650–651; 1965 [1922], 32–33, 195–196; Perham 1960, 40). Thus, though Lugard made significant alterations in these earlier versions of indirect rule to suit what he perceived to be the situation in Northern Nigeria, his pivotal advocacy of the preservation of indigenous elites, from the court at Sokoto downward, and the restoration of what he believed to be authentic Hausa-Fulani culture were the products of a cumulative process that extended back at least as far as the era of the rise of British hegemony in eighteenth-century India and perhaps that of the Dutch on Java in the preceding century.

The cross-colony linkages that are so apparent in the genesis of the Lugardian variant of indirect rule exemplified a broader exchange of ideas and precedents between policy makers running the different European colonial empires in this era. Just as French administrators and politicians drew on Dutch and British models in arguing for a shift from assimilation to association (Betts 1961, chap. 2; Harmand 1910, 259–277), British advocates of indirect rule cited the findings of French ethnographers and linguists, which linked the pace of evolutionary advance displayed by different colonized peoples to the forms of colonial governance that were suitable for them (Lugard 1965 [1922], 197–198; Smith 1926, 53–54). Perhaps more critically, a general and spreading crisis of imperialism, engendered, among other things, by market dislocations and the rising challenges of Western-educated professionals among the colonized, pushed British officials in widely divergent colonial contexts to efforts to shore up the position of collaborateur African and Asian elites and indigenous cultural traditions. Whether bolstering the Khedival regime in Cairo and excavating the ruins of pharaonic Egypt, staging grandiose (and very costly) durbars in Delhi, or confirming the authority of the Sultan of Sokoto, British colonial administrators acted out of a common concern to counteract the disintegrative forces of change that they believed were undermining the very foundations of the European colonial order. As the influence of social evolutionist thinking noted above also suggests, ideas emanating from Europe itself were also a significant factor behind the colonizers' projects of cultural preservation and reconstruction before and after World War I. In some cases arguments for the evolutionary limitations of colonized peoples were counterbalanced by the admiration for their past cultural achievements prompted by the revived, late nineteenth-century Orientalist interest in India, the findings of the first generation of anthropologists, and the "discovery" of African art by major painters like Picasso and Braque (Adas 1989, 350–356).

II

Whatever the specific factors operating in particular colonial contexts to bolster the colonizers' campaigns for the reconstruction of indigenous cultural traditions, all these efforts were grounded in a more general crisis of the British empire. Key manifestations of this crisis included the eroding authority of collaborateur princes, landlords, and "chiefs"; spreading unrest—at times erupting into confrontational protest—in peasant societies long buffeted by the vagaries of the international market system; urban workers' agitation; and rapidly mounting challenges from Western-educated leaders of emerging nationalist movements. In long-established portions of the empire, most notably India, British administrators struggled to shore up the position of threatened indigenous elite groups, to preserve the "timeless" peasant village communities—which, in fact, were often invented or reconstructed by the colonizers (Bremen 1987)—and to fix, through censuses and other forms of official codification, religious, ethnic, and caste divisions among the subject populace (for examples of the former, see Fox 1985; on codification strategies, see Cohn 1984).

Compared to India, where the reconstruction of tradition involved mainly strengthening indigenous allies and cultural practices that the colonizers had sought to preserve and fix for decades, the British who undertook similar projects of reconstruction in West Africa faced considerably more daunting challenges. To begin with, in most areas of West Africa they struggled to establish stable administrative foundations for colonial rule in societies that had for generations been disrupted and transformed by external forces and internal struggles. In overlapping waves the shocks of centuries of the slave trade, the mid-nineteenth-century shift to the production of export crops like palm oil and groundnuts, and the European conquest in the last decades of the century skewed and eroded indigenous cultures. This made it difficult for even the best informed British officials to get a clear fix on configurations of traditional culture that they presumed could be codified and preserved or restored. Even before conquest and annexation, market inroads had seriously disrupted indigenous social and economic arrangements, rendering the societies the British captured in all but the most isolated of areas more the products of externally induced forces than internally induced change.

The breakdown of African social systems and the steady erosion of African cultures was an almost obsessive concern of British officials and ethnographers throughout sub-Saharan Africa in the decades on either side of World War I. Lugard wrote in 1902 that one of the chief rationales for the spread of British colonial control was that it slowed or altogether arrested this process of "disintegration" and made it possible to "build up again what is best in the social and political organization of conquered dynasties" (quoted in Perham 1960, 148). Lugard's pronouncements did much to draw the attention of British policy makers to social dislocations in newly colonized areas in Africa in the early 1900s. But no one worked harder in these years than the explorer and self-trained ethnographer, Mary Kingsley, to convince a skeptical British public of the dangers of the corrosive effects on African society and culture of intolerant and "reform"-minded missionaries and other agents of Westernizing change (Kingsley 1897, esp. 20, 30, 403; 1901, 326–329).

Ironically, perhaps no subsequent observer explored the effects of missionary activities, as well as those of Western commerce that Kingsley somewhat contradictorily defended, on "traditional" African culture as fully as Edwin Smith, a missionary stationed in the Gold Coast in the 1920s. Smith began his account of conditions in the region with a tale that illustrated both the disrespect that many Africans displayed even for the most sacred of symbols of traditional authority, such as the Golden Stool of the Asante (Ashanti) monarchs, and the ways in which Western imports, in this case whiskey, had debased African religious ceremonies (Smith 1926, 1–12, 17). Smith saw the rapid pace of change generated by European colonialism as the central cause of the breakdown of African institutions and cultural traditions. He lamented the breakup of African communities and the weakening of "tribal" restraints (49–50, 203–204); the decline of African craft production (67–68); the disrespect that particularly African youths displayed toward the "traditional chiefs"; and the triumph of self-seeking individualism over the gemeinschaft sensibility he believed had tempered social relations in precolonial African societies (214, 266).

Smith's concerns were widely shared by missionaries and British officials throughout sub-Saharan Africa in the years before and after World War I. They were underscored by the spate of ethnological studies by colonial administrators which appeared in the years just after the end of the war (see, for example, Hobley 1967 [1922], 281–282, 288–289; Melland 1923, 207–

208, 296–297, 305–306; Orde Browne 1925, 260–261, 272). In their 1932 plan for future research the anthropologists at the influential International Institute of African Languages and Cultures emphasized the dangers of the "complete disintegration" of African society and the need for field research aimed at discovering and understanding "factors of social cohesion in *original* African society" and the ways these had been eroded due to new economic and cultural forces (quoted in Kuper 1973, 130–133).

Without a doubt, missionaries, colonial officials, and ethnographers alike saw a clear connection between the preservation and reconstruction of what they argued were authentic African cultural traditions and social systems and the establishment and maintenance of colonial control in the newly claimed areas of West Africa. At one level, administrators like Lugard were very much aware of manpower and financial constraints. They were also cognizant of the manifold advantages of ruling through the indigenous elites. With the "traditional" rulers left in place, the colonizers could cut administrative costs, deflect popular dissent resulting from unpopular policies from themselves to indigenous leaders, and ideally minimize the sort of social dislocations that made for the unrest in the first place—unrest that led to embarrassing headlines at home and necessitated costly military interventions in the colonies. But as official and civilian writings on Africa in the pre- and postwar eras demonstrate, the colonizers' advocacy of indirect rule was prompted by convictions and concerns that extended beyond these manipulative strategies for social control or approached them in a less cynical way.

To begin with, the advocates of indirect rule stressed that to succeed, this approach to colonial administration had to be firmly grounded in extensive knowledge of and sensitivity to the cultures and social systems of the colonized. Early twentieth-century writers on colonial affairs repeatedly stressed that official ignorance of indigenous beliefs and customs and the affronts that often resulted were a major source of local disturbances as well as sustained protest that periodically disrupted the *pax imperium*. F. M. Hodgson's subordinates and his successor as governor of the Gold Coast identified the folly of Hodgson's attempts to seize the revered Golden Stool of the Asante monarch and his announcement that he himself intended to sit upon it as the key to the Asante disturbances in 1900 (Tordoff 1965, 103–106). The commission enquiring into the 1929 Aba riots in southeast Nigeria blamed them on the attempt to introduce indirect rule in the area despite an appalling official ignorance regarding Ibo society and culture (Lackner 1973, 126–127). Fortifying his case with examples of cross-cultural clashes arising from glaring miscues in British colonies in the South Pacific, Arthur Grimble declared in 1921 that "good knowledge of native custom is apt to be better than the best intentions without knowledge." He concluded that ignorance of "native custom" was invariably the source of

"dangerous little mistakes" that produced "friction" between British officials and the colonized and observed that offended subject peoples had a
tendency to either retreat into "sullen silence" or to rise up in rebellion
(Grimble 1921, 765–768).

The need for the able colonial administrator to be well-informed regarding "native customs" and to "understand" the ways of thinking and modes
of behavior of the colonized was usually linked in this period to affirmations
of the importance of the new discipline of anthropology in the maintenance
of European colonial domination. Whatever the intentions of official ethnographers and early British social anthropologists who carried out their
field research in colonial settings, their findings were viewed by both sympathetic administrators and civilians (who were very often in the minority of
the European community in a given colony) and some of the anthropologists themselves as vital to just and effective government in the colonies.
Though Lugard expressed a strong preference in the 1920s for having district officials rather than professional anthropologists carry out ethnographic surveys (Lackner 1973, 134–135), he stressed that for indirect rule
to be successfully implemented, it was imperative that "native etiquette and
ceremonial ... be carefully studied and observed in order that unintended
offense may be avoided" (Lugard 1965 [1922], 212, also 193). Lugard's successors often divided on the issue of whether trained bureaucrats or professional anthropologists attached to the colonial administration should carry
out the fieldwork. But there was considerable agreement that when the
introduction of indirect rule failed, it did so because of insufficient knowledge of the beliefs and customs of the societies to which the system was extended (Lackner 1973, 131–138). In fact, Lugard's successor as Governor of
Nigeria, Hugh Clifford, explicitly linked the failure of the introduction of
indirect rule in Benin in the Niger delta area to the lack of a proper investigation into the "native system of government." He regretted the rather cav-
alier way in which a system that had been originally formulated in the very
different circumstances of the northern emirates was imposed with little or
no adjustment on the peoples of the south (Nigerian Council 1920, 35–36).

Edwin Smith, who has himself a self-trained ethnographer, was more direct in his advocacy of anthropological expertise in colonial governance. He
contrasted the peaceful settlement of a potentially explosive situation in the
1920s, which resulted from the accidental finding of the hidden Golden
Stool of the Asante Asantehene, with the revolt two decades earlier that
had been touched off in large part by the governor's obtuse handling of the
stool question. The key to the difference, Smith (1926, 13–14) argued, was
that in 1920 government officials thought to consult with and follow the advice of R. S. Rattray, then considered the premier anthropological expert
on the Asante people. Smith's conviction that anthropological expertise was
critical to the maintenance of social peace in the Gold Coast was affirmed

by both official ethnographers and social anthropologists, including such luminaries as Bronislaw Malinowski, working throughout sub-Saharan Africa and further afield in the empire in the post–World War I decades (see Hobley 1967 [1922], 283–285; James 1973, 42–46, 54–55; Lackner 1973, 147–148; Melland 1923, 7–8). By the 1920s, these trained experts in "native affairs" were widely considered essential to the task of reconstructing tradition, which was in turn regarded as a vital concomitant of the successful exercise of indirect rule over the colonized.

The advocates of the preservation or reconstruction of "tradition" that underlay the application of the Lugardian principles of indirect rule emphasized advantages of this approach to colonial administration that extended far beyond budget considerations and the pliability of collaborateur princes and local notables. From the backward savages depicted in much of the nineteenth-century travel literature, African peoples, particularly those living in centralized states, were elevated at the turn of the century by influential policy makers like Lugard to the status of "advanced" peoples of "exceptional intelligence" and potential for self-administration under British supervision (Lugard 1965 [1922], 200, 203–204). Lugard and his disciples argued that such peoples were best ruled by their own leaders because the indigenous lords were more sensitive to their subjects' needs and less likely to implement policies that violated long-standing customs, religious taboos, and perceptions of justice, which were alien to even the best trained British official (Lugard 1965 [1922], 211–212; Ranger 1973, 249–250). With its emphasis on the preservation and restoration of tradition, indirect rule, its defenders argued, reinforced social control because it upheld the moral restraints that they had come to believe inhered in "tribal" law, "native" beliefs, and even practices such as sorcery that the British and other European observers had once seen as the very epitome of savagery and superstition. For administrators and official ethnologists in the 1920s, detribalization was anathema. Consequently, African migration to the rapidly growing towns, where "traditional" sanctions had little effect, was increasingly viewed as a major source of cultural dissolution and social unrest among the colonized (Hobley 1967 [1922], 281–282, 288–289; James 1973, 45; Melland 1923, 301, 306–307; Orde Browne 1925, 262–265).

Advocates of indirect rule placed great stress on the preservation or restoration of the rituals and symbols of authority that buttressed the legitimacy of African rules and local "chiefs." In the original formulation of the system for West Africa, Lugard was attentive to the manner in which the emirs and "chiefs" were graded. He prescribed which grades should be given a staff of office and which a simple baton, and within each level of administration he noted which rank should have a silver staff and which should be allotted one made merely of brass. He stressed the symbolic importance of a grand installation ceremony for the sultan and the emirs, complete with a parade and a formal ritual in which the British Resident presented the new ruler with a parchment scroll listing the terms of his tenure of office and administered a "native" oath on the Qur'an (Lugard 1965 [1922], 212). As the references in Governor Clifford's annual address in 1920 to official tours and the "barbaric display" of "durbars" held at the courts of various southern Nigerian rulers make clear, if anything, the ceremonial dimensions of "native" administration were enhanced as indirect rule spread to different parts of the colony. In a rather startling moment of public candor, Clifford went so far as to admit that the splendid pomp and ceremony that surrounded his audience with the Oba of Benin lent an impression of power and prestige that far exceeded the reality of the Oba's nominal authority (Nigerian Council 1920, 35–37). Like contemporary officials working with the Asante in the Gold Coast colony (Crowder 1968, 224; Tordoff 1965, 179–181, 205, 213, 289), Clifford singled out the Oba's stool as a symbol of authority of special importance and thus as a piece of the colonized's "traditional" culture that ought to be treated by British administrators with special deference.

The advocates of indirect rule also sought to justify what was in effect a retreat into the past by invoking ideas linked to several overlapping themes in intellectual discourse in Great Britain itself in this era. The first of these was the medieval revival that had preoccupied elements of the aristocratic and middle classes throughout much of the nineteenth century. The kingdoms of the emirs of Northern Nigeria had great appeal for colonial administrators who longed for the imagined world of the European Middle Ages, where hierarchy and deference to one's superiors informed a social order in which everyone had his or her place, allotted tasks, and obligations (Delheim 1982, esp. 13–16; Girouard 1981, chap. 14). In fact, in celebration of the British preservation of emirates, Governor Clifford invoked the "exact parallel" between the societies of Northern Nigeria and "the Medieval Kingdoms of Europe in the days of the Crusades" (Nigerian Council 1920, 24). For nineteenth-century Britons, who concurred with the critiques of the industrial order that had found so many adherents among the English upper classes and who grew anxious about the social upheavals that the upsurge of democracy and socialism portended (Weiner 1981), "feudal" societies like those found in Northern Nigeria promised refuge from the anomie, competition, class conflict, and mass-produced mediocrity of the modern era. As Lugard (1965 [1922], 213–214) opined, the true English gentleman would have no difficulty understanding and working with the dignified, etiquette-conscious, and thoroughly paternalistic emirs of Northern Nigeria.

Upholding the emirs would in turn promote the preservation or restoration of what colonial officials believed to be the gemeinschaft ethos, which formed the peasant base of precolonial kingdoms. These communities were touted by district officers and European ethnographers as the repositories of the "traditional" craft skills and customs of African and other colonized peoples. Warnings that African handicraft skills were declining or dying out as a result of competition from shoddy, machine-manufactured goods from the West (Smith 1926, 69ff.) were extensions of a century-long craft revival movement in England itself, championed in successive generations by critics of industrialization and artists of the stature of John Ruskin, William Morris, and Bernard Leach (Thompson 1955, 65–67, 120–132). As with their counterparts in England and America (Lears 1981, chap. 2), the concern of official ethnographers to record and sustain African handicraft techniques arose from a determination to uphold the authentic in defiance of a flood of cheap, alien, and often ersatz imports from industrial Europe.

The analogies drawn by British colonial officials between societies like the emirates of Northern Nigeria and medieval Europe represented one of the more significant applications of the concept of recapitulation to the actual practice of colonial rule. The notion of recapitulation, which gained wide currency among European intellectuals in the nineteenth century (Adas 1989, 164–165, 172–173), held that peoples and societies whom the Europeans regarded as primitive, savage, or barbaric represented earlier stages in human development; stages that the Europeans themselves had gone through in the distant past. Thus, the equivalent of European medieval society achieved by the Nigerian emirates, or Indian civilization in the view of writers like Henry Maine, meant that they had advanced much further than most of the peoples in the Niger delta area, whom the British saw as exemplars of their prehistoric origins. This ranking of colonized peoples in terms of what European observers judged to be their level of social and cultural development was a product of the social evolutionist theorizing that had become a major force in British and especially French thinking on colonial issues by the late 1890s. Lugard, Clifford, and other advocates of indirect rule argued that because this approach to administration was premised upon the preservation or reconstruction of "traditional" African societies and cultures, it was the best adaptation to the level of evolutionary development that a particular people had achieved. The wide latitude for self-rule through their own leaders and institutions that indirect rule permitted meant that each colonized people could advance at its own pace rather than being forced to adjust to expectations and demands geared to societies at a higher level of evolutionary development (Lugard 1965 [1922], 193, 198; Nigerian Council 1920, 28–29).

In the view of those who championed indirect rule, encouraging colonized peoples to break abruptly from their natural evolutionary trajectory and to leap within a generation from the traditional village to the lifestyle of middle-class Europeans unleashed forces that were inimical to social peace in the colonies and the continuation of European domination. Lugard and his disciples made little secret of their hostility to the Western-educated classes in the urban centers of Africa or to their counterparts elsewhere in the empire. The Native States of India, Lugard charged, were the appropriate model for administrators in Africa, while the growing nationalist challenge in areas of the subcontinent that were under direct rule and extensively Westernized testified to the dangers of too rapid a pace of change. Given Nigeria's deep "tribal" divisions, he concluded, the minuscule Western-educated classes of the coastal towns could not possibly represent national interests as they claimed. The only genuine representatives of the diverse Nigerian peoples were their traditional rulers and "chiefs" (Lugard 1965 [1922], 195–196, 226).

Just after the war, Lugard's successor, Hugh Clifford, contrasted what he characterized as the artificial and unrepresentative nationalism of the Western-educated professionals of the Aborigines Rights Protection Society with the authentic national bonds that he believed linked the different peoples of Nigeria with their own traditional rulers and local notables. Noting the recent disturbances in Egbaland that he claimed had been set off by the corruption and insensitivity of Western-educated officials who had infiltrated into the government of the traditional rulers, Clifford argued that the time-tested policies of their "natural" rulers rather than Westernizing innovations were the key to good government in the colonies. Allegiance to the imaginary nation envisioned by increasingly vocal, urban professionals, he claimed, could not begin to compete with the peoples' attachment to the natural rulers of the diverse multitude of internally homogenous "nations" that were linked only by British colonial rule (Nigerian Council 1920, 18–19, 22–23, 27–28).

CONCLUSION

The nature of the effects of indirect rule on postcolonial African history has been a subject of considerable and continuing controversy, with views ranging from those who see the Lugardian approach to colonial governance as a key contributor to the rise of African self-government and sense of social responsibility (Hogbin and Kirk-Greene 1966, 133) to those who dismiss it as a breeding ground for autocracy, conservatism, and resistance to the forces of modernism (Crowder 1968, 137, 198–199, 220–221). Whatever its impact on recent African history, the widespread imposition of systems of indirect rule has profoundly influenced the way African cultures and societies have been studied and thought about through much of the twentieth century. The extensive project of reconstructing traditional cultures, which was central to the thinking of British colonial policy makers who shaped systems of indirect rule, both fossilized and essentialized the African societies and cultures to which the system was applied. They were seen as static configurations with definite "tribal" boundaries and timeless customs, rituals, and patterns of behavior rooted in tribal identities and institutions. This view was, of course, quite consistent with the notion of recapitulation that informed colonial thinking, and it served to justify the efforts of successive administrators to isolate *their* "native preserves" from the disruptive forces emanating from the rapidly changing, heavily Westernized towns. Nowhere was this isolation more vigorously pursued than in the seedbed of Lugard's vision of indirect rule, Northern Nigeria, which was shielded even from missionary education that was a key agent of change in much of the rest of British West (and South and East) Africa.

From the observations of colonial administrators and often more discerning official ethnographers and independent anthropologists, a reified and eternal essence of African societies and cultures was distilled in the decades when indirect rule was in vogue. The African societies incorporated into the colonial order in this way were seen, for example, to be consensual, oriented to collectivity and hierarchy, and profoundly conservative (Asad 1973, 114–115; Orde Browne 1925, 258–259; Ranger 1983, 247). Not coincidentally, all these attributes made these societies more amenable to rule by colonial overlords, provided they were willing to work through the indigenous elites and existing institutions. The application of indirect rule made the identification, fixing, and preservation of these imagined social qualities and the cultural configurations that had nurtured them the central tasks of European administrators. Ironically, the colonizers were often so successful at essentializing and reifying that key elements of the cultures they reconstructed or invented were appropriated by emerging African nationalist leaders anxious to associate their movements with evocative and legitimizing symbols, beliefs, and political rituals.

The effects of the project of reconstruction and invention associated with the introduction of indirect rule in different colonized areas were felt beyond the arenas where colonizers and emergent nationalists vied for political influence. The ahistorical quality of the British perception of "traditional" societies and cultures incorporated into the colonial order had much to do with the overwhelmingly synchronic nature of British social anthropology. Perhaps less directly but often equally critically, it also accounts for the absence of a meaningful diachronic dimension to most anthropological studies until recent decades (Ortner 1984, 141–143). This pattern was mirrored in historical research by a prevailing tendency to associate process, dynamism, and forces that made for cultural transformation with the coming of the West, whether through the slave trade, the spread of the postslaving market economy, or the imposition of colonial rule. These were seen to act upon "traditional" African societies and cultures that were essentially closed, discrete, and static entities, rather than malleable configurations with imperatives and processual histories of their own.

All this brings us back to Eric Wolf's observation about the colonizers and missed cultural cues in responding to the colonized or the Europeans' tendency to ignore them altogether. Much of the colonial experience would bear this observation out, particularly when it is applied to the groups that were Wolf's main concern—peasant farmers, tenants, rural laborers, and other social groups without a history, about whom for all their paternalistic pretensions most of the colonizers knew little. But in certain time periods and colonial locales, particularly in the decades on either side of World War I in much of the British empire, great energy was expended by both official and civilian colonizers to study and perpetuate the cultural scripts and stage moves of colonized peoples. As I have tried to show in this essay, their motives for this enterprise were complex and mixed—though all ultimately led back to the desire to shore up what was perceived to be a crumbling colonial edifice.

Whatever their intent, the effort proved futile. Conquest and alien rule inevitably altered indigenous cultural performances and drained them of much of their meaning and thus their capacity to hold the attention of important segments of the peasant audience, much less urban laborers and the emerging middle classes. At the same time, indigenous challengers to the colonial overlords laid claim to the "authentic" configurations of cultural tradition that were so often the product of the reconstruction projects of European administrators and ethnographers. They and successive generations of "modernization"-minded social scientists have very often inherited the stultified and essentialized visions of "traditional" African and Asian culture that these reconstruction projects yielded. It should not surprise us then that cultural cues continue to be missed, that grand development schemes have too often been pushed by postcolonial elites and world agencies that have made little provision for the social disruption and human displacement they were bound to engender.

NINETEEN

Who Were the Bushmen?
Historical Process in the Creation of
an Ethnic Construct

Edwin N. Wilmsen

Isaac Schapera noted, forty years ago, that Tswana "tribes" (Ngwato, Kgatla, Kwena, Ngwaketse, Rolong, Tawana, etc.) in the Bechuanaland Protectorate, now Botswana, were neither ethnically nor linguistically homogeneous.[1] He also noted that an anomaly existed in the 1946 Census of the Protectorate, that is, although people called Bayei then (as they do today) constituted a majority of the population in the northwestern district, Ngamiland, there were very few Yei wards (Schapera 1952, 68–102). Bayei are Western Bantu-speaking riverine people whose ancestors have lived in the Okavango-Chobe river system for several centuries; they were subjugated by Batawana, a junior branch of Eastern Bantu-speaking Tswana agropastoralists, in the early decades of the nineteenth century. The anomaly noted by Schapera came about because subjugated non-Tswana peoples were, more so in the past than now, incorporated by Batswana into a regional *morafe* (pl., *merafe*, usually glossed "tribes"; I prefer "polities") by creating separate *tebelo* (wards, putatively kin-based administrative subunits of merafe) for them under the administration of a junior elite member of the local Tswana morafe appointed as headman by his *kgosi* (chief). Members of a ward are by Setswana definition members of their headman's morafe; in the past, it would seem this also conferred Tswana (in this case, Tawana) identity on those peoples, hence they became Batswana of the appropriate morafe.[2] That this was no longer the case in mid-twentieth century and Yei members of the Tawana "tribe" now retain "ethnic" Yei identity underscores the processes of ethnicization I shall discuss in this essay.

It also underscores my argument that, however embellished by expressive signs or shielded in clouds of symbolic values, the essence of ethnic existence lies in differential access to means of production and rights to shares in production returns. The terms, both as name and as condition, of ethnic identification are always given from outside (Mudimbe 1989). It is not necessary, perhaps not usual, that a designating term is itself introduced by a dominant authority; the name will likely have an older usage quite independent of its transformed application. But its acquired ethnic form and content are determined by relative position in a power context. Furthermore, dominant groups are never ethnicities; they are in control. Successful national states employ their power of cultural hegemony to facilitate renewal of forms of involuntary ascription, such as ethnicity; these forms can coexist with a national consciousness precisely because they are cultural, that is, ascribed (see Vail 1989, 10), and therefore can appear both natural and national from the perspective of individuals. In political discourse, perhaps particularly in times of crisis, the established status of these ethnic terms often provides the most readily available avenue for collective self-identification and action. This helps to explain why today in southern Africa many people who are not in power attach great significance to the "facts" of cultural difference, even though this plays directly into the segregating ideology of the dominant nationalist power structure. These "facts" are drawn from histories both imagined and actual; they are thus available as the basis for the formation of groups whose members are perceived to share a common culture (Wilmsen in press *a*).

The function of ethnic terms in condensing previously independent social features into a coherent set of generalized symbols with which individuals can identify does appear to be internal to the ideology of individuals who thereby anchor a collective sense of selfhood (Galaty 1982, 17). The resulting identity nucleus transposes and attempts to transcend, for its constituent members, collective and individual partitioning from the encompassing social formation. Thus ideologically centered, the ethnic nucleus with its icons and lexicon, with its indexical signs perpetually pointing to its legitimate ontology, serves as internal rationale for individual peripheral position in a social formation.

But it is just those partitive structures of the social formation that are prior to ethnic logics and creations; they include the economic and political power structures in which partitioning takes place. Consequently, these prior structures must constrain the forms into which previously independent features may be condensed; they also constrain the parameters of generalized identity and collective sense of selfhood. That is to say, although the "ethnic" function of constructing a collective identity center may appear to be self-motivated and self-motivating, it is actually dictated by the material conditions in which the ethnicizing function is realized. This is the role of ideology in local and regional factionalism today.

Ethnicity, thus, is a feature of class domination by means of which subordinate "groups" are kept in conflict with each other; ethnicities grow out of this conflict. J. Galaty (1982, 17) concludes that it represents one of the most accessible and easiest levels of discourse regarding general identity. Although this often appears to be true, ethnicity and identity refer to diametrically opposite processes of locating individuals within a social formation, the one to objective conditions of inequality in an arena of social power, the other to subjective classification on a stage of social practice. As John L. Comaroff (1987, 302) puts it, "ethnicity takes on a cogent existential and experiential reality when sociocultural features are reified into a justificatory premise for inequality." Thus, ethnic consciousness and class (to paraphrase Sydel Silverman [1976, 633]) "represent two entangled systems of stratification." Ethnic identity arises when—and if—these processes intersect; it is constituted in partitive ideologies within the framework of class struggle (see Friedrich 1989). The accompanying discourse is ideologically embedded in a wider cultural discourse in which ethnic divisions are fluid and shaped by objective (or, objectively perceived) positions of persons in a social field.

J. O'Brien (1986, 899), however, calls attention to the fact that a primordialist notion of ethnicity remains strong in vernacular imaginations, and, indeed, "seems implicit in the concrete analyses of some anthropologists" up to the present day—analyses, moreover, in which emphasis is more often placed on symbols and rituals (the putative culturally distinctive markers of groups) than on the economics and politics of subordinated lives. It seems self-evident that an ambiguous theoretical stance that qualifies any minority group phenomenon as ethnic must feed a primordialist philosophy of division because "it makes it all too easy to explain away any material that doesn't 'fit'" (Silverman 1976, 626); worse, it allows *any* material to fit. For example, even in some excellent recent works on the creation of tribes in Africa, ethnicity and tribalism are conflated (e.g., Vail 1989). But tribes, as L. Vail's authors make abundantly clear, are a product of colonial engagement; they are essentially administrative constructs. By contrast, ethnicity as a central logic emerged out of conflicts engendered in competition for favored positions among these tribal constructs. The emergent ethnicities were formulated out of an amalgam of preexisting indigenous and inserted colonial partitive ideologies. A dominant class—in colonial Africa, this was often an ascendent "tribal" aristocracy—defined and determined the terms of subordinate class competition, which is the seedbed of ethnicizing processes. It is particularly important to stress this at a time when a philosophy of primordial ethnicity is being widely reasserted as a form of neoracism to justify new or continued suppression of dispossessed ethnic groups. As Comaroff (1987, 320) observes: "So long as social practice continues to be pursued *as if* ethnicity did hold the key to the structures of inequality, the protectionism of the dominant and the responses of the dominated alike serve to reproduce an ethnically ordered world."

ETHNIC ANTECEDENTS

With this framework of ethnicizing processes in mind, I turn now to the discourse of ethnicity in Botswana and trace some trajectories along which individual and group identities became homogenized.[3] I argue that the inter-section of ethnicity and class lies in the creation of what Eric R. Wolf (1982*a*, 380) has called "a 'disposable mass' of laborers out of diverse populations." In this creation, the basic relation between capital and labor is reproduced at the same time that the heterogeneity of labor sources is reinforced. This is accomplished "by ordering the groups and categories of laborers hierarchi-cally with respect to one another, and by continuously producing and re-creating symbolically marked 'cultural' distinctions among them" (Wolf 1982*a*, 380). It was in just this intersection that indigenous Tswana and colonial European partitive ideologies converged to create the class struc-ture with its ethnic divisions found in Botswana today.

Thus, although the Bantu- and Khoisan-speaking peoples of Botswana now rearrange their divisions according to a logic long internal to them-selves, they do so with respect to relative positions of power in an overarch-ing social formation that is itself the creation of colonial and postcolonial power relations. The resultant constructed ethnicities rarely conform to a people's prior self-identification. For example, during the past one hundred and fifty years or so, all Khoisan languages spoken in the Kalahari region, of which as many as ten are mutually unintelligible, have been lumped undif-ferentially by Setswana under a single term, Sesarwa (the language of Bush-men), whereas the speakers of these languages became undifferentially marked as Basarwa (the Bushmen/San of ethnography).[4] In like manner, independent eponymous Sekgalagadi-speaking Bangologa, Bakgwatheng, Bashaga, Baloongwe, and others living in the dry sandveld were undifferen-tiated as Bakgalagadi (people of the desert) when they were reduced to sub-ordinate status (Ncgoncgo 1977; Okihiro 1976; Schapera 1942). Again, when Batawana established themselves on Lake Ngami in about 1795, they rather quickly subordinated indigenous Bayei and other Okavango Delta peoples who were collectively, and disparagingly, called Makoba (accord-ing to some Batawana this means "slaves" but it is more usually glossed "those who lag behind"), a term often still applied to them today (Tlou 1979). Even weaker Tswana-speaking peoples, more distantly related to the emerging hegemonic polities (principally Ngwato and Kwena) could be categorized according to the dictates of hegemonic Tswana merafe. Thus, small groups of Tswana-speaking Bapedi were gradually dominated by Bangwato and subjected to tribute levies, labor extraction, land appropria-tion, and resettlement in the Tswapong Hills where they, along with subju-gated Bakaa, Bakhurutse, and other Tswana speakers acquired the designa-tion, Batswapo, as a mark of their collective subordination (Motzafi-Haller 1987). Delmos Jones and Jacqueline Hill-Burnett (1982, 218) argue that it is just this homogeneous treatment of diverse peoples that brings about the formative stage of ethnicity.

Two initially separate but ultimately converging processes combined to create the ethnic distinctions currently found in Botswana. The cumulative effect of these congruent processes has been the consolidation of a colonially inspired generalized ethnic inequality inserted into precolonially existing structures of inequality. These latter preexisting structures were overridden when local group autonomy was subverted beginning in the early nineteenth century by the stereotyping recategorization that was a salient feature of Tswana hegemonic consolidation, as the foregoing examples illustrate. This itself reflects the ethnopolitical state formation of the Tswana polity (Cooper 1977, 4). As Wolf (1982a, 381) has noted, "Such ethnicities are therefore not 'primordial' social relationships. They are historical products of labor market segmentation under the capitalist mode."

That European colonial administrative order created tribes where it could not discover them has been given much attention and will not detain us. This was essentially a labor process designed more or less consciously to relegate stigmatized peoples to lower echelons in the labor pool while insulating through the legal structure erected by colonial administration hegemonically higher strata from lower echelon competition. For example, official British policy in the 1920s announced that if Basarwa were allowed to leave their masters they should do so only in a recognized and controlled manner (Gadibolae 1985, 28).

In order to link the developing capitalist and indigenous Tswana modes of social division, however, it is necessary to examine in greater detail the prior process that brought about ethnicization in Botswana; this lies on a trajectory of social relations with ancient roots in the region.[5] When premetallurgical pastoralist economies were absorbed into southern Africa two thousand years ago, the social groups involved were almost surely not markedly differentiated among themselves. We can be reasonably confident that among those groups were indigenous Khoisan-speaking foragers and pastroforagers. There is also fairly strong circumstantial evidence that non-Bantu-speaking black peoples were involved; it is possible that their descendants are to be found among the Khoe-speaking peoples (the so-called Black Bushmen) who still live in a wide arch across northern Namibia, southern Angola, the top of Botswana, and western Zambia and Zimbabwe. There is reason to think that Khoisan-speaking peoples then constituted the higher status economic and political groups. In the subsequent period (A.D. 600–1000) when Bantu-speaking peoples who were agropastoralists and metallurgists spread throughout southern Africa, a regional differentiation of settlement organization and an associated difference in social formations can be discerned in the archaeological record. In the east there was clearly an appropriation of Khoisan-speaking forager/pastroforager systems by Bantu-speaking agropastoral metallurgists who within about three centuries established a hierarchy of settlements around their central towns. It appears that by the end of the first millennium A.D. eastern Kalahari communities were differentiated socially and economically in a manner similar to that of later historically known and contemporary social formations found in that same region.

In the western half of the subcontinent, full agropastoralist economies with metalworking and transcontinental exchange networks were introduced at the same time as in the east. Bantu-speaking peoples were surely involved in the process in the northern peripheral zones where transmission must have taken place and there is some historical evidence to suggest that they penetrated much further south. But Bantu hegemony as it now exists was not established in the western Kalahari until shortly after the mid-nineteenth century, and at first only to a limited extent. It appears, rather, that early agropastoral economies were transferred among indigenous cattle-keeping pastroforagers, who could only have been Khoisan speakers, and entering Bantu-speaking small stock herding and horticultural metalworkers. The mechanisms for these transfers are not yet entirely clear but probably followed long-established lines of interaction and then became internally differentiated according to local conditions. Forager and herder polities were less hegemonically structured in this area than in the east, as they are known not to have been in historic time until disrupted in the nineteenth century, first by Batswana and then by European capitalism.

In the twelfth century as trade with the Indian Ocean, which had then been important in the Kalahari for at least two hundred years, grew in scale, peoples on the eastern highlands (for example, at Great Zimbabwe) exploited their geographical advantage with respect to the east coast trading entrepots and centralized trading networks to their own benefit. From then on, the Kalahari as a whole was reduced to the status of producer rather than receiver in the Asian trade and local eastern Kalahari polities appear to have become internally less stratified under the hegemony of the Zimbabwean highland states. A series of sites dating from the twelfth to the nineteenth centuries documents the continuity of these small-scale ceramic- and metal-using agropastoralists into the time of recorded history (Denbow and Wilmsen 1986).

Before the later nineteenth century, there was no overarching Tswana category (Denbow, Kiyaga-Mulindwa, and Parsons 1985; Murray 1986), only several independent polities whose leaders were descendants of eponymous Tswana founders. Shula Marks (1982, 10) calls attention to the manifest fluidity of political boundaries in the region at that time, when the objectives of leaders and societies were to "secure a certain degree of control over people, followers, not units of wage labour. In this situation, amongst Africans ethnicity would appear to have been of relatively little significance." That is, historically constructed assumptions about individual and group identity associations were, in practice as well as in ideology, what Peter Worsley (1984, 242) has labeled "relative, situational categories." We have the testimony of Tshekedi Khama, regent of Bangwato, that when the forebears of present-day Batswana entered what is now Botswana at mid-eighteenth century, there was "no question of overlordship of one people over another ... we had no strength by which we could force them

[Basarwa] to become our servants." Alluding to the Boer extermination of "Bushmen" in South Africa, Khama continued candidly: "If we had had such power the history of our contact with them would have been similar to the history of the white people with them" (see Joyce 1938).

These ancient roots came to a crisis during the so-called difaqane wars[6] of the early nineteenth century when a large proportion of southern Africa's peoples became realigned socially and politically. In the Kalahari, a particular class structure along with its attendant property and surplus extraction relations was established, initially with the *kgamelo* (milk-jug) system instituted by Kgari, kgosi of Bangwato, in about 1826–1828 (Parsons 1977). Through this system, older forms of property relations were replaced by stronger suzerainty of Tswana royals and for the first time the formerly bipartite royal/commoner division of Tswana social order based on intersecting kinship was expanded to include an intermediate administrator class and an underclass of *malata*, serfs, incorporated mainly from peoples outside recognized Tswana merafe (Mautle 1986, 23). Whereas exchange relations between indigenous peoples and Batswana appear to have been previously reasonably balanced, from the second quarter of the nineteenth century direct force was increasingly applied to extract ever larger levies of "ground rent" (in the form of tusks, furs, feathers, hides, livestock, and labor) from increasingly dispossessed non-Tswana Bantu- as well as Khoisan-speaking peoples.

As Khama suggests, coercive means were seldom available and rarely needed to recruit autonomous, self-sufficient foragers and pastroforagers into becoming commodity producers through hunting ivory, furs, and ostrich feathers; similarly, resident pastoralists were apparently readily induced to take on the daily maintenance of Tswana cattle. The transfer of livestock work to other groups by ruling Batswana took two forms. In one, cattle were taken to distant water sources and left in the care of resident people; this would seem to have been a form of *mafisa* (a patron-client relationship). Subsequently, young men and women were taken from their homes and transported to established Tswana locations where they were used as herdboys, milkmaids, domestic servants, and hunters. This transpositioning of labor appears to have been initially mutually agreed upon and perhaps mutually useful.

From mid-nineteenth century onward, however, Batswana imposed a form of native colonialism upon subordinated peoples, expropriating the productive capacity of their land as well as their labor. This happened in even the distant corners of the Kalahari: "They put us under the carrying yoke," as a Dobe Zhu man graphically phrased his recollection of the time to Richard B. Lee (1979, 78; the German geographer, Siegfried Passarge, gives illuminating descriptions of the situation in the 1890s [Wilmsen in press *b*]). The transferred value for labor, usually in the form of payments in kind, was less than the cost to laborers of their social reproduction, forcing them deeper into varying degrees of serfdom or clientship. Foraging offered an option to escape this dependency, but it was an incomplete one that had become a condition of poverty in the overall social formation and was not open to all; those who fell into this form of subsistence depression were further removed from participation in the political economy and became the "Bushmen" of modern ethnography.

The consolidation of power in a few Tswana hands coincided with, and was in large measure stimulated by, the insertion of European mercantile capital into the region. It was as a consequence of struggles to control commodity production for the newly created market, that is, to control labor units, and to channel access of the resultant product to its market that secondary rationalizations (Worsley 1984, 235) were invoked to first concretize ideologically then stigmatize in practice those peoples who became progressively more disenfranchised. As part of this process, the mobility of increasingly dependent peoples became a function of the wishes of Tswana administrators and masters, preventing thereby the growth of a free labor market that might have given those peoples some advantage.

The history of labor migration in Botswana reveals that a multitiered system of reserves was required in the Protectorate to free Tswana men from otherwise inescapable duties in domestic production and allow them to take advantage of cash income opportunities on the mines and farms of South Africa (Wilmsen 1982). One subordinate tier in this system is the female-headed household that is especially prevalent in the southern and eastern parts of the country from whence the greater proportion of migrant labor is drawn. The major burden of reproducing labor migrants' social relations of production falls on such households. A second subordinate tier is composed of ethnicized minorities, among whom Khoisan-speakers are prominent but hardly alone. The initial stages of subjugation of these "minorities" (who are in the majority in some districts, as are Bayei in the Northwest) were completed in their essentials by the middle of the nineteenth century. Necessary to the process of subordination was an undermining of self-sufficiency, due not so much to a loss of indigenous productive capacity by the natural environment (although loss, particularly through commodity hunting of animal species, did occur) as to a reorientation of relations of production stimulated by competition for favored positions in the only available labor market. It is, consequently, readily apparent why members of the rural underclass, mainly Basarwa but also substantial numbers of Bakgalagadi, Bayei, and others should compete for available labor positions as herdsmen. The collapse of ivory and feather markets quite suddenly alienated their labor from the land more thoroughly than had been possible either in the pre-European indigenous social formation or in its nineteenth-century transformation by merchant capital. Through this alienation, a surplus labor pool was created with essentially only one outlet. Those who could capture a cattlepost position obtained a measure of security in the system—at the bottom of the heap, but in it.

The dependency of Batswana developed as the obverse of that of dispossessed minorities and was one over which they retained for themselves a large measure of control within their own political sphere while becoming, in their turn, subjugated to the labor needs of industrializing South Africa. The contradictions inherent in serfdom keyed to land-based relations of extraction came to a crisis with the opening of South African diamond and gold mines, followed by demand for an ever-larger labor force to work the mines as well as the farms straining to supply the burgeoning need for provisions to feed mine labor. Serfdom inhibited the creation of a reserve of labor by restraining the response of potential workers in the Protectorate. In this atmosphere Khama, kgosi of Bangwato, ostensibly "freed" serfs in 1875, giving them the right to dispose of their labor in their own interests; in 1891, Sekgoma Letsholathebe, kgosi of Batawana, adopted this policy in Ngamiland. In fact, the conditions in which serfs found themselves had deteriorated. In the economic reality shaped by Tswana self-interest, there were very limited opportunities for freed serf labor aside from Tswana cattleposts where terms of employment were easily manipulated by elites who owned the means of production. As primary producers during the years of mercantile hunting, Bushmen had had some bargaining power in the disposal of their product. This power declined as state capital consolidated its strength and hunting became less remunerative; now, as obligatory herders, and also as subsistence foragers, they were completely at the mercy of their masters.

The imposition by British administration of a hut tax in 1899 increased the pressure (Massey 1980, 11). Tswana household heads found themselves in need of immediate cash, which the poorer among them could obtain only through migration to jobs principally in mines and on farms in South Africa but also on the productive farms in the southern parts of the Protectorate. At least part of their consequently absent domestic labor had to be replaced. As J. Parson (1984, 25) observes, this quickly created a pattern of oscillating migratory labor that touched almost all the people who lived in the Protectorate. Thus began the transformation of the rural poor, among whom serfs and clients were among the very poorest, into what Parson (1981, 240; see also Cooper 1982, 297; Marks 1982) has called a peasantariat, a proletarian industrial working class with a retained agricultural base. In this transformation, Sarwa and Kgalagadi serfs, who had nothing to offer but their labor, increasingly found their place in this partly proletarianized agricultural arena; they filled the homestead labor gap created by absent Tswana migrants. As a result, the 1937 Bushman Survey reported that there were hundreds of cattleposts in the Bangwato Reserve at most of which Masarwa were found. Significantly, J. Joyce (1938, 15) did not include Bateti among the Bushmen of this survey because he said that economically they could not be distinguished from their Tswana and Kalanga neighbors, though "in appearance and language they were Masarwa." Forty years later, R. Hitchcock (1978) excluded Bateti from his socioeconomic survey for the same reasons.

Force was sometimes necessary to keep Sarwa labor on a particular cattlepost. In 1930, Tshekedi Khama testified at the trial of a Mongwato accused of killing his runaway Sarwa serf that "Masarwa were deserting their lords and masters in Bamangwato Reserve and finding work or squatting in Northeast District"; he said that Bangwato go on "slave hunting" tours to return them, and kill them sometimes if they resist too much (Joyce 1938). Siegfried Passarge (1907) in 1897 noted similar conditions in western Ngamiland and seventy years later Lee (1979, 396) recorded Zhu memories of this "rough frontier justice" at Dobe, as did I at CaeCae in the 1970s. Less harsh, perhaps, but at least equally effective was the decision taken ten years later to confiscate all Sarwa firearms in Central District, thus forcing Sarwa men to seek out work on cattleposts. Indeed, Basarwa and Bakgalagadi were the only peoples available to be hired in any numbers; in large measure, this is why they are to be found on almost every cattlepost, rather than only those of the wealthy, in the region today. In this labor climate, an emergent Tswana aristocracy gained ascendency not only over minority peoples but over peripheral branches of its own linguistic affiliates. The large economic differences found today between patron villages and remote rural client settlements can be traced directly to this historically developed ecologic-ethnic pattern.

ETHNIC LEGACIES

This brief overview of the past two thousand years of Kalahari history has traced the trajectories along which economically, politically, and linguistically diverse Khoisan-speaking peoples were subordinated and transformed ideologically into an undifferentiated "ethnic" category. None of this occurred automatically or uniformly throughout the region. Rather, it came about through episodic transformations in power relations involving political and economic struggles among many peoples spanning centuries in an encompassing historical sense and decades in a more restricted colonial sense. The structure of ethnic class relations in the regional economy is rooted in these specific conditions of production and accumulation. These relations have been defined in a particular history of political struggle over access to the disposal of labor as well as to land resources and products along with the attendant power to manipulate the disposal of these products. Thus, in Wolf's (1982*a*, 380) words, the intersection of ethnicity and class in the Kalahari lies in the creation of "a 'disposable mass' of laborers out of diverse populations." In this creation, the basic relation between capital and labor is reproduced at the same time that the heterogeneity of labor sources is reinforced. This is accomplished, as Wolf says, "by ordering the groups and categories of laborers hierarchically with respect to one another, and by continuously producing and recreating symbolically marked 'cultural' distinctions among them." It was just in this intersection that indigenous and colonial European partitive ideologies converged to create the class structure with its ethnic divisions found in Botswana today.

Earlier chiefdom-states were tied together by lopsided but nonetheless mutual mafisa and kinship relations and were regulated by tributary mechanisms passing domestic products and exchange commodities up and down the hierarchical line (Nangati 1982, 140). With the penetration of mercantile capitalism, this preexisting structure of reciprocity, which had articulated the state hierarchy with various forms of communal property relations, was at first strengthened in order to facilitate the flow of commodities from producers to merchants. As the nineteenth century entered its third quarter, those in the higher echelons of the political hierarchy found it increasingly easier to siphon off for themselves an ever-larger fraction of the reverse flow of exchange value. Thus, former relations of reciprocity were transformed into exploitative relations for purposes of profit in the modern cash nexus. In the process, the dues and privileges of earlier elites (in theory, simply their share of community property) were increasingly translated into private family fortunes of a colonially favored aristocracy. Previously flexible relations of production were transformed into ethnic categories defined by criteria of race, language, and economic status. Although self-referent names of Khoisan-speaking peoples (Zhu, Gcwi, Gxana, Deti, Qoo, and a dozen others) continue to function as self-identity terms, the imposed Tswana term, Basarwa, is today favored as the global referent in national discourse; the state fosters the use of Basarwa and suppresses self-referents in the schools (Vossen 1988). This is at base a racial classification stereotyped in images of supposed neotenic physiognomy, atavistic culture, homogeneous social institutions, and inferior language, although this is masked by the rhetoric of ethnicity within the class structure of Botswana.

In this atmosphere, the native category, Basarwa (which in its root connotation of aboriginality was neutral, or perhaps positive), retains its acquired negative denotations. Historically, these denotations became reciprocally marked in symbolic ordering, with Basarwa "Bushmen" increasingly consigned to a peripheral wild, uncontrolled "nature" in Tswana ideology, whereas in much, but by no means all, San ideology Batswana took on the central attributes of overlordship. Other groups were drawn into positions between these polar nodes.

Some examples will illuminate the process by which perpetuation of this segmentation is assured. The first concerns District Land Boards which, in order to safeguard increasingly scarce land for centrally perceived Tswana morafe constituencies, today often resort to dubious measures to discourage applications from stigmatized class cum ethnic persons seeking a parcel of arable land. That is to say, land allocation continues to follow the precolonial pattern of land control. In 1977, a Mosarwa man (whose linguistic affiliation is not identified) employed by a Motswana in that part of Kgatleng District designated remote applied to the Sub-District Land Board for a field to plow; after questioning designed to undermine his credibility, he was told that before further action could be taken he must return to the place of his birth where he had not been since childhood and obtain there a letter of identification, because "as you are not a Mokgatla you cannot be allocated land in Kgatleng District" (Worby n.d.). L. Wily (1979, 183) says this was not an isolated case and that local land boards routinely claim that peoples classed as Basarwa are not members of the Tswana polity in which they live, even if such peoples speak no San language. D. Cooper (1980, 130) points to the mutually reinforcing nature of this practice in which preestablished social divisions are partly reproduced because land allocation based on them is continuously partly reproduced.

In the second example, P. Motzafi-Haller (Motzafi 1986) documents a three-generation reproduction of socially isolated and economically depressed households at Tamasane in eastern Botswana; the members of these households speak only Setswana but are classified locally as Basarwa. All but two of these households are female-headed because Sarwa men are forced to seek labor opportunities in the only places available to them, invariably at distant cattleposts. Consequently, these men are rarely present in the village, and the women say of themselves "we are born alone," that is, without men. These women are vulnerable to the demands of other men who father their children but seldom acknowledge or support either the mothers or their progeny. These are acted out instances of the saying "Mosarwa ke yo motonanyana yo monamagadi ke Mongwato [The real Bushman is the male one, the female one is a Mongwato]" (Gadibolae 1985). What is meant here is that sexual pollution is not part of the stigmata of female lower social class; on the contrary, Tswana (and other) men are granted cost-free access to still another service of the submerged class. The result is a truncated Sarwa household development cycle that reproduces social marginality with its attendant economic poverty, coupled with stigmatized group identification. In the process, the unserviced, voiceless labor pool is kept full and available at little cost to the ruling class that thus reproduces—in both dimensions of this term—itself.

Finally, at CaeCae today about two-thirds of all Zhu households are incapable of securing social reproduction; this inability is grounded in the historical development of local social interaction as well as of production. All

these households have come to CaeCae during this century and have no entitlement to land or its products there. Most starkly notable is their inability
to contract footholds through marriage in the CaeCae landowning households, all of which have recognized, generations-long entitlements to that
place. This failure is not the consequence of a paucity of members of mar-
riageable age or of the capabilities of such persons in the excluded households. In the first half of the 1970s, they had several capable persons of both
sexes but made no marriages in the community. These otherwise desirable
persons were thoroughly dispossessed and could offer no security—either in
access to cowherd jobs or, now of secondary but still significant importance,
to foraging grounds; they were, therefore, of no interest to landholding
households. The persons in these landless households, especially the men
(for whom there is a potentially wide range of job categories), have become
freed labor in Marx's sense of being dispossessed from land; they are seeking
markets elsewhere for their labor. In contrast, during the same five-year period, a single homestead of landowning households made four lasting marriages and realized eight births. This homestead plus its kindred in the local
descent group thus has the potential to consolidate its tenurial entitlement
to CaeCae for another generation. It is also significant that all eleven of the
children born at CaeCae in the early 1980s who were fathered by transient
Tswana men were borne by unwed and unbetrothed teenaged and young
adult Zhu women from landless households. Neither the mothers nor the
children will derive any social or material support from the fathers. Furthermore, the children have no claim on their paternal family or its land; this
places them at a severe disadvantage with respect to those children in the
community who can call upon full kindred support. Although a few of these
"fatherless" children may overcome their disadvantage, most will probably
live a life of poverty. They will be forced, as are their older cousins now,
into an overly full labor pool where the ethnic label, Basarwa, will deepen
their disadvantage.

To a large degree, conditions of class poverty are shared today by rural
poor Batswana irrespective of ethnic labeling. These ethnic categorizations,
moreover, are, as in the past, neither homogeneous nor immutable, and, as
earlier, they act as masks for underlying class conflicts. It is important to
realize as well that there are as yet no internal social forces or entities corresponding to the labels Basarwa, Bakgalagadi, Batswapo, or Makoba,
integrating ideologically or politically the persons encompassed by these
terms. And it is useful to reiterate for emphasis that neither is each linguistically homogeneous. There are no commonly held Sarwa expressive signs
or symbolic values, no shared conception of a common Sarwa cultural heritage. Individuals and local groups accept, passively and negatively for the
most part, externally imposed Sarwa designation, but they do not yet recognize a global Sarwa "ethnicity" as an element in their perceived identity
structure.

Indeed, there is growing evidence that as objective conditions of inequality within Botswana locate particularized groups further out on the margins of the state formation, the subjective practice of members of those groups may subvert current indexical ethnic markers that are a function of marginalization. As class interests of peoples whose imposed identity is subsumed under labels such as Basarwa and Bakgalagadi become more explicitly aligned with those of other of Botswana's rural poor, these ethnic labels are likely to become submerged and ultimately replaced by self-designated terms of more meaningful content to the bearers. In this atmosphere, a tension develops between the need to join in a consolidation of security through shared identity—even if doing so guarantees continued economic marginalization—and the need to join the economic mainstream in order to escape marginality. The terms for joining are determined by a dominant class, which thereby defines the terms in which subordinate class competition may take place. Elsewhere (Wilmsen 1989; Wilmsen and Vossen 1990), I demonstrate that in the competition to enter those avenues, rural non-Tswana minorities lose out more frequently and more thoroughly than do those whose identification as Tswana goes unchallenged. This is simply a specific instance of a general process that has left myriad diverse and diversifying scars on the cultural edifice of capitalism. In Botswana, this has led to ethnicization of Basarwa along with other marked peoples as a means of coordinating and controlling class factions.

NOTES

1. This paper was written in the summer of 1989, about six months before President F. W. de Klerk effectively ended white rule in South Africa; consequently, some references to then active events no longer apply. However, an international conference on "Ethnicity, Identity, and Nationalism" which I co-organized in South Africa in April 1993 revealed that the paper's argument is, if anything, more cogent now than when it was written.

2. Bantu languages attach prefixes to noun roots to specify meaning domains. I use the following throughout this paper: Mo = single, Ba = plural person/s; Bo = locative; Se = linguistic-cognitive. Thus, Batswana are the Setswana-speaking/thinking people of Botswana; roots used as adjectives (Tswana people) have no prefix.

3. Citations to archival and other primary sources are not given in this section; they may be found in Wilmsen 1989.

4. Until recently, Masarwa was the form most frequently used; the prefix, Ma, refers to foreigners and persons of undesirable character.

5. This brief sketch of pre-nineteenth-century history is fully developed in Denbow and Wilmsen in press.

6. The difaqane/mfecane period has come under severe question; the fact of widespread, disruptive violence is not disputed, but whether this was a single coherent phenomenon or grew out of many local combinations of indigenous and introduced forces is intensely debated, much as is the "Bushman" question (see Cobbing 1988; Hamilton and Wright in press).

TWENTY

Amazonian Windows to the Past: Recovering Women's Histories from the Ecuadorean Upper Amazon

Blanca M. Muratorio

After a critical reassessment of Claude Lévi-Strauss's distinction between "cold" and "hot" societies, some Amazonian scholars have turned their attention to the creativity shown by Amazonian indigenous peoples in incorporating their particular experiences of colonial contact into their mythical narratives (Hill 1988; Hugh-Jones 1988), recognizing that myth and history are complementary modes of historical consciousness (Turner 1988). Without overlooking the importance of mythic narratives in Amazonian societies, I have chosen to examine the issue of historical consciousness in a group of Amazonian women through the narrative genre of daily conversation. This topic raises the problem of the relationship between gender ideologies, culture, and consciousness in an ethnographic area where this theoretical concern remains relatively unexplored.

In Latin American and Mediterranean Catholic societies, "Marianismo," as an ideology of female spiritual superiority modeled on the ideal figure of the Virgin Mary, has been used to explain important aspects of the dynamics of gender relations. Evelyn P. Stevens (1973), who introduced the concept in the North American literature on Latin American women, claimed that Marianismo as a form of female power was able to counterbalance the exacerbated virility and mastery of men over women commonly known as "machismo." Since the 1970s, further research on gender ideologies has questioned, directly or indirectly, the ahistorical character of this version of Marianismo and has explored its changing meanings in relation to considerations of class, ethnicity, and historical change (e.g., for the Mediterranean, see Collier 1986; for Latin America, Harris 1978, 1980; Martin 1990; Silverblatt 1980, 1987). I am unable to discuss at length here all the theoretical implications of this literature. In the case of the Amazonian indigenous women whom I am examining, however, one small clarification about the applicability of this concept of Marianismo to different culture areas is in order.

Unlike the more general connotations of sexual behavior explicit in the term "machismo," Marianismo is specifically tied to one religious figure—the Virgin Mary—who plays an important role only in the Catholic version of Christianity. Although it is possible to say that Catholicism was adopted in regions of the European Mediterranean and in white and mestizo America as an integral component of their own Western culture, in the indigenous populations of the Americas, it was imposed by force as part of a larger cultural and material colonial project. Any ideologies derived from Catholicism and said to influence the consciousness of indigenous peoples have to be analyzed in this light. Furthermore, in her article on the transformations suffered by Marianismo in contemporary rural Spain, Jane F. Collier (1986) has rightly argued that gender conceptions of different peoples not only have a different material basis, but have to be understood in relation to the specific historical experiences of these peoples. Here I will look at Marianismo as a historically specific gender ideological construction used by Catholic missionaries, along with other evangelical strategies, to try to enforce upon Napo Quichua women of the Ecuadorean tropical forest a particular way of being women, and to colonize their consciousness into the missionaries' own version of Christian and civilized gender behavior.

To interpret this colonial ideological construction as the reality of women's self-perception and practice would be to fall into the same Eurocentric discourse that denied indigenous women their own histories. Instead, in this article I will explore in particular the way gender mediates in the shaping of indigenous historical consciousness. By uncovering a significant facet of the active history of these "people without history" (Wolf 1982a), I will examine how Napo Quichua women borrowed those cultural categories and images of the colonial discourse specifically related to their subordination, reinterpreted the meaning of those images to suit their own cultural needs, and in the process managed to question some of the most important premises of Catholic dogma.

THE COLONIAL ENCOUNTERS

The Napo Quichua of the Upper Napo belong to a long-established tropical forest culture of the Ecuadorean Amazon, a culture that they share in different degrees with thousands of other lowland Quichua (Quechua) speakers. Traditionally all Napo Quichua were hunter-gatherers and swidden horticulturalists. Throughout the four hundred years of their contacts first with the Spanish conquistadors and later with the Ecuadorean national society, they have adapted their subsistence strategies to deal with *encomiendas*, labor tribute, gold panning, and rubber tapping under an exploitative system of debt-peonage controlled by traders and patrons. Since the 1940s, large-scale colonization, oil exploration and development, and small-town urban growth have impinged as well. Since the middle of the sixteenth century, European colonialism of this area was followed by Christian missionaries keen on civilizing and evangelizing the "savages." Looking for the best route to their mission in Maynas, the Jesuits established themselves in Napo Quichua territory in the seventeenth century where they remained until they were expelled from the Americas in 1768. Under the auspices of a conservative government, they returned to the area in 1869 and established a mission along with the Good Shepherd nuns, until they were expelled thirty years later by a liberal government.

The process of economic and spiritual conquest was not easily accomplished, and the colonial powers faced several Indian rebellions, the earliest of which took place in 1562. As late as the middle of the nineteenth century the Napo Quichua were described by a surprised foreign traveler as showing "a great disdain for religion" (Osculati 1854, 103–104). By 1922 the government was willing to try again and collaborated with the Italian Catholic Josephine Order and with the Dorothean and Murialdin nuns to establish a mission that remains, to this day, in the core of Napo Quichua territory. They were soon followed by a series of Evangelical Protestant missionaries, primarily from the United States.

As a people, the Napo Quichua were in many ways constituted by their historical encounter with the first European expansion into the Amazon region in the middle of the sixteenth century. The expansion constitutes their history as well (see Wolf 1982*a*, 385), even if they did not share equal power with the Europeans in determining the main story line (see Asad 1987, 604). Out of a multitude of different ethnic and language groups in the area of the Upper Napo prior to the Spanish conquest (Lemus y de Andrade 1965; Ortegón 1973), the Napo Quichua emerged identifying themselves as *Runa*, the Quicha term for "human being." In the oral history of their origin, the Runa themselves construct their identity with categories borrowed from the colonial discourse: as "salt-eaters" and "baptized" Indians, the Runa distinguish themselves from the *auca* ("savage" in Quichua), that is, from all other peoples who refused those and other "gifts" of civilization. But a closer probe into the different cultural forms of Napo Quichua historical consciousness at different time periods, including the present, shows that European history is not *equally* their own. In the past four hundred years the Napo Quichua have struggled to accommodate to, and resist, the different colonial constructions of their identity within the unequal social and economic conditions created by their historically specific colonial encounters (see Muratorio 1991). By taking into consideration the power of the European colonial discourse about authority, Christianity, and capital, as well as the historical dynamism of indigenous systems of meanings—and by analyzing this dialogue in detail for different historical periods—we can begin to unravel the processes by which indigenous peoples make their own histories. In order to examine the significance of gender in the shaping of these histories, I have chosen to discuss here an instance of the lived experience of women in the present. From it women select, structure, or restructure past events and ideas in order to account for their differential presents. Sometimes indigenous histories are made within the colonial discourse, at other times essentially outside of it; and at others still, they subvert the very categories sanctioned by that discourse. If, as Eric R. Wolf (1982a) points out, the incorporation of different populations into global capitalism did not occur only along one unalterable road, neither did Christian conversion nor the first attempts of Spanish colonial civilization to articulate indigenous peoples into its empire.

Like the Jesuits before them, the main objective of the Josephine missionaries is to radically change and monitor the Indians' symbolic systems and ways of life. They have been keen to promote the cult of the Virgin Mary as a symbol of feminine subservient demeanor and maternal devotion and the image of the Holy Family as a paradigm for conceptions of kinship and gender dualism. Following the hierarchical gender system of all Catholic institutions, the Dorothean and Murialdin Sisters were put in charge of the local boarding schools for indigenous women. The nuns were supposed to embody the Marian virtues of submissiveness and devotion to males and thus to represent gender models for the indigenous interns. The objective of the boarding schools was to "mold" Napo Quichua women into "proper Christian ladies," a task at which they have hardly succeeded, at least among the generational group of women with whom I worked. Here I will concentrate on discussing how these women were able to do an alternative and contested reading of that hegemonic Christian message, thus refracting the power of the missionaries to determine their histories.

The problem is not only whether unique historical events—and specifically the encounter with the colonial Other—affect women differently from men (see Silverblatt 1980, 1987, for Andean women; Nash 1980 for Aztec women) or whether the colonizers constructed separate subjectivities for men and women in their many attempts to change and restructure the cultures of the colonized (see Anderson 1988; Comaroff and Comaroff 1986; Leacock 1980) but if and how indigenous women experience and understand the past differently from men and the variety of narrative and other genres they use to express and convey that historical consciousness to the next generation.

Among the Napo Quichua, traditional songs, the social discussion of everyday dreams, the telling of myths, ritual wailing, and a series of oral narratives associated with life crisis, are all forms by which women express important aspects of their consciousness of history, establishing connections between past and present to convey their own making and understanding of the social world.[1]

The specific case I will discuss here involves a conversation between three Napo Quichua women in my house by the Pano River. The topic of religion was prompted by a sermon they had heard delivered in the Catholic church by a bishop, soon after the Napo province suffered a strong earthquake in March 1987. The bishop's "medieval" explanation of this earthquake as God's punishment for their sins motivated a lively conversation among these women, who drew on their own oral traditions not only to criticize the bishop's explanation but also to deal with a traumatic event in their lives. In addition to suffering the aftermath of the earthquake in their own communities, they still did not know the fate of several of their relatives living in a colonization area much closer to the epicenter. Many of the issues these three women talked about on that occasion would be relevant for an exploration into historical consciousness. I have chosen to concentrate on the narratives that dealt with Christian conceptions of good and evil as represented by the myth of Creation and the Fall, and particularly with the Christian gender models of Eve and the Virgin Mary. By appropriating and reworking the categories imposed by the Christian missionaries, these indigenous women selectively incorporate the past in the present to account for the contradictory and conflictive experiences of evangelization and conversion.

VIRGIN MAMA AND MAMA IBA

The two central female figures of the Christian pantheon—Eve and the Virgin Mary—have always dominated the missionaries' discourse about the role of women in what G. W. Trompf (1989, 634) characterizes as the "mythological macrohistories" of Creation, Paradise, the Fall, and Redemption. Missionaries everywhere have used these global paradigms to incorporate indigenous "pagan" subjects into the cultural history of humankind as defined by the West. These two female figures also turn up in the narratives of Napo Quichua women who define themselves as Catholic, although they can hardly compete in frequency of appearance and richness of details with the many *supai huarmi* (female spirits) who populate almost all forms of women's oral narratives and songs (see also Harrison 1989).

The nuns, as models for female gender roles or as embodiments of these two Christian figures, can be dealt with briefly. Napo Quichua women of this generation (between forty and sixty years of age) have little contact with the conservatively oriented nuns of the Josephine mission and still view them as a kind of "human hybrid," referring to them as *huarmi padres* (women-fathers), a mere "reproduction" of the male priests. The nuns are regarded precisely as the opposite of Eve and the Virgin Mary, who are associated in Napo Quichua women's consciousness with the idea of motherhood and referred to as Virgin Mama and Mama Iba.

Unlike the Highland Catholic Quichua peasants in Ecuador and elsewhere in the Andes, the Napo Quichua have no cult of the saints or of the Virgin Mary, no icons of the Virgin or altars dedicated to her, nor indigenous sponsored fiestas around those cults. Runa women grant recognition and respect the Virgin Mary primarily because she evokes the image of motherhood. Her reality is revealed and confirmed by the fact that she gave birth to a child in pain, raised him, and, most important, was at his side and talked to him at the time of his death. According to the women, before dying, *Cristu* (Christ) blew his *samai* (spirit force) on his mother Mary, thus empowering her to cure the sick as he had done. As it will become clear in the discussion below, however, he was only returning to her a power she had given him when he was born. Nevertheless, although the roles are here reversed, the custom of dying parents blowing their samai on those children who have cared for them during their lifetime is an important symbolic gesture of historical continuity in Napo Quichua families.

Although significant, the image of the Virgin Mary among Napo Quichua women is not as unidimensional as the orthodox Catholic one: a *mater dolorosa* representing above all the values of female submission, suffering, and moral superiority. On the contrary, the Virgin Mary is a powerful woman in her own right. She is the mother of a son, Cristu, whose significance is considered to reside not so much in the fact that he is presented as a god in the Christian pantheon, but on his transformed image as a Quichua culture hero who gave indigenous people agriculture, teaching them to cultivate manioc, the basis of their subsistence.

Native women compare the Virgin Mary only to the mothers of the most powerful shamans known as *bancu*. These women are able to transmit part of their own powers to their sons through breastfeeding. Thus, the Virgin Mary is considered to be responsible for an important part of her son's powers as a life-giver, especially because the women have a hard time figuring out the role of the father. In Christian doctrine, Saint Joseph is already a minor figure, but Napo Quichua women have downgraded him to the role of a total outsider. Not only is he a mere "adoptive" father of Cristu, but his marginality is accentuated by the fact that he is by profession a carpenter. In some of the contemporary images of him in the mission's literature, he is also shown wearing a poncho. These two characteristics immediately identify him in the women's eyes as an *ahuallacta* (highlander; also foreigner), somebody alien to the Napo Quichua culture group.

The mystery of Mary's virginity—so important in Catholic doctrine—is a matter of controversy among Napo Quichua women. In their culture, premarital virginity is neither a problem nor a value; premarital sexual relations are allowed on the understanding that they will lead to a "proper" Quichua marriage, which does not necessarily include a church wedding. When one of the women mentioned the issue of virginity in relation to the figure of Mary, the others discussed the comment with a certain degree of whimsical skepticism until they arrived at an explanation that seemed to settle the issue essentially within the framework provided by traditional Quichua cultural codes. After discarding a possible version that Christ was the son of the wind, the women agreed on the more credible idea that Mary became pregnant on her wedding night when Joseph's knee touched her belly. The "truth" of this second version was confirmed to me, the foreign listener in the conversation, by explaining that a woman may become pregnant by a powerful spirit (*supai*) in her own bed, when that spirit is trying to teach her to become a shaman. If the woman gives birth to a spirit child (*supai huahua*), the alleged "virgin" sexual contact becomes a source of her own future power as a shaman.

The subordinate role the Virgin Mary plays in Christian theology as mediator between humans and God has been upgraded by Napo Quichua women to an important position in their own vision of the Christian pantheon. She has been transformed into a female culture hero who teaches and reinforces female cultural norms about the domestic division of labor, marriage, and postmarital behavior. Unlike Cristu, who is believed to have visited the Ecuadorean tropical forest a long time ago and therefore is incorporated into "mythic time" (see Muratorio 1989), the Virgin Mama still maintains a contemporary presence. The women commented that she comes to visit Quichua homes very early in the morning to breastfeed little babies and that she particularly likes to help women who have many children, and who are diligent and generous housekeepers, thus confirming and legitimizing some of the most important values that define the ideal woman (of this generation) in Napo Quichua culture.

Finally, in the course of their conversation the women even pointed out some of the implicit contradictions—or "mysteries"—in the version of mythological macrohistory taught by the missionaries. Thus, the mystery of the Holy Trinity was regarded as an "erroneous" temporal relation between a universal God and a universal Mother. Their conclusions on this thorny issue are condensed in the following thought which puzzled one of the women: "If God the Son was Mary's son, he could not have been there first as the Fathers say."

EVE AND THE CREATION STORY

The figure of Eve as the original woman in the Christian myth of Creation and Paradise was compared to, or simply just assimilated into, the Virgin Mary. However, the parallel the Napo Quichua women made between Eve and Mary was based on their common condition of motherhood, not on the contrast between obedience and rebellion to God which is the main symbolic structure of binary opposition in the missionaries' teachings. Under no circumstances was Eve associated with the idea of original sin, or with women as the cause of evil, a conception that has played such an important role in determining the low status and the subordination of women in Western culture. In her fascinating study of the intellectual history of this Western myth, the theologian Elaine Pagels forcefully makes this point:

> If any of us could come to our own culture as a foreign anthropologist and observe traditional Christian attitudes toward sexuality and gender, and how we view "human nature" in relation to politics, philosophy, and psychology, we might well be astonished at attitudes that we take for granted. Augustine, one of the greatest teachers of western Christianity, derived many of these attitudes from the story of Adam and Eve: that sexual desire is sinful; that infants are infected from the moment of conception with the disease of original sin; and that Adam's sin corrupted the whole of nature itself. Even those who think of Genesis only as literature, and those who are not Christian, live in a culture indelibly shaped by such interpretations as these. (1988, xix)

The Napo Quichua women, masterfully playing the role of foreign anthropologists, challenged the symbolism of the Christian creation story and the Fall, using a variety of expressive forms. First, the issue was discussed in what I read to be an ironic, light, and rather humorous mood. In that spirit, the association of eating the fruit with the origin of evil was considered ridiculous and totally alien to Quichua thought and way of life. The women commented that in "their part of the world," the apple particularly is a fruit imported from the Highlands, which makes it expensive to buy and is offered to children as a treat for good behavior. The "absurdity" of the thought that an edible fruit could be connected with evil was expressed by one of the women in the following words: "If the reason why Eve sinned is because she ate the apple, why are white people so stupid and continue to plant and harvest apples?" In a more serious tone, these Quichua women's moral philosophical arguments rejected outright the hegemonic gender models in the episodes of Creation and the Fall, and the Christian idea of the original corruption of human nature through sin, that is, the underlying themes of the bishop's sermon. These two arguments need further elucidation, taking into account related themes in Napo Quichua cultural tradition.

As many other missionaries before them, the Josephines use the creation myth of Adam and Eve as a "true historical" account of the origin of all human beings and as a model of gender relations dramatizing the subordination and inferiority of women. Throughout time, the Napo Quichua have elaborated several versions of that same Christian myth, but the hierarchy of gender roles in the native versions is significantly changed. When discussing them in the course of their conversation, the indigenous women acknowledged that the creation of Eve—secondhand, so to speak—from Adam's rib, may have given women in general a weaker soul than men. Nevertheless, the reason these women gave for God's creation of Eve emphasizes an important aspect of the complementarity of gender roles within Quichua marriage and the domestic sphere. The women argued that, feeling very lonely, Adam asked God to give him another thinking person as a companion with whom he could discuss his thoughts and dreams—an interpretation that makes Adam and Eve at least intellectual equals. In Napo Quichua culture, this source of gender equality cannot be underestimated. The capacity to interpret dreams and thoughtful verbal ability are considered to be critical sources of power, and those who excel in these qualities—women as well as men—may be transformed after death into jaguar spirits, one of the most significant symbols of power in Amazonian indigenous societies.

I have argued that the women's narratives in the conversation analyzed here represent a contested reading of the causal explanations offered by the missionaries to account for fundamental issues concerning human origins, gender relations, and ultimate redemption. Implicit in those narratives is also a critique of the Judeo-Christian conception of unilineal time and of the Western linear record of history as the only possible paradigms to interpret the past and give meaning to the present. The Napo Quichua have their own competing versions of mythic-historical truth that I am unable to discuss in detail. But of particular interest to us here is the myth about the "cataclysms" (in Oriente Quichua, *iyus*, or judgments) that are believed to unleash the destruction and successive creations of different groups of human and other beings and of the worlds they live in.

The Napo Quichua distinguish at least four of these cataclysms: the great flood or judgment of water, the judgment of fire, the great hurricane, and the judgment of darkness. All of them are reckoned in mythic time, which is cyclical, since the history of the world is considered to be constantly renewed. In contrast to the unilineal conception of a single origin of all humanity, posited by the Christian story of Adam and Eve, the Napo Quichua myth postulates the multiple origins of humanity. In each cycle, human beings become perfected by turning into more rational beings endowed with the gift of speech, differentiating into separate ethnic groups, and dispersing themselves throughout the tropical forest. Thus in the myth, God creates society by establishing kinship norms and property and land-use rights, and by organizing nature as the protector of those human beings who take good care of her. The main cause of divine punishment administered to any of the humanities in each cycle is incest (see also Mercier 1979, 154, 155, 165; Ortíz de Villalba 1976, 143), a "social" sin par excellence that destroys society and produces the return to a state of nature by transforming humans into different kinds of animals. The idea of any cataclysm as a punishment for individual sins and the notion of guilt in the Christian sense are completely absent from the native narratives of the creation myth.

But the Napo Quichua have also accepted the linear conception of time introduced through the Judeo-Christian worldview. Thus, they give a certain finality to the "time of the Christians" (*cristianu tiempu*), while at the same time incorporating it as one of the mythical cataclysms, as is obvious in the following statement by an indigenous woman: "Since the time of the Christians our beliefs were erased, the trees do not speak to us any more, and the spirits have gone into hiding." This flexibility and relativism in their conceptions of time allow the Napo Quichua to give coherent cultural solutions to new, conflictual, or traumatic situations such as the one produced by the earthquake.

In one of the many group discussions about the 1987 earthquake that took place in Quichua homes and at which I was present, some old men and women agreed on an explanation of the painful event that not only defied the one supplied by the bishop but also recast the traditional myth about cataclysms to accommodate it to modern times. I will sum up their thoughts with the words of an old woman who said: "Now that the hills have moved and the rivers flooded, there will be new and richer land, manioc will grow better, and more and different people will go there to plant and harvest it. In our present times there are too many people without land. When our ancestors had plenty of land and did not work it well, the great flood came." The idea of an unjust distribution of resources as the origin of a chaos that has to be solved by the inversion of that "world turned upside down" is the underlying theme of the old woman's statement. The three women protagonists of the conversation questioned the connection made by the bishop in his sermon between a natural disaster as divine punishment and what he considered to be individual "female" sins. To them this was "irrational," "excessive," and "unjust." By rejecting or by being skeptical or ironic about the priest's explanation of their world, the Napo Quichua women distanced themselves from the subservient and guilt-ridden gender roles that a male-dominated society still wishes to assign to them. Sometimes they even throw the guilt back at the men, including God himself, as it is clear in the final explanation of the earthquake humorously provided by one of the women:

> The Monseigneur told us that the earthquake was caused by the weight of our sins. He said that this is why we women should continue to be Christians, go to hear Mass, and not have children if we are not properly married. I rather think that what really happens is that God is tired of holding the world in one hand, and suddenly changes it to the other. From time to time he gets arthritic pains; that's why the earth moves and we have an earthquake.

GENDER AND COLONIAL RELIGIOUS IDEOLOGIES

Women's ways of understanding their own role within Christianity contrasts with those of both Napo Quichua men and foreign missionaries. In closely associating the two most central religious images of Mary and Eve with childbirth and motherhood, women exclude men from their cultural reinterpretation of the Christian figures. They seldom mention them in their religious discourse but, if questioned directly, they would recite the orthodox version of the Virgin Mary as the mother of Christ and Eve as the origin of sin in the Fall. This fact per se is not very revealing, since in Napo Quichua male culture, women of any kind are not considered a worthy topic of conversation. Female power figures in the Catholic discourse are thus perfunctorily dismissed by men with the official story. This and other aspects of gender inequality in Napo Quichua culture make it highly unlikely that men would find a form of social religious identity through female principles. The reinterpretation of God the Father and of Jesus Christ as tropical forest culture heroes, however, is an integral part of the men's religious discourse (Muratorio 1989).

To understand why women rather than men have chosen to appropriate and reinterpret female Christian figures as an act of their own empowerment, one has to go beyond the confines of the religious discourse and its meaning. It is necessary to locate that discourse in reference to the roles that have been assigned to indigenous men and women within the institutional practices of Catholic and Protestant churches, as well as in reference to the cultural and material transformations suffered by the Napo Quichua as a result of the colonial encounter. It is, of course, impossible to do justice to the complexity of these issues in the context of this article. I will concentrate, therefore, on a brief examination of the possible reasons why indigenous men have found their own means of empowerment through the *practices* of Protestantism whereas women have centered on specific female figures within the Catholic *message*.

In the nineteenth century the Jesuits were unable to sustain their own continuity in this area of the Amazon or the necessary native cooperation to establish a fiesta system comparable to that of the Highlands. Due to the specific character of their evangelization strategy, based primarily on pragmatic development and not on baroque ritual, the Josephine missionaries never attempted a fiesta cycle at all. Thus, the absence of a folk cult of the saints or of the Virgin deprived Napo Quichua men of the powerful formal offices in religious hierarchies and ritual celebrations that men all over the Andes and even in other areas of the Ecuadorean Amazon generally monopolize (for the latter, see Reeve 1985; Whitten 1976).

Furthermore, since their arrival in 1922, the Josephines were perceived by indigenous people to be closely tied to the white political and economic system of domination. The Protestant message that soon followed was accepted by the first converts as a form of protest against the whole local structure of spiritual and material oppression and as a possible alternative for changing their predicament. But for reasons that pertain to the fundamentalist and patriarchal ideology of the North American Protestant missionaries who first came to this area, and to initial Napo Quichua resistance to allowing women to attend Protestant schools, only the men found in this church a public domain in which some of them were assured formal leadership roles. At first they were educated to become pastors and preachers. Later on they also came to lead the indigenous political organizations that organized people of the same Evangelical Protestant affiliation to fight for secular demands—a situation that persists to this day. An important factor that contributed to indigenous women's initial support for the Protestant church was its success in partially controlling men's alcoholism which, in turn, contributed to diminishing domestic physical violence against women. But like their Catholic counterpart, all Protestant churches in this area have consistently excluded women from positions of authority and from the control of symbolic resources.[2] That may partially explain why women searched for a spiritual identity primarily through the power of the Virgin Mary, who is privileged in the Catholic message, and seem to resent the indifference shown towards her in the Evangelical Protestant discourse. However, after more than four hundred years of evangelization, neither form of Christianity has provided Napo Quichua men or women with a version of the absolute truth as was the missionaries' intention, and Christianity coexists in intricate articulations with indigenous symbolic systems.

By associating the Virgin Mary with shamanism, Napo Quichua women also manage to assert their own "hidden" (because private) powers as shamans and curers,[3] thus defying the fact that only men have these roles publicly recognized within their culture and by outsiders. Furthermore, since the seventeenth century, all missionaries working among Amazonian people have constructed shamanism as an "oppressive" system of meanings and practices that allegedly keeps men and women in "a state of constant fear," and as a sign of "barbarism" of an entire cultural tradition. The Josephine missionaries always considered the elimination of shamanism as an important step in their endless task of civilizing indigenous modes of consciousness. Their evangelization strategy continues to be a Eurocentric monologue oblivious to the cultural dialogic unleashed by Liberation Theology in the Amazon and elsewhere that brought about what Judith Shapiro (1987, 133) calls a "culturally relative missionary practice." For the Josephines, Napo Quichua religious culture is voiceless, and the Josephines' rigid proselytizing certainly does not sensitize them to the silent voices of indigenous women or to the type of religious discourse I have tried to uncover here. Finally, by providing their own reinterpretation of the Christian dogma, the women symbolically empower themselves and articulate an inner moral protest against the negative and passive roles assigned to them in both Catholic and Protestant churches active in this area of the Napo.

CONCLUSION

Napo Quichua women were forced to submit to Christian evangelization as part of the larger colonial project of incorporating them into Western civilization. They adopted several of the official rituals of the Catholic church such as the mass and church marriage, but they certainly did not accept without intellectual criticism the culturally and historically bounded social ideologies implicit in the heavily male-oriented teachings and strategies of the Jesuit and Josephine missionaries. These indigenous women managed to turn the orthodox image of the Virgin Mary on its head and to transform a religious figure who is supposed to be the archetype of women's submissiveness, devotion, and acceptance of the hegemonic gender system into the very source of women's power, independence, and cultural assertiveness. It is then significant that the women also associated the Virgin Mary with the image of the shaman, and with the symbolic powers and the social values that still make of shamanism the core of ethnic identity in Napo Quichua culture (see Muratorio 1991). Moreover, the women used the categories and narrative genres of their own culture with creative imagination to construct a powerful sense of themselves and to express their own historical consciousness, implicitly showing the same spirit of irreverent submission that the men like to display in more public and explicit forms. As noted above, indigenous men do not share women's beliefs about Eve and the Virgin Mary or women's views about their own powers, a fact that in no way has deterred women from evoking and manipulating those images and ideas about themselves and about the role of women in Napo Quichua culture, in different historical contexts, and with varying degrees of success.

As Collier (1986) has suggested, we need further exploration of specific historical experiences where concepts of masculinity and femininity are used to negotiate practical social relations. Here I have tried to show that by highlighting the importance of gender to understand historical consciousness in relation to a specific traumatic event such as the earthquake, it is possible to reach a more nuanced understanding of gender ideologies in a context of colonialism and to avoid hastily imposed Western European notions of feminism. The meaning women attach to the two female figures of Mary and Eve provides a different gender paradigm that supersedes the simple dichotomy between machismo and Marianismo. The inspired subversion of indigenous women in response to a Catholic and colonial construction of their world shows the need for the deconstruction of the still current anthropological categorization of Latin American women's consciousness as dominated by "Marianismo," a Catholic and therefore colonial concept that, by depicting women as "spiritually superior" but nevertheless "consenting passive victims," actually turns them into people without history.

NOTES

This chapter is based on data I collected in fieldwork among Napo Quichua women, Napo, Ecuador, from 1986 to 1990. I gratefully acknowledge the generous grants from the Social Sciences and Research Council of Canada which made this research possible.

1. I do not claim that these narrative genres and vocal styles are exclusively female ones. However, they are used in different contexts by men and women. Men usually sing in ritual weddings and, of course, during shamanic sessions, whereas women seem to prefer more private occasions (see Harrison 1989). Ritual wailing as part of everyday conversation seems to be primarily a female expressive form (see Urban 1988 for an analysis of ritual wailing in Amerindian Brazil). For a culture area of the Ecuadorean Amazon similar to that of the Napo Quichua, the work of Dorothea and Norman Whitten (1988) has demonstrated how art, particularly ceramics, is a medium through which Canelos Quichua women express a sense of continuity with the past and the experiences of the most recent changes that are affecting them. In her work among Athapaskan women from the Northern Yukon, Julie Cruikshank (1988) shows how these women use traditional narratives with different meanings and in different contexts than men.

2. Only the Episcopalian church is headed by a woman, and she is a white person not born in this area. There are no indigenous women pastors in any of the Evangelical churches. In almost seventy years of missionary practice the Josephines have not recruited any indigenous woman to become a nun, the only institutional female role of some authority recognized by the Catholic church.

3. In the area of the Napo I know best (Tena-Archidona), there is only one indigenous woman who practices shamanism publicly and who has regular clients. Many other women, however, have shamanic powers but only reveal their knowledge to those they trust. Women also have a profound knowledge of tropical plants and their curative properties. Many of them have told me that they do not reveal the extent of their knowledge to outsiders for fear of being accused of witchcraft.

TWENTY-ONE

Ethnic Segmentation of the Labor Market and the "Work Site Animal": Fragmentation and Reconstruction of Identities within the World System

Gustavo Lins Ribeiro

Highly skilled and well-paid engineers and technicians who are recruited to work on large-scale projects around the world comprise a little studied segment of the global labor market. A large-scale project is a world-system happening, enticing to the civil engineering industry. The construction of hydroelectric dams is a good example. High-powered national and international corporations compete intensely for the contracts to build them. Once begun, construction takes an average of ten years and involves thousands of workers, recruited from geographically and ethnically varied sources. Residential camps—"small villages of the world system"—house the resulting multiethnic, predominantly male, labor force. Also present, on the site, are the trappings of communities, created by the companies in order to service, and thereby retain, the engineers or technicians and their families. Of interest to this paper are the processes of identity formation that characterize these well-paid specialists as they enter into circuits that are more or less detached from their country of origin.

Anthropology is increasingly equipped with concepts and methods appropriate for addressing the postmodern condition of global capitalism, argued to emphasize flexible accumulation and the compression of time and space (Harvey 1989); to foster homogenization in an apparently shrinking world, yet simultaneously to exaggerate localisms; and to produce fragmented, deterritorialized, and ambiguous identities, or "homeless minds" (Marcus 1990, 4; see also Laclau 1991). A preliminary concept, useful for my purposes, is that of the ethnically segmented labor market. This concept originated in sociological analyses of industrial employment, where it shed light on the role of racial or ethnic factors in the allocation of labor market positions (see Bonacich 1972; Gordon 1972). A plastic notion, it can be applied to complex units of analysis, whether nation-states, given industrial plants, or large-scale projects (Ribeiro 1988). In his *Europe and the People without History*, Eric R. Wolf (1982*a*) firmly placed the concept within the body of anthropological literature.

Interested in the "juxtaposition of groups of different social and cultural origins" (1982*a*, 379–381), Wolf stressed the ethnic underpinning of the formation of labor markets worldwide. Using the concept of ethnic segmentation as a systemic notion, he drew attention to global migratory processes provoked by the expansion of capitalism and showed how different ethnic groups occupy positions that have varied in historical time. His analysis condensed historical and anthropological visions of the structured formation of contemporary human populations, helping us see that with capitalist development, the complexity of ethnically segmented arrangements increased enormously, creating interethnic systems with multiple interactions. The proximity and interdependence of differences are factors that contribute both to the perception of the "shrinking" of the contemporary world and to the fragmentation of individual perceptions, in a double movement of homogenization and heterogenization. The simultaneous exposure to a "same," shared reality by people whose perspectives are clearly differentiated fosters both.

Europe and the People without History is a comprehensive historical and anthropological contribution to the understanding of the formation of the world system. It shows how in the creation of a global political economy the powerful forces that produced homogeneous relationships had, to a lesser or greater degree, to adjust to the diversity of local realities, generating a most difficult paradox for anthropological analysis: the need to understand realities that are homogeneous and heterogeneous at the same time. Indeed, it can be said that the interplay between heterogeneous realities and homogeneous ones (in)forms a set of basic anthropological preoccupations. These are reflected in subjects that are recurrent and structuring of the discipline; for instance: the tension universalism/particularism; relativism; cultural pluralism and identity formation. Besides addressing main anthropological questions, Wolf's book reveals how some important issues of our times originated and developed. Two of them, central to understanding the present configuration of the world system, are critical for this paper: (1) increasing ethnic diversity under the umbrella of a similar set of powerful constraints; and (2) the acceleration of the circulation of people, things, and information on a global scale.

LARGE-SCALE PROJECTS: SOME GENERAL CHARACTERISTICS

Large-scale projects have particular characteristics as forms of production linked to the expansion of political-economic systems. These characteristics can be synthetically grouped under three dimensions: gigantism, isolation, and temporariness (Ribeiro 1987). The construction of such projects brings together a vast array of workers for periods of up to ten years or more. The labor market is structured both by the hierarchy typical of the civil engineering industry and by the ethnic segmentation caused by the recruiting and migratory processes associated with the project. Spatial mobility is a central feature of the engineering industry, since the mobility of investments induces the rotation of the labor force (Panaia 1985, 11ff.).

Migrant labor, directly associated with this industrial branch, is especially evident when construction is being done in isolated areas. Every time a new job begins in such places, contractors have to transfer the labor force and equipment to the new working site. The formation of a large-scale project labor market entails several migratory movements and associated social changes. Corporations either transfer personnel who are already working within the system or recruit new people who may then migrate, following their employers' investments. A characteristic of the resulting population is a skewed gender distribution reflected in the majority presence of adult men to the detriment of women and children. Skilled workers, including managers and engineers, tend to rotate faster and, therefore, to have a shorter stay in any given project. As we will see, they are more likely than the waged workers to have their families with them.

Large corporations that operate in large-scale project markets develop several sites at once as well as over time. The simultaneous maintenance of multiple construction projects is as important as a sequence of projects. Corporations, from their national or world headquarters, constantly maximize their fixed and variable capital by transferring equipment and people from one project to another on a global or national scale. Each project represents the intersection of national and international migratory circuits. In the case in point, I will limit myself to the experience of skilled workers who exemplify the essence of the turnover between projects.

The transference of people, especially of skilled workers, is a kind of occupational migration that I call "the large-scale projects migratory circuit" (Ribeiro 1988), a form of industrial nomadism. It is characteristic not only of engineering but also, for instance, of the oil industry (see Olien and Olien 1982).[1] In reality, industrial nomadism is closely related to the spatial dynamics of these economic activities, but mitigated by the need of industrial capital to establish a stable labor force. A way of confronting cost overruns caused by turnover is through what José Sérgio Leite Lopes (1979) calls the immobilization of the labor force: corporations foster housing quarters and company towns designed to keep labor engaged. Living quarters are conceived as a way of concentrating workers so that they become dependent upon management not only through wages but also through housing. Housing is seen as an effective way of maintaining a population constantly present and available for productive ends. It also facilitates the political control of employees since quarters may be used as another element of pressure and negotiation.

Both unskilled and skilled workers are exposed to a sui generis daily life (evidently with different contents) typical of a labor force immobilized via housing (Ribeiro 1989). Life in a large-scale project camp is penetrated in all its spheres by the interests and needs of the work, monitored by a central management as in a total institution. But collective and individual experiences vary according to one's position within the hierarchy of the labor market. Unskilled workers are subject to greater control. For instance, they cannot have their families with them since the project only offers them the possibility of living in collective dormitories for "singles." Skilled workers, by contrast, are given conditions of social reproduction that include the presence of their families. Corporations must invest in keeping skilled workers, who are highly valued in the civil engineering labor market. The cost of losing people from this segment is the principal factor leading to investments in an infrastructure of individual residences, social clubs, and, more important, schools for their children.

LARGE-SCALE PROJECTS: AN ETHNOGRAPHIC EXAMPLE

Since I consider anthropology's strongest contribution to social theory to be based on ethnographic examples, I will turn my attention to a large-scale project on the Parana River, bordering Argentina and Paraguay: the Yacyreta Hydroelectric Dam (4,100 MW). A complete description of the project based on fieldwork from the mid-1980s can be found in my earlier work (Ribeiro 1988). In Yacyreta, a binational project, the ethnic segmentation of the labor market is expressed first in the presence of two large Argentinian and Paraguayan segments. As of February 1986, the consortium ERIDAY, the main contractor that is building the dam, employed 1,808 bearers of Argentinian contracts and 1,448 bearers of Paraguayan contracts. Next, in decreasing order, there were Uruguayans and Europeans—mainly Italian, French, and German. My analysis focuses on the European segment of skilled workers, specifically the group of Italian origin, since they were the largest and the most powerful contingent. It is an Italian contractor that leads the consortium ERIDAY.

Expatriates are a common presence in large-scale projects worldwide (Murphy 1983, 32). Here their distinct treatment is visible within ERIDAY's administrative structure. A separate department of personnel deals with the specific needs of the European staff. In Yacyreta the European segment (there is a clear overlap between ethnicity and higher-level hierarchical positions) received differentiated treatment that included: a separate club where rituals of identity reinforcement were performed (religious celebrations, national holidays, etc.), two-way trips to their country of origin, access to

Italian videotapes, magazines, and newspapers (the installation of a parabolic antenna was being considered). In 1987 there were three European schools, one Italian, one French, and one German. The Italian school was the largest, covering kindergarten to the last year of high school.

The internal composition of the European segment of Yacyreta's labor market replicates the arrangement among the several European contractors involved in the creation of ERIDAY. Italians represent the largest population of foreigners in the project, followed by French. The importance of holders of European labor contracts stems not from their numbers but from the fact that they form a closed managerial power elite. As of 28 February 1986, there were 140 Europeans, less than 4 percent of ERIDAY's labor force, living in Yacyreta. Their nationalities were distributed as follows: 83 Italian; 45 French; 10 German; and 2 Austrian.

It is not only because of differential access of managerial power that ethnicity is an issue among these managers. Indeed, ethnic identities always arise in a contrastive context. Italian and French managers whom I interviewed perceived each other in terms of their nationalities and what that meant for the daily administration of the project. Italian managers, for instance, think of themselves as more pragmatic, less bureaucratic, and more site-oriented than others—professionals who can make decisions onsite without engaging in further studies in the office. They often talk about their personnel at the construction site as if they were a family. By contrast, French managers see themselves as more acquainted with modern corporate ideas and with an impersonal concept of management. Both Italians and French tended to blame each other for daily administrative problems. They seldom socialized together. In fact, Italians, French, and Germans tended to form separate closed groups.

Daily life in a camp is highly organized by the powerful "General Services" section that takes care of such diverse things as fixing electrical appliances, house maintenance, and the reservation of flights and migration paperwork—important details for a population that is frequently traveling. General Services is a strategic agency in the transformation of individuals into "corporation brats." Its action contributes to the perception that life outside camp is more difficult than life inside.

Several of the technical and managerial elite of the Yacyreta project have graduate degrees. In a large-scale project, a foreman or an engineer can accumulate impressive personal power. Some command several hundred men in activities that presuppose a complex articulation of factors of production, giant equipment, and daily risk. In fact, the synergy of the work site, together with the mobilization of power attached to the top hierarchical positions, is often mentioned (over and above good pay) as a factor in keeping people in the migratory circuits of large-scale projects.

ERIDAY's Italian personnel have been transferred by Impregilo, the Italian firm that leads the consortium, from several large-scale projects, most of them located in Argentina and other Latin American countries.[2] In June 1986, out of 86 Italians working in Yacyreta, 77 (89.5 percent) had previously participated in at least one project. Reflecting Impregilo's long-standing presence in the Argentine market, 52 had come from the Salto Grande (17) and Alicura (35) projects in Argentina. A group of 10 had come from Pakistan, and the remaining 15 had previously worked in construction projects in Peru, Ecuador, Colombia, Panama, Venezuela, and in Itaipu (Brazil/Paraguay).

Expatriates who have worked in different countries under different working conditions are highly regarded in the labor market and can only be held, as a minimum condition, by the immediate comparative economic advantage of higher wages and such fringe benefits as free housing. In Yacyreta, an Italian technician, for instance, may earn three times more than in his home country. Furthermore, expatriates receive an extra payment—the *carovita*, or pocket money—intended to cover local expenses. For some of Yacyreta's expatriates, the "pocket money" paid was not sufficient, forcing them to use part of their regular wages for daily costs. Most expatriates, however, could save their entire wage or a substantial part of it, making investments in their home country. Saving is possible not only because of fringe benefits and higher wages, but also because living in a work site community reduces the overall cost of social reproduction. The temptations of sophisticated markets and consumption patterns are absent from these isolated areas. Indeed, as one informant told me: "Living in Ituzaingo makes me feel like a peasant when I go to Posadas [the capital of Misiones and the largest city close to Yacyreta] and see all those stores."

Although it is true that most expatriates become "nomads" for monetary reasons, their motivation cannot be reduced to economic calculation alone. Managers, increasingly aware that the large-scale project environment is likely to generate social conflict, go out of their way to foster the creation of a "community sense" among the labor force. This, indeed, is part of the internal managerial rationale in developing a large-scale project.[3] Perhaps we could put it this way: expatriates do enter the large-scale project migration circuit for economic reasons, but they remain in it for several reasons. Some, in fact, live their whole labor life within it. Among the skilled workers of Italian origin were cases of third-generation people who live permanently linked to large-scale projects. Such people, born and raised in camps throughout the world, and assuming these camps and the migratory circuit that connects them as the main markers of their personal identities, may be taken as archetypical of the problems of identity formation here addressed.

BECOMING A BICHO-DE-OBRA

Significantly, the expatriate skilled workers of the hydroelectric dam project that I studied refer to themselves as *bicho-de-obra*, which translates literally as "work site insect." However, the American expression "party animal" captures well certain aspects of their existence, and I adopt the label "work site animal" as the best translation of their self-categorization. As we have seen, the typical bicho-de-obra first enters the large-scale migratory circuit because it offers the economic opportunity for saving money and enhancing the quality of the reproduction of his/her domestic group.[4] The would-be bicho-de-obra conceives of what is actually the first step of a long migratory sequence as a temporary move. The hardships of the first project's surrounding environment, together with the peculiarities of living in an isolated company town, negate conceptualizing the coming experience as a permanent condition of working life.

Whether a given migratory experience is permanent or temporary is an important issue that has been analyzed in different migratory contexts. It has been shown, for instance, that a substantial part of Portuguese migrant labor to West Germany conceives of its stay as a temporary one, despite the fact that "going back home" is either a decision constantly postponed or never made (Klimt 1987*a*, 1987*b*). Concerning large-scale projects, though, it must be remembered that "temporariness" is a defining feature: the projects are eventually finished, forcing segments of the labor force to move from one site to another.

It is hard, and perhaps impossible, to demarcate from the outset the limits of a migrant's definition of the economic rewards sought, for goals often expand once the circuit is entered. It is not uncommon to find among the skilled segment of the labor force bichos-de-obra who have fulfilled their previous economic goals, usually by accumulating a sizable quantity of money and making investments in their home countries, but who nonetheless do not want to leave the circuit. In such cases, the logic of the occupation has taken over the migrants' initial intentions. In fact, the very idea of a career in engineering may naturalize a person's understanding of the occupational migratory circuit. But there are also other factors that intervene. I will first consider how the logic of the occupation may restrain a person from leaving the large-scale project migratory circuit, then describe mechanisms that derive from broader social determinants.

First, by participating in one large-scale project, a person acquires an occupational background that makes him a specialist in certain tasks and/or a desirable commodity in the labor market for large-scale projects in general. Such a person will either consider participating in another project or—in case he considers leaving the circuit—will be approached by his employers with an offer of better wages and/or a better position in the next job. Since large-scale projects are the cream of the construction industry market, wages and fringe benefits are already highly attractive, making it hard to locate equally rewarding jobs in the home town or country. It is likely that our hypothetical person will find the home-country wages no match for those he was used to receiving, especially if fringe benefits such as free housing are considered. Moreover, since this person has been working for several years in an isolated area, he has lost access to the social networks that would facilitate entrance in a given urban labor market. In these crucial moments of a person's labor trajectory, it is not uncommon to decide to get engaged in another large-scale project. Projects, anyhow, are temporary jobs.

This critical turning point indicates a major restructuring of the subjectivity and intersubjectivity of the would-be work site animal: the loss of the social networks that this person used to have "back home." To the constituents of these networks, he begins to lose meaning as a concrete actor, becoming an image, a memory. This gradual process entails different moments and decisions by the migrant. Going "back home" to reaffirm his membership in his original network is usually what the young bicho-de-obra does during vacation time. Gradually he begins to perceive that his vacations are degenerating into mandatory visits to the houses of relatives with different psychological and social costs for himself and his family. The passage of time tends to intensify his alienation. The already bicho-de-obra increasingly realizes that the quality of his membership in the original network is changing in problematic ways. He begins to conceive of himself as "uprooted." Visiting his family/home town becomes a secondary option during his vacations. He wants to have *real* vacations, he wants to *rest* from his work. Parallel to this process of loss of a migrant's previous social identity, there develops a new process of identification. The large-scale project camp slowly becomes "home," and he begins to consider the people he interacts with on a daily basis in the project environment as his "original" social network.

Ambiguity installs itself. The bicho-de-obra is still an individual from a certain country, or from a certain province, but he feels like a stranger when he goes back to his original place. Some friends and relatives have died, others have changed their positions within the kinship system (marriages, divorces, births). He himself might have gotten married to a citizen of the country where the construction is being carried out, or to a neighbor in the company town. In their "homelands" these migrants face the results of the unfolding of developmental cycles of many domestic groups. Since they could not participate in those unfoldings, they find that their original place is not the same anymore. Indeed, removal from a given social network for a lengthy period of time means the impossibility of accompanying the daily, multiple, and differentiated interactions that make social actors meaningful to each other.[5] Briefly, the migrant loses what Anthony Giddens calls "practical consciousness."[6] However, "practical consciousness" is a characteristic of social life anywhere; as the expatriate loses practical consciousness of his Italian town, he "acquires" another: that of the large-scale project migratory circuit.

"NEITHER FISH NOR FOWL": LIFE AS A BICHO-DE-OBRA

In addition to bicho-de-obra, some of the labels these migrants use to classify themselves, such as "uprooted," "expatriate," and "gypsies," indicate consciousness of the migratory experience as implied by working in a large-scale project. Furthermore, they indicate a perception that combines nomadism and ambiguity. "Uprooted," for instance, is the most frequent category that Argentine work site animals use to classify their experience. Its metaphorical power alludes to the loss of a previous stable and grounded situation that is replaced by a new environment, demanding readaptation. Since the Argentines are working in their own country, nationality is not the issue that it apparently is for expatriates. "Expatriate" also alludes to a loss, in this case of a homeland, and tends to approximate negative connotations such as forced resettlement or exile. In this sense, both "uprooted" and "expatriate" evoke experiences that social actors wish would be temporary. However, "gypsy," a category employed by both national and international migrants, is indicative of the assumption of temporariness as permanent, of nomadism becoming a lifestyle. Indeed, this is the case for many bichos-de-obra.

In Yacyreta, I met—and was told of their existence in other working sites—several individuals who had spent their whole working life within the large-scale project migratory circuit. Their trajectories varied according to whether they were in the Argentine or international circuits. But most of them had participated in six or more projects, in a manner similar to a long step-migration chain. Furthermore, many had raised their children in a series of projects in Argentina or around the world. I also met third-generation bichos-de-obra, a clear demonstration of intergenerational continuity. For a family living in a large-scale project, the crucial moment is when its young members have—for educational or occupational reasons—to leave the circuit. Among the Italian segment in Yacyreta, this was often a two-moment sequence, the first being when the child entered secondary level education. Despite the existence of Italian schools in all the projects they had participated in, some people considered that their children could receive a better education "back home." The separation of parents and teenagers is common. Indeed, there are few teenagers in Yacyreta's *Villa Permanente* or *Mil Viviendas*. If the teenager has remained with his or her parents, attending the camp's secondary school, the hard separation decision may be faced later, at the point of entering higher education or employment. Going "back home" can happen then. However, the presence of second- and even third-generation bichos-de-obra in Yacyreta shows that not all of them leave the system. Furthermore, and more interestingly, it is not uncommon to leave it and come back.

In one family whose members had been exposed to large-scale projects for more than three decades, the children were working or living in different projects around the world. One of them had married within the migratory circuit, a fact that is not uncommon. It is interesting to note that although the children are second-generation work site animals, like other migrants who conceive their experiences as temporary (Klimt 1987a), they still think of Italy as their "homeland."[7]

I met young people who had tried to live in Italy and failed. They said they were not satisfied with the provincial vision of the world Italian youth seemed to have, nor with their low wages and extremely competitive daily lives. They also considered that after living for so long under a corporation's influence, they had become "corporation brats." Spoiled by General Services, the community action department of the contractor, they had also been given more attention than children in other contexts because of their parents feeling guilty for raising them in adverse circumstances.[8] After several years of feeling like strangers in Italy, these young adults decided they belonged to construction sites and reentered the circuit. A young woman who had spent her whole life in projects and was about to return to Italy doubted whether she could remain there. She considered making an attempt because she could always go back to a project, obtaining work in the corporation's onsite office. A young Argentine man, second-generation work site animal and the father of two children, also doubted he would ever leave the circuit.

These examples are not exclusive to the second generation of bichos-de-obra. Cases of first-generation individuals who had failed to settle down in an urban environment at some point in their migratory experience were frequently reported. The explanations for these failures varied from inability to readapt to urban environments (although large-scale projects' housing areas resemble small villages, they represent unique residential experiences), to the absence of a daily life marked both by a clear-cut structure of privileges and the synergy of the large-scale construction project.[9]

Intergenerational continuity and the potential for bicho-de-obra inbreeding or occupational endogamy are factors that reinforce a conceptualization of them as a permanent migratory population, attracted and created by the logic of the large-scale project migratory circuit, both national and international. In this sense, it does not matter whether retiring individuals leave the circuit. They will carry their identities in ways analogous to retired military personnel or diplomats. As long as large-scale projects exist, so will bichos-de-obra.

FROM MODERNITY TO POSTMODERNITY: SOME CENTRAL CHARACTERISTICS IN THE CONSTRUCTION OF PERMANENT AMBIGUITY

Work site animals are "deterritorialized" people, in the sense that they lose the possibility of realizing a univocal identification between territory/culture/

nation/identity, a fact expressed in the labels they use to describe themselves: uprooted, expatriated, gypsies, citizens of the world. However, daily human activities need a place or a set of places definable as a "territory," in which the reproduction of life can unfold with greater or lesser stability. Typically, work site animals treat as theirs the territories of large-scale projects. Moreover the camps—small villages of the world system—are a space made homogeneous by the process of time-space compression. In other words, a territorialization defined by the labor sphere compensates for cultural deterritorialization, a fact expressed in the label *work site* animal.

A large-scale project is a space without a sui generis cultural identity. Intending to reproduce the totality of an urban environment, it is planned and managed by a central bureaucracy along lines defined by the necessities of flexible accumulation. This is why the qualities of spatial organization are "the same" from project to project, delimited by the requirements of the productive process regardless of what part of the world. It is *as if* it were the same for the work to be in Argentina, Pakistan, or Nigeria.

In such a universe, the transnational corporation, maximizing flexible accumulation, fosters an accelerated turnover of its employees within the circuits of the world system and ends up being the principal organizer of the formal processes of socialization. Ironically this includes the (re)creation and maintenance of the set of factors determinant of national identity. In a world where the contradictions between globalism and localism are many and have affected the system of nation-states in various ways (see Szentes 1988), the transnational corporation becomes responsible for fixing concepts of the nation in situations of strong ethnic segmentation. In the case being considered here, it is the corporation that circulates information from Italy (videos, magazines, and newspapers), and promotes or stimulates the celebration of national and religious holidays. More important, it is the corporation that manages the *Italian school*, a fundamental place for the socialization of the children of work site animals, many of them with a future similar to that of their parents.

In the school there develop phenomena of the "as if" type—a mark of ambiguity typical of postmodern time-space compression (Harvey 1989). A child studies to be an Italian citizen *as if* he or she were in Italy, so much so that the calendar is inverted. When it is winter in Italy, in the northern hemisphere, it is summer in Argentina. However, at the Italian school during the Argentine summer, classes are held *as if* it were Italian winter, the children of the work site animals learning about snowstorms and life under cold weather in the Alps. The school day over, they confront the hot and humid weather of northeastern Argentina, by the Parana River, on the border with Paraguay. This is the most visible example of the mismatch between the transmission of a national identity and the reality experienced in the project's territory.

Given the ethnic segmentation of the labor market, large-scale projects are a universe where bilingualism and multilingualism are common. In Yacyreta, for instance, and in order of importance, at least the following languages are spoken: Spanish, Guarani, Italian, French, English, and German. Evidently, Spanish is the language that predominates in the area both because it is spoken in Argentina and Paraguay and because it is the "official" language of the project or the lingua franca between the several ethnic segments. In addition, Spanish is the language of the mass media in the region.

As a result of participation in the migratory circuit of large-scale projects, it is common for work site animals to marry natives of the countries where they have worked, forming interethnic couples. The child's first language, in such cases, tends to be that of the mother. Because of the fact that the Italian corporation has participated in other Latin American projects and has been operating in Argentina for many years, there were in Yacyreta a number of Italian/South American couples. Here children's Spanish is reinforced by the presence of native maids as well as by local television broadcasting. Italian becomes a second language learned in school, for some children with difficulty. The result is linguistic ambivalence, as well as a heightened experience of cultural fragmentation. In the end, Italy represents a lived trajectory only for the father of the family. For mother and children it is a foreign country, a special one without any doubt, but a country that is not directly known so much as it is apprehended through institutions (the school and the corporation) or through political kin and other work site animals of Italian origin.

In the case of children of Italian couples, although exposed for years to Italian schools in the camps, ambiguity is present also because they do not identify themselves with who they suppose to be typical Italian youngsters. Their daily social networks are marked by the totalizing experience of living in large-scale project environments. As mentioned before, I met young people who had tried to live in Italy, but whose maladjustment, in their own words, to Italian reality had led them to reenter the large-scale project migratory circuit, this time not as dependents but as full-fledged work site animals.

CONCLUSION

The processes of socialization internal to the domestic group are responsible to a great extent for the construction of individual identities. For work site animals these are affected by company housing, ethnic segmentation, and continuous migration. In the end, the work site animal assumes as a fundamental dimension of his/her identity the facets associated with the labor sphere. Although other agencies of identity formation are present, they are hegemonized by the world of labor, especially its conditions of time-space compression.

As we have seen, a work site animal of Italian origin is different from another of French origin. For this reason, we must acknowledge that the agencies and processes of national identity formation have kept their efficacy. They have done so, however, within a situation where there is a change in the hierarchy of their relative powers of structuration, this hierarchy being subjected to the totalizing characteristics of the working universe where the daily lives of these social actors unfold. In this situation of high fragmentation and deterritorialization, we find social actors dominated by their professional occupation. Separated from a cultural and ethnic identity, they conceive of themselves as citizens of the world—citizens of a world system increasingly more homogeneous, yet promoting the interaction/integration of heterogeneous population segments at the same time.

In today's world, change has accelerated in contexts of ever more complex social and communicative encounters. People undergo multiple exposures to socializing and normative agencies, themselves also traveling through an accelerated trajectory of change. In this situation, an identity can only be the fragmented synthesis of multiple alterities constructed from a great number of interactive contexts. Instead of an irreducible essence, identity in modern/postmodern situations is for many people multifaceted, subject to both negotiations and rigidity. Although most of the time, interactive contexts are institutionally regulated by a socializing and/or normative agency (for a similar position see Marcus 1990, 29), this is only part of what we need to know. On the one hand, the fragmented identity is lived as a given, a reality that structures the subject. On the other hand, it is a set characteristic of the subject, yes, but undergoing constant change as one or another of its multiple facets, or an aggregate of them, becomes hegemonic in relation to the rest, according to the context. Under conditions of extreme change, the defining arrangement of collective and individual identities may go through radical transformations, even leading to a redefinition —a *reconstruction*—of the relationships of hegemony between the constituent parts.

Because of ethnic segmentation, large-scale projects like the Yacyreta dam examined here foster interactive contexts of dual potentiality. Social actors can emphasize distinctiveness via the classic mechanism of contrast made explicit by difference, or they can discover a repertoire of alliances in situations of cooperation or conflict. Interethnic contexts are characterized by ongoing political, cultural, and linguistic processes relevant to the question of ethnic identity. Also relevant is the domain of kinship—above all interethnic marriage and the exchange of women—which is fundamental to the reinforcement or reconstruction of identities. The greater the ethnic segmentation, the greater the fragmentation provoked by the interethnic system, and the greater the importance of processes associated with this situation in actors' daily lives.

NOTES

1. In volume 1 of *Capital*, Karl Marx mentioned the existence of a "nomad proletariat" typical of large-scale construction projects such as railroads. It is true that "industrial nomadism" is a condition that affects workers, but it is not exclusive to them. Often, as in this case study, the segment of the labor force that most fully lives within the limits of a closed migratory system is composed of skilled workers, technicians, and professionals.

2. I believe international contractors tend to transfer their personnel within a single world region not only because of cost efficiency, but also because knowledge of the local language is a valuable asset in the working site.

3. In her book for managers involved in large-scale projects' administration, Kathleen Murphy states the following: "The expatriates—or 'expats,' as they frequently call themselves—are out of their element, living on the fringes of a strange environment. The conditions are tough; the climate is often hot; tropical diseases are common. Medical problems are intensified, due to a shortage of doctors and hospitals.... As is common in most 'marginal' situations, social unrest is widespread, leading to alcoholism, divorce, boredom, supermarket complaints, fist-fights, and sometimes even murder. Thus, the project manager must somehow create a sense of community among these expats to diminish the sense of social isolation" (Murphy 1983, 32). She also considers that creating "a sense of community" is a way to minimize turnover (166).

4. Since construction is almost exclusively a male occupation, I will consider the typical bicho-de-obra as being a man. That does not mean that there are no women participating in the large-scale projects migratory circuit. Women's most typical insertion, though, is in the position of relatives (wives and daughters) of employed men. Some of these women may be hired in the working site to do administrative work or to teach at a camp school.

5. What is difficult to estimate here is the amount of time this process takes to unfold fully. It certainly varies according to individuals. During my research in Yacyreta, I was frequently led to question whether the reasons for becoming a bicho-de-obra (beyond professional-economic considerations) were not also related to conflictive relationships being developed by the would-be migrant within his original network. Furthermore, disliking large urban environments was another recurrent characteristic among some of these persons.

6. Practical consciousness is a notion that refers to the routinization of social actions and the predictability that it entails in daily social interactions. In this sense it is a basic constituent of social actors since it allows for a necessary margin of predictability in individuals' mutual monitoring of their actions, and conveys a sense of security and stability in the system of interactions. Giddens considers that "routinization is vital to the psychological mechanisms whereby a sense of trust or ontological security is sustained in the daily activities of social life. Carried primarily in practical consciousness, routine drives a wedge between the potentially explosive content of

the unconscious and the reflexive monitoring of action which agents display" (Giddens 1984, xxiii).

7. In this case, the role that mutual-aid associations often play in the maintenance of migrant identities (see, e.g., Maeyama 1979; Szuchman 1980) is performed by services the corporation provides (such as the distribution of Italian papers and videotapes) and—more important—by the school (see next section). Interestingly enough, Uruguayans, a sizable foreign population in Yacyreta, did not count on any separate school for their children but did have a mutual-aid association. The European segment of the labor force carries out national-related celebrations in their *Club Hípico*, which is assisted by the corporation.

8. For the skilled segment of the labor force the sense of "Big Brother is watching you," mentioned by Murphy (1983, 167), goes together with a sense of "Big Brother is helping you," or, better, of "company paternalism," something typical of industries with immobilization of labor force via housing (Leite Lopes 1979; Tilly 1985).

9. Life and work in construction sites involve a great deal of outdoors activity, hectic interaction, cooperation with several labor teams, and a clear sense of accomplishment. Most of the professionals, technicians, and workers described their jobs as fulfilling a need for concrete achievement. As an engineer told me: "When we come to a place there is nothing. While we are working we see the transformation and accumulation of our work. Once we are finished, it is as if we face dead work. It is time to move again." They talked about nature as a powerful entity that needed to be understood in order to be tamed. Damming a river is seen as a challenge undertaken to benefit the progress of civilization. Engineers, technicians, and foremen are also powerful actors on project sites, sometimes commanding hundreds of men. For the transformation of engineers into the Messiah of a messianic movement of natives affected by a hydroelectric project in Mexico, see Barabas 1977.

WORKS BY ERIC R. WOLF

Reprints are not noted unless cited by the contributors to this volume.

BOOKS AND EDITED COLLECTIONS

1959a   *Sons of the Shaking Earth*. Chicago: University of Chicago Press. (Translations: French, Spanish.)

1964   *Anthropology*. Englewood Cliffs, N.J.: Prentice-Hall. (Paperback edition, with a new introduction, 1974. New York: W. W. Norton.)

1966a   *Peasants*. Englewood Cliffs, N.J.: Prentice-Hall. (Translations: Danish, French, Hungarian, Indonesian, Japanese, Portuguese, Spanish, Swedish.)

1969a   *Peasant Wars of the Twentieth Century*. New York: Harper and Row. (Translations: French, Italian, Spanish.)

1976   Ed. *The Valley of Mexico: Studies in Ecology and Society*. Albuquerque: University of New Mexico Press.

1982a   *Europe and the People without History*. Berkeley, Los Angeles, London: University of California Press. (Translations: German, Italian, Spanish.)

1984a   Ed. *Religion, Power and Protest in Local Communities*. New York: Mouton.

1991a   Ed. *Religious Regimes and State Formation*. Albany: State University of New York Press.

CO-AUTHORED BOOKS

1972   with Edward C. Hansen. *The Human Condition in Latin America*. New York: Oxford University Press.

1972   with Angel Palerm. *Agricultura y civilización en Mesoamérica*. Mexico D.F.: Sep Setentas.

1974   with John W. Cole. *The Hidden Frontier: Ecology and Ethnicity in an Alpine Valley*. New York: Academic Press. (Translation: Italian.)

ARTICLES, ESSAYS, CHAPTERS

1951   "The Social Organization of Mecca and the Origins of Islam," *Southwestern Journal of Anthropology* 7:329–356. (Translation: Arabic.)

1953   "La formación de la nación," *Ciencias Sociales* 4:50–62, 98–111, 146–171.

1955a   "The Mexican Bajío in the Eighteenth Century: An Analysis of Cultural Integration." In *Synoptic Studies of Mexican Culture*, 177–199. Middle American Research Institute Publication 17, Tulane University. (Translation: Spanish.)

1955b   "Types of Latin American Peasantry," *American Anthropologist* 57:452–471. (Translations: Italian, Spanish.)

1956a   "Aspects of Group Relations in a Complex Society: Mexico," *American Anthropologist* 58:1065–1078.

1956b   "San José: Subcultures of a Traditional Coffee Municipality." In *The People of Puerto Rico: A Study in Social Anthropology*, by Julian H. Steward et al., pt. 7, 171–264. Urbana: University of Illinois Press.

1957   "Closed Corporate Peasant Communities in Mesoamerica and Central Java," *Southwestern Journal of Anthropology* 13:1–18. (Translation: Spanish.)

1958   "The Virgin of Guadalupe," *Journal of American Folklore* 71:34–39. (Translation: Spanish.)

1959b/ "Specific Aspects of Plantation Systems in the New World: Community
1971   Subcultures and Social Class." In *Plantation Systems in the New World*, ed. Angel Palerm and Vera Rubin, 136–146. Social Science Monograph 7, Pan American Union, Washington, D.C. (Translation: Spanish.) Reprinted in *Peoples and Cultures of the Caribbean*, ed. M. Horowitz, 163–178. Garden City, N.Y.: Natural History Press.

1960   "The Indian in Mexican Society," *Alpha Kappa Deltan* 30:3–6.

1961   "Concluding Comments." In *The Evolution of Horticultural Systems in Native South America*, ed. Johannes Wilbert, 37–41. *Antropológica*, Supplement Publication 2, Caracas.

1962a   "Reply to Howard Cline's Review," *American Anthropologist* 64:374.

1962b   "Cultural Dissonance in the Italian Alps," *Comparative Studies in Society and History* 5:1–14.

1962c   "The Study of Evolution." In *Horizons of Anthropology*, ed. Sol Tax, 108–119. Chicago: Aldine.

1962d   "Santa Claus: Notes on a Collective Representation." In *Process and Pattern in Culture*, ed. Robert A. Manners, 147–155. Chicago: Aldine.

1965   "Intellectuels Americains contre la guerre du Vietnam," *Les Temps Modernes* 21(235):1093–1109.

1966b   "Kinship, Friendship, and Patron-Client Relations in Complex Societies." In *The Social Anthropology of Complex Societies*, ed. Michael Banton, 1–22. Association of Social Anthropologists Monograph. London: Tavistock Publications.

1967a   "Introduction to the National Teach-In." In *Teach-Ins*, ed. L. Menashe and R. Radosh, 158. New York: Praeger.

1967b   "Understanding Civilization," *Comparative Studies in Society and History* 9:446–465.

1967c   "Levels of Communal Relations." In *Handbook of Middle American Indians*, Vol. 6, *Social Anthropology*, ed. Manning Nash, 299–316. Austin: University of Texas Press.

1967*d*   "Patrones políticos entre campesinos Latinoamericanos." In *Colloques Internationaux du Centre National des Recherches Scientifiques*, 181–191. Les Problemes Agraires des Amériques Latines, Editions du Centre Nationale por Recherche Scientifique, Paris.

1968   "Introductory Remarks." Symposium 17: Comparative Analysis of Complex Societies, 8th International Congress of Anthropological and Ethnological Sciences, Science Council of Japan, Tokyo, Proceedings, Vol. 3, 456–457.

1969*b*   "On Peasant Rebellions," *International Journal of Social Sciences* 21:286–293. (Translations: French, Portuguese.)

1969*c*   "American Anthropologists and American Society." In *Concepts and Assumptions in Contemporary Anthropology*, ed. Stephen A. Tyler, 3–11. Southern Anthropological Society Proceedings, no. 3. Athens: University of Georgia Press.

1969*d*   "Society and Symbols in Latin Europe and in the Islamic Near East," *Anthropological Quarterly* 42(3):287–301.

1969*e*   "Editorial," *Comparative Studies in Society and History* 11:476–479.

1970*a*   "The Inheritance of Land Among Bavarian and Tyrolese Peasants," *Anthropologica* 12:99–114.

1970*b*   "Algerian Peasant Revolt," *Transaction* 7:33–46.

1971*a*   "Introduction." In *National Liberation*, ed. Norman Miller and Roderick Aya, 1–13. New York: Free Press.

1971*b*   "Peasant Rebellion and Revolution." In *National Liberation*, ed. Norman Miller and Roderick Aya, 48–67. New York: Free Press.

1971*c*   "Preface." In the British edition of Wolf's *Peasant Wars of the Twentieth Century*, ix-xi. London: Faber and Faber.

1971*d*   "Obituary: Hortense Powdermaker," *American Anthropologist* 73:783–786.

1971*e*   "Los Hidalgos de Indias." Michigan Papers in Anthropology, no. 1.

1972*a*   "Comments on 'Peasantries in Anthropology and History' by George Dalton," *Current Anthropology* 13:410–411.

1972*b*   "Ownership and Political Ecology," *Anthropological Quarterly* 45:201–205.

1972*c*   "The Pre-Columbian Collection." In *Pre-Columbian, African, and Oceanic Art from the Collection of Mrs. Henry Testut-Obstfield*, 3–4. Catalogue, The Gallery, Lehman College.

1973   "Die Phasen des ländlichen Protestes in Lateinamerika." In *Gewalt und Ausbeutung*, ed. Ernest Feder, 273–286. Hamburg: Hoffman und Campe Verlag. (Translation: Spanish.)

1974*a*   "Foreword." In *In Search of the Primitive*, by Stanley Diamond, xi-xiii. New Brunswick, N.J.: Transaction Books.

1974*b*   "Introduction." In the paperback edition of Wolf's *Anthropology*, ix-xii. New York: W. W. Norton.

1975*a*   "Comments." Symposium on Revolutionary Directions in Intellectual and Cultural Production, 10th Anniversary Convocation, City University of New York, Proceedings, 50–53.

1975*b*   "Introduction: Peasants and Political Mobilization," *Comparative Studies in Society and History* 17:385–388.

1977*a*   "Introduction." In *Society and History: Essays by Sylvia L. Thrupp*, ed. Raymond Grew and Nicholas H. Steneck, pt. 4: Social Change, 193–197. Ann Arbor: University of Michigan Press.

1977*b* "Encounter with Norbert Elias." In *Human Figurations: Essays for Norbert Elias*, ed. Peter R. Gleichmann, Johan Goudsblom, and Hermann Korte, 28–35. Amsterdam: Amsterdam Sociologisch Tijdschrift.

1977*c* "Killing the Aché: Comments on a Case of Genocide." In *Genocide in Paraguay*, ed. Richard Arens, 46–57. Philadelphia: Temple University Press.

1977*d* "Foreword." In *Networks and Marginality: Life in a Mexican Shantytown*, by Larissa Lomnitz, xi–xiii. New York: Academic Press.

1978 "Remarks on the People of Puerto Rico," *Revista Interamericana / Interamerican Review* 8:17–25.

1980*a* "They Divide and Subdivide, and Call It Anthropology," *New York Times* (30 November):E9.

1980*b* "The United States: The Cultural Predicament of the Anthropologist." In *Anthropology: Ancestors and Heirs*, ed. Stanley Diamond, 455–462. The Hague: Mouton.

1981*a* "A. L. Kroeber." In *Totems and Teachers: Perspectives on the History of Anthropology*, ed. Sydel Silverman, 35–64. New York: Columbia University Press.

1981*b* "The Mills of Inequality: A Marxian Approach." In *Social Inequality: Comparative and Developmental Approaches*, ed. Gerald Berreman, 41–57. New York: Academic Press.

1981*c* "Obituary: Angel Palerm Vich," *American Anthropologist* 83:612–615.

1982*b* "Culture: Panacea or Problem?" *Northeastern Anthropological Association Newsletter* (Fall):1–10.

1983*a* "Introduction." In *Bonds of Mutual Trust*, by Carlos Vélez-Ibañez, xiii–xv. New Brunswick, N.J.: Rutgers University Press.

1983*b* "Prólogo." In *Génesis de una revolución: Análisis del surgimiento de la organización campesina en El Salvador*, by Carlos Rafael Cabarrús Pellecer, 9–12. Centro de Investigaciones y Estudios Superiores en Antropología Social, Ediciones de la Casa Chata, México, D.F.

1983*c* "On Peasant Rent." In *Social Anthropology of Peasantry*, ed. Joan Mencher, 48–59. Bombay: Somaiya Publications.

1983*d* "A Summing Up." In *Social Anthropology of Peasantry*, ed. Joan Mencher, 345–351. Bombay: Somaiya Publications.

1983*e* "Culture: Panacea or Problem?" *American Antiquity* 49:393–400.

1984*b* "Introduction." In *Religion, Power and Protest in Local Communities*, ed. Eric R. Wolf, 1–14. New York: Mouton.

1984*c* "Angel Palerm Vich (1917–1980)." In *Histori i Antropologia: A la memoria d' Angel Palerm*, ed. Neus Escandell and Ignaci Terradas, 21–27. Montserrat: Publicacions de l'Abadia de Montserrat.

1984*d* "Incorporation and Identity in the Making of the Modern World," *Suomen Antropologi* 3:82–92.

1986*a* "Foreword." In *The House That Giacomo Built*, by Donald Pitkin, ix–x. London: Cambridge University Press.

1986*b* "The Vicissitudes of the Closed Corporate Peasant Community," *American Ethnologist* 13:325–329.

1987*a* "Cycles of Violence: The Anthropology of War and Peace." In *Waymarks*, ed. Kenneth Moore, 127–150. Notre Dame: University of Notre Dame Press.

1987*b* "Peasant War in Germany: Engels as Social Historian," *Science and Society* 51:82–92.

1987*c* "Cultura e ideología: Un ensayo dedicado a Angel Palerm." In *La heterodoxia recuperada: En torno a Angel Palerm*, ed. Susana Glantz, 582–596. México, D.F: Fondo de Cultura Económica.

1988*a* "Foreword." In *A Negotiated World: Three Centuries of Change in a French Alpine Community*, by Harriet G. Rosenberg, ix–x. Toronto: University of Toronto Press.

1988*b* "Reply to Alan R. Beals, 'On Eric Wolf and the North Berkeley Gang,'" *Current Anthropology* 29:306–307.

1988*c* "Afterword," Bureau of Applied Research in Anthropology, Special Issue on Indigenous Responses to Economic Development, ed. Jack Rollwagen, *Urban Anthropology/Studies of Cultural Systems and World Economic Change* 17: 105–109.

1988*d* "Inventing Society," *American Ethnologist* 15:752–761.

1988*e* "Ethnicity and Nationhood," *Journal of Ethnic Studies* (Revija za narodnostna vprasanja, Ljubljana, Treatises and Documents) 21:27–32.

1989 "La Poule aux Oeufs d'Or: Les Voies de la richesse et du pouvoir en Amérique Centrale au debut de la colonisation," *Les Temps Modernes* (Paris) 44(517/518, "Amérique Centrale"):38–58.

1990*a* "Freedom and Freedoms: Anthropological Perspectives." 29th T. B. Davie Memorial Lecture, University of Cape Town, South Africa.

1990*b* "Distinguished Lecture: Facing Power—Old Insights, New Questions," *American Anthropologist* 92:586–596.

1991*b* "Prefacio." In *Empresas transnacionais: Un grande projeto por dentro*, by Gustavo Lins Ribeiro, 7–9. São Paulo: Editora Marco Zero e Anpocs.

CO-AUTHORED ARTICLES, ESSAYS, CHAPTERS

1950 with Sidney W. Mintz, "An Analysis of Ritual Co-Parenthood (Compadrazgo)," *Southwestern Journal of Anthropology* 6:341–368. (Translation: Spanish.)

1956*a* with Angel Palerm, "Irrigation in the Old Alcohua Domain, Mexico," *Southwestern Journal of Anthropology* 11:265–281.

1956*b* with Angel Palerm, "El desarrollo del área clave del Imperio Texcocano," *Revista Mexicana de Estudios Antropológicos* 14:337–349.

1956 with Pedro Armillas and Angel Palerm, "A Small Irrigation System in the Valley of Teotihuacán," *American Antiquity* 21:396–399.

1957 with Angel Palerm, "Ecological Potential and Cultural Development in Mesoamerica." In *Studies in Human Ecology*, 1–37. Social Science Monograph 3, Pan American Union, Washington, D.C.

1957 with Sidney W. Mintz, "Haciendas and Plantations in Middle America and the Antilles," *Social and Economic Studies* 6:380–412. (Translation: Spanish.)

1959 with Sidney W. Mintz, "Ethnology: Middle America and the West Indies." In *Handbook of Latin America Studies, Vol. 21*, ed. Nathan A. Haverstock, 26–31. Gainesville: University of Florida Press.

1960   with Sidney W. Mintz, "Ethnology: Middle America and the West Indies."
        In *Handbook of Latin American Studies, Vol. 22*, ed. Nathan A. Haverstock, 26–
        29. Gainesville: University of Florida Press.
1961   with Angel Palerm, "La agricultura y el desarrollo de la civilización en
        Mesoamérica," *Revista Interamericana de Ciencias Sociales* 1(2).
1961   with Sidney W. Mintz, "Ethnology: Middle America and the West Indies."
        In *Handbook of Latin American Studies, Vol. 23*, ed. Nathan A. Haverstock and
        Earl J. Pariseau, 37–41. Gainesville: University of Florida Press.
1962   with Sidney W. Mintz, "Ethnology: Middle America and the West Indies."
        In *Handbook of Latin American Studies, Vol. 24*, ed. Earl J. Pariseau, 39–49.
        Gainesville: University of Florida Press.
1965   with Marshall D. Sahlins, "The Tragedy of American Unreason," *Michigan
        Daily* 76, no. 39(13 October):6.
1966   with Thomas Harding, "Conference: The Evolutionary Interpretation of
        Culture," *Current Anthropology* 8:127–129.
1967   with Edward C. Hansen, "Caudillo Politics," *Comparative Studies in Society and
        History* 9:168–179.
1969   with William Schorger, "Preface," *Anthropological Quarterly* 42:107–108.
1970   with Joseph C. Jorgensen, "Anthropology on the Warpath in Thailand,"
        New York Review of Books (19 November):26–35. (Translations: French, Span-
        ish.)
1971   with Joseph C. Jorgensen, "Anthropology on the Warpath: An Exchange,"
        New York Review of Books (8 April):45–46 and (22 July):38. (Translation:
        French.)
1975   with Bob Scholte and Stanley Diamond, "Anti-Kaplan," *American Anthropol-
        ogist* 77:870–876.
1989   with Sidney W. Mintz, "Reply to Michael Taussig," *Critique of Anthropology*
        9:25–31.

UNPUBLISHED PAPERS CITED IN TEXT

1950   "The Formation of the Nation." (Published in Spanish; see 1953.)
1982c   "Culture and Ideology: An Essay in Honor of Angel Palerm." (Published in
        Spanish; see 1987c.)
1983f   "The People without History." Lecture to the University Faculty Senate,
        125th Plenary Session, City University of New York, 13 December.
1985   "Ideas and Power: An Essay in Honor of Elman Service."
1987d   "Capitalism, Nation-Formation and Ethnicity." Session 3-012: Confronting
        Capital, Annual Meeting of the American Anthropological Association,
        Chicago, 21 November.
1992a   "Perilous Ideas: Race, Culture, People." Inaugural Lecture to Honor Sid-
        ney Mintz, The Johns Hopkins University, 16 November.
1992b   "Aspects of the German Catastrophe." Brockway Lecture on the Anthro-
        pology of Crisis, Ph.D. Program in Anthropology, City University of New
        York, 11 December.

REFERENCES

Abel, Wilhelm
  1964   *Die Drei Epochen der deutschen Agrargeschichte.* Hannover: Schaper.
  1980   *Agricultural Fluctuations in Europe.* New York: St. Martin's Press.
Adams, Richard N.
  1975   *Energy and Structure: A Theory of Social Power.* Austin: University of
            Texas Press.
  1991   "Strategies of Ethnic Survival in Central America." In *Nation-States
            and Indians in Latin America*, ed. Greg Urban and Joel Sherzer, 181–
            206. Austin: University of Texas Press.
Adas, Michael
  1989   *Machines as the Measure of Men: Science, Technology and Ideologies of Western
            Dominance.* Ithaca: Cornell University Press.
Aguirre Beltràn, Gonzalo
  1973   "Regiones de refugio: El desarrollo de la comunidad y el proceso
            dominical en mestizo America, Mexico: Instituto Nacional Indige-
            nista." Serie de Antropología Social, no. 17.
Alavi, Hamza
  1965   "Peasants and Revolution." In *The Socialist Register*, ed. R. Miliband
            and J. Saville, 241–277. London: Merlin Press.
Althusser, Louis
  1979   "The Crisis of Marxism." In Proceedings of the meeting of *Il mani-
            festo, Potere e Opposizione nelle Società post-rivoluzionare: Una discussione
            della Sinistra.* London: Links. (Orig. Rome: Alfani, 1977.)
Alvarez, Elena
  1983   *Política económica y agricultura en el Perú.* Lima: Instituto de Estudios Per-
            uanos.
Anagnost, Ann
  1988   "Defining the Socialist Imaginary: The 'Civilized Village' Campaign
            in Post-Mao China." Paper presented at the Annual Meeting of the
            American Anthropological Association, Phoenix, Ariz.

Anderson, Benedict
1983   *Imagined Communities: Reflections on the Origin and Spread of Nationalism.*
            London: Verso.
Anderson, Karen
1988   "As Gentle as Little Lambs: Images of Huron and Montagnais-
            Naskapi Women in the Writings of the 17th-Century Jesuits," *Cana-
            dian Review of Sociology and Anthropology* 25:560–576.
Andolf, Göran
1985   "Nationalism och objektivitet i historieböckerna," *Att vara svensk*
            (Kungl. Vitterhets, Historie och Antikvitets Akademin, Konferenser)
            13:3–22.
Andrade, Maria Cecilia
1986   "Calendario y memoria colectiva Mixe." Tesis para la maestria
            en etnohistoria, Escuela Nacional de Antropología e Historia,
            Mexico.
Ardener, Shirley
1986   "The Representation of Women in Academic Models." In *Visibility
            and Power: Essays on Women and Society and Development*, ed. Leela
            Duke, Eleanor Leacock, and Shirley Ardener, 3–14. Delhi: Oxford
            University Press.
Arizona Daily Star (Tucson)
1985*a*   "Smelter Foes of Every Stripe Dominate Douglas Town Hall," *Ari-
            zona Daily Star* (18 January):G2.
1985*b*   "Tucson Chosen as Next Site for Douglas Smelter Meeting," *Arizona
            Daily Star* (9 April):C11.
Arnstberg, Karl-Olov
1989   *Svenskheten: Den erfarenhetsförnekande kulturen.* Stockholm: Carlssons.
Asad, Talal
1973   "Two European Images of Non-European Rule." In *Anthropology and
            the Colonial Encounter*, ed. Talal Asad, 103–121. New York: Humani-
            ties Press.
1987   "Are There Histories of People without Europe? A Review Article,"
            Comparative Studies in Society and History 29:594–607.
Ashcraft, Norman, and Cedric Grant
1968   "The Development and Organization of Education in British Hon-
            duras," *Comparative Education Review* 12:171–179.
Auletta, K.
1983   *The Underclass.* New York: Simon and Schuster.
Aulette, Judy, and Trudy Mills
1988   "Something Old, Somthing New: Auxiliary Work in the 1983–1986
            Copper Strike," *Feminist Studies* 14:251–268.
Baird, P. A.
1990   "Genetics and Health Care: A Paradigm Shift," *Perspectives in Biology
            and Medicine* 33:203–213.
Ballon, E., and A. Filomeno
1981   "Los movimientos regionales: ¿Hacía donde van?" *Que Hacer*
            11(Julio):77–103.

Banks, David J.
1990   "Resurgent Islam and Malay Rural Culture: Malay Novelists and the Invention of Culture," *American Ethnologist* 17:531–548.

Barabas, Alicia Mabel
1977   "Chinantec Messianism: The Mediator of the Divine." In *Western Expansion and Indigenous Peoples*, ed. Elias Sevilla-Casas, 221–254. Amsterdam: Mouton.

Bardella, Gustavo
1964   *Setenta y cinco años de vida económica del Perú, 1889–1964*. Lima: Banco de Crédito del Perú.

Barrow, Lennox
1970   "The Uses of Money in Mid-Nineteenth Century Ireland," *Studies: An Irish Quarterly Review* 59:81–86.

Basadre, Jorge
1968–   *Historia de la República del Perú 1822–1933*. 6th ed. 17 vols. Lima: Editorial Universitaria.
1969
1980   *Elecciones y centralismo en el Perú*. Lima: Centro de Investigación de la Universidad del Pacífico.

Batteau, Allen W.
1990   *The Invention of Appalachia*. Tucson: University of Arizona Press.

Bauman, Zygmunt
1990   "Identity and Ambivalence," *Theory, Culture and Society* 7:143–170.

Baumgart, P.
1966   *Erscheinungsformen des preussischen Absolutismus*. Berlin: Stahlmann.

Beals, Ralph L.
1942   "Ethnology of the Western Mixe." University of California [Berkeley] Publications in American Archaeology and Ethnology, no. 42(1).

Beck, Ulrich
1986   *Risikogesellschaft auf dem Weg in eine andere Moderne*. Frankfurt: Suhrkamp.

Belize Labor Force Survey
1983–   "Preliminary Report, August 1984." Central Statistical Office, Ministry of Economic Development, Belmopan, Belize.
1984

Bendix, Reinhard, ed.
1964   *Nation-Building and Citizenship*. New York: Wiley.

Bentley, G. Carter
1987   "Ethnicity and Practice," *Comparative Studies in Society and History* 29:24–55.

Beresford, Melanie
1988   *Vietnam: Politics, Economics and Society*. New York: Pinter Publishers.

Berger, Suzanne
1972   *Peasants against Politics*. Cambridge: Harvard University Press.

Berlin, Gordon
1991   "The Poverty among Families: A Service Decategorization Response." Photocopied report, Manpower Demonstration Research Corporation, New York.

Betts, Raymond
    1961   *Assimilation and Association in French Colonial Theory.* New York: Colum-
                bia University Press.
Biklen, Douglas
    1987   *Images of the Disabled/Disabling Images.* New York: Praeger.
Black, R. D. Collinson
    1960   *Economic Thought and the Irish Question, 1817–1870.* Cambridge: Cam-
                bridge University Press.
Blickle, Peter
    1973   *Landschaften im alten Reich.* Munich: Beck.
Bloch, Marc
    1966   *French Rural History.* Berkeley: University of California Press. (Orig.
                1931.)
Bloch, Maurice
    1989   "The Symbolism of Money in Imerina." In *Money and Morality of Ex-
                change,* ed. Jonathan Parry and Maurice Bloch, 165–190. New York:
                Cambridge University Press.
Block, Alan A., and Frank R. Scarpitti
    1985   *Poisoning for Profit: The Mafia and Toxic Waste in America.* New York:
                Morrow.
Bluebond-Langner, Myra
    1991   "Living with Cystic Fibrosis," *Medical Anthropology Quarterly* 5:99–132.
Blumberg, P.
    1980   *Inequality in an Age of Decline.* New York: Oxford University Press.
Bolland, O. Nigel
    1986   *Belize: A New Nation in Central America.* Boulder, Colo.: Westview Press.
Bonacich, E.
    1972   "A Theory of Ethnic Antagonism: The Split-Labor Market," *Ameri-
                can Sociological Review* 5:533–547.
Bonilla, Heraclio
    1972   *La Independencia en el Perú.* Lima: Instituto de Estudios Peruanos.
Booth, David, and Bernardo Sorj, eds.
    1983   *Military Reformism and Social Classes: The Peruvian Experience, 1968–
                1980.* New York: St. Martin's Press.
Borneman, John
    1992   *Belonging in the Two Berlins: Kin, State, Nation.* Cambridge: Cambridge
                University Press.
Bourdieu, Pierre
    1977   *Outline of a Theory of Practice.* Trans. Richard Nice. Cambridge: Cam-
                bridge University Press.
Bourgois, Philippe
    1989   "Crack in Spanish Harlem: Culture and Economy in the Inner
                City," *Anthropology Today* 5:6–11.
    in press   *In Search of Respect: Selling Crack in Spanish Harlem.* New York: Cam-
                bridge University Press.
Bradford, George
    1989a   "Return of the Son of Deep Ecology: The Ethics of Permanent Crisis
                and the Permanent Crisis in Ethics," *Fifth Estate* 24(Spring):5–38.

1989*b*   *How Deep Is Deep Ecology? With an Essay Review of Woman's Freedom.*
          Novato, Calif.: Times Change Press.

Bramwell, Anna
1989   *Ecology in the Twentieth Century: A History.* New Haven: Yale University
          Press.

Brandes, Stanley
1988   *Power and Persuasion: Fiestas and Social Control in Rural Mexico.* Philadel-
          phia: University of Pennsylvania Press.

Bratring, F. W. A.
1968   *Statistisch-Topographische Beschreibung der Mark Brandenburg 1804–1809.*
          Ed. Otto Büsch and Gerd Heinrich. Berlin: de Gruyter.

Bremen, Jan
1987   *The Shattered Image: Construction and Deconstruction of the Village in Colonial
          Asia.* Amsterdam: Center for Asian Studies, University of Amster-
          dam.

Brenneis, Don, and Fred Myers, eds.
1984   *Dangerous Words.* New York: New York University Press.

Bridenthal, Renate, Atina Grossman, and Marion Kaplan, eds.
1984   *When Biology Became Destiny: Women in Weimar and Nazi Germany.* New
          York: Monthly Review Press.

Brown, Michael H.
1981   *Laying Waste: The Poisoning of America by Toxic Chemicals.* New York:
          Pocket Books.

Brown, Phil, and Edwin J. Mikkelsen
1990   *No Safe Place: Toxic Waste, Leukemia, and Community Action.* Berkeley, Los
          Angeles, London: University of California Press.

Bullard, Robert D.
1990   *Dumping in Dixie: Race, Class and Environmental Quality.* Boulder, Colo.:
          Westview Press.

Bulmer, M. I. A.
1975   "Sociological Models of the Mining Community," *Sociological Review*
          23:61–92.

Burawoy, Michael, and János Lukács
1992   *The Radiant Past: Ideology and Reality in Hungary's Road to Capitalism.*
          Chicago: University of Chicago Press.

Burga, Manuel, and Alberto Flores Galindo
1979   *Apogeo y crisis de la república aristocrática.* Lima: Instituto de Estudios
          Peruanos.

Bynum, Caroline Walker
1986   "Introduction: The Complexity of Symbols." In *Gender and Religion:
          On the Complexity of Symbols*, ed. Caroline Walker Bynum, Sevan Har-
          rell, and Paula Richman, 1–22. Boston: Beacon Press.

Cancian, Frank
1965   *Economics and Prestige in a Maya Community: The Religious Cargo System of
          Zinacantan.* Stanford: Stanford University Press.

Caravedo, Baltazar
1979   "Poder central y decentralización: Perú, 1931," *Apuntes* 5(9):111–
          129.

1983   *El problema del descentralismo.* Lima: Centro de Investigación de la Universidad del Pacífico.

Carmel Chamber of Commerce (New York)

1990   *Real Estate in Putnam County.* Chamber of Commerce, Carmel, N.Y.

Carsten, F. L.

1947   "The Origins of the Junkers," *English Historical Review* 62:145–178.

1959   *Princes and Parliaments in Germany.* Oxford: Clarendon.

1989   *A History of the Prussian Junkers.* Aldershot, Hampshire, U.K.: Scolar.

Cayetano, E. Roy

1982   "A Garifuna Orthography." Paper presented at 44th International Congress of Americanists, Manchester, England.

Cazdan, Courtney

1979   "Language in Education: Variation in the Teacher-Talk Register." In *Language in Public Life,* ed. J. E. Alatis and R. Tucker, 144–162. Georgetown University Round Table on Languages and Linguistics. Washington, D.C.: Georgetown University Press.

Center for Investigative Reporting (CIR) and Bill Moyers

1990   *Global Dumping Ground: The International Traffic in Hazardous Waste.* Washington, D.C.: Seven Locks Press.

Cerrell Associates

1984   *Political Difficulties Facing Waste to Energy Conversion Plant Siting.* Los Angeles: California Waste Management Board.

Chance, John K.

1990   "Changes in Twentieth-Century Mesoamerican Cargo Systems." In *Class, Politics, and Popular Religion in Mexico and Central America,* ed. Lynn Stephen and James Dow, 27–42. Washington, D.C.: American Anthropological Association.

Chance, John K., and William B. Taylor

1985   "Cofradías and Cargos: A Historical Perspective on the Mesoamerican Civil-Religious Hierarchy," *American Ethnologist* 12:1–26.

Cipolla, Carlo

1976   *Before the Industrial Revolution.* New York: W.W. Norton.

Citizen's Clearing House for Hazardous Wastes

1988   *Action Bulletin,* no. 19 (July).

Clayton, Ellen Wright

1993   "Reproductive Genetic Testing: Regulatory and Liability Issues," *Fetal Diagnosis and Therapy* 8(supp. 1):39–59.

Clements, Lord

1838   *The Present Poverty of Ireland.* London: Charles Knight.

Cobbing, J.

1988   "The Mfecane as Alibi: Thoughts on Dithakong and Mbolompo," *Journal of African History* 29:487–519.

Cohen, Abner

1985   *The Symbolic Construction of Community.* Chichester, U.K.: Horwood.

Cohn, Bernard

1983   "Representing Authority in Victorian India." In *The Invention of Tradition,* ed. Eric Hobsbawm and Terence Ranger, 165–211. Cambridge: Cambridge University Press.

1984   "The Census, Social Structure and Objectification in South Asia,"
            Folk 26:1–10.
Cole, John W., and Eric R. Wolf
1974   *The Hidden Frontier: Ecology and Ethnicity in an Alpine Valley.* New York:
            Academic Press.
Collette, Will
1988   *Waste Managment, Inc.: A Corporate Profile.* Arlington, Va.: Citizen's
            Clearinghouse for Hazardous Wastes.
Colletti, Lucio
1974   *From Rousseau to Lenin: Studies in Ideology and Society.* New York:
            Monthly Review Press.
Collier, Jane F.
1986   "From Mary to Modern Woman: The Material Basis of Marianismo
            and Its Transformations in a Spanish Village," *American Ethnologist*
            13:100–107.
Collins, E. J. T.
1976   "Migrant Labour in British Agriculture in the Nineteenth Century,"
            Economic History Review, 2d series, 29:38–59.
Colmenares, German
1985   "La nación y la historia regional en los países andinos, 1870–1930,"
            Revista Andina 3(2):311-330.
Comaroff, Jean, and John L. Comaroff
1986   "Christianity and Colonialism in South Africa," *American Ethnologist*
            13:1–22.
1991   *Of Revelation and Revolution: Christianity, Colonialism, and Consciousness in
            South Africa.* Vol. 1. Chicago: University of Chicago Press.
Comaroff, John L.
1987   "Of Totemism and Ethnicity: Consciousness, Practice, and the Signs
            of Inequality," *Ethnos* 52:301–323.
Commission for Racial Justice, United Church of Christ
1987   *Toxic Wastes and Race in the United States: A National Report on the Racial
            and Socio-Economic Characteristics of Communities with Hazardous Waste
            Sites.* New York: Public Data Access.
Cooper, D.
1977   "Some Preliminary Perspectives on Social Stratification in Selebi-
            Phikwe." Working Paper, Sociology Department, Birmingham Uni-
            versity.
1980   "How Urban Workers in Botswana Manage Their Cattle and
            Lands." National Migration Study Working Paper 4. Gaborone,
            Botswana: Central Statistics Office.
1982   "Socio-economic and Regional Factors of Wage Migration and Em-
            ployment." In *Migration in Botswana: Patterns, Causes, and Consequences*,
            ed. C. Kerven, 297–336. Gaborone, Botswana: Government Printer.
Cooper, Frederick, and Ann L. Stoler
1989   "Tensions of Empire: Colonial Control and Visions of Rule," *Ameri-
            can Ethnologist* 16:609–621.
Cornejo Koster, Enrique
1968   "Cronica del movimiento estudiantil Peruano." In *La Reforma Univer-*

sidad, ed. Gabriel del Mazo. Lima: Instituto de Estudios Peruanos.

Cotler, Julio
1978   *Clases, Estado y Nación*. Lima: Instituto de Estudios Peruanos.

Cowan, Ruth Schwartz
1991   "The History of Prenatal Testing." Presentation at the Conference "Genetic Testing: Impact on Women," National Institutes of Health, Bethesda, Md., 21–23 November.
1992   "Genetic Technology and Reproductive Choice: An Ethics for Autonomy." In *The Code of Codes*, ed. Daniel Kevles and Leroy Hood, 244–263. Cambridge: Harvard University Press.

Crawford, Michael, ed.
1984   *Current Developments in Anthropological Genetics*. Vol. 3, *Black Caribs: A Case Study in Biocultural Adaptation*. New York: Plenum Press.

Crenson, Matthew A.
1971   *The Un-Politics of Air Pollution: A Study of Non-Decisionmaking in the Cities*. Baltimore: Johns Hopkins University Press.

Crooks, Harold
1982   *Dirty Business: The Inside Story of the Garbage Agglomerates*. Toronto: Lorimer.

Crowder, Michael
1968   *West Africa under Colonial Rule*. London: Hutchinson.

Cruikshank, Julie
1988   "Myth and Tradition as Narrative Framework: Oral Histories from Northern Canada," *International Journal of Oral History* 9:198–214.

Cumings, Bruce
1981   "Interest and Ideology in the Study of Agrarian Politics," *Politics and Society* 10:467–495.

Dao Hung
1991   "Spring Festivals in Northern Vietnam," *Vietnam Courier* 16(February):12.

Daston, Lorraine
1987   "The Domestication of Risk: Mathematical Probability and Insurance, 1650–1830." In *The Probabilistic Revolution*, Vol. 1, *Ideas in History*, ed. Lorenz Kruger, Lorraine J. Daston, and Michael Heidelberger, 237–260. Cambridge: MIT Press.

Davidson, O.
1990   *Broken Heartland: The Rise of America's Rural Ghetto*. New York: Free Press.

Davin, Anna
1978   "Imperialism and Motherhood," *History Workshop*, no. 5(Spring):9–66.

DeGregori, Carlos Ivan
1990   *El surgimiento de Sendero Luminoso. Ayacucho 1969–1979*. Lima: Instituto de Estudios Peruanos.

Dehavenon, Anna Lou, ed.
n.d.   *There Is No Place Like Home: The Anthropology of United States Homelessness and Housing*. Unpublished manuscript.

Delheim, Charles
1982   *The Face of the Past*. Cambridge: Cambridge University Press.

Denbow, J., D. Kiyaga-Mulindwa, and N. Parsons
1985   "Historical and Archaeological Research in Botswana." History Workshop, Botswana Society Symposium on Research and Development, University of Zimbabwe.
Denbow, J., and E. Wilmsen
1986   "The Advent and Course of Pastoralism in the Kalahari," *Science* 234:1509–1515.
in press   *Cattle, Copper, and Capital in the Transformation of Southern African Communities: A Political Economy of the Past 2000 Years.* Chicago: University of Chicago Press.
Devall, Bill, and George Sessions
1985   *Deep Ecology.* Salt Lake City: G. M. Smith.
DeWalt, Billie
1975   "Changes in the Cargo Systems of Mesoamerica," *Anthropological Quarterly* 45:87–105.
Dodgshon, Robert
1975   "The Landholding Foundations of the Open-Field System," *Past and Present* 67:1–29.
Doke, Joseph J.
1967   *M. K. Gandhi, An Indian Patriot in South Africa.* Delhi: Ministry of Information and Broadcasting, Government of India. (Orig. 1909.)
Dominguez, Marcelino
1987   "Nax Kajpn Tunip: Comunalidad, El Caso de Cacalotepec Mixe, Oaxaca." Tesis para la licenciatura en etnolinguistica, Centro de Investigaciones y Estudios Superiores en Antropología Social, Apetatitlan, Tlaxcala.
Dow, James
1974   *Santos y sobrevivencia: Funciones de la religión en una comunidad Otomí.* Mexico: Instituto Nacional Indigenista, Secretaría de Educación Pública.
Edelman, Murray
1985   *The Symbolic Uses of Politics.* Urbana: University of Illinois Press.
Edelstein, Michael R.
1988   *Contaminated Communities: The Social and Psychological Impacts of Residential Toxic Exposure.* Boulder, Colo.: Westview Press.
Ehn, Billy
1983   *Ska vi leka tiger? Daghemsliv ur kulturell synvinkel.* Malmö, Sweden: Liber.
1989   "National Feeling in Sport," *Ethnologia Europaea* 19:57–68.
Elliott, Gregory
1987   *Althusser: A Detour of Theory.* London: Verso.
Engels, Friedrich
1975   *Marx and Engels Collected Works.* Vol. 4, *The Condition of the Working Class in England: From Personal Observation and Authentic Sources.* London: Lawrence and Wishart. (Orig. 1845.)
Enzensberger, Hans Magnus
1982   "A Critique of Political Economy." In his *Critical Essays,* ed. Reinhold Grimm, 186–223. New York: Continuum.

Epstein, A. L.
1958   *Politics in an Urban African Community.* Manchester: Manchester University Press.
Everyone's Backyard
1991   "Editorial," 9(1 October).
Falcon, Angelo
1992   "Puerto Ricans and Other Latinos in New York City Today: A Statistical Profile." Pamphlet, Institute for Puerto Rican Policy, New York.
Favre, Henri
1965   "La evolución de la situación de las haciendas en la región de Huancavelica." Serie Mesas Redondas, no. a. Lima: Instituto de Estudios Peruanos.
Finer, Samuel E.
1955   *The Life and Times of Sir Edwin Chadwick.* London: Methuen.
Finger, Ann
1984   "Claiming All of Our Bodies: Reproductive Rights and Disabilities." In *Test Tube Women,* ed. Rita Arditti, Renate Duelli-Klein, and Shelley Minden, 281–297. Boston: Routledge and Kegan Paul.
Fitzpatrick, David
1989   "'A Peculiar Tramping People': The Irish in Britain, 1801–1870." In *A New History of Ireland,* Vol. 5, *Ireland under the Union, I. 1801–1870,* ed. W. E. Vaughan, 623–660. Oxford: Clarendon Press.
Flores, Augustin, and Gasper Martin
1975   *Luwani Garifuna.* Dangriga: Settlement Day Committee.
Flores-Galindo, Alberto
1977   *Arequipa y el Sur Andina: Siglos XVII-XX.* Lima: Horizonte.
Foley, Doug
1990   *Learning Capitalist Culture: Deep in the Heart of Tejas.* Philadelphia: University of Pennsylvania Press.
Fordham, Signithia
1988   "Racelessness as a Factor in Black Students' School Success: Pragmatic Strategy or Pyrrhic Victory?" *Harvard Educational Review* 53: 257–293.
Foster, George
1967   *Tzintzuntzan: Mexican Peasants in a Changing World.* Boston: Little, Brown.
Foster, Mary LeCron
1988   "Conclusion: Expanding the Anthropology of Peace and Conflict." In *The Social Dynamics of Peace and Conflict,* ed. Robert A. Rubinstein and Mary LeCron Foster, 179–189. Boulder, Colo.: Westview Press.
Foster, Mary LeCron, and Robert A. Rubinstein
1986   "Introduction." In *Peace and War, Cross-Cultural Perspectives,* ed. Mary LeCron Foster and Robert A. Rubinstein, xi–xviii. New Brunswick, N.J.: Transaction Books.
Foucault, Michel
1979   "On Governmentality," *Ideology and Consciousness* 6:5–22.

Fox, Richard G.
1985   *Lions of the Punjab: Culture in the Making.* Berkeley, Los Angeles, London: University of California Press.
1989   *Gandhian Utopia: Experiments with Culture.* Boston: Beacon Press.
1990*a*   "Hindu Nationalism in the Making." In *Nationalist Ideologies and the Production of National Culture,* ed. Richard G. Fox, 63–80. [New] Monograph Series, no. 2. Washington, D.C.: American Anthropological Association.
1990*b*   "Introduction." In *Nationalist Ideologies and the Production of National Culture,* ed. Richard G. Fox, 1–14. [New] Monograph Series, no. 2. Washington, D.C.: American Anthropological Association.
1991   "For a Nearly New Culture History." In *Recapturing Anthropology: Working in the Present,* ed. Richard G. Fox, 93–114. Santa Fe: School of American Research Press.
Fox, Richard G., ed.
1990*c*   *Nationalist Ideologies and the Production of National Culture.* [New] Monograph Series, no. 2. Washington, D.C.: American Anthropological Association.
Frank, Andre Gunder
1966   *The Development of Underdevelopment.* New York: Monthly Review Press.
1978   *World Accumulation 1492–1789.* New York: Monthly Review Press.
Freeman, Thomas W.
1957   *Pre-famine Ireland: A Study in Historical Geography.* Manchester: Manchester University Press.
Freudenberg, Nicholas
1984   *Not in Our Backyards: Community Action for Health and the Environment.* New York: Monthly Review Press.
Fried, Morton H., Marvin Harris, and Robert Murphy, eds.
1968   *War: The Anthropology of Armed Conflict and Aggression.* Garden City, N.Y.: Natural History Press.
Friedrich, P.
1989   "Language, Ideology, and Political Economy," *American Anthropologist* 91:295–312.
Frykman, Jonas
1992   "In Motion: Body and Modernity in Sweden between the World Wars," *Ethnologia Scandinavica* 22:22–47.
Fulford, Roger
1948   *Votes for Women.* London: Faber and Faber.
Gadibolae, M.
1985   "Serfdom (Bolata) in the Nata Area." *Botswana Notes and Records* 17:25–32.
Gal, Susan
1989   "Language and Political Economy," *Annual Review of Anthropology* 18:345–367.
1991   "Bartók's Funeral: Representations of Europe in Hungarian Political Rhetoric," *American Ethnologist* 18:440–459.

Galaty, J.
1982   "Being 'Maasai': Being People of Cattle: Ethnic Shifters in East Africa," *American Ethnologist* 9:1–20.

Gamson, William
1991   "Commitment and Agency in Social Movements," *Sociological Forum* 6:27–50.

Gandhi, Mohandas K.
1972   *Satyagraha in South Africa*. Weare, N.H.: Greenleaf Books. (Orig. 1928.)

1983   *The Collected Works of Mahatma Gandhi*. New Delhi: Government of India, Publications Division, Ministry of Information and Broadcasting.

Gaventa, John
1980   *Power and Powerlessness: Quiescence and Rebellion in an Appalachian Valley*. Urbana: University of Illinois Press.

Geary, William N. M.
1965   *Nigeria under British Rule*. London: Cass.

Geertz, Clifford
1960   "Javanese Kijaji: The Changing Role of a Cultural Broker," *Comparative Studies in Society and History* 2:228–249.

1961   "Studies in Peasant Life: Community and Society." In *Biennial Review of Anthropology*, ed. Bernard J. Siegel, 1–41. Stanford: Stanford University Press.

1973   "After the Revolution: The Fate of Nationalism in the New States." In his *The Interpretation of Cultures*, 234–254. New York: Basic Books.

Ghani, Ashraf
1987   "A Conversation with Eric Wolf," *American Ethnologist* 14:346–367.

n.d.   *Production and Domination: Afghanistan 1747–1901*. Unpublished manuscript.

Gibbs, Lois M.
1982   *Love Canal: My Story*. Albany: State University of New York Press.

Giddens, Anthony
1984   *The Constitution of Society: Outline of the Theory of Structuration*. Berkeley, Los Angeles, London: University of California Press.

Gilder, George
1982   *Wealth and Poverty*. New York: Bantam.

Gillin, John
1947   *Moche: A Peruvian Coastal Community*. Washington, D.C.: Government Printing Office.

Gimpel, Jean
1977   *The Medieval Machine*. Harmondsworth, U.K.: Penguin.

Girouard, Mark
1981   *The Return to Camelot: Chivalry and the English Gentleman*. New Haven: Yale University Press.

Gonzales, Michael J.
1985   "Plantation Agriculture and Social Control in Northern Peru, 1875–1933." Latin American Monographs, no. 62, Institute of Latin American Studies, University of Texas, Austin.

Gonzalez, Nancie L.
1969   *Black Carib Household Organization.* Seattle: University of Washington Press.
1970   "The Neoteric Society," *Comparative Studies in Society and History* 12:1–13.
1988   *Sojourners of the Caribbean: Ethnogenesis and Ethnohistory of the Garifuna.* Urbana: University of Illinois Press.
González Villanueva, Pedro
1989   *El sacrificio Mixe: Rumbos para una antropología religiosa indígena.* Mexico: Ediciones Don Bosco, S.A.
Gordon, David M.
1972   *Theories of Poverty and Underemployment: Orthodox, Radical and Dual Labor Market Perspectives.* Lexington, Mass.: Lexington Books, D. C. Heath.
Gorman, Stephen
1979   "The State, Elite and Export in Nineteenth-Century Peru," *Journal of Interamerican Studies and World Affairs* 21:395–418.
Gouldner, Alvin
1979   *The Future of Intellectuals and the Rise of the New Class.* New York: Oxford University Press.
Gramsci, Antonio
1971   *Selections from the Prison Notebooks.* New York: International Publishers.
Grant, Cedric
1966   "The Civil Service Strike in British Honduras: A Case Study of Politics and the Civil Service," *Caribbean Quarterly* 12:37–49.
1976   *The Making of Modern Belize: Politics, Society and British Colonialism in Central America.* Cambridge: Cambridge University Press.
Greenberg, James B.
1981   *Santiago's Sword: Chatino Peasant Religion and Economics.* Berkeley, Los Angeles, London: University of California Press.
Greenhouse, Carol J.
1986   "Fighting for Peace." In *Peace and War, Cross-Cultural Perspectives,* ed. Mary LeCron Foster and Robert A. Rubinstein, 49–60. New Brunswick, N.J.: Transaction Books.
1987   "Cultural Perspectives on War." In *The Quest for Peace,* ed. Raimo Väyrynen with Dieter Senghaas and Christian Schmidt, 32–47. Beverly Hills, Calif.: Sage.
Greenpeace
1990   "Special Issue: The Next Ten Years," 15, no. 1(January/February).
Grimble, Arthur
1921   "Administrators and Anthropologists," *United Empire* (December): 765–769.
Gutman, Herbert G.
1977   "Two Lockouts in Pennsylvania, 1873–1874." In his *Work, Culture, and Society in Industrializing America,* 321–343. New York: Vintage Books.
Hacking, Ian
1990   *The Taming of Chance.* Cambridge: Cambridge University Press.

Hagen, William W.
1985 "How Mighty the Junkers? Peasant Rents and Seigneurial Profits in Sixteenth-Century Brandenburg," *Past and Present* 108:80–116.
1986*a* "The Junkers' Faithless Servants: Peasant Insubordination and the Breakdown of Serfdom in Brandenburg-Prussia, 1763–1811." In *The German Peasantry*, ed. Richard J. Evans and W. R. Lee, 71–101. London: Croom Helm.
1986*b* "Working for the Junker: The Standard of Living of Manorial Laborers in Brandenburg, 1584–1810," *Journal of Modern History* 58: 143–158.
1989 "Seventeenth-Century Crisis in Brandenburg: The Thirty Years' War, the Destabilization of Serfdom, and the Rise of Absolutism," *American Historical Review* 94:303–335.

Hahn, Harlan
1988 "Can Disability Be Beautiful?" *Social Policy* (Winter):26–31.

Hall, Gwendolyn Miello
1992 *Africans in Colonial Louisiana: The Formation of Afro-Creole Culture in the Eighteenth Century*. Baton Rouge: Louisiana State University Press.

Hamilton, C., and J. Wright, eds.
in press *The Mfecane Aftermath: Papers from the Conference.* Johannesburg and Durban: University of Witwatersrand and University of Natal Presses.

Hamilton, Cynthia
1990 "Women, Home and the Community: The Struggle in an Urban Environment." In *Reweaving the World: The Emergence of Ecofeminism*, ed. I. Diamond and G. Orenstein, 215–222. San Francisco: Sierra Club Books.

Hammar, Tomas
1990 *Democracy and the Nation State*. Aldershot, Hampshire (U.K.): Avebury.

Handler, Richard, and Jocelyn Linnekin
1984 "Tradition, Genuine or Spurious," *American Journal of Folklore* 97:273–290.

Handley, James Edmund
1945 *The Irish in Scotland, 1799–1845*. Cork: Cork University Press.

Hanks, William
1987 "Discourse Genres in a Theory of Practice," *American Ethnologist* 14:668–692.

Hann, Chris
1993 "Property Relations in the New Eastern Europe: The Case of Specialist Cooperatives in Hungary." In *The Curtain Rises: Rethinking Culture, Ideology and the State in Eastern Europe*, ed. Hermine De Soto and David G. Anderson, 99–119. Atlantic Highlands, N.J.: Humanities Press.
n.d. "From Production to Property: Decollectivization and the Human-Land Relationship in Contemporary Eastern Europe." Unpublished manuscript.

Haraldsson, Désirée
1987 *Skydda vår natur! Svenska Naturskydds föreningens framväxt och tidiga utveck-*

ling. Bibliotheca Historica Lundensis, 63. Lund, Sweden: Lund University Press.

Haraway, Donna
1988   "The Biopolitics of Postmodern Bodies: Determinations of Self in Immune System Discourse," *Difference* 1:3–44.

Harmand, Jules
1910   *Domination et Colonisation.* Paris: Flammarion.

Harris, Marvin
1964   *Patterns of Race in the Americas.* New York: Walker.

Harris, Olivia
1978   "Complementarity and Conflict: An Andean View of Women and Men." In *Sex and Age as Principles of Social Differentiation,* ed. J. S. La Fontaine, 21–40. New York: Academic Press.
1980   "The Power of Signs: Gender, Culture and the Wild in the Bolivian Andes." In *Nature, Culture and Gender,* ed. Carol P. MacCormack and Marilyn Strathern, 70–95. Cambridge: Cambridge University Press.

Harris, Ruth-Ann Mellish
1980   "The Nearest Place that Wasn't Ireland: A Study of Prefamine Irish Circular Migration to Britain." Ph.D. diss., Tufts University.

Harrison, Regina
1989   *Signs, Songs, and Memory in the Andes: Translating Quechua Language and Culture.* Austin: University of Texas Press.

Harvey, David
1989   *The Condition of Post-Modernity.* Oxford: Basil Blackwell.

Helms, Mary
1981   "Black Carib Domestic Organization in Historical Perspective: Traditional Origins of Contemporary Patterns," *Ethnology* 20:77–86.

Heyman, Josiah M.
1991   *Life and Labor on the Border: Working People of Northeastern Sonora, Mexico, 1886–1986.* Tucson: University of Arizona Press.

Hill, Jonathan D.
1988   *Rethinking History and Myth: Indigenous South American Perspectives on the Past.* Urbana: University of Illinois Press.

Hintze, Otto
1975   *The Historical Essays of Otto Hintze.* Ed. Felix Gilbert with Robert Berdahl. New York: Oxford University Press.

Hitchcock, R.
1978   *Kalahari Cattle Posts: A Regional Study of Hunter-Gatherers, Pastoralists, and Agriculturalists in the Western Sandveld Region.* Gaborone, Botswana: Government Printer.

Hobley, C. W.
1967   *Bantu Beliefs and Magic.* 2nd ed. London: Witherby. (Orig. 1922.)

Hobsbawm, Eric
1983   "Introduction: Inventing Traditions." In *The Invention of Tradition,* ed. Eric Hobsbawm and Terence Ranger, 1–15. Cambridge: Cambridge University Press.

Hobsbawm, Eric, and Terence Ranger, eds.
1983   *The Invention of Tradition.* Cambridge: Cambridge University Press.

Hoffman, Richard C.
  1975   "Medieval Origins of the Common Fields." In *European Peasants and Their Markets*, ed. William Parker and Eric Jones, 23–71. Princeton: Princeton University Press.

Hogbin, S. J., and Kirk-Greene, A. H. M.
  1966   *The Emirates of Northern Nigeria*. London: Oxford University Press.

Homans, George
  1953   "The Rural Sociology of Medieval England," *Past and Present* 4:32–43.

Hoopes, Townsend
  1971   *The Limits of Intervention: An Inside Account of How the Johnson Policy of Escalation in Vietnam Was Reversed*. New York: W. W. Norton.

Hopkins, Raul
  1981   *Desarrollo desigual y crisis en la agricultura Peruana, 1944–1969*. Lima: Instituto de Estudios Peruanos.

Hoszowski, Stanislas
  1972   "Central Europe and the Sixteenth- and Seventeenth-Century Price Revolution." In *Economy and Society in Early Modern Europe*, ed. Peter Earle, 85–103. New York: Harper and Row.

Huggett, Frank
  1975   *The Land Question*. London: Thames and Hudson.

Hugh-Jones, Stephen
  1988   "The Gun and the Bow: Myths of White Men and Indians," *L'Homme* 23:138–155.

Hunt, David
  1974   "Villagers at War: The National Liberation Front in My Tho Province, 1965–1967," *Radical America* 8(January–April):3–184.
  1982   "Village Culture and the Vietnamese Revolution," *Past and Present* 94:131–157.
  1988*a*   "From the Millennial to the Everyday: James Scott's Search for the Essence of Peasant Politics," *Radical History Review* 42:155–172.
  1988*b*   "Peasant Movements and Communal Property during the French Revolution," *Theory and Society* 17:255–283.

Hunt, James D.
  1986   *Gandhi and the Nonconformists: Encounters in South Africa*. New Delhi: Promilla.

Hunt, Lynn
  1989   "Introduction: History, Culture, Text." In *The New Cultural History*, ed. Lynn Hunt, 1–24. Berkeley, Los Angeles, London: University of California Press.

Hy Van Luong
  n.d.   "Economic Reforms and the Resurgence of Local Tradition in a North Vietnamese Village (1980–1990)." Unpublished manuscript. (Available from the author, Department of Anthropology, University of Toronto.)

Ibsen, Henrik
  1966   *Ghosts and Three Other Plays by Henrik Ibsen*. Trans. Michael Meyer. Garden City, N.Y.: Anchor Books.

India, Government of
1975   *The Disorders Inquiry Committee Evidence.* Vol. 6, *Committee on Disturbances in Bombay, Delhi, and the Punjab,* ed. V. N. Datta. Simla: Indian Institute of Advanced Study. (Orig. 1920.)
Indian National Congress
1976   *Punjab Disturbances 1919–1920.* Vol. 1, *Indian Perspectives.* New Delhi: Deep. (Orig. 1920.)
Ingenieros, José, and Victor Raul Haya de la Torre
1928   *Teoría y táctica de la acción renovadora antimperialista de la juventud en América latina.* Buenos Aires: Talleres gráficos argentinos de L. J. Rosso y Cía.
Jackson, John, Phil Weller, and the Waterloo Public Interest Research Group
1982   *Chemical Nightmare: The Unnecessary Legacy of Toxic Wastes.* Toronto: Between the Lines.
Jacobsen, Nils
1988   "Free Trade, Regional Elites and the Internal Market in Southern Peru, 1895–1932." In *Guiding the Invisible Hand,* ed. Joseph L. Love and Nils Jacobsen, 145–176. New York: Praeger.
Jakobson, Roman
1960   "Closing Statement: Linguistics and Poetics." In *Style in Language,* ed. Thomas Sebeok, 350–377. Cambridge: MIT Press.
1971   "The Metaphoric and Metonymic Poles" (Pt. 4 of "Two Aspects of Language"). In *Selected Writings,* Vol. 2, *Word and Language,* 254–259. The Hague: Mouton.
James, Wendy
1973   "The Anthropologist as Reluctant Imperialist." In *Anthropology and the Colonial Encounter,* ed. Talal Asad, 41–71. New York: Humanities Press.
Jeffrey, Robert S.
1951   "The History of Douglas, Arizona." Master's thesis, University of Arizona, Tucson.
Jones, Delmos, and Jacqueline Hill-Burnett
1982   "The Political Context of Ethnogenesis: An Australian Example." In *Aboriginal Power in Australian Society,* ed. M. Howard, 214–246. Honolulu: University of Hawaii Press.
Joyce, J.
1938   "Masarwa Report." Botswana National Archives S360/1.
Kaprow, M.
1991   "Magical Work: Firefighters in New York," *Human Organization* 50:97–103.
Katz, Michael B.
1989   *The Undeserving Poor: From the War on Poverty to the War on Welfare.* New York: Pantheon Press.
Kehoe, Alice B.
1986   "Christianity and War." In *Peace and War, Cross-Cultural Perspectives,* ed. Mary LeCron Foster and Robert A. Rubinstein, 153–173. New Brunswick, N.J.: Transaction Books.
Kemesis, Paul
1990   "Court Nixes Alabama Waste Ban," *Chemical Week* (22 August):40.

Kent Board of Education (New York)
    1991   *Annual Report.* Brewster, N.Y.: Southeast Lithographics.

Kerns, Virginia
    1983   *Women and the Ancestors: Black Carib Kinship and Ritual.* Urbana: University of Illinois Press.
    1985   "Sexuality and Social Control among the Garifuna." In *In Her Prime: A New View of Middle-aged Women,* ed. Virginia Kerns and Judith Brown, 87–100. South Hadley, Mass.: Bergin and Garvey Publishers.

Kevles, Daniel
    1985   *In the Name of Eugenics.* New York: Knopf.

Keyes, Charles
    1981   "The Dialectic of Ethnic Change." In *Ethnic Change,* ed. Charles F. Keyes, 3–30. Seattle: University of Washington Press.

Khan, Aisha
    1982   "Garifuna Vendedoras: Survival in the Informal Labor Sector, La Cieba, Honduras." Master's thesis, San Francisco State University.
    1987   "Migration and Life Cycle among Garifuna (Black Carib) Street Vendors," *Women's Studies: An Interdisciplinary Journal* 13:183–198.

Kideckel, David
    1990   "The Politics of Decollectivization in Romania after Ceauşescu." Paper presented at the Annual Meeting of the American Anthropological Association, New Orleans.
    1991   "Rural Romania in Transition: Civil Society or the Politics of Privatism?" In *Romania after Tyranny,* ed. Daniel Nelson. Boulder, Colo.: Westview Press.

Kilpatrick, David
    1990   "Environmentalism: The New Crusade," *Fortune* 121, no. 4(12 February):44–55.

Kingsley, Mary
    1897   *Travels in West Africa.* London: Macmillan.
    1901   *West African Studies.* London: Macmillan.

Kingsolver, Barbara
    1989   *Holding the Line: Women in the Great Arizona Mine Strike of 1983.* Ithaca, N.Y.: ILR Press.

Klaren, Peter F.
    1973   "Modernization, Dislocation and Aprismo." Latin American Monographs, no. 32, Latin American Studies, University of Texas, Austin.
    1988   "The Origins of Modern Peru, 1880–1930." In *The Cambridge Economic History of Latin America,* Vol. 5, *c. 1870–1930,* ed. Leslie Bethell, 587–639. Cambridge: Cambridge University Press.

Klimt, Andrea
    1987*a*   "'Temporary' and 'Permanent' Lives: Portuguese Migrants in Germany." Paper presented at the Sixth International Conference of Europeanists, Washington, D.C.
    1987*b*   "Building a 'Home'—Portuguese Migrant Notions of Temporariness, Permanence and Commitment." Paper presented at the Annual Meeting of the American Anthropological Association, Chicago.

Knight, Rolf
1975   *Work Camps and Company Towns in Canada and the U.S.: An Annotated Bibliography.* Vancouver: New Star.
Kohn, H.
1989   *The Last Farmer: An American Memoir.* New York: Harper and Row.
Kolko, Gabriel
1985   *Anatomy of a War: Vietnam, the United States, and the Modern Historical Experience.* New York: Pantheon Books.
Komlos, John
1989   *Nutrition and Economic Development in the Eighteenth-Century Habsburg Monarchy: An Anthropometric History.* Princeton: Princeton University Press.
Kopf, David
1969   *British Orientalism and the Bengal Renaissance.* Berkeley: University of California Press.
Kuper, Adam
1973   *Anthropologists and Anthropology: The British School 1922–1972.* New York: Pica Press.
Kuroda, Etsuko
1984   "Under Mt. Zempoaltépetl: Highland Mixe Society and Ritual." Senri Ethnological Studies, no. 12. Osaka: National Museum of Ethnology.
Lackner, Helen
1973   "Social Anthropology and Indirect Rule. The Colonial Administration and Anthropology in Eastern Nigeria: 1920–1940." In *Anthropology and the Colonial Encounter*, ed. Talal Asad, 123–153. New York: Humanities Press.
Laclau, Ernesto
1991   "A política e os limites da pós-modernidade." In *Pós-Modernismo e Política*, ed. Heloisa Buarque de Hollanda. Rio de Janeiro: Rocco.
Laclau, Ernesto, and Chantal Mouffe
1985   *Hegemony and Socialist Strategy: Towards a Radical Democratic Politics.* New York: Verso.
Ladies Home Journal
1989   [Advertisement], 106(November):188.
Lambert, Bruce
1990   "AIDS Travels New York-Puerto Rico 'Air Bridge,'" *New York Times* (15 June):B1.
Lamme, Ary J., III
1989   *America's Historic Landscapes: Community Power and the Preservation of Four National Historic Sites.* Knoxville: University of Tennessee Press.
Lane, Frederic C.
1975   "The Role of Governments in Economic Growth in Early Modern Times," *Journal of Economic History* 3:8–17.
Lankton, Larry
1991   *Cradle to Grave: Life, Work, and Death at the Lake Superior Copper Mines.* New York: Oxford University Press.

Latour, Bruno
1988   *The Pasteurization of France.* Trans. Alan Sheridan and John Law.
            Cambridge: Harvard University Press.
Lauria, Anthony, Jr.
1964   "'Respeto,' 'Relajo,' and Inter-Personal Relations in Puerto Rico."
            Anthropological Quarterly 37(2):53–67.
Leacock, Eleanor
1980   "Montagnais Women and the Jesuit Program for Colonization." In
            Women and Colonization, ed. Mona Etienne and Eleanor Leacock, 25–
            42. New York: Praeger.
Lears, Jackson
1981   *No Place of Grace: Antimodernism and the Transformation of American Culture.*
            New York: Random House.
Leclerc, Gérard
1972   *Anthropologie et colonialisme: Essai sur l'histoire de l'africanisme.* Paris: Fayard.
Ledesma Ruiz, Norma Leticia, and Enrique Rebollar Dominguez
1988   "Los Mixes: Geografía de un grupo etnico en el estado de Oaxaca."
            Tesis para la Licenciatura en Geografía, Universidad Nacional
            Autonoma de México.
Lee, Richard B.
1979   *The !Kung San: Men, Women, and Work in a Foraging Society.* New York:
            Cambridge University Press.
Leite Lopes, José Sérgio
1979   "Fábrica e Vila Operária: Considerações sobre uma Forma de
            Subordinação Burguesa." In *Mudança Social no Nordeste. A Reprodu-
            ção da Subordinação,* ed. J. S. Leite Lopes et al. Rio de Janeiro: Paz
            e Terra.
Lemus y de Andrade, Conde de
1965   "Descripción de la Provincia de Quixos (1608)." In *Relaciones Geográ-
            ficas de Indias,* ed. Marcos Jiménez de la Espada. Biblioteca de Au-
            tores Españoles, vol. 183. Madrid: Ediciones Atlas.
Lesser, Alexander
1978   *The Pawnee Ghost Dance Hand Game.* Madison: University of Wisconsin
            Press. (Orig. 1933.)
1985   "Social Fields and the Evolution of Society." In *History, Evolution, and
            the Concept of Culture,* ed. Sidney Mintz, 92–99. New York: Cambridge
            University Press. (Orig. 1960.)
Levine, Adeline
1982   *Love Canal: Science, Politics and People.* Lexington, Mass.: Heath.
Lévi-Strauss, Claude
1966   *The Savage Mind.* London: Weidenfeld and Nicolson.
Lewis, Marcela, E. Roy Cayetano, and Fabian Cayetano
1977   *Chülüa Dan (It's About Time) Dangriga.* Belize: Pelican Beach Motel.
Lipp, Frank Joseph
1982   "The Mixe Calendrical System: Concepts and Behavior." Ph.D.
            diss., New School for Social Research, New York.
Lippman, Abby
1991   "Prenatal Genetic Testing and Screening: Constructing Needs and

Reinforcing Inequities," *American Journal of Law and Medicine* 17:15–50.

Löfgren, Orvar
1989   "The Nationalization of Culture," *Ethnologia Europaea* 19:5–23.
1990   "Landscapes and Mindscapes," *Folk* 31:183–208.
1992   "Modernizing the Nation—Nationalizing Modernity." Paper presented at the workshop "Defining the National," Lund University, Sweden.

Lowenthal, Abraham F., ed.
1975   *The Peruvian Experiment: Continuity and Change Under Military Rule.* Princeton: Princeton University Press.

Lowenthal, David
1983   *The Past Is a Foreign Country.* London: Cambridge University Press.

Lucas, John
1992   *England and Englishness: Ideas of Nationhood in English Poetry, 1688–1900.* Iowa City: University of Iowa Press.

Lugard, F. D.
1965   *The Dual Mandate in British Tropical Africa.* London: Cass. (Orig. 1922.)
1968   *The Rise of Our East African Empire.* London: Cass. (Orig. 1893.)

Lukes, Steven
1974   *Power: A Radical View.* London: Macmillan.

Lundberg, Ingrid, and Ingvar Svanberg
in press "Turkish Immigrant Associations in Metropolitan Stockholm," *Migration: A European Journal of International Migration and Ethnic Relations.*

Lundberg, P. A.
1978   "Barranco: A Sketch of a Belizean Garifuna (Black Carib) Habitat." Master's thesis, University of California, Riverside.

Lyon, Margot L.
1993   "Psychoneuroimmunology: The Problem of the Situatedness of Illness and the Conceptualization of Healing," *Culture, Medicine, and Psychiatry* 17:77–98.

McDonough, Peggy
1990   "Congenital Disability and Medical Research: The Development of Amniocentesis," *Women and Health* 16:137–153.

MacLeod, Jay
1987   *Ain't No Makin' It: Leveled Aspirations in a Low-Income Neighborhood.* Boulder, Colo.: Westview Press.

McPhee, Peter
1989   "The French Revolution, Peasants, and Capitalism," *American Historical Review* 94:1265–1280.

Madisso, Urmass
1984   *An Annotated Bibliography of the Literature on the Social and Psychological Effects of Exposure to Hazardous Substances.* Ottawa, Ontario: Environment Canada, Inland Waters Directorate.
1985   *A Synthesis of Social and Psychological Effects of Exposure to Hazardous Substances.* Ottawa, Ontario: Environment Canada, Inland Waters Directorate.

Maeyama, T.
    1979   "Ethnicity, Secret Societies and Associations: The Japanese in Bra-
               zil," *Comparative Studies in Society and History* 21:589–610.

Maine, Henry Sumner
    1872   *Village Communities in the East and West.* 2d ed. London: John Murray.
    1986   *Ancient Law.* Tucson: University of Arizona Press. (Orig. 1861.)

Malinowski, Bronislaw
    1935   *Coral Gardens and Their Magic: A Study of the Methods of Tilling the Soil and
               of Agricultural Rites in the Trobriand Islands.* New York: American Book
               Company.
    1984   *Argonauts of the Western Pacific: An Account of Native Enterprise and Adventure
               in the Archipelagoes of Melanesian New Guinea.* London: Routledge. (Orig.
               1922.)

Mallon, Florencia E.
    1983*a*   "Murder in the Andes: Patrons, Clients and the Impact of Foreign
               Capital, 1860–1922," *Radical History Review* 27:79–98.
    1983*b*   *The Defense of Community in Peru's Central Highlands.* Princeton: Prince-
               ton University Press.

Mandel, Ernest
    1978   *Late Capitalism.* London: Verso.

Marcus, George
    1990   "Past, Present, and Emergent Identities: Requirements for Ethnogra-
               phies of Late Twentieth Century Modernity Worldwide." Unpub-
               lished manuscript.

Marfatia, Lavania, Diana Punales-Morejon, and Rayna Rapp
    1990   "Counseling the Underserved: When an Old Reproductive Technol-
               ogy Becomes a New Reproductive Technology," *Birth Defects*
               26:109–126.

Marks, Shula
    1982   "Industrialization and Social Change: Some Thoughts on Class For-
               mation and Political Consciousness in South Africa, 1870–1920."
               Walter Rodney Seminar, African Studies Center, Boston University.

Marr, David, and Christine White, eds.
    1988   *Postwar Vietnam: Dilemmas in Socialist Development.* Ithaca: Cornell
               Southeast Asia Program.

Martin, Emily
    1990   "Toward an Anthropology of Immunology: The Body as Nation
               State," *Medical Anthropology Quarterly* 4:410–426.

Martin, Joann
    1990   "Motherhood and Power: The Production of a Women's Culture
               of Politics in a Mexican Community," *American Ethnologist* 17:470–490.

Martinez, Daniel Perez
    1987   "Tu'ukni"ïmt Ayuuk Jyujky'ajti"ïn (Religion Ayuuk de Tamazula-
               pam)." Tesis para la licenciatura en etnolinguistica, Centro de Inves-
               tigación y Estudios Superiores en Antropología Social, Apetatitlan,
               Tlaxcala.

Marx, Karl
    1959   *Capital: A Critique of Political Economy.* Vol. 3. London: Lawrence and

Wishart. (Orig. 1894.)
1967a   *Das Kapital.* Vol. 1. Frankfurt: Europäische Verlagsanstalt. (Orig. 1867.)
1967b   *Capital: A Critique of Political Economy.* Vol. 3. New York: International Publishers. (Orig. 1894.)
1971   *Theories of Surplus Value.* Vol. 3. Moscow: Progess Publishers.
1975   *Capital: A Critique of Political Economy.* Vol. 1. New York: International Publishers. (Orig. 1867.)

Massey, D.
1980   "The Development of a Labor Reserve: The Impact of Colonial Rule in Botswana." Working Paper 34, African Studies Center, Boston University.

Mathews, Holly F.
1985   "We Are Mayordomo: A Reinterpretation of Women's Roles in the Mexican Cargo System," *American Ethnologist* 12:285–301.

Mautle, G.
1986   "Bakgalagadi-Bakwena Relationship: A Case of Slavery, c. 1840– c. 1930," *Botswana Notes and Records* 18:19–32.

Meinig, Donald W.
1979   "Symbolic Landscapes: Some Idealizations of American Communities." In *The Interpretation of Ordinary Landscapes,* ed. Donald W. Meinig, 164–191. Oxford: Oxford University Press.

Melland, F. H.
1923   *In Witch-Bound Africa.* London: Seeley, Service.

Mercier, Juan Marcos
1979   *Nosotros los Napo Runas. Mitos e historias.* Iquitos, Peru: Publicaciones CETA.

Miller, Peter, and Nikolas Rose
1990   "Governing Economic Life," *Economy and Society* 19:1–31.

Miller, Rory
1982   "The Coastal Elite and Peruvian Politics, 1895–1919," *Journal of Latin American Studies* 14:97–120.

Mills, C. Wright
1961   *The Sociological Imagination.* New York: Grove Press.

Milow, Cynthia
1904   *Älskar du ditt fosterland?* Pamphlet. Stockholm: Swedish Society for Temperance and Popular Education.

Mintz, Sidney W.
1972   *Caribbean Transformations.* Chicago: Aldine.
1975   *Worker in the Cane.* New York: W. W. Norton. (Orig. 1960.)
1982   "Afterword: Peasantries and the Rural Sector—Notes on a Discovery." In *Power and Protest in the Countryside: Studies of Rural Unrest in Asia, Europe, and Latin America,* ed. Robert Weller and Scott Guggenheim, 180–188. Durham: Duke University Press.
1989   *Caribbean Transformations.* New York: Columbia University Press. (Orig. 1972.)

Miringoff, Marque-Luisa
1991   *The Social Costs of Genetic Welfare.* New Brunswick, N.J.: Rutgers University Press.

Mitchell, Edward
    1968   "Inequality and Insurgency: A Statistical Study of South Vietnam,"
                World Politics 20:421–438.
Monaghan, John
    1990   "Reciprocity, Redistribution, and the Transaction of Value in the
                Mesoamerican Fiesta," *American Ethnologist* 17:758–774.
Montgomery, Scott L.
    1991   "Codes and Combat in Biomedical Discourse," *Science as Culture*
                2:341–390.
Moody's Investors Service
    1987   *Handbook of Common Stocks.* Vol. 4. New York: Moody's Investors Ser-
                vice Publications.
Moore, Barrington
    1966   *Social Origins of Dictatorship and Democracy: Lord and Peasant in the Making
                of the Modern World.* Boston: Beacon Press.
Mosse, George L.
    1975   *The Nationalization of the Masses.* New York: Howard Fertig.
    1985   *Nationalism and Sexuality: Respectability and Abnormal Sexuality in Modern
                Europe.* New York: Howard Fertig.
Motolinía, Fray Toribio de Benavente
    1971   *Memoriales.* Mexico: UNAM.
Motzafi, P.
    1986   "Whither the 'True Bushmen': The Dynamics of Perpetual Margin-
                ality," Proceedings of the International Symposium on African
                Hunters and Gatherers, ed. Sankt Augustin, F. Rottland, and R.
                Vossen, *Sprache und Geschichte in Afrika* 7(1):295–328.
Motzafi-Haller, P.
    1987   "Transformations in the Tswapong Region, Central Botswana:
                National Policies and Local Realities." Ph.D. diss., Brandeis Univer-
                sity.
Mudimbe, V.
    1988   *The Invention of Africa.* Bloomington: Indiana University Press.
Mueller, P. S.
    1990   "Corporate Corner: Carbide Apologizes to CCHW for McCarthyite
                Smear," *Everyone's Backyard* 8(June):18.
Muratorio, Blanca
    1989   "Dios en la selva: Aculturación cristiana y resistencia cultural entre
                los Napo Quichua de la Alta Amazonía Ecuatoriana." In *Las Reli-
                giones Amerindias 500 Años Después,* ed. SS.AA. Quito, Ecuador: Abya-
                Yala.
    1991   *The Life and Times of Grandfather Alonso: Culture and History in the Upper
                Amazon.* New Brunswick, N.J.: Rutgers University Press.
Murphy, Kathleen J.
    1983   *Macroproject Development in the Third World: An Analysis of Transnational
                Partnerships.* Boulder, Colo.: Westview Press.
Murphy, Robert
    1987   *The Body Silent.* New York: Henry Holt.

Murray, A.
1986   "Social and Economic History in Botswana." Joint History Departments Seminar (Regional), University of Zambia, Lusaka.

Murray, Charles
1984   *Losing Ground: American Social Policy 1950–1980.* New York: Basic Books.

Nader, Laura
1989   "The Drift to War." In *The Anthropology of War and Peace, Perspectives on the Nuclear Age*, ed. Paul R. Turner and David Pitt, 79–86. Granby, Mass.: Bergin and Garvey.

Nahmad, Salomón
1965   *Los Mixes: Estudio social y cultural de la región del Zempoaltépetl y del Istmo de Tehuantepec.* Memorias del Instituto Nacional Indigenista, vol. 11.

Nangati, F.
1982   "Early Capitalist Penetration: The Impact of Precolonial Trade in Kweneng (1840–1876)." In *Settlement in Botswana*, ed. Renee Hitchcock and M. Smith, 140–147. Marshalltown, Iowa: Heinemann.

Nasaw, David
1985   *Children of the City: At Work and at Play.* Garden City, N.Y.: Anchor Press/Doubleday.

Nash, June
1979   *We Eat the Mines and the Mines Eat Us: Dependency and Exploitation in the Bolivian Tin Mines.* New York: Columbia University Press.
1980   "Aztec Women: The Transition from Status to Class in Empire and Colony." In *Women and Colonization*, ed. Mona Etienne and Eleanor Leacock, 134–148. New York: Praeger.

Ncgoncgo, L.
1977   "Aspects of the History of the Bangwaketse to 1910." Ph.D. diss., University of Dalhousie, Halifax, Nova Scotia.

Nehru, Jawaharlal
1930   *An Autobiography.* New Delhi: Allied.

Nelson, Lin
1990   "The Place of Women in Polluted Places." In *Reweaving the World: The Emergence of Ecofeminism*, ed. I. Diamond and G. Orenstein, 173–188. San Francisco: Sierra Club Books.

Newman, K.
1987   *Falling from Grace.* New York: Columbia University Press.

New York State
1990a   "Census 1980–1990." Office of the Census, Albany, N.Y.
1990b   "Employment in New York (1970–1990)." Annual Reports, Department of Labor, Albany, N.Y.

New York Times
1977   "Fire Destroys Main Street Carmel," *New York Times* (8 February): A1.

Ngo Vinh Long
1990   "Communal Property and Peasant Struggles in Vietnam," *Peasant Studies* 17:121–140.

Nicholson, F.
1969   *The Administration of Nigeria 1900–1960*. Oxford: Oxford University Press.
Nigerian Council
1920   *Address by the Governor, Sir Hugh Clifford*. Lagos: Government of Nigeria.
Noble, Kingsley
1965   *Proto-Arawakan and Its Descendants*. Bloomington: Indiana University Press.
Nolasco, Margarita
1972   "Oaxaca indígena: Problemas de aculturación en el estado de Oaxaca y sub-àreas culturales." Series Investigaciones, no. 1, Instituto de Investigación e Integración Social del Estado de Oaxaca, Mexico.
North, Michael
1983   "Untersuchungen zur adlingen Gutswirtschaft im Herzogtum Preussen des 16. Jahrhunderts," *Vierteljahrschrift für Sozial- und Wirtschaftsgeschichte* 70:1–20.
Nugent, David
1988   "The Mercantile Transformation of Provincial Urban Life: Labor, Value and Time in the Northern Peruvian Sierra." Ph.D. diss., Columbia University.
1991   "Control of Space, Stability of Time: The State as Arbiter of Surplus Flows." In *Marxist Approaches in Economic Anthropology*, ed. Hill Gates and Alice Littlefield, 161–185. Lanham, Md.: University Press of America.
O'Brien, J.
1986   "Toward a Reconstitution of Ethnicity: Capitalist Expansion and Cultural Dynamics in Sudan," *American Anthropologist* 88:898–907.
Ochs, Elinor
1988   *Culture and Language Development: Language Acquisition and Language Socialization in a Samoan Village*. New York: Cambridge University Press.
O'Dowd, Anne
1991   *Spalpeens and Tattie Hokers: History and Folklore of the Irish Migratory Agricultural Worker in Ireland and Britain*. Dublin: Irish University Press.
O'Grada, Cormac
1989*a*   "Poverty, Population, and Agriculture, 1801–45." In *A New History of Ireland*, Vol. 5, *Ireland under the Union, 1801–1870*, ed. W. E. Vaughan, 108–103. Oxford: Clarendon Press.
1989*b*   *The Great Irish Famine*. London: Macmillan.
Okihiro, G.
1976   "Hunters, Herders, Cultivators, and Traders: Interaction and Change in the Kalakgadi, Nineteenth Century." Ph.D. diss., University of California, Los Angeles.
Olien, Michael
1987   "Micro/Macro-Level Linkages: Regional Political Structures on the Mosquito Coast, 1845–1864," *Ethnohistory* 34:257–287.
Olien, Roger M., and Diana D. Olien
1982   *Oil Booms: Social Change in Five Texas Towns*. Lincoln: University of Nebraska Press.

Orde Browne, G. St. John
1925   *The Vanishing Tribes of Kenya.* London: Seeley, Service.
Ortegón, Diego de
1973   "Descripción de la hobernación de Quijos, sumaco y La canela por el Lcdo. Diego de Ortegón, oidor de la Real Audiencia de Quito." *Cuadernos de Historia y Arqueología* 22(40):11–27.
Ortíz de Villalba, Juan
1976   *Sacha Pacha. El mundo de la selva.* Pompeya: CICAME.
Ortner, Sherry
1984   "Theory in Anthropology Since the Sixties," *Comparative Studies in Society and History* 26:126–166.
1991   "Reading America: Preliminary Notes on Class and Culture." In *Recapturing Anthropology: Working in the Present*, ed. Richard Fox, 163–190. Santa Fe: School of American Research Press.
Osculati, Gaetano
1854   *Esplorazioni delle regioni equatoriali lunghi il Napo e dei fiumi delle Amazzoni. Frammento di un viaggio fatto nelle due Americhe negli anni 1846–47–48.* Milano: Fratelli Centenari e Compagni.
Otterbein, Keith F.
1970   *The Evolution of War.* New Haven: HRAF Press.
Ozouf, Mona
1988   *Festivals and the French Revolution.* Trans. Alan Sheridan. Cambridge: Harvard University Press.
Pagels, Elaine
1988   *Adam, Eve, and the Serpent.* New York: Random House.
Paige, Jeffery
1975   *Agrarian Revolution: Social Movements and Export Agriculture in the Underdeveloped World.* New York: Free Press.
Palacio, Joseph O.
1982   "Food and Social Relations in a Garifuna Village." Ph.D. diss., University of California, Berkeley.
1987   "Age as a Source of Differentiation within a Garifuna Village in Southern Belize," *America Indigena* 47:97–118.
1990   *Socioeconomic Integration of Central American Immigrants in Belize.* Belize City: Society for Promotion of Education and Research.
Panaia, Marta
1985   *Los trabajadores de la construcción. Cambios y evolución del empleo en la indústria de la construcción Argentina.* Buenos Aires: Ediciones del IDES.
Pankhurst, E. Sylvia
1936   *The Life of Emmeline Pankhurst.* Boston: Houghton Mifflin.
Pardo, Mary
1990   "Mexican American Women Grassroots Community Activists: 'Mothers of East Los Angeles,'" *Frontiers* 11(1):1–7.
Park, Joseph F.
1961   "The History of Mexican Labor in Arizona during the Territorial Period." Master's thesis, University of Arizona, Tucson.
Parliamentary Papers
1836   "Third Report of the Commissioners for Inquiring into the Condi-

tion of the Poorer Classes in Ireland." London: House of Commons.
Parry, Jonathan, and Maurice Bloch, eds.
   1989   *Money and the Morality of Exchange.* Cambridge: Cambridge University
                Press.
Parson, J.
   1981   "Cattle, Class, and the State in Rural Botswana," *Journal of Southern
                African Studies* 7:236–255.
   1984   *Botswana: Liberal Democracy and the Labor Reserve in Southern Africa.* Boul-
                der, Colo.: Westview Press.
Parsons, Howard L., ed.
   1977   *Marx and Engels on Ecology.* Westport, Conn.: Greenwood Press.
Parsons, N.
   1977   "The Economic History of Khama's Country in Botswana, 1844–
                1930." In *The Roots of Rural Poverty in Central and Southern Africa*, ed.
                R. Palmer and N. Parsons, 113–143. Berkeley, Los Angeles, Lon-
                don: University of California Press.
Passarge, Siegfried
   1907   *Die Buschmänner.* Berlin: Dietrich Reimer.
Paz Soldan, Carlos Enrique
   1919   *De la inquietud a la revolución: Diez años de rebeldías universitarias (1909–
                1919).* Lima: Bibiloteca de "La Riforma Medica."
Perelman, Michael
   1984   *Classical Political Economy: Primitive Accumulation and the Social Division of
                Labor.* London: Pinter Publishers.
Perham, Margery
   1960   *Lugard: The Years of Authority, 1898–1945.* London: Collins.
Perry, Lewis
   1984   *Intellectual Life in America.* Chicago: University of Chicago Press.
Pike, Douglas
   1966   *Viet Cong: The Organization and Techniques of the National Liberation Front
                of South Vietnam.* Cambridge: MIT Press.
Pike, Frederick B.
   1967   *The Modern History of Peru.* London: Weidenfeld and Nicholson.
Pitt, David
   1989   "Introduction." In *The Anthropology of War and Peace: Perspectives on the
                Nuclear Age*, by Paul R. Turner et al., xiii–xiv. Granby, Mass.: Bergin
                and Garvey.
Plakans, Andrejs
   1975   "Seigneurial Authority and Peasant Family Life: The Baltic Area in
                the 18th Century," *Journal of Interdisciplinary History* 5:629–654.
Polanyi, K.
   1957   *The Great Transformation.* Boston: Beacon Press.
Popkin, Samuel
   1979   *The Rational Peasant: The Political Economy of Rural Society in Vietnam.*
                Berkeley, Los Angeles, London: University of California Press.
Porter, Dorothy, and Roy Porter
   1988   "What Was Social Medicine? An Historiographical Essay," *Journal of
                Historical Sociology* 1:90–106.

Poulantzas, Nicos
1978   *State, Power, Socialism.* London: New Left Books.
Puerrefoy, D.
1956   *History of the Town of Southeast Brewster.* New York: Brewster Litho-
            graphics.
Raab, Diana
1987   *Getting Pregnant and Staying Pregnant.* Montreal: Sirdan.
Rand Corporation
1971   "Interviews in Vietnam, Series DT: Activities of the Viet Cong
            within Dinh-Tuong Province." Santa Monica: Rand Corporation
            Publications.
Ranger, Terence
1983   "The Invention of Tradition in Colonial Africa." In *The Invention of
            Tradition,* ed. E. J. Hobsbawm and Terence Ranger, 211-263. Cam-
            bridge: Cambridge University Press.
Rapp, Rayna
1988   "Chromosomes and Communication: The Discourse of Genetic
            Counseling," *Medical Anthropology Quarterly* 2:143–157.
Rawls, T.
1990   *Small Places: In Search of a Vanishing America.* Boston: Little, Brown.
Reddy, William
1987   *Money and Liberty in Modern Europe: A Critique of Historical Understanding.*
            Cambridge: Cambridge University Press.
Redfield, Robert
1956   *Peasant Society and Culture.* Chicago: University of Chicago Press.
Reeve, Mary-Elizabeth
1985   "Identity and Process: The Meaning of Runapura for Quichua
            Speakers of the Curaray River, Eastern Ecuador." Ph.D. diss., Uni-
            versity of Illinois at Urbana-Champaign.
Reich, Robin M.
1981   "Toxic Politics: A Comparative Study of Public and Private Respon-
            ses to Chemical Disasters in the United States, Italy and Japan."
            Ph.D. diss., Yale University.
Reif, Heinz
1979   *Westfälischer Adel, 1770–1860.* Göttingen: Vandenhoeck and Ru-
            precht.
Remy, María Isabel, ed.
1985   *Promoción campesina, regionalización y movimientos sociales.* Lima: DESCO.
Revans, John
n.d.   *Evils of the State of Ireland: Their Causes and Their Remedy—A Poor Law.*
            London: John Hatchard.
Ribeiro, Gustavo Lins
1987   "Cuanto Más Grande Mejor? Proyectos de Gran Escala: Una Forma
            de Producción Vinculada a la Expansión de Sistemas Económicos,"
            Desarrollo Económico 105:3–27.
1988   "Developing the Moonland: The Yacyreta Hydroelectric High Dam
            and Economic Expansion in Argentina." Ph.D. diss., City University
            of New York.

1989   "Acampamento de Grande Projeto, una Forma de Imobilizaçâo da
              Força de Trabalho pela Moradia." Série Antropologia, no. 84, Uni-
              versidade de Brasília.

Ridgeway, James
1970   *The Politics of Ecology.* New York: Dutton.

Rodriguez, Clara E.
1989   *Puerto Ricans: Born in the U.S.A..* Winchester, Mass.: Unwin Hyman.

Rogers, Jasper
1847   *The Potato Truck System of Ireland: The Main Cause of the Periodical Famines
              and the Non-payment of the Rents.* London: James Ridgway.

Romo, Frank, and Michael Schwartz
1993   "The Coming of Post-Industrial Society Revisited: Manufacturing
              and the Prospects for a Service-based Economy." In *Explorations in
              Economic Sociology,* ed. Richard Swedburg, 335–373. New York:
              Russell Sage Foundation.

Rosdolsky, R.
1951   "The Distribution of the Agrarian Product in Feudalism," *Journal of
              Economic History* 11:247–265.

Rose, Daniel
1989   *Patterns of American Culture: Ethnography and Estrangement.* Philadelphia:
              University of Pennsylvania Press.

Roseberry, William
1978   "Historical Materialism and the People of Puerto Rico," *Revista/Re-
              view Interamericana* 8:26–36.

1989   *Anthropologies and Histories: Essays in Culture, History, and Political Econ-
              omy.* New Brunswick, N.J.: Rutgers University Press.

Rosenbaum, David E.
1989   "Bush and Congress Reach Accord Raising Minimum Wage to
              $4.25." *New York Times* (1 November):A1–A2.

Rosenberg, Hans
1958   *Bureaucracy, Aristocracy, Autocracy: The Prussian Experience, 1660–1815.*
              New York: Beacon Press.

1978   *Machteliten und Wirtschaftskonjunkturen.* Göttingen: Vandenhoeck and
              Ruprecht.

Rosenberg, Harriet G.
1988   *A Negotiated World: Three Centuries of Change in a French Alpine Community.*
              Toronto: University of Toronto Press.

1990*a*   "The Home Is the Workplace: Stress, Hazards and Pollutants in the
              Household." In *Through the Kitchen Window: The Politics of Home and
              Family,* ed. M. Luxton, H. Rosenberg, and S. Arat-Koc, 57–80. Tor-
              onto: Garamond Press.

1990*b*   "The Kitchen and the Multinational Corporation: An Analysis of the
              Links between the Household and Global Corporations." In *Through
              the Kitchen Window: The Politics of Home and Family,* ed. M. Luxton, H.
              Rosenberg, and S. Arat-Koc, 123–150. Toronto: Garamond Press.

Rotman, David
1990   "Chemical Firms Move to Turn Waste to Profit," *Chemical Week* (22
              August):23.

Runblom, Harald
  1985   "Emigranten och fosterlandet. Svenskamerikanarnas bild av Sver-
             ige," *Att vara svensk* (Kungl. Vitterhets, Historie och Antikvitets Aka-
             demin, Konferenser) 13:131–150.
Russ, Jan, and Robert Wasserstrom
  1980   "Civil-Religious Hierarchies in Central Chiapas: A Critical Perspec-
             tive," *American Ethnologist* 7:466–478.
Russell, Dick
  1989   "Exporting Cancer," *New Internationalist*, no. 198 (August):10–11.
Sabean, David
  1984   *Power in the Blood.* Cambridge: Cambridge University Press.
Sachs, Wolfgang
  1990   "The Age of Ecology." Transcript of Canadian Broadcasting Cor-
             poration Radio Broadcast, "Ideas" Series, 18 June.
Sahlins, Marshall
  1981   *Historical Metaphors and Mythical Realities: Structure in the Early History of
             the Sandwich Islands Kingdom.* Ann Arbor: University of Michigan Press.
Sajó, András
  1990   "Diffuse Rights in Search of an Agent: A Property Rights Analysis of
             the Firm in the Socialist Market Economy," *International Review of Law
             and Economics* 10:41–59.
Sanford, Margaret
  1974   "Revitalization Movements as Indicators of Completed Accultura-
             tion," *Comparative Studies in Society and History* 16:504–518.
Schapera, Isaac
  1942   "A Short History of the Bangwaketse," *African Studies* 1:2–3.
  1952   *The Ethnic Composition of Tswana Tribes.* Monographs on Social
             Anthropology 11. London: London School of Economics.
Schneider, Jane
  1971   "Of Vigilance and Virgins: Honor, Shame and Access to Resources
             in Mediterranean Societies," *Ethnology* 10:1–24.
Schneider, Jane, and Peter Schneider
  1976   *Culture and Political Economy in Western Sicily.* New York: Academic
             Press.
Schneider, Peter, Jane Schneider, and Edward Hansen
  1974   "Modernization and Development: The Role of Regional Elites and
             Noncorporate Groups in the European Mediterranean," *Comparative
             Studies in Society and History* 14:328–350.
Scotch, R. K.
  1984   *From Good Will to Civil Rights: Transforming Federal Disability Policy.* Phil-
             adelphia: Temple University Press.
Scott, James C.
  1976   *The Moral Economy of the Peasant: Rebellion and Subsistence in Southeast
             Asia.* New Haven: Yale University Press.
  1985   *Weapons of the Weak: Everyday Forms of Peasant Resistance.* New Haven:
             Yale University Press.
Scott, Joan
  1988   *Gender and the Politics of History.* New York: Columbia University Press.

Scribner, Robert
   1975   "Civic Unity and the Reformation in Erfurt," *Past and Present* 66:29–
               60.
Shapiro, Judith
   1987   "From Tupa to the Land without Evil: The Christianization of Tupi-
               Guarani Cosmology," *American Ethnologist* 14:126–139.
Shipton, Parker
   1989   *Bitter Money: Cultural Economy and Some African Meanings of Forbidden
               Commodities*. American Ethnological Society Monograph Series, no.
               1. Washington, D.C.: American Anthropological Association.
Silverblatt, Irene
   1980   "The Universe Has Turned Inside Out. There Is No Justice for Us
               Here: Andean Women Under Spanish Rule." In *Women and Coloniza-
               tion*, ed. Mona Etienne and Eleanor Leacock, 149–185. New York:
               Praeger.
   1987   *Moon, Sun, and Witches: Gender Ideologies and Class in Inca and Colonial
               Peru*. Princeton: Princeton University Press.
Silverman, Sydel
   1976   "Ethnicity as Adaptation: Strategies and Systems," *Reviews in Anthro-
               pology* 3:626–636.
   1979   "The Peasant Concept in Anthropology," *Journal of Peasant Studies*
               7:49–69.
Slater, David
   1989   *Territory and State Power in Latin America*. New York: St. Martin's Press.
Slicher van Bath, B. H.
   1963*a*   *The Agrarian History of Western Europe, A.D. 500–1850*. London: E. Ar-
               nold.
   1963*b*   "Yield Ratios 1810–1820," *Afdeling Agrarische Geschiedenis Bijdragen* 10.
Smith, Anthony
   1983   *Theories of Nationalism*. 2d ed. New York: Holmes and Meier.
Smith, Carol A.
   1984   "Local History in Global Context: Social and Economic Transitions
               in Western Guatemala," *Comparative Studies in Society and History*
               26:193–228.
   1990   "Failed Nationalist Movements in 19th-Century Guatemala: A Para-
               ble for the Third World." In *Nationalist Ideologies and the Production of
               National Cultures*, ed. Richard G. Fox, 148–178. [New] Monograph
               Series, no. 2. Washington, D.C.: American Anthropological Associa-
               tion.
   1992   *Guatemalan Indians and the State: 1540–1988*. Austin: University of
               Texas Press.
Smith, Edwin W.
   1926   *The Golden Stool: Some Aspects of the Conflict of Cultures in Modern Africa*.
               London: Holborn.
Smith, Waldemar
   1977   *The Fiesta System and Economic Change*. New York: Columbia University
               Press.

Sörlin, Sverker
  1988   *Framtidslandet. Debatten om Norrland och naturresurserna under det industriella genombrottet.* Stockholm: Carlssons.
Spivak, Gayatri Chakravorty
  1987   "Speculations on Reading Marx: After Reading Derrida." In *Post-Structuralism and the Question of History*, ed. Derek Attridge, Geoff Bennington, and Robert Young, 30–62. Cambridge: Cambridge University Press.
Staniszkis, Jadwiga
  1991a   "Political Capitalism in Poland," *Eastern European Politics and Societies* 5:127–141.
  1991b   *The Dynamics of the Breakthrough in Eastern Europe.* Berkeley, Los Angeles, Oxford: University of California Press.
Stark, David
  1990   "Privatization in Hungary: From Plan to Market or from Plan to Clan?" *Eastern European Politics and Societies* 4:351–392.
  1991   "Privatization Strategies in East Central Europe." Working Papers on Transitions from State Socialism, no. 91-6, Cornell Project on Comparative Institutional Analysis, Cornell University.
Starr, Paul
  1982   *The Transformation of American Medicine.* New York: Basic Books.
Stein, Steve
  1980   *Populism in Peru: The Emergence of the Masses and the Politics of Social Control.* Madison: University of Wisconsin Press.
Stephen, Lynn, and James Dow
  1990   "The Politics of Ritual: The Mexican State and Zapotec Autonomy." In *Class, Politics, and Popular Religion in Mexico and Central America*, ed. L. Stephen and J. Dow, 63–76. Washington, D.C.: American Anthropological Association.
Stevens, Evelyn P.
  1973   "Marianismo: The Other Face of Machismo in Latin America." In *Female and Male in Latin America*, ed. Ann Pescatello, 89–101. Pittsburgh: University of Pittsburgh Press.
Steward, Julian H.
  1950   *Area Research: Theory and Practice.* Bulletin 63. New York: Social Science Research Council.
  1955   *Theory of Culture Change: The Methodology of Multilinear Evolution.* Urbana: University of Illinois Press.
  1956   "Introduction." In *The People of Puerto Rico: A Study in Social Anthropology*, by Julian H. Steward et al., 1–27. Urbana: University of Illinois Press.
Steward, Julian H., ed.
  1967   *Contemporary Change in Traditional Societies.* 3 vols. Urbana: University of Illinois Press.
Steward, Julian H., Robert A. Manners, Eric R. Wolf, Elena Padilla Seda, Sidney W. Mintz, and Raymond L. Scheele
  1956a   "The Cultural Historical Approach." In *The People of Puerto Rico: A*

          Study in Social Anthropology, by Julian H. Steward et al., 31–33. Ur-
          bana: University of Illinois Press.
1956*b*   *The People of Puerto Rico: A Study in Social Anthropology*. Urbana: Univer-
          sity of Illinois Press.
Stocking, George
1987   *Victorian Anthropology*. New York: Free Press.
Stoeltje, Beverly
1981   "Making the Frontier Myth: Folklore Process in a Modern Nation,"
          Western Folklore 46:235–253.
Stoler, Ann L.
1989   "Making Empire Respectable: The Politics of Race and Sexual Mor-
          ality in 20th-Century Colonial Cultures," *American Ethnologist* 16:
          634–660.
1992   "Sexual Affronts and Racial Frontiers: European Identities and the
          Cultural Politics of Exclusion in Colonial South East Asia," *Com-
          parative Studies in Society and History* 34:514–551.
Stone, Michael Cutler
1989   "Backabush: Settlement on the Belmopan Periphery and the
          Challenge to Rural Development in Belize," *SPEAR Reports* 6:82–
          134.
Susman, Warren I.
1984   *Culture as History: The Transformation of American Society in the Twentieth
          Century*. New York: Pantheon Books.
Suter, Andreas
1985   *'Troublen' im Fürstbistum Basel (1726–1740)*. Göttingen: Vandenhoeck
          and Ruprecht.
Sutherland, Neil
1976   *Children in English-Canadian Society: Framing the Twentieth Century Consen-
          sus*. Toronto: University of Toronto Press.
Szelényi, Balázs, and Iván Szelényi
1991   "The Social Impact of Agrarian Reform: Social and Political Con-
          flicts in the Post-Communist Transformation of Hungarian Agricul-
          ture," *Anthropology of East Europe Review* 10:12–24.
Szentes, Tamás
1988   *The Transformation of the World Economy: New Directions and New Interests*.
          London: Zed Books.
Szuchman, Mark D.
1980   *Mobility and Integration in Urban Argentina: Cordoba in the Liberal Era*. Aus-
          tin: University of Texas Press.
Taussig, Michael T.
1980   *The Devil and Commodity Fetishism in South America*. Chapel Hill: Univer-
          sity of North Carolina Press.
Taylor, Douglas
1951   *The Black Caribbean of British Honduras*. New York: Wenner-Gren
          Foundation.
1977   *Languages of the West Indies*. Baltimore: Johns Hopkins University Press.

Taylor, Lewis
   1986   *Bandits and Politics in Peru: Landlord and Peasant Violence in Hualgayoc*
               1900–1930. Center of Latin American Studies, University of Cam-
               bridge.
Taylor, Peter J.
   1991   "If Cold War Is the Problem, Is Hot Peace the Solution." In *The*
               Political Geography of Conflict and Peace, ed. Nurit Kliot and Stanley
               Waterman, 78–92. London: Belhaven.
Thirsk, Joan
   1964   "The Common Fields," *Past and Present* 29:3–25.
   1966   "The Origin of the Common Fields," *Past and Present* 33:142–147.
Thompson, E. P.
   1955   *William Morris: Romantic to Revolutionary.* London: Lawrence and Wise-
               hart.
Thompson, Noel
   1984   *The People's Science: The Popular Political Economy of Exploitation and Crisis*
               1816–34. Cambridge: Cambridge University Press.
Thorp, Rosemary, and Geoffry Bertram
   1978   *Peru 1890–1977: Growth and Policy in an Open Economy.* New York:
               Columbia University Press.
Tilly, Louise A.
   1981   "Paths of Proletarianization: Organization of Production, Sexual
               Division of Labor, and Women's Collective Action," *Signs: Journal of*
               Women in Culture and Society 7:400–417.
   1985   "Coping with Company Paternalism: Family Strategies of Coal
               Miners in Nineteenth-Century France," *Theory and Society* 14:403–417.
Titow, J. Z.
   1965   "Medieval England and the Open-Field System," *Past and Present* 32:
               86–102.
Tlou, T.
   1979   "Servility and Political Control: Botlhanka among the BaTawana of
               Northwestern Botswana, ca. 1750–1906." In *Slavery in Africa,* ed. S.
               Miers and I. Kopytoff, 367–390. Madison: University of Wisconsin
               Press.
Tocqueville, A. de
   1945   *Democracy in America.* 2 vols. New York: Vintage Books. (Orig. 1835,
               1840.)
Todd, Alexandra Dundas
   1990   "Ending the War on Disease," *Socialist Review* 20:99–114.
Tordoff, William
   1965   *Ashanti under the Prempehs: 1888–1935.* London: Oxford University
               Press.
Trompf, G. W.
   1989   "Macrohistory and Acculturation: Between Myth and History in
               Modern Melanesian Adjustments and Ancient Gnosticism," *Compara-*
               tive Studies in Society and History 31:621–648.

Turner, Paul
1989   "Conclusion." In *The Anthropology of War and Peace, Perspectives on the Nuclear Age*, ed. Paul R. Turner and David Pitt, 174–178. Granby, Mass.: Bergin and Garvey.

Turner, Terence
1988   "Ethno-Ethnohistory: Myth and History in Native South American Representations of Contact with Western Societies." In *Rethinking History and Myth: Indigenous South American Perspectives on the Past*, ed. Jonathan D. Hill, 195–213. Urbana: University of Illinois Press.

Urban, Greg
1988   "Ritual Wailing in Amerindian Brazil," *American Anthropologist* 90:385–400.

Vail, L., ed.
1989   *The Creation of Tribalism in Southern Africa*. London: James Curry.

Vallette, Jim
1987   *Waste Management, Inc.* Washington, D.C.: The Greenpeace Report.

Vann, James Allen
1984   *The Making of a State: Württemberg, 1593–1793*. Ithaca: Cornell University Press.

Van Velsen, J.
1967   "The Extended Case Method and Situational Analysis." In *The Craft of Social Anthropology*, ed. A. L. Epstein, 129–149. London: Tavistock Publications.

Vélez-Ibañez, Carlos G.
1983   *Rituals of Marginality: Politics, Process, and Culture Change in Central Urban Mexico, 1969–1974*. Berkeley, Los Angeles, London: University of California Press.

Verdery, Katherine
1990   "The Production and Defense of 'The Romanian Nation,' 1900 to World War II." In *Nationalist Ideologies and the Production of National Cultures*, ed. Richard G. Fox, 81–111. [New] Monograph Series, no. 2. Washington, D.C.: American Anthropological Association.

1991a   *National Ideology under Socialism: Identity and Cultural Politics in Ceaușescu's Romania*. Berkeley, Los Angeles, Oxford: University of California Press.

1991b   "Theorizing Socialism: A Prologue to the 'Transition,'" *American Ethnologist* 18:419–439.

1992   "The 'Etatization' of Time in Socialist Romania." In *The Politics of Time*, ed. Henry Rutz, 37–61. American Ethnological Society Monograph Series, no. 4. Washington, D.C.: American Anthropological Association.

Vincent, Joan
1977   "Agrarian Society as Organized Flow: Processes of Development Past and Present," *Peasant Studies* 6:56–65.

1990   *Anthropology and Politics: Visions, Traditions, and Trends*. Tucson: University of Arizona Press.

1992   "A Political Orchestration of the Irish Famine: County Fermanagh,
              May 1847." In *Approaching the Past: Historical Anthropology through Irish
              Case Studies*, ed. Philip Gulliver and Marilyn Silverman, 75–98. New
              York: Columbia University Press.

Vossen, R.
1988   "Patterns of Language Knowledge and Language Use in Ngamiland
              Botswana." Bayreuth [Bavaria] African Studies Series 13.

Vyner, Henry M.
1988   *Invisible Trauma: The Psychosocial Effects of Invisible Environmental Contami-
              nants.* Lexington, Mass.: Lexington Books.

Wakin, Eric
1992   *Anthropology Goes to War: Professional Ethics and Counterinsurgency in Thai-
              land.* Monograph 7. Madison: Center for Southeast Asian Studies,
              University of Wisconsin.

Walkowitz, Daniel J.
1978   *Worker City, Company Town: Iron and Cotton Worker Protest in Troy and
              Cohoes, New York, 1855–1884.* Urbana: University of Illinois Press.

Wallace, Anthony F. C.
1961   *Culture and Personality.* New York: Random House.
1978   *Rockdale.* New York: Knopf.

Wallerstein, Immanuel
1974   *The Modern World System: Capitalist Agriculture and the Origins of the
              European World-Economy in the Sixteenth Century.* New York: Academic
              Press.

Weber, Eugen
1976   *Peasants into Frenchmen.* Stanford: Stanford University Press.

Weber, Max
1958   "Capitalism and Rural Society in Germany." In *From Max Weber*, ed.
              H. H. Gerth and C. Wright Mills, 363–385. New York: Oxford Uni-
              versity Press.
1980   *Wirtschaft und Gesellschaft.* Tübingen: Mohr. (Orig. 1925.)

Weiner, Martin
1981   *English Culture and the Decline of the Industrial Spirit, 1850–1980.* Cam-
              bridge: Cambridge University Press.

Weir, David, and Mark Schapiro
1981   *Circle of Poison.* San Francisco: Center for Investigative Reporting, In-
              stitute for Food and Development Policy.

Whisnant, David E.
1983   *All That Is Native and Fine: The Politics of Culture in an American Region.*
              Chapel Hill: University of North Carolina Press.

White, Hayden
1973   *Metahistory: The Historical Imagination in Nineteenth-Century Europe.* Balti-
              more: Johns Hopkins University Press.

Whitehead, Neil L.
1988   *Lords of the Tiger Spirit: A History of the Caribs in Colonial Venezuela and
              Guyana 1498–1820.* Dordrecht: Foris.

Whitten, Dorothea S., and Norman E. Whitten, Jr.

1988   *From Myth to Creation: Art and Adaptation of Ecuadorian Jungle Quichua.* Urbana: University of Illinois Press.

Whitten, Norman E., Jr.

1976   *Sacha Runa: Ethnicity and Adaptation of Ecuadorian Jungle Quichua.* Urbana: University of Illinois Press.

Wiegersma, Nancy

1988   *Vietnam Peasant Land, Peasant Revolution: Patriarchy and Collectivity in the Rural Economy.* New York: St. Martin's Press.

Williams, Brackette

1989   "A Class Act: Anthropology and the Race to Nation across Ethnic Terrain," *Annual Review of Anthropology* 18:401–444.

1990   "Nationalism, Traditionalism, and the Problem of Cultural Inauthenticity." In *Nationalist Ideologies and the Production of National Cultures,* ed. Richard G. Fox, 112–129. [New] Monograph Series, no. 2. Washington, D.C.: American Anthropological Association.

Williams, Raymond

1977   *Marxism and Literature.* Oxford: Oxford University Press.

Willis, Paul

1977   *Learning to Labor: How Working Class Kids Get Working Class Jobs.* New York: Columbia University Press.

Wilmsen, E.

1982   "Migration Patterns of Remote Area Dwellers." In *Migration in Botswana: Patterns, Causes, and Consequences,* ed. C. Kerven, 337–376. Gaborone, Botswana: Central Statistics Office.

1989   *Land Filled with Flies: A Political Economy of the Kalahari.* Chicago: University of Chicago Press.

in press *a*   "Auxiliary Units of Labor: The Homogenization of Diversity in Ethnic Discourse." In *The Politics of Difference: Ethnic Premises in a World of Power,* ed. E. Wilmsen and P. McAllister. Chicago: University of Chicago Press.

in press *b*   *The Kalahari Ethnographies of Siegfried Passarge.* Ann Arbor: University of Michigan Press.

Wilmsen, E., and R. Vossen

1990   "Labour, Language, and Power in the Construction of Ethnicity in Botswana," *Critique of Anthropology* 10:7–38.

Wilson, Fiona

1982   "Property and Ideology: A Regional Oligarchy in the Central Andes in the Nineteenth Century." In *Ecology and Exchange in the Andes,* ed. David Lehman, 191–210. Cambridge: Cambridge University Press.

Wilson, Patricia, and Baltazar Caravedo, eds.

1984   *La crítica del centralismo y la cuestión regional.* Lima: CEDESA.

Wilson, William Julius

1987   *The Truly Disadvantaged: The Inner City, the Underclass, and Public Policy.* Chicago: University of Chicago Press.

Wily, L.

1979   "Official Policy Toward San (Bushmen) Hunter-Gatherers in Modern Botswana: 1966–1978." Gaborone, Botswana: National Institute of Development and Cultural Research.

Worby, E.
n.d.   "Not to Plow my Master's Field: Discourses of Ethnicity and the Pro-
            duction of Inequality in Botswana." Unpublished manuscript. (On
            file at the Department of Anthropology, McGill University.)

Worsley, P.
1984   *The Three Worlds.* Chicago: University of Chicago Press.

Wright, Pamela
1986   "Language Shift and the Redefinition of Social Boundaries Among
            the Carib of Belize." Ph.D. diss., Department of Anthropology,
            Graduate Center of the City University of New York.

1990   "The Metonymy of Ethnicity: Public Sector Work and Intergenera-
            tional Language Shift Among the Garifuna of Belize." Paper pre-
            sented at the Social Sciences History Conference, St. Paul, Minn.

1991   "Terms of Identity: Two Schemata for the Carib from the Fifteenth
            Century to the Present." Paper prepared for Wenner-Gren confer-
            ence no. 112, "Rethinking Linguistic Relativity," Ocho Rios, Ja-
            maica, 3–11 May.

1993   "Sencillamente adecuado para una pelea a cucillo: Las peleas en
            publico entre mujeres, apropriada que contrarresta el revalorizado
            poder domestico en Andalusia," *Antropología* 4–5:103–141.

Wrigley, E. A.
1989   "Some Reflections on Corn Yields and Prices in Preindustrial Econo-
            mies." In *Famine, Disease, and the Social Order in Early Modern Society,* ed.
            John Walter and Roger Schofield, 235–278. Cambridge: Cambridge
            University Press.

Wunder, Heide
1975   "Zur Mentalität aufständischer Bauern." In *Der deutsche Bauernkrieg,
            1524–1526,* ed. H. U. Wehler, 9–37. Göttingen: Vanderhoeck and
            Ruprecht.

Yanigasako, Sylvia Junko, and Jane Fishburne Collier
1987   "Toward a Unified Analysis of Gender and Kinship." In *Gender and
            Kinship: Essays Toward a Unified Analysis,* ed. Jane Fishburne Collier and
            Sylvia Junko Yanigasako, 14–53. Stanford: Stanford University Press.

Yepes del Castillo, Ernesto
1980   "Los inicios de la expansión mercantil capitalista en el Perú (1890–
            1930)," *Historia del Perú* (ed. Juan Mejía Baca) 7:305–403.

Young, Nigel
1990   "On The Study of Peace Movements." In *Towards a Comparative Anal-
            ysis of Peace Movements,* ed. Katsuya Kodama and Unto Vesa, 3–14.
            Brookfield, Vt.: Gower.

Zapata, Francisco
1977   "Enclaves y sistemas de relaciones industriales en America Latina,"
            Revista Mexicana de Sociología 39:719–731.

Zapata Cesti, Victor A.
1949   *Historia de la policía del Perú.* Lima: Empresa Editora Peruana.

Zeff, Robin Lee, Marsha Love, and Karen Stults
    1989   *Empowering Ourselves: Women and Toxics Organizing.* Arlington, Va.: Citizen's Clearinghouse for Hazardous Wastes.
Zelinsky, Wilbur
    1983   "Nationalism in the American Place-Name Cover," *Names* 31:1–28.
    1986   "The Changing Face of Nationalism in the American Landscape," *Canadian Geographer* 30:171–217.
Zelizer, Viviana
    1985   *Pricing the Priceless Child: The Changing Social Value of Children.* New York: Basic Books.

CONTRIBUTORS

Michael Adas is professor of comparative and European colonial history at Rutgers University at New Brunswick. His most recent books include *Machines as the Measure of Men: Science, Technology and Ideologies of Western Dominance* and (with Peter Stearns and Stuart Schwartz) *Turbulent Passage: A Global History of the Twentieth Century*. Among his current research projects is a study of World War I and its contribution to the decline of the British Empire.

Philippe Bourgois is associate professor of anthropology at San Francisco State University. His study on social marginalization in East Harlem, *In Search of Respect: Selling Crack in El Barrio*, is forthcoming; his earlier book is *Ethnicity at Work: Divided Labor on a Central American Banana Plantation*.

Richard G. Fox is professor of anthropology at Washington University in St. Louis and editor of *Current Anthropology*. Among his recent books are *Gandhian Utopia: Experiments with Culture, Lions of the Punjab: Culture in the Making*, and the edited collections, *Recapturing Anthropology: Working in the Present* and *Nationalist Ideologies and the Production of National Culture*.

Ashraf Ghani has carried out fieldwork in Afghanistan and Pakistan and has written articles on the history of anthropology, gender, religion, and cultural theories of power and state; his forthcoming book is entitled *Production of Domination: Afghanistan 1747–1901*. He has taught at the University of Kabul; University of Aarhus, Denmark; University of California, Berkeley; and Johns Hopkins University, where he is currently adjunct associate professor.

James B. Greenberg is associate research anthropologist with the Bureau of Applied Research in Anthropology at the University of Arizona, and head of its Borderlands section. He has researched peasant economies and conflict in Oaxaca, Mexico, and household economies in the borderlands. His publications include *Santiago's Sword: Chatino Peasant Religion and Economics* and *Blood Ties: Life and Violence in Rural Mexico*. In 1990 and 1991, as a Fulbright Scholar, he carried out fieldwork among the Mixe of Oaxaca.

Edward C. Hansen is professor of anthropology at Queens College of the City University of New York. Field research in Catalonia during the 1960s led to his book *Rural Catalonia under the Franco Regime: The Fate of Regional Culture since the Spanish Civil War*. More recently he has been researching and writing on social class in America. He is the co-author (with Eric Wolf) of *The Human Condition in Latin America* and of an article on caudillo politics.

Josiah M. Heyman is assistant professor of anthropology and science, technology, and society at Michigan Technological University in Houghton, Michigan. He is the author of *Life and Labor on the Border: Working People of Northeastern Sonora, Mexico, 1886–1986*. His current research is on the U.S. Immigration and Naturalization Service at the Mexico–United States border and on approaches to state workers, bureaucracies, and power.

David Hunt is associate professor of history at the University of Massachusetts at Boston. He has published extensively on peasants and revolutions in France and Vietnam. He is the author of *Parents and Children in History* and *Villagers at War: The NLF in My Tho Province, 1965-1967*, and co-editor (with Jayne Werner) of *The American War in Vietnam*.

Orvar Löfgren is professor of European ethnology at the University of Lund, Sweden. He has published a number of works on class and culture in Swedish society, including (with Jonas Frykman) *Culture Builders: A Historical Anthropology of Middle-Class Life*, and is currently involved in a comparative project on national and transnational cultural processes.

Blanca M. Muratorio is associate professor of anthropology and sociology at the University of British Columbia and research associate at the Latin American School of Social Sciences (FLACSO, Ecuador). She is the author of *Etnicidad, evangelización y protesta en Ecuador: Una perspectiva antropológica* and *The Life and Times of Grandfather Alonso: Culture and History in the Upper Amazon*. She is currently editing *Images of Ecuadorean Indians and Their Imagemakers* and completing research on Napo Quichua women's work and symbolic universe.

David Nugent is assistant professor of anthropology at Colby College. He has done fieldwork in northern Peru and coastal Kenya on political economy and social movements. Recent publications include "Property Relations, Production Relations and Inequality: Anthropology, Political Economy and the Blackfeet," *American Ethnologist*, and "Building the State-making Nation: The Bases and Limits of State Centralization in Modern Peru," *American Anthropologist*. He is currently finishing *Modern Projects: State, Individual and*

Nation in Contemporary Peru, in which he focuses on the forces behind the consolidation and fragmentation of the Peruvian state and of a national culture during the last one hundred years.

Rayna Rapp is professor of anthropology and chair of the Graduate Program in Gender Studies and Feminist Theory at the New School for Social Research. She has edited *Toward an Anthropology of Women* and co-edited (with Marilyn Young and Sonia Kruks) *Promissory Notes: Women in Transition to Socialism* and (with Faye Ginsburg) *Conceiving the New World Order: The Global Politics of Reproduction*. Currently, she is completing a book on the social impact and cultural meaning of prenatal diagnosis, one of the new reproductive technologies. She has been active in the movement for reproductive rights and the movement to establish women's studies for over twenty years.

Hermann Rebel teaches on European cultural history at the University of Arizona. He has published books and articles on Austrian and German peasant society, folktales, the history of the family, and the cultural dimensions of technological development. Recently he has turned toward theorizing interdisciplinary research in history and anthropology and is working on a book about the long-term origins of Austrian fascism.

Gustavo Lins Ribeiro is associate professor of anthropology at the University of Brasilia and the author of a prize-winning book on a large-scale infrastructure project, studied anthropologically from within. Recently translated from the Portuguese, this book has appeared in English as *Transnational Capitalism and Hydropolitics in Argentina: The Yacyreta Dam*.

William Roseberry is professor and chair of the Anthropology Department at the New School for Social Research. He is the author of *Coffee and Capitalism in the Venezuelan Andes*, *Anthropologies and Histories*, the co-editor (with Jay O'Brien) of *Golden Ages, Dark Ages: Imagining the Past in Anthropology and History*, and one of the authors of *Confronting Historical Paradigms*.

Harriet G. Rosenberg is associate dean in the Faculty of Arts at York University (Toronto, Canada) where she is associate professor in the Division of Social Science. She is the author of three books: *Surviving in the City: Urbanization in the Third World* (with M. FitzGerald); *A Negotiated World: Three Centuries of Change in a French Alpine Village*; and *Through the Kitchen Window: The Politics of Home and Family* (with M. Luxton and S. Arat-Koc). She has done fieldwork in France, North America, and Botswana and is interested in social reproduction and resistance in households and communities.

Jane Schneider has been writing, with Peter Schneider, on peasant and urban Sicily since the 1960s, focusing at first on agrarian social life, then on the social class dynamics of the island's "demographic transition," and most recently on the changing relationship of mafia to anti-mafia in Palermo. She is the author of several articles on cloth and cloth history and co-editor (with Annette Weiner) of *Cloth and Human Experience*. She is a professor of anthropology at the Graduate School of CUNY.

Katherine Verdery has been working in Romania since her first fieldwork in 1973–1974. She has published two books on that country, *Transylvanian Villagers: Three Centuries of Political, Economic, and Ethnic Change* and *National Ideology under Socialism: Identity and Cultural Politics in Ceauşescu's Romania*, as well as a number of articles. Since 1977 she has been a member of the Anthropology Department at Johns Hopkins University.

Joan Vincent has conducted field research in Uganda and Ireland. Her books include *African Elite: The Big Men of a Small Town*, *Teso in Transformation: Peasant and Class in Eastern Africa*, and *Anthropology and Politics: Visions, Traditions and Trends*. She has also written on Irish culture and politics.

Edwin N. Wilmsen is research fellow in the Department of Anthropology, University of Texas–Austin. Since 1973, he has worked with Zhu, Herero, and Tswana peoples in Botswana and has represented them in petitions to District and Ministry agencies. In 1981, he wrote an analysis of "Remote Area" peoples for the National Migration Study which served as a source for the subsequent sixth National Development Plan of Botswana. His book, *Land Filled with Flies: A Political Economy of the Kalahari*, won the 1990 Herskovits Prize of the African Studies Association (U.S.A.) and the 1992 Graham Prize of the School of Oriental and African Studies (London).

Pamela Wright is a linguistic anthropologist teaching at the New School for Social Research. She specializes in issues of language, gender, and education. Her field areas are in Central America and Europe.

Designer: U.C. Press Staff
Compositor: Asco Trade Typesetting Ltd.
Text: 10/12 Baskerville
Display: Baskerville
Printer: Maple-Vail Book Manufacturing Group
Binder: Maple-Vail Book Manufacturing Group